Donated
in
Memory of ⸱

Mildred Kieser
1995

Cities of the Mississippi

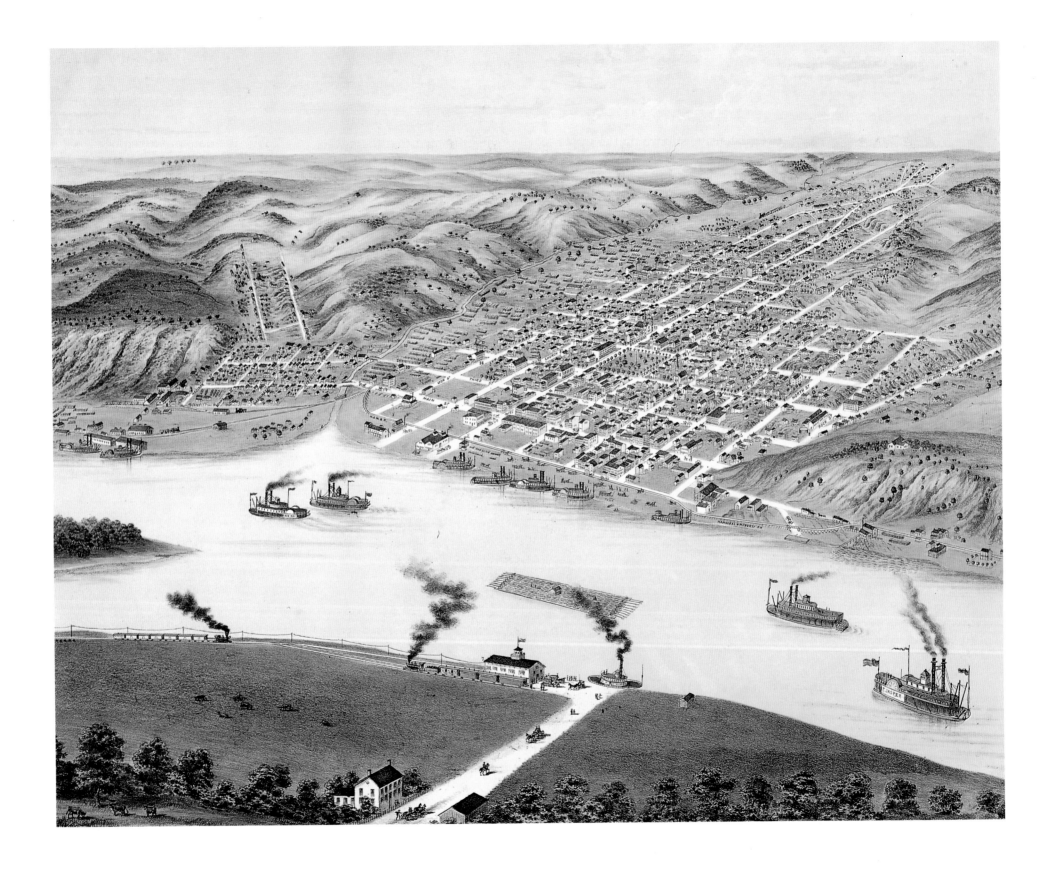

Cities of the Mississippi

Nineteenth-Century Images of Urban Development

John W. Reps

With Modern Photographs from the Air
by Alex MacLean

University of Missouri Press • Columbia and London

76543

Copyright © 1994 by
The Curators of the University of Missouri
University of Missouri Press, Columbia, Missouri 65201
Printed and bound in China
All rights reserved
5 4 3 2 1   98 97 96 95 94

Library of Congress Cataloging-in-Publication Data

Reps, John William.
  Cities of the Mississippi : nineteenth-century images
of urban development / John W. Reps ; with modern
photographs from the air by Alex MacLean.
      p.   cm.
  Includes bibliographical references and index.
  ISBN 0-8262-0939-4
  1. Cities and towns—Mississippi River valley—
History—19th century.   2. Cities and towns—
Mississippi River Valley—History—19th century—
Pictorial works.   3. Mississippi River Valley—History—
Pictorial works.   I. Title.
F353.R47 1994
977′.03—dc20   93–44630
                                                         CIP

♾ This paper meets the requirements of the American
National Standard for Permanence of Paper for Printed
Library Materials, Z39.48, 1984.

Designer: Rhonda Miller
Typesetter: Bookcomp, Grand Rapids, Michigan
Printer and binder: Regent
Typefaces: Palatino and Centaur

The publication of this book has been supported by a grant
from the National Endowment for the Humanities, an
independent federal agency.

To the memory of the victims and to those who survived the Mississippi River floods of 1993

The University of Missouri Press gratefully acknowledges the support for its ongoing work in the humanities provided by Boatmen's Banks and their particular endorsement of John W. Reps's *Cities of the Mississippi*.

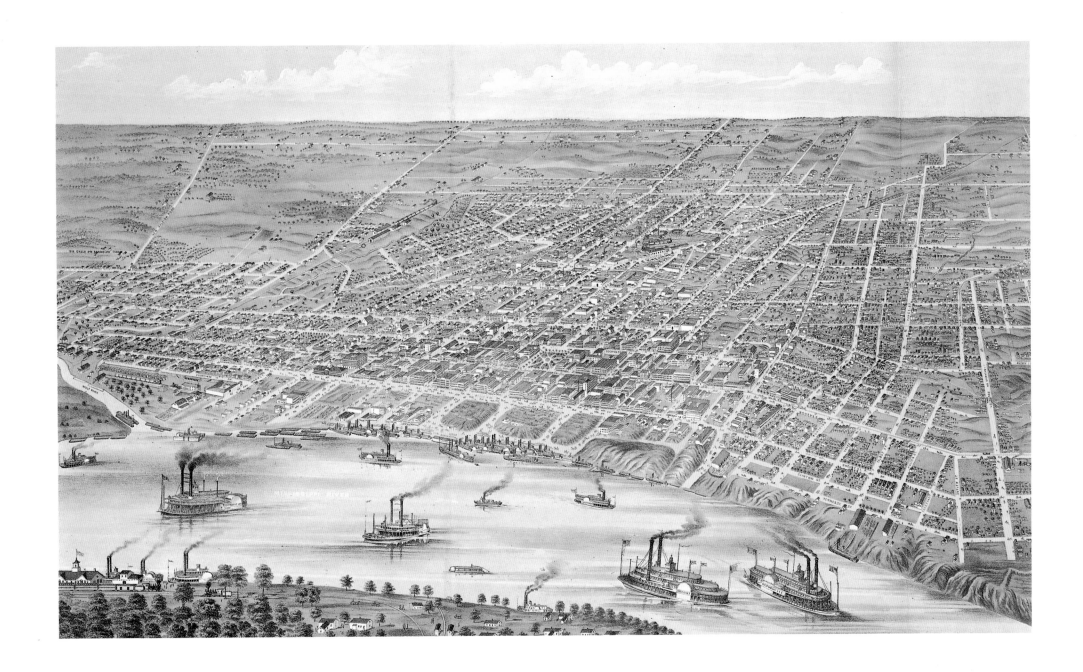

Contents

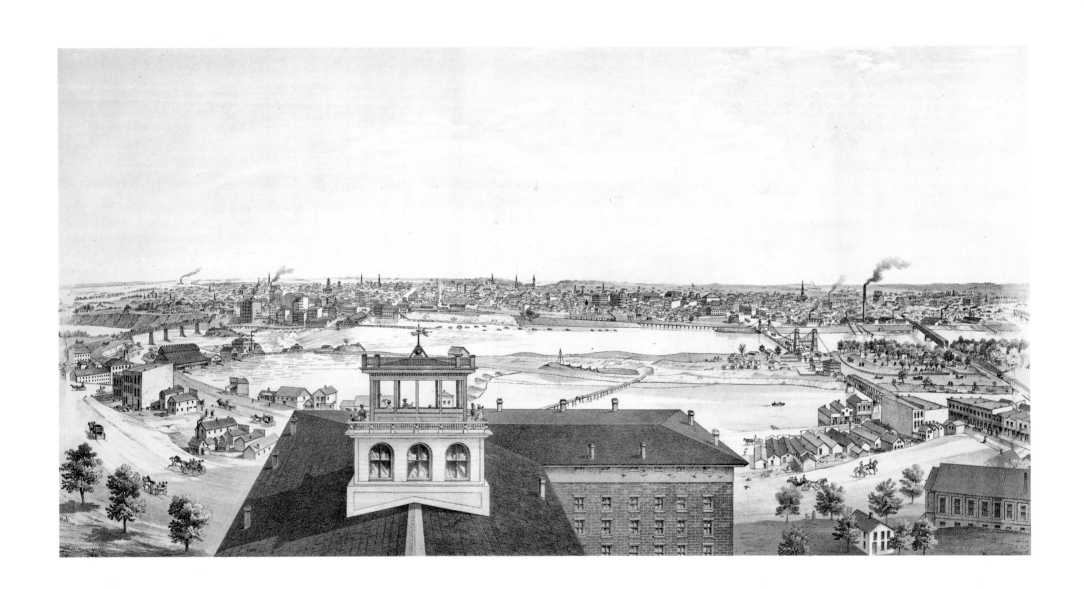

Introduction

This book takes readers on several voyages up and down the Mississippi River in the nineteenth century. Each trip offers at least a brief—and, often, a more extended—stopover at the dozens of towns along the river from New Orleans in Louisiana to St. Cloud in Minnesota. Helping to guide these tours and supplementing the author's eight chapters are the works of a great many artists and authors of the last century. They drew the images of, or described in words, the towns and cities they visited or lived in at various periods throughout the century.

The illustrations the artists produced and the descriptions written by observers combine to provide valuable and fascinating insights into the nature of urban communities along the Mississippi a century and more ago. Their work allows us to understand and appreciate the special character of the towns that trade, manufacturing, and commerce created on the country's great inland water transportation corridor.

The book's eight chapters begin with an exploration of the early towns on the river and an introduction to the pioneering viewmakers in the first decades of the nineteenth century who captured on paper and in print the images of these fledgling communities. Subsequent chapters explore the expanding network of towns and cities and the widening popularity of a variety of printed urban views that recorded their appearance. The text presents events in chronological order, although the last portion of Chapter III follows one type of city view well beyond the period where the next chapter begins. Throughout, there are frequent references to the illustrations contained in the "folios" that compose the second part of the book.

These folios begin after the final chapter and present the joint contributions of nineteenth-century authors and artists. Each folio begins with a text page containing extracts from descriptions of the town by residents or visitors at some period in its development. Printed illustrations of the town at that time appear on the facing page and often on two or four additional pages that reproduce other images of the community.

While the chapters treat the subject chronologically, the illustrations and their accompanying travel accounts, descriptions, and explanations in the folios are arranged geographically, beginning with New Orleans and proceeding up the river. Multiple images of most places drawn and published at various times of the city's life allow the reader to observe the changes that took place over time by comparing earlier with later views of the same city. It is thus possible for a reader less concerned with or already well informed about the artists and printmakers who produced urban views along the Mississippi to proceed at once to the folios for a sequential visit to the river's towns and cities. Or, the reader can seek out a particular place and examine how it was described by writers and depicted by artists at one or more times during its existence. Still others may prefer to compare the appearance of and changes in two or more towns by consulting the appropriate pairs of folios.

A special feature of many of the folios are modern aerial photographs duplicating as nearly as possible the perspective views drawn by the bird's-eye-view artists of the nineteenth century. These photographs of twenty-three river towns are the work of Alex MacLean. He took them almost exactly a century after Henry Wellge, very nearly the last artist of his kind in this region, toured the river at the beginning of the 1890s.

Seeing together on opposite pages nineteenth-century views and matching modern air photos makes one appreciate how much the two-dimensional structure of the core of every modern community is a child of its historic ancestor. Streets, parks, church sites, public building locations, and residential and commercial lots for the most part remain little changed from the town's plat as first laid out by its founders and as enlarged later in the nineteenth century by adjacent landowners subdividing their land for urban purposes.

Only in exceptional cases have public officials or private developers succeeded in obliterating traces of the original town plan. The old views and the modern photograph of St. Louis clearly illustrate the most dramatic example: the wholesale clearing of forty blocks of the old French portion of St. Louis for the Jefferson National Expansion Memorial National Historic Site. Of all the structures that once stood here only the Old Courthouse and the Old Cathedral remain—buildings dwarfed by but giving scale to the great parabolic arch that exceeds in height the Washington Monument in the national capital.

Even such a disaster as the Mississippi River flood of 1993 will probably not change the basic patterns of land division in the many cities affected by this unprecedented catastrophe. It is likely, therefore, that most rebuilding and reconstruction will leave largely intact the preflood boundaries of lots, blocks, and streets. So, although the aerial photographs in this book portray cities before the flood and are thus themselves part of the historic record, they can still be examined as generally reliable guides to the cities they depict.

The artists who created the other images reproduced in this book remain virtually unknown, although scholarly work on a few of them has put some biographical flesh on what for so long consisted of little more than bare bones. As a result, we now can appreciate better the backgrounds of and works by such itinerant artists as Henry Lewis, Frederick Piercy, John Caspar Wild, and Alfred Waud, each of whom visited and drew several cities along the Mississippi.[1]

A few additional studies exist of artists who contributed only one or two views of Mississippi River cities, most notably Edwin Whitefield. For the rest, one must rely on a few lines in specialized biographical dictionaries or brief biographical notes in works on American historical or popular prints. These entries often do little more than list the prints associated with the artist's name, provide the dates when they appeared, and assemble meager bits of real information about the artist culled from a variety of sources.[2]

The same limitations apply to the information available on most of the engravers, lithographers, printers, and publishers who converted artists' sketches into finished illustrations, book plates, or separately issued prints. Their contributions are important, and it is a pity that so little has been written about the roles they played in creating the images reproduced in this volume.

It may be too early to judge whether this paucity of information results from a genuine lack of data about these urban viewmakers or a failure to search long and well enough to discover them. Certainly the author's meagerly rewarded efforts to gather available material and to uncover additional facts concerning artists, printmakers, printers, and publishers suggest the task will not be easy. It would be helpful if curators of graphic arts in museums as well as academic historians of American art could be persuaded to show a greater interest in such investigations. That by and large they have not reflects in part their disdain of images produced for utilitarian purposes or created for commercial reasons.

Certainly the artists who drew cities for wood engravings in *Gleason's Pictorial, Harper's Weekly, Frank Leslie's Illustrated Newspaper, Every Saturday,* and other periodicals did so because editors and publishers believed these illustration would attract readers and thus help sales. Commercial imperatives also influenced artistic style, especially after the Civil War. Most city-view artists at that time used a bird's-eye perspective because in this way they could include far more buildings than in a conventional skyline townscape, and they knew that each building's owner was a potential customer.

1. For Lewis, see the introductory material by Bertha L. Heilbron in the modern reprint of Lewis's *The Valley of the Mississippi Illustrated.* Jonathan Fairbanks provides useful information about Piercy in "The Great Platte River Trail in 1853: The Drawings and Sketches of Frederick Piercy." Chap. 3 of John W. Reps, *Saint Louis Illustrated,* 29–51, presents what is known about John Caspar Wild as revealed by the studies of John Francis McDermott and Martin Synder. For Waud, see Historic New Orleans Collection, *Alfred R. Waud, Special Artist on Assignment: Profiles of American Towns and Cities, 1850–1880,* and Frederic E. Ray, *Alfred R. Waud: Civil War Artist.*

2. Whitefield's career is the subject of Bettina A. Norton, *Edwin Whitefield: Nineteenth-Century North American Scenery.* John W. Reps, *Views and Viewmakers of Urban America: Lithographs of Towns and Cities in the United States and Canada, Notes on the Artists and Publishers, and a Union Catalog of Their Work, 1825–1925,* 159–217, provides biographical notes on several of the artists active along the Mississippi; some of these, however, offer little more information than the artist's dates of activity and the places visited and drawn.

Artists and publishers of city views often included border vignettes showing places of business, homes, churches, and factories. Although some of these vignettes display public buildings and churches that would doubtless have been included by the artist, the images of privately owned buildings probably resulted from fees paid by those whose homes and places of business received special recognition in this way.

Curators and art historians also have applied only conventional standards of artistic judgment in approaching (or, far more often, drawing back from) the printed images of cities produced in the nineteenth century. They look with scorn at the numerous bird's-eye views that present a city tilted up before us like a slab of beef in a butcher shop. Seemingly these stretch the rules of linear perspective to the vanishing point of disbelief and indicate lack of artistic training.

In fact, artists depicted cities in this way, not through ignorance of perspective theory and practice, but because they wished to achieve an important goal. To market as many views as possible, they needed to show clearly and with as much detail as they could all or nearly all the buildings in the community. A conventional perspective with vanishing points on the horizon would have resulted in images of buildings in the background too small for recognition.

Conversely, vanishing points well beyond the horizon or far to one side of the picture border produced in the perspective system lines that did not converge nearly so sharply as in a drawing that followed drawing-book rules. This meant that images on the drawing of, for example, three-story houses in the background would be nearly as large as the corresponding foreground images of structures of similar size. The practical effect was to increase the number of potential customers who could recognize their homes, places of business or industry, churches, schools, and other features no matter where they might be located in real space.

This helps to explain why views like this possess cartographic characteristics that often overshadow their artistic qualities. Unlike a conventional townscape painted from eye level or from a slight elevation, bird's-eye views display the street pattern, depict every building, reveal spatial relationships, and record the natural setting and geographic features of the cities they portray. Such prints thus inform the mind more than they delight the eye, and they must be judged by standards of historians and geographers as well as by those of art critics.

Perhaps the time is coming when such distinctions will no longer be made automatically. If so, we will be returning to standards prevailing in seventeenth-century Holland. In her remarkable study, *The Art of Describing: Dutch Art in the Seventeenth Century*, Svetlana Alpers notes that at that time "botanical description, maps, topography, and costume study all were tasks for the artist as illustrator." According to Alpers, it is only in our era that

> art historians have tended to separate high art, on the one hand, from image-making as a craft with utilitarian uses. The line is drawn so that what is considered to be a craft has not been considered to be art. What happens . . . to the interest in mapping, archaeology, and botany that are present in a landscape by Van Goyen, a church interior by Saenredam, or a vase of flowers by Bosschaert? Artful images such as these make it hard to dismiss pictorial craft.[3]

Perhaps few of the images reproduced in this book could stand comparison with the examples offered by Alpers. Nevertheless, many display features that cannot be dismissed easily as the work of artists with no redeeming talent. Whatever merits they may possess as judged by more conventional standards, they have an undeniable role in documenting the character of urban places along the Mississippi.

3. *Art of Describing*, 24.

I

Urban Artists on the Mississippi Frontier, 1803–1839

By the middle of the nineteenth century scores of towns and cities lined the banks of the Mississippi River. Town life flourished especially from the mouth of the Ohio River to St. Paul and Minneapolis and even farther up the river to St. Cloud. Although a shortage of suitable sites and the prevailing plantation economy confined significant urban development along the lower river to fewer locations, this region included such cities as New Orleans, Baton Rouge, Natchez, Vicksburg, and Memphis. Here, too, one could find other much smaller towns and hamlets clustered tightly around lands frequented by river steamboats.

In 1846 that indefatigable observer, recorder, and booster of economic development of the South and West, J. D. B. de Bow, recalled the rapid process of urbanization in the Mississippi valley:

> The growth of the various cities which scatter themselves throughout the valley of the Ohio and Mississippi rivers, has been so rapid and extraordinary, as scarcely to be credited by those whose minds have been educated in other sections of the world. We may suppose if the same ratio of increase is preserved, that in progress of time towns and cities will rear themselves among us which will vie in populousness with those of Asiatic climes. If the West continues its rapid progress for the next fifty years unabated, and the same proportion of population at the expiration of that period reside in cities, it has been computed by an intelligent writer that there will be at least twenty cities westward of the Allegheny mountains with a population of half a million of human beings each.[1]

Dozens of artists visited these places in the nineteenth century to record their appearance in sketches, drawings, and paintings. Although some of these images were never published, countless others served as sources for a wide variety of printed urban portraits. They appeared at a time when Americans hungered for information about the development of their country, and these multiple images thus proved especially popular. Engravings on copper, wood, and steel supplied illustrations for books, magazines, reports, and newspapers. Lithographs also served as plates in books or as pages in atlases but more commonly took the form of larger, separately issued prints.

Owners of these latter prints displayed them on the walls of parlors, offices, and such public places as banks, hotels, and government buildings. Everyone regarded these urban views as convincing evidence of their city's prosperity and importance and looked on them with pride, consulted them for information, sent them to friends, or admired them as decorations for their homes or places of business.

Although book plates depicting river cities were not usually so impressive, volumes containing such images seem to have been eagerly bought and added to home libraries. City views in the several illustrated periodicals of the time often enjoyed shorter lives, but these were printed in enormous editions, and a surprisingly large number

---

1. "Cities of the Valley of the Mississippi and Ohio," 145. This article, presumably

written by the editor and proprietor of *The Commercial Review of the South and West*, J. D. B. de Bow, appeared in the second issue of his journal. The first issue contained an article on the "rise and progress of New Orleans in wealth and opulence."

of impressions have survived—an indication of how popular they must have been.

Our generation can use these views in different ways. They provide windows through which we can peer into another era and examine urban life along the Mississippi. Such opportunities are almost endless, for scores of images exist of places ranging in size from small towns to major urban centers. These printed views of river towns first appeared shortly after the beginning of the nineteenth century, became enormously popular in the two decades before and after the Civil War, and survived into the first decade of the twentieth century.

By that time photographic halftone and gravure illustrations had largely replaced hand-drawn city views. Like the great river steamboats so many of the views portray, city views were made obsolete by changes in technology. But what a record of urban life along the Mississippi this body of graphic images comprises! We shall begin our exploration of them with an examination of the earliest examples, those produced by the pioneer viewmakers of the region practicing their craft before 1840.

Few artists and publishers of this early period documented in print the faces presented to the world by the towns on the Mississippi. It was no wonder, for aside from New Orleans, with a population in 1820 of just over 27,000, only a limited number of places existed to provide either inspiration or market for an artist attempting to earn a livelihood through his art. Baton Rouge consisted of little more than a military post and a steamboat landing. While Natchez could also boast of its eighteenth-century origins, it remained quite small and was divided between its untidy and rowdy lower settlement at the river's edge and its respectable upper town some distance away on the bluff above. Vicksburg, planned in 1811, was too tiny and insignificant to attract any attention.

Memphis, surveyed into streets and lots in 1819, consisted of only a handful of cabins. Far to the north at the mouth of the Ohio an attempt to create a town in 1818 failed dismally, and it was not until the late 1830s that Cairo, Illinois, finally came into existence as anything more than a cluster of shacks around the wharfboats that served as its steamboat landing. To the north the old French settlement of Cahokia, Illinois, began in 1699 as a French mission. Although it gradually took on the appearance of a village, Cahokia hardly provided a suitable subject for an artist's townscape. Its somewhat younger sister community at Kaskaskia also exhibited few true urban characteristics.

On the Missouri side of the river, New Madrid, dating from 1789, suffered first from continual erosion of its platted land and then was devastated by the great earthquake of 1811 to which the scruffy little town gave its name, even though it had little else to offer the world. Upriver, Cape Girardeau had been platted as early as 1806, but the government's refusal to recognize the Spanish land title of its proprietor condemned this former military and trading post to thirty years of stagnation before development resumed after the government reversed its original decision.

Early visitors to Missouri found Ste. Genevieve, across from Kaskaskia, far more impressive and citylike than New Madrid or Cape Girardeau. It first occupied a site that proved too flood-prone, and in 1785 its residents began moving to a new and much higher location four miles northwest. For a time Ste. Genevieve rivaled St. Louis, but as the fur trade moved west and local deposits of salt and lead neared exhaustion, its population began to decline. As early as 1772 on its first site the city's population reached nearly 700. In 1800 the new town numbered only 806 residents, almost exactly the population in 1836.[2]

Even St. Louis, by far the largest and most populous place on the river above New Orleans, had a population in 1820 of only 4,600—not a particularly impressive record for a town founded more than a half-century earlier. Most of the city's growth had taken place in the previous decade, for in 1810 the census counted only 1,400 residents. Caleb Atwater reported that when he visited St. Louis in 1829 it was "a town containing, now, I presume about 7000 inhabitants . . . [and] . . . 40 stores." It was clear that St. Louis had not yet attained any significant urban stature or character.[3]

Across the river from St. Louis travelers to and from the east passed through Illinois Town, a small, unattractive village where lots had been first auctioned in 1816 for what became a ferry station serving travelers and freight bound for St. Louis. It was not until the arrival of the Ohio and Mississippi Railroad in 1855 that this site succeeded in attracting any number of people. Two years after landowners to the northeast platted East St. Louis, the two places became a single municipality under the name of the newer community.

2. The founding and early years of this town are ably treated in Carl J. Ekberg, *Colonial Ste. Genevieve.*
3. *Remarks Made on a Tour to Prairie du Chien: Thence to Washington City, in 1829,* 42.

A few miles north of St. Louis on the north bank of the Missouri River stood St. Charles. The French established this town near the mouth of the Missouri in 1780, but it had been largely eclipsed by the growth of St. Louis. Then, after the admission of Missouri to the Union in 1821, legislators chose St. Charles to serve as the new state's temporary capital while a permanent capital was being constructed near the center of the state. Five years later, when the legislature moved to Jefferson City, St. Charles resumed its life as a river town of minor importance.

A few other small towns at this time clung to precarious life above St. Louis. In 1829 Atwater visited many of them briefly as he traveled up the river in his capacity as a commissioner appointed by the government to negotiate the acquisition of land from the Indians. From his descriptions one can appreciate why no artists found it worthwhile to record the towns' appearance.

Leaving St. Louis, Atwater soon came to Alton on the Illinois side of the Mississippi, a community that began its existence in 1816-1818 when rival adjoining landowners and speculators platted three contiguous towns. Atwater noted, "The State is building . . . a State Penitentiary here. Several steam mills, &c. are here, and the place is rapidly rising up to some importance." Atwater may have been more optimistic than accurate, for after twenty-one more years of growth Alton could claim a population of only 3,585 in 1850.[4]

Continuing his trip, Atwater mentioned several new towns that speculators had laid out in Illinois and Missouri:

> Early in the morning of the first day of July . . . we stopped a moment to land passengers at a nominal village, called, if my memory serves me, Passage des Sioux. . . .
> We again moved forward, stopping at Clarksville, Louisiana and Hannibal, small towns on the Missouri side of the river, and tarried longer in the day time, at a little town called Quincey [sic], two hundred miles perhaps, above St. Louis. . . .
> The towns we had passed, were all small ones, and newly built.[5]

Clarksville was a tiny village where a few pioneers first settled in 1816, and Louisiana was a place of similar size and age. Hannibal began when one Abraham Bird platted the town in 1819 on land acquired in

exchange for property that the earthquake of 1811 destroyed at New Madrid. At the time of Atwater's visit the town consisted of far more vacant lots than houses and stores.

Quincy enjoyed a more orderly origin than Illinoistown, Alton, or the three villages mentioned by Atwater. It began in 1822 as a hamlet called The Bluffs, but when the state legislature created Adams County in 1825 and appointed commissioners to choose a location for a county seat The Bluffs found itself the favored site. On level land at the top of the slope leading to the river the commissioners laid out a town with wide streets, large lots, and a public square near its center. Officials of the county named it Quincy in honor of President John Quincy Adams. To make this connection more apparent they called the large public square John's Square, a name eventually replaced by the more dignified Washington Square.[6]

Not mentioned by Atwater, probably because it was of too little consequence, was Alexandria, Missouri, standing near the northern boundary of the state. When Atwater passed it by it was only four years old, the creation of a ferry operator who had established his enterprise south of the mouth of the Des Moines River. In Illinois across from the mouth of the Des Moines River, Atwater stopped at Fort Edwards, "located on a high bluff, that juts out into the river." Below the fort the little town of Warsaw, Illinois, would soon begin its existence, but in 1829 this site remained unplatted for urban use.

On the opposite side of the Mississippi and above the mouth of the Des Moines River, Atwater came to Keokuk. He observed, "The village is a small one, containing twenty families perhaps. The American Fur Company have a store here." The company doubtless selected this site because the rapids in the Mississippi at this point required boats to be at least partially unloaded during periods of low water in order to proceed farther north.[7]

North of Keokuk, Atwater arrived at Fort Armstrong, located at the lower end of Rock Island in the middle of the river. Here, the site of what are now called the Quad Cities (Davenport, Moline, Rock Island, and Bettendorf), he noted that a "village adjoins the fort on the north, and a few families live here. Mr. Davenport, who keeps a store for the American Fur Company, being a principal man among them. The

4. Ibid., 56.
5. Ibid., 57.

6. Henry Asbury, *Reminiscences of Quincy, Illinois, Containing Historical Events, Anecdotes, Matters Concerning Old Settlers and Old Times, Etc.*, 29–31.
7. *Remarks*, 58.

sutler has a store here in addition to the company's store." In short, this settlement was essentially a military post with a few civilians engaged in trade with the Indians and in selling goods to the soldiers stationed at the fort. Town founding at this vicinity still lay in the future.

Still farther north, just a few miles up the Fever River, the discovery of lead at what became Galena, Illinois, resulted in the platting of a town in 1826. Atwater visited it three years later and reported that it was "the largest town in Illinois." He described its appearance:

> When we arrived there, it had been settled about three years. It contained several taverns, a considerable number of stores, about a dozen lawyers, four or five physicians, with little to do, as the country is healthy. There were three religious congregations in the place—Methodists, Roman Catholics and Presbyterians. The town is built on the side hill, in the form of a crescent, on the north side of Fever river, and contains, perhaps one thousand inhabitants.[8]

Before 1830 no other nucleated settlements existed in this region aside from the hamlets that could be found at a few trading stations or military posts. Among the latter were Fort Crawford at what became Prairie du Chien, Wisconsin, and Fort Snelling in Minnesota near the site where St. Paul would be established. It was not until a part of eastern Iowa came into the public domain in June 1833 after the Black Hawk War that formal settlement began on the Iowa side of the river. Then a frenzy of town founding in Iowa and during the following decade in Wisconsin and Minnesota quickly added many new names to the roster of Mississippi River communities with results that later chapters will explore.

Because in their early years these towns on the upper river were still so new and small, no artist sought them as subjects for printed images. For the first third of the nineteenth century, therefore, it is to the towns of the lower river from St. Louis to New Orleans that we must turn in our search for the earliest printed images of river cities.

Travelers entering the Mississippi from the Gulf of Mexico passed by one small town before reaching New Orleans: The Balize, or Pilot's Town, a peculiar collection of huts, watchtowers, and a lighthouse that accommodated the pilots needed to guide vessels up and down the tortuous and ever-changing channels that together constituted the mouth of the Mississippi. In a book describing his travels to America in 1822–1824, Paul Wilhelm Friedrich, Herzog von Württemberg, recorded one of the earliest of many impressions of this squalid settlement.

The duke referred to The Balize as composed of a "few wooden houses that . . . stand on piles in the midst of the water and slime, between high reeds." He noted that "one house can be reached only from another along plank footpaths." He drew what he saw, the view reproduced in Folio 1 that the Royal Lithographic Establishment in Württemberg printed sometime between 1828 and 1835.[9]

A decade or so earlier another artist produced the first printed view of New Orleans, the largest and by far the most important economic, social, and political center of the area. This pioneer image came from an artist about whom very little can be found. Indeed, even the correct spelling of his rather difficult name remains in doubt; it appears as Boquet de Woiseri on his earliest known print, the view of New Orleans late in 1803 reproduced in Folio 2.[10]

John L. Boqueta de Woiseri (as he is now identified) evidently came to New Orleans earlier that year, announcing his arrival in the city by advertising in the New Orleans *Le Moniteur* on May 28. It is possible, however, that he had lived there previously, a claim he made in 1804 when he stated in the Philadelphia *General Advertiser Aurora* on February 21 that for "a number of years" he was a New Orleans resident. It was in this newspaper that de Woiseri claimed to be a "designer, drawer, geographer, and engineer." In addition to practicing as an artist, engraver, and "hair worker," de Woiseri evidently taught art during his stay in New Orleans.[11]

---

8. Ibid., 66.

9. The quotation is from *Erste Reise nach dem Nördlichen Amerika in den Jahren 1822 bis 1824.*, as quoted in Gloria Gilda Deák, *Picturing America, 1497–1899: Prints, Maps, and Drawings Bearing on the New World Discoveries and on the Developments of the Territory That Is Now the United States . . .*, entry 334, 1:228. The lithograph may have been used in the duke's book, but it is not found in the copy at the New York Public Library.

10. On a watercolor version of this view at the Mariners' Museum in Newport News, Virginia, the artist's name appears as Boqueto de Woieseri. This information appears in Perry T. Rathbone, ed., *Mississippi Panorama: The Life and Landscape of the Father of Waters and Its Great Tributary, the Missouri; . . .*, 67. The watercolor is illustrated on p. 69. Unlike nearly all other works of art listed by Rathbone, the size of the watercolor is omitted. This watercolor may have served as the basis for the aquatint evidently printed in Philadelphia rather than the large oil painting of the same image in the collection of the Chicago Historical Society that is usually cited in this connection.

11. John T. Magill, "Pelican's-eye Views of New Orleans," 30, n. 5; Historic New Orleans Collection, *Encyclopaedia of New Orleans Artists, 1718–1918*, 46. I have relied on these two sources extensively in my treatment not only of the de Woiseri view but of most of the New Orleans views discussed elsewhere in this and other chapters.

The city had already expanded well beyond its original French colonial limits. In 1806 an English traveler, Thomas Ashe, noted that "New Orleans . . . extends nearly a mile along the river . . . but there is an extensive suburb on the upper side." Ashe estimated that there were then "about fifteen hundred houses in the city and suburbs," containing a population of approximately "fifteen thousand, including the garrison and Africans." He observed approvingly that "most of the houses have open galleries, and gardens abounding with flowering shrubs and rich bearing orange-trees. These give the city a cool and lively appearance." Certainly at that time no other city of the Mississippi could boast of such a distinctly urban character.[12] Nevertheless, New Orleans evidently did not yet provide the engraving and printing facilities that de Woiseri needed, and it was probably in search of these that the artist came to Philadelphia. It was there that he first announced he had painted a view of New Orleans, had drawn a plan of the city, and was preparing engravings of both.

It may have been at this time that he also executed his watercolor and gouache painting of Philadelphia, one of several other cities that he depicted in paintings, including Richmond and Boston. He probably executed similar works of Charleston, Baltimore, and New York. These are the six cities whose views engraved by "Boquet" can be seen on a sectioned single-sheet aquatint measuring about eighteen by twenty-seven inches that appeared around 1817, possibly slightly earlier.[13]

12. *Travel in America, Performed in 1806 . . .*, 332–33.

13. Anglo-American Art Museum, Louisiana State University, *The Louisiana Landscape, 1800–1969*, note for entry 2, mentions that the artist "painted a huge mural-sized view of New Orleans now in the possession of the Chicago Historical Society, which served as a model for the engraving." Entries 266 and 270 in Deák, *Picturing America*, 1:176–79, locate the other paintings. The Philadelphia painting is in the Stokes Collection of the New York Public Library; that of Richmond can be found in the Virginia Historical Society; a Boston view, Deák states, is "owned in that city" (presumably the one at the Boston Athenaeum), and a larger, redrawn version is in the Garvan Collection at the Yale University Art Gallery. The aquatint images in the print of Philadelphia, Richmond, and Boston closely resemble the paintings, and it is a reasonable assumption that the artist painted the other three places as well. Although the print identifies Boqueta only as the engraver, he surely drew the images, and he probably published the print as well. Deák, in her helpful notes to entry 270, presents the evidence that there were at least two states of this view. Apparently its place of publication has not yet been established. Of the artist's career during the period between the publication of his New Orleans view and that of the six cities we know only that the city directories of New York from 1807 to 1811 identify him as "painter and engraver."

De Woiseri's New Orleans view, reproduced in Folio 2, celebrates the transfer of sovereignty for New Orleans and all the Louisiana Territory from France to the United States. The imprint below the image includes the date of November 1803, and it was on the last day of that month that the official ceremony transferring the flag took place. De Woiseri predicted what this would mean for the future of the city by crowning the view with a banner in the sky carried by a huge American eagle. It proudly announces that "under my wings every thing prospers," a slogan that de Woiseri doubtless hoped would attract patriotic Americans to purchase copies of his print.

In this the artist must have been disappointed if the great rarity of this view is a reliable indication. It seems unlikely that he sold many copies in New Orleans, in Philadelphia, where his aquatint was probably printed, or elsewhere. For reasons that will never be known, de Woiseri chose to portray the city from the Marigny Plantation, located a short distance from the downriver end of the French Quarter, whose linear grid of streets dates from a survey of 1722. It is the lower portion of this section of New Orleans that stretches off to the distance where one can just barely see the more imposing public buildings on and near the old Place d'Armes, now Jackson Square.

Valuable today as a document that reveals much about the architecture of several types of Creole buildings, this view of New Orleans could have had only limited appeal to a general purchaser. Certainly in New Orleans the established Creole residents, unenthusiastic about becoming subjects of the United States, would not have been eager customers. Possibly the artist-publisher recognized that its unmistakably chauvinistic slogan displayed so prominently would limit sales in New Orleans and for that reason and the availability of printing facilities went to Philadelphia to advertise his work and have it printed there.

However, he apparently failed to realize that to attract purchasers among persons in the East unfamiliar with the city he would need to produce an image with far great pictorial appeal than the one he hopefully offered to the public. The scene he presents to us is an odd combination: a bucolic foreground with ships on one side of a vanishing street and on the other a seemingly disordered collection of buildings. To eastern eyes, these strange buildings must have seemed outlandish, awkward, and unprepossessing. Nor is the quality of the aquatint particularly meritorious. Taken together, these characteristics combined to prevent de Woiseri's print from achieving the popularity he surely sought.

Fourteen years after de Woiseri produced his pioneering view of New Orleans, a French artist and traveler named Edouard de Montulé made his way up the Mississippi to Natchez. There in 1817 he sketched what is known as the lower town, occupying a narrow river terrace at the foot of a towering bluff. On his return to France, Montulé used his drawing to prepare a lithograph for his book published in Paris in 1821. Folio 11 reproduces this rather crude little illustration.[14]

This and a companion view of New York City by Montulé in the same work may be the first views of cities in the United States to be done in the relatively new medium of lithography. In this connection, the first paragraph of Montulé's foreword is of interest:

> I should not have published these letters without the aid of lithography. The easy execution of this process suggested to me the idea of passing along to my friends and to the public some of the sketches I have made in different countries. Several persons of some repute in the arts have assured me that a collection of views of America . . . would not be without interest; that is what made me decide to have them printed and to accompany them with these explanatory letters.[15]

For some reason, Montulé did not provide his readers with an illustration of the upper town of Natchez, a place the author described as consisting of "perhaps three hundred houses" and "still in its infancy," but where at the time of his visit he saw "new buildings . . . being erected on all sides." Instead, he drew Natchez-under-the Hill, seen here in its early years before it achieved notoriety as a settlement of saloons, gambling halls, and brothels frequented by drunken and brawling rivermen.

The respectable town of Natchez stood on top of the bluff near the site of a fort that the French and then the Spanish once occupied. The fort's location and that of the town in its early period appear on the plan reproduced in Folio 11. This folio includes a view of the fort from the same source, the atlas volume of General Victor Collot's report on the Ohio and Mississippi valleys. Although not published until 1826, this work contains notes and drawings made thirty years earlier.[16]

A better-known Frenchman, Charles-Alexandre Lesueur (1778–1846), drew Natchez ten years after Montulé, although he shows us few details in his distant townscape, also illustrated in Folio 11. Lesueur received his training in drawing and painting at a French military school and was able as a young man of twenty-three to put his talents to work on a French exploratory voyage to the South Pacific in 1800. His work won him recognition as a respected naturalist, and a chance meeting in Paris with William Maclure, then planning a geological survey of the United States, resulted in his commission to prepare the natural history drawings and to be responsible for preserving specimens collected by the expedition.[17]

---

14. The view is reproduced—not very well—in Montulé's *Travels in America, 1816–1817.*

15. This passage is from *Travels in America.* Both English and French versions were in two volumes, and were published in 1821. The French title reads *Voyage en Amérique, en Italie, en Sicile et en Egypte, pendant les Années 1816, 1817, 1818 et 1819.* The English version, published in London by Sir R. Phillips and Co., bears the title *A Voyage to North America and the West Indies in 1817* and has etched illustrations interleaved with the text. The illustrations of the French edition were published in a separate atlas volume titled *Recueil des Cartes et des Vues du Voyage en Amérique, en Italie . . . par Edouard de Montulé.* For a reproduction of the two-stone lithograph of New York City in that volume, see Reps, *Saint Louis Illustrated,* fig. 1–16, p. 12. Montulé is another of these river artists whose life remains unknown. Not even dates of birth or death have been determined, although in his narrative he states that he was a native of Le Mans, France, and claims that he was a chevalier of the Legion of Honor. The editor and translator of the modern edition reports his failure to find any biographical information in his search of French sources. See his note 1, p. 10.

16. The earliest views of Natchez are mentioned in the brief essay by Maurice R. Scharff, "Collecting Views of Natchez." Collot served during the American Revolution on the staff of General Rochambeau. He undertook his reconnaissance of the American interior in 1796 when the French minister in this country asked him to observe and report on "the political, commercial and military state of the western part" of the United States. Georges Henri Victor Collot, *A Journey in North America, Containing a Survey of the Countries Watered by the Mississippi, Ohio, Missouri, and Other Affluing Rivers. . . .* The French edition, *Voyage dans l'Amérique Septentrionale; ou, Description des Pays Arrosés par le Mississippi, l'Ohio, le Missouri, et autres Rivières . . . ,* was published the same year. In 1924 O. Lange of Florence, Italy, published a facsimile of the English edition. In Collot's work, the names of cartographers do not appear on the many finely drawn and engraved strip maps of the Ohio and Mississippi rivers or on those of towns and forts. However, several manuscripts in the Chicago Historical Society and elsewhere of plates appearing in Collot's book bear the name of George Bois St. Lys. At least one other, the view of Pittsburgh, is the work of Joseph Warin, who also accompanied Collot on his trip. Collot himself may have drawn one or more of the other illustrations that make the atlas volume of his work such a cartographic treasure. The original drawing for the view of Pittsburgh is now in the Stokes Collection of the New York Public Library and is signed on the back by Joseph Warin, identified by the editor of the 1924 edition of Collot's book as Adjudant [*sic*] General Warin. For a description of this wash drawing and further information on Collot, see Deák, *Picturing America,* entry 214.

17. The best account of Lesueur's American career is R. W. G. Vail, "The American Sketchbooks of a French Naturalist, 1816–1837: A Description of the Charles Alexandre

In 1816 Lesueur came to Philadelphia to continue his career as a scientist and to teach drawing, moving in 1825 to New Harmony, Indiana, as one of the intellectuals caught up in Robert Owen's project for a model community. Despite the early breakup of the Owenites as an organized body, Lesueur spent the next dozen years in New Harmony, which he used as a base for numerous trips into the interior of America on sketching and collecting trips. It was on one of those trips, probably in the spring of 1828, that he sketched Natchez.

Lesueur returned to France in 1837, and it was there that he used some of his American sketches for lithographs. In addition to the view of Natchez, these included a Memphis view and ten others, among them a few that depict small settlements on the river, each with a tiny cluster of buildings: Iron Bank, Randolph, Grand Gulf, and Petit Gulf. At first glance the Natchez view seems to show nothing more than the fort occupying a commanding site atop the bluff at the left. For some reason the artist elected not to include the upper town, which would have appeared beyond where Lesueur ruled his left border. One needs to look carefully to discern the image of the lower town whose buildings stretched along the narrow shelf of land near the water's edge.[18]

Lesueur's Memphis view (Folio 18) provides a somewhat better record of conditions in this community, which was then less than ten years old. In his analysis of this printed view and several other Lesueur sketches from the vicinity, James Roper tells us what can be learned from the artist's depiction of frontier Memphis:

> It would seem that Lesueur is sketching at about where Riverside Drive meets Front Street today, just west of City Hall. The line of buildings in the distance runs east-west at about Market Street. The tall house near the bluff edge is probably Mayor Winchester's imposing residence, known to have

had an upper story which he a little later converted into a lecture hall . . . and a ballroom. It was located near Jackson and Front Streets, the latter being then known as Chickasaw.[19]

The only other views of this early period portray the dominant community of the upper river, St. Louis. Its earliest printed image appeared in 1817 on a banknote issued in St. Louis but engraved in New York by William L. Leney and William Rollison and doubtless printed there. This partial skyline panorama in Folio 25 gives us our first glimpse of what soon would become the busy and thriving gateway to the West. Modern scholars have provided a key that identifies the buildings on this rare engraving, and it is clear from that analysis that the anonymous artist knew St. Louis and, within the restricted confines available to him for the illustration, supplied a reasonably accurate portrait of the little city's business core.[20]

Beyond St. Louis there were no places sufficiently large or with features interesting enough to attract early viewmakers, and itinerant artists would have found it inconvenient and uncomfortable to venture further upstream even if suitable subjects existed. Roads were few in number and poorly maintained, no railroads had yet arrived in the region, and while by 1830 steamboats had clearly triumphed over competing types of rivercraft on the lower river, their use remained limited north of the mouth of the Missouri River a few miles beyond St. Louis.

At St. Louis, however, steamboat transportation promised to transform this frontier outpost into an inland metropolis just as it stimulated the development of dozens of smaller and less important places. Appropriately enough, the second oldest printed view of St. Louis provides the background of an advertisement for the *Peoria*, a vessel that served the city during the years 1832–1834. Folio 25 reproduces this view along

Lesueur Collection, with a Brief Account of the Artist." Vail provides a list of all the American sketches now at the Natural History Museum in Le Havre where Lesueur spent the last two years of his life as director. A bibliography of Lesueur literature can be found in Jacqueline Bonnemains, "Charles-Alexandre Lesueur en Amérique du Nord (1816–1837)."

18. Reproductions of twelve lithographs made from Lesueur's drawings appear in E.-T. Hamy, *Les Voyages du naturaliste Ch. Alex. Lesueur Dans L'Amérique du' Nord (1815–1837)....* Two of Lesueur's sketches showing the lower town in more detail from closer vantage points are reproduced in James Register, *Views of Old Natchez [Early 1800s]*, unpaged. Apparently the lithographs were never published but were simply made by Lesueur for private purposes. I am indebted to Mme J. Bonnemains, Conservateur de la Coll. Lesueur, Museum d'Histoire Naturelle, Le Havre, for a number of references and additional information in a letter to me of September 3, 1992.

19. "The Earliest Pictures of Memphis: Charles Lesueur's Drawings, 1828–1830," 15–16.

20. I have reproduced the banknote illustration and the diagrammatic key in *Saint Louis Illustrated*, 17. There I mention that "the buildings represented in the view belonged to the most prominent and wealthy families of St. Louis, so obviously the engraving illustrates the largest and most impressive buildings the artist could find in the little city. In addition, six of the buildings shown in the view belonged to persons who joined in incorporating the Bank of St. Louis in 1813, and perhaps they determined both the focus and the limits of the engraving." The banknote is known only from the unique impression in the Eric and Evelyn Newman Collection in St. Louis. The diagrammatic analysis of this view and explanatory text appeared in Stella M. Drumm and Isaac H. Lionberger, "Earliest Picture of St. Louis."

with a map of the city published in 1822. This map depicts the large and rigidly rectangular addition that had increased substantially the size of the city that originated as a linear French settlement along the river, extending only four blocks inland to the west.[21]

It is this expanded community that both George Catlin and Leon Pomarede saw and drew in 1832, although printed versions of the images they created were not published until three and four decades later. Folio 26 reproduces both of these prints, a distant view of St. Louis from the southeast by Catlin and a more detailed glimpse of the city's waterfront from the ferry landing across the river in Illinois by Pomarede. On the occasion of the publication of the lithographic version of the latter view its publishers provided this description:

> The steam ferry-boat . . . has made its landing at the eastern bank. . . . Across the river, the eye takes in a goodly town, with market house standing on the spot where . . . Laclede [the city's founder] landed sixty-eight years before. . . . The spire of the Cathedral, on Walnut Street, was then the only one of which the city could boast. . . . The low round domes of the Baptist Church, on the corner of Third and Chestnut, and Dr. Bullard's on the corner of Fourth and Washington, are landmarks that a few old citizens will recognize.[22]

Catlin and Pomarede came from quite different backgrounds. George Catlin (1796–1872) was born in Pennsylvania; he studied law but soon turned to painting, first in Philadelphia and then in New York. In the latter city he produced several crude lithographic views. These were used in a volume celebrating the opening of the Erie Canal and are among the very first American prints executed in this new medium of printmaking.[23]

Starting in 1829 he began what became a collection of some six hundred portraits of Indians and Indian scenes. It was in St. Louis during his many years of life in or near the Indian tribes of the Midwest that he produced two essentially identical paintings of St. Louis, one of which served as the basis for the lithograph reproduced in Folio 26.[24]

Leon Pomarede (ca. 1807–1892) probably studied in France before coming to New Orleans in 1830. There he sharpened his artistic skills under two theatrical scene painters before traveling to St. Louis in 1832 to work on murals in the old cathedral. It was in that year or shortly thereafter that he painted the view that was reproduced as a lithograph in 1875. After returning to New Orleans in 1837 to open a studio, he came back to St. Louis six years later. There he began work on a great panorama of the Mississippi River, first with Henry Lewis, and then on his own after their association ended.[25]

In 1849 and 1850 Pomarede began a tour of his panorama with showings in St. Louis, New Orleans, and some eastern cities. This venture ended when a fire in Newark destroyed the huge painting on which Pomarede had worked so long. He spent the rest of his life in St. Louis as a painter, mainly of religious subjects, dying at the age of eighty-five after falling from a scaffold while decorating a church ceiling in Hannibal, Missouri.

For a return trip from St. Louis to New Orleans with viewmakers in the 1830s we need make only two stops, beginning with Cairo, Illinois. This seemingly favorable spot for urban development in the heart of the continent and at the mouth of the Ohio River bore the curse of its low-lying site, which flooded almost every year. As noted previously, efforts of townsite promoters to create a city here had begun as early as 1818 but had come to nothing.

By the mid-1830s one Darius Holbrook had gained control of the site, a spot he intended as the southern terminus for his Illinois Central Rail Road, a venture chartered by the state legislature in January 1836. Like most frontier promoters, Holbrook possessed far more ideas than wealth, and to seek the latter he set off for London to borrow money.

21. This same image of St. Louis provided an identical background illustration for a broadside advertising the steamboat *Yellow Stone*. An impression of this is in the InterNorth collection on permanent loan to the Joslyn Art Museum in Omaha, Nebraska. I came across a small illustration of this recently when looking at a folder describing the superb exhibit "Views of a Vanishing Frontier," held at the Joslyn Museum a few years ago.

22. "Historical Sketch of the City of Saint Louis," in Camille N. Dry and Richard J. Compton, *Pictorial St. Louis: The Great Metropolis of the Mississippi Valley*, 10. In 1950 Pomarede's oil painting measuring 29 x 39 inches was part of an exhibit at the St. Louis Art Museum. See entry 82, p. 110, and a small reproduction on the facing page in Rathbone, ed., *Mississippi Panorama*.

23. Cadwallader Colden, *Memoir Prepared at the Request of the Committee of the Common Council of the City of New York . . . at the Celebration of the Completion of the New York Canal*, appeared in 1826 with Catlin's two views of Lockport and two of Buffalo. One of the Lockport views is reproduced in Reps, *Saint Louis Illustrated*, as fig. 1–17.

24. The painting used for the lithograph printed sometime between 1865 and 1869 is in the collection of the Missouri Historical Society in St. Louis. The other is in the National Museum of American Art in Washington, D.C. For Catlin's career see Loyd Haberly, *Pursuit of the Horizon, a Life of George Catlin, Painter & Recorder of the American Indian*, and Joseph R. Millichap, *George Catlin*.

25. John Francis McDermott, "Leon Pomarede, 'Our Parisian Knight of the Easel'" and "Portrait of the Father of Waters: Leon Pomarede's Panorama of the Mississippi."

He departed carrying with him two items that he relied on to help his cause. One was a detailed engineering and planning study of the site that he commissioned from an English engineer and geologist, Richard Taylor, and a well-known American architect, William Strickland.[26]

Their study concluded that the site could be protected from flooding and recommended the development of a compact town consisting of blocks about five hundred feet square formed by the gridiron street pattern. The plan showed the city divided into six sections, each focusing on a public square the same size as the standard city blocks. This drawing, signed by both consultants, showed one of these sections shaded, doubtless indicating a policy of phased development that would allow the town to expand one or more sections at a time in an orderly fashion that would minimize the cost of land filling called for in the report.[27]

Holbrook's other weapon was an impressive lithographic view drawn by Strickland showing how this first section of the city would appear if built according to plan. Folio 22 reproduces this view, skillfully put on stone in Philadelphia by Alfred Hoffy and printed in 1838 at the lithographic establishment of Peter S. Duval. Holbrook's glib tongue, the seemingly sound technical report he had commissioned, and Strickland's attractive portrayal of the future city combined to win the approval of London bankers to underwrite an issue of Cairo City bonds. In February 1839 Holbrook revealed that he had obtained $1.5 million from Wright and Company of London.[28]

Whatever funds Holbrook actually spent on improvements at Cairo seem to have been wasted. An English visitor who passed by Cairo in 1845 referred to Strickland's view showing "domes, spires, and cupolas, hotels, warehouses, and lines of steamboats along both rivers. How fair—how magnificent it all looked on the India paper!" Instead of this vision, he found almost nothing:

> You should see the result. . . . Cairo is a swamp, overflowed by every rise of either river. The large hotel, one of the two buildings erected, is slowly sinking below the surface. The heaps of railroad iron sent out from England for the great central road to Chicago, of which this was to be the depot, are many feet beneath the surface. Piles . . . however deep they are driven, sink still deeper. The present business of the place, consisting of selling supplies to steamboats, and transferring passengers from the down to the up-river boats, is done on floating store boats, made fast to the shore.[29]

In contrast to Strickland's prospective view of Cairo—an image that bore no resemblance to the community then or anytime since—the handsome portrayal of Natchez in Folio 12 probably records with fair accuracy the appearance of this center of Mississippi culture. James Tooley (1816–1844) drew this view, which was printed in New York about 1835. The artist was not more than twenty when he or some anonymous publisher sent his work to Charles Risso and William R. Browne to be put on stone and printed at their New York City lithographic establishment.[30]

Tooley's original sketch or painting evidently has not survived, and one can judge his abilities as an artist only from the lithograph. Unfortunately, this is not always a reliable measure since skillful lithographers could and often did transform an indifferent sketch into an attractive print. The view, however, does possess a character that can be compared favorably with an earlier painting of 1822, an almost identical composition by a far more well-known and admired artist, John James Audubon. The similarity of the two suggests at least the possibility that

26. Before Strickland began the independent practice of architecture he made his living as an artist and engraver. For his career, see Agnes Addison, *William Strickland: Architect and Engineer, 1788–1854.*

27. The plan is reproduced as fig. 227 in John W. Reps, *The Making of Urban America: A History of City Planning in the United States,* 384. See also Reps, "Great Expectations and Hard Times: The Planning of Cairo, Illinois." The standard history of early Cairo from which much of the above was derived is John M. Landsden, *A History of the City of Cairo, Illinois.*

28. Cephas G. Childs, one of the pioneers of Philadelphia lithography, brought Duval to the city from France in 1831, as Duval recalled it "to take charge of Messers. Childs & [Henry] Inman's lithographic establishment." Duval is quoted in Nicholas B. Wainwright's important study of this form of printing in Philadelphia, *Philadelphia in the Romantic Age of Lithography: An Illustrated History of Early Lithography in Philadelphia with a Descriptive List of Philadelphia Scenes made by Philadelphia Lithographers before 1866,* 22. After 1835 when Duval and George Lehman took over the business of Childs and Inman, and especially beginning in 1838 when he became sole proprietor of the enterprise, Duval gained a reputation as the most accomplished lithographer in the city. The Holbrook-Strickland view of Cairo was thus one of the first produced by the firm under his sole direction.

29. Thomas L. Nichols, *Forty Years of American Life,* 1:168–69.

30. Risso and Browne began their association in 1832 and continued in business together until 1838. Deák follows I. N. Phelps Stokes in assigning a conjectural date of ca. 1835 to the Tooley view. In her notes to entry 448 in her *Picturing America,* 1:302–3, she provides this information about buildings appearing in the print: "The large house with columns at the left is 'Rosalie,' the home of the Rumble family, built around 1820. . . . The building with the dome, in the center of the view, is the Court House, remodeled in 1926. The steeple at the right of the view is that of the First Presbyterian Church, built in 1830 and still in active service more than 150 years later."

young Tooley saw Audubon's painting and based his sketch on that more experienced artist's work.[31]

Of Tooley himself almost nothing is known except that he was a painter of miniatures and landscapes whose presence in Natchez has been established at the time this view appeared and again in 1842–1843. In 1839 the New Orleans *Daily Picayune* carried a brief notice reading: "Miniature Painting. James Tooley, Jr.—Miniature painter, room No. 5, Camp Street, up-stairs." Before his second visit or stay in Natchez, he was in Philadelphia for at least part of 1842 and 1843.[32]

Henry B. Miller, who visited Natchez in 1838, just a few years after Tooley saw the city, described it as "a regular laid out town of about one mile square; the streets are of a good width & intersect each other at right angles; the side walks are generally paved with Bricks with Brick gutters." He provided what must be an almost complete catalog of Natchez's major buildings: "a Court house & jail, a Market house, Masonic Hall, three Churches, two Hotels, Mansion House, three Banks, & the Theatre," not all of which Tooley could capture in his view.

Miller began his verbal tour with the courthouse on State Street, the domed building near the center of Tooley's view. He found this "beautifully situated on a square Plat of ground planted with ornamental trees; the House is built of Brick with a cupola & Bell." Miller called "the jail . . . opposite the court House (on the west side of State street)" only "a tolerable Brick building." The market building "south of the Court house on the same square" impressed him as "a fine building." He passed no judgment on the city hall, noting only that "the building is plastered & finished in imitation of stone work."

He also recorded his impressions of some of the town's other buildings:

> The Masonic Hall is situated on the corner of Main & Union streets (North west corner); and is quite a respectable Brick Building; the front is Plaster in imitation of Stone work, with Corinthian Colums [sic] & pilasters; the Post Office is kept in one part of the Lower story and the Institute & Lyceum have the other room; the Masonic Lodge is up stairs. . . . The Theatre is

situated on Main street near Pine; this is rather an indifferent concern; it is fitted out with considerable taste but is rather small . . . ; it is, however, large enough for the accommodation except on rare occasions.[33]

One other urban view published before 1840 needs to be examined. Reproduced in Folio 4, this New Orleans scene bears the name of a distinguished and prolific French artist of marine views, Ambroise Louis Garneray (1783–1857). While still very young Garneray began a life devoted to maritime affairs, shipping out on a French vessel when only thirteen. Eventually he turned to drawing and painting, doubtless influenced by his father, who also was an artist. Garneray published the bulk of his printed work in a five-volume set under the title *Vues des Cotes de France dans l'Océan et dans la Méditerranée* between 1830 and 1835. The final volume contained prints of important ports in the Western Hemisphere, including Philadelphia, New York, and New Orleans.[34]

The view in Folio 4, like the other American ports by Garneray, was engraved by Sigismond Himely. While the quality of this aquatint cannot be faulted as an example of fine printmaking, the view itself resembles more an elevation drawing by an architect than a work of art by a townscape painter. There is no record of Garneray coming to America, and the unconvincing character of this view probably stems from the sketch by an unknown artist from which Garneray worked. The date of depiction may have been as early as 1825 but was more likely around 1830.[35]

The view is disappointing in another way, for it shows little more of the city than the immediate surroundings of the old French Place d'Armes, by that time renamed Jackson Square for the hero of the Battle of New Orleans. Even so, it offers a useful if not necessarily entirely accurate record of the appearance of the cathedral with its two flanking buildings housing the offices of the church on the right, or downriver, side in the Presbytère and the civil offices of the local government on the other side in the Hotel de Ville, or city hall.

---

33. "The Journal of Henry B. Miller," 281–83.

34. Almost all of my information about Garneray comes from entries 432 and 433, 1:291–92, in Deák, *Picturing America*.

35. In Historic New Orleans Collection, *Encyclopaedia of New Orleans Artists*, the entry under Garneray states that the artist prepared his collection of aquatint marine views during 1821–1832. Deák's *Picturing America* puts the publication dates as ca. 1830–1835. The Historic New Orleans Collection dates its impression of the view ca. 1825. The collection also has a smaller (10 3/8 x 14 5/8 inches) version printed by lithography. Curators have assigned a questioned date of 1830–1835 to this version of the print.

31. Audubon's painting of Natchez in 1822 has been reproduced in several books, but perhaps the best is the double-page color plate following p. 120 in Rathbone, ed., *Mississippi Panorama*. See also the color reproduction in Donald Culross Peattie, ed., *Audubon's America: The Narratives and Experiences of John James Audubon*. Both Tooley's and Audubon's views, along with several others of Natchez, are reproduced uncolored in Scharff, "Collecting Views of Natchez."

32. Historic New Orleans Collection, *Encyclopaedia of New Orleans Artists*, 377.

Few visitors to New Orleans came away from this part of the city unimpressed by this square and its surrounding buildings. Louis Fitzgerald Tasistro admired what he saw on his visit in 1840: "The most remarkable buildings here are the ancient Cathedral, somewhat the worse for age, built in the old quiet style of French architecture; and the famous *Calaboose*, the terror of all evil-doers. . . . There is, besides, the Town Hall, and the Court of Law, with their venerable stone walls, harmonizing, not inelegantly, with the rest."[36]

This first reconnaissance to the urban Mississippi as revealed in prints of the time has been necessarily brief. In the following years leading up to the Civil War, however, more towns came into existence along the Mississippi, especially in the hitherto only sparsely settled stretch of the river serving Iowa, Wisconsin, and Minnesota. Alive to the possibility of profits from town founding and urban land promotion, townsite developers and speculators came to the upper Mississippi in increasing numbers.

One early report on possible sites for successful towns provided a useful guide to would-be town founders. It came from Lieutenant Albert M. Lea, an officer of the U.S. government carrying out mapping duties as part of an official reconnaissance mission of the upper river. Lea's observations on potential town sites must have seemed almost like a governmental endorsement, even though it was Lea himself who published the book in which they appeared. Moreover, Lea was also investing in Iowa lands, so his assessments of various sites were not entirely unbiased, although subsequent events were to prove his judgment sound.

A graduate of West Point in 1831, Lea served with the army topographical engineers for several years before joining the command of Lieutenant Colonel Stephan Kearney and participating as a topographer in the reconnaissance of parts of Wisconsin Territory in 1835 that included what is now Iowa, Wisconsin, and Minnesota. In February of the following year Lea resigned from the army at Fort Des Moines, visited many sites in Iowa along the Mississippi, purchased some land there, and journeyed to Philadelphia to arrange for the publication of his report and map of the region.[37]

Published in 1836, Lea's book contained a chapter titled "Remarks upon Towns, Landings, and Roads." It began with these words: "In this embryo State, those interested are anxiously looking out for places where are to be the future cities to do the trade and manufacturing of the country. I propose making a few remarks upon places that have attracted most attention." He mentioned Keokuk as a place where "a mile square was laid off . . . for a town-site" to help settle land claims of those within the so-called Half-Breed tract.

Lea described what became the town of Fort Madison as a place "nature seems to have designed . . . for the trade of an extensive back country." He noted that "this place was laid out in lots in November, 1835; the lots were immediately sold out, and building is now rapidly progressing." Of Burlington he had this to say: "This place has a good landing, and a tolerable site for building. There is a fine quarry of sandstone within the town. The first settlement was made here in 1833, and the town was laid out in 1834. It contained about 400 inhabitants at the close of 1835."

He observed that the intended "town at the head of the Muscatine Slue" [*sic*] would have "an excellent landing, and . . . a fine back country; but the bluff . . . approaches the river very abruptly, allowing little room for building below it." Nevertheless, Lea concluded, "It must be a place of considerable trade; as it is the first place above Burlington, where a town can be built on the west bank of the Mississippi, thus leaving an interval between these two places of forty miles on the river."

Lea considered Davenport's site attractive and that its location at the lower end of the rapids, "where navigation is much obstructed, will cause it to be resorted to as a place of shipment, both for persons and freight." He wrote that the town had been planned "on a liberal scale" and that "three public squares have been reserved from sale, one of which, it is supposed . . . will be occupied by the public buildings of the future State of Iowa." Of this possibility and knowing of his own involvement in a town on the Iowa River that became Iowa City and the first territorial capital, Lea commented: *"Nous verrons."*

He liked Bellevue because the "place has a good landing," although "there is no room for building near the water's edge, in consequence of the proximity of the bluff to the river." Lea noted that the town had been "laid out in 1835, and immediately [there]after several houses were erected." He confidently predicted, "It must soon be a place of much trade."

36. *Random Shots and Southern Breezes, Containing Critical Remarks on the Southern States . . .*, 1:94.
37. Lea's career is the subject of Robert M. Merryman, *A Hero Nonetheless: Albert Miller Lea, 1808–1891.*

It was Dubuque, however, that he found most advanced, the city having been surveyed in 1833. When he visited it two years later he found
"about twenty-five dry good stores, numerous groceries, four taverns,
a court-house, a jail, and three churches. One of these, the Catholic, is
a beautiful little building. Ten steam-boats, which run between this and
Saint Louis, are partly owned here, and there is also here a steam-ferry-
boat. The site of the town is very handsome, and building materials
and fuel are convenient."[38]

As these and other places on the upper river grew, several artists
found them suitable outlets for their talents and depicted their images
in a variety of prints. And—as the tempo of urban development ac-
celerated with westward expansion of the nation—later artists found
more and more subjects whose portraits seemed worth recording. In the
chapter to follow we will look at the first results of their activities.

38. *Notes on Wisconsin Territory, with a Map.* See pp. 148–55 for the passages quoted.

II

Mississippi Views in the 1840s

The Urban World of John Caspar Wild and Henry Lewis

Throughout most of the 1840s artists in two cities—New Orleans and St. Louis—dominated urban viewmaking along the Mississippi. One aquatint of New Orleans from a sketch by Antoine Mondelli at the beginning of the decade demonstrated the highest qualities of that method of creating multiple images and offered its owners or others seeing it an impressive portrait of the city's busy waterfront. Shortly thereafter Paul Cavailler, an artist-lithographer—not the most skilled who ever practiced this trade—created a semi-panorama of the city in three related lithographs that provided convincing graphic evidence of how New Orleans had grown up- and downriver from its original compact core.

At the same time in St. Louis the talented and prolific John Caspar Wild arrived to live for a time and to draw, lithograph, and publish a superb set of views of his adopted city. He then produced a less impressive series of illustrations of smaller places in Missouri and Illinois before moving upriver to create the first printed images of places in Iowa as well as the earliest such view of Galena, Illinois.

Closely following Wild and perhaps influenced by him came Henry Lewis, who also lived for a time in St. Louis. In the late 1840s Lewis fulfilled his ambition to create a huge, moving panorama of the entire Mississippi. This enormously long, painted canvas could be unrolled before an audience as scenes on the canvas passed through a large frame that functioned like a motion picture screen.

A decade later Lewis used the sketches made for the panorama by him and others to produce a cornucopia of more than thirty printed views of cities on the Mississippi from Minnesota to the Gulf of Mexico. This chapter will explore the work of these artists who helped bring the images of river cities to the attention of both residents of the region and those who lived elsewhere.

We can begin with one of the most prized views of New Orleans, one that Antoine Mondelli (ca. 1799–?) sketched for the aquatint of the city in 1841 reproduced in Folio 5. An Italian artist whose career in New Orleans spanned thirty-three years beginning in 1821, Mondelli like many other artists of the period in this country found it necessary to engage in a number of related activities. Thus at one time or another he taught art, painted signs, worked as a gilder and glazier, created stage scenery, and operated an art store.[1]

William James Bennett (178?–1844), one of the foremost practitioners of aquatint, ably transformed Mondelli's sketch into a painting and from that finished image created his aquatint print. Bennett's New Orleans view was one of nineteen portraits of American cities similar in

1. Historic New Orleans Collection, *Encyclopaedia of New Orleans Artists*, 269–70, lists his major works and provides references to the sources from which the entry was prepared and which this paragraph summarizes. Leon Pomarede, the artist of the view of St. Louis in 1832 mentioned in the previous chapter, was one of Mondelli's students as well as his son-in-law, and the two worked together for a time in St. Louis. Mondelli received many commissions in New Orleans to decorate churches, and he also designed two important cenotaphs, prepared architectural plans for the U.S. Marine Hospital, and painted other scenic works of New Orleans as well as of Cincinnati, Nashville, and Mobile.

character and format that Bennett produced after his arrival in America from England, where he had studied at the Royal Academy and had acquired a substantial reputation.[2]

In 1826 as he approached forty Bennett decided to come to the United States to continue his career in a country that offered fresh subjects for his talents. Often, as he did for his New Orleans print, he based his prints on the work of other artists. For such places as Boston, Baltimore, and Detroit he was the artist as well as the printmaker, using the painstaking and exacting process of aquatint etching and engraving. Bennett himself may also have colored many impressions of the prints with the transparent watercolors that so beautifully complement and enhance the aquatints.[3]

The print is undeniably attractive, although the foreground figures and the ships and rivercraft either at anchor or moving downstream almost overwhelm the skyline of New Orleans in the background. Even so, several buildings can be identified. The two most obvious are St. Patrick's Catholic Church of 1837, whose towering spire extends well into the dramatic sky, and the imposing dome of the Exchange (later the St. Charles) Hotel, finished in 1837 but burned in 1851. In between

one can see the spires of the Presbyterian and the Methodist Episcopal churches.[4]

Not all visitors to New Orleans at this time found it so attractive, at least not at first sight. In 1840 Louis Fitzgerald Tasistro set down his initial impressions:

> New-Orleans . . . seemed, at first, to contain all the horrors of New-York, without any of its general character of external grandeur. The filth of the streets, and the eternal din of carts loaded with cotton . . . struck me as truly execrable. The endless succession of plain, brown, dirty-looking bricks piled up for houses, with plain, square holes for windows and doors, equally execrable!

Tasistro evidently began his inspection of the city in the American quarter, for when he "crossed the line" and strolled down the rue de Chartres, he found himself struck by the "balconies with which the houses are decorated" and "the elegant forms that here and there stood revealed in all their singularity of beauty and attire." Soon he "began to think New-Orleans a very fine place indeed—perhaps the only one in America fit for a gentleman to live in."[5]

A few years before Tasistro's visit and the appearance of the Mondelli-Bennett view of New Orleans, the legislature in 1836 divided the city into three coequal municipalities. Thus began an interesting and unusual experiment in structuring local government to provide a measure of independence for the three major ethnic sections of the city. It reflected both the cosmopolitan nature of New Orleans's population and the substantial amount of self-imposed and forced segregation that prevailed.

The First Municipality encompassed the original French town between Canal and Esplanade and occupied the central location among the three constituent parts of the new city government. This portion of the city remained strongly Creole in composition, inhabited by descendants of earlier French and Spanish settlers as well as some newer arrivals from French- and Spanish-speaking lands. The Second Municipality extended upriver from Canal Street to Felicity Street, an area consisting largely of Anglo-American residents. The Third Municipality

2. According to one writer, Bennett "first exhibited at London in 1808, and contributed to the exhibitions of the Water Colour Society from 1819 to 1825." Frank Rutter, "Rare American Colour Prints: Early Views of American Cities now in Favour with Collectors: W. J. Bennett—a Notable English Craftsman among Makers of American Prints," 331.

3. In his article on Bennett's views and other contemporary aquatints, the then Curator of the Department of Prints at the Metropolitan Museum of Art in New York explains the aquatint process: "To make an aquatint the outlines of the picture are first etched on copper, as a guide in laying the tones. The copper is then evenly dusted with rosin power, which sticks to the metal when gently heated. Next, the copper plate is placed in an acid bath and acid eats around the protective rosin grains, eroding irregular canyons around mesas so that the copper surface somewhat resembles sandpaper. Printer's ink is then rubbed into the canyons, and wiped off the tops of the mesas. The plate thus prints irregular white dots on a dark ground, and the two blend at a distance into an even tone like that of an ink wash. . . . To reproduce a wash drawing with many gradations of tone takes great skill and patience. First of all the areas of pure white must be protected altogether from any acid by being painted with stopping-out varnish. After the plate has had a brief bath in etching acid, the palest tone is stopped out, and so on with gradually darker tones. This process of stopping out parts of the plate and lightly etching the rest may have to be repeated a couple of dozen times to achieve subtle transitions of tone from lightest to darkest. . . . Because the process itself is so complex, few aquatinters also learned how to draw interesting pictures." A. Hyatt Mayor, "Aquatint Views of Our Infant Cities," 314.

4. For an informative note about this view see Deák, *Picturing America*, entry 512, 1:344–45. She notes that one English visitor at midcentury compared the domed hotel to St. Peter's in Rome.

5. *Random Shots and Southern Breezes*, 1:54, 83–84.

lay downriver from Esplanade. Its population included large numbers of recent arrivals from Italy, Germany, and other European countries.[6]

These three parts of the city and additional tracts of subdivided land beyond them can best be understood by an examination of the Map of New Orleans reproduced in Folio 3. Jacques Tanesse, the city surveyor, drew this in 1815 to show lands within the city and its suburbs that had then been laid out in streets and lots. Probably the majority of the lots thus created still lay vacant, including some of those that Tanesse shows in darker tones to indicate where development was most intense.

The sections that from 1836 to 1852 became for a time separate municipalities can be easily identified on Tanesse's map. The First Municipality comprised the blocks in the central rectangle that the map shows bordered by three wide, tree-lined streets. Its upriver boundary (to the left on the map) was Canal Street. The Second Municipality extended beyond to Felicity Street, the last long thoroughfare on the map leading back from the river. The Third Municipality lay below Esplanade, the street bounding the First Municipality on the downriver side.[7]

Perhaps inspired by the division of the city in this manner, Paul Cavailler (ca. 1813–1854 or after) drew and put on stone for publication in 1843 the three views found in Folio 6, each showing one of the three municipalities. Cavailler may have arrived in New Orleans only the year before these three prints were published, for they represent the first appearance of his name in a New Orleans context. A few city directory listings of him as a lithographer and his name on a view of Tivoli Gardens and on some sheet-music covers exhaust the known facts of his life and career. The excessive rarity of the three prints suggests also that his efforts as an artist went largely unrewarded.[8]

Possibly sales would have been greater if Cavailler had drawn the prints so that they could have been joined together as one continuous panorama. Instead, sharp breaks in the large foreground details make this impossible. If an owner had wished to join the three to make a single print for framing, these discontinuities would have severely detracted from the resulting image. It would also have been helpful if Cavailler had provided a legend below the lower border so that the very small images of the buildings could be readily identified.

Indeed, the three prints are more valuable as a record of activities at Algiers, the community directly across the Mississippi from Jackson Square and the cathedral, which appear at the center of the lithograph of the First Municipality. At Algiers lumberyards, warehouses, and ship-building enterprises occupied sites along the river, and all three prints provide excellent views of these waterfront activities.

One also finds in these views informative images of the working boats of a major seaport. In the Third Municipality print the sidewheel steamer *Panther* advertises itself as a towboat. In the print of the Second Municipality another boat of this type makes its way upstream with a three-masted schooner made fast on its starboard side and a smaller sailing vessel toward us on the port side. At other places in this set

---

6. The portion of the Third Municipality between Esplanade and the Elysian Fields was known as Little Saxony because of the preponderance of German settlers there. Elysian Fields was the wide street running inland from the river and bisecting the former Marigny Plantation. The ethnic divisions of New Orleans at this time were, of course, far from fixed, for many Germans, particularly those who had been among the early arrivals, lived in the Second Municipality or farther upriver in what was incorporated in 1833 as the City of Lafayette. See John Fredrick Nau, *The German People of New Orleans, 1850–1900*, 16–17.

7. In addition to its clear delineation of the city's streets and civic squares, this engraving provides an excellent catalog of the principal buildings of the city as they existed early in the nineteenth century. Few American cities had as many impressive structures as those that gave New Orleans its distinctive character. Tanesse himself designed one of the most important, the long market illustrated in the vignette at the upper left corner of the engraving. The map's publishers, Charles Del Vecchio of New York and P. Maspero of New Orleans, had the engraving done in New York by William Rollinson, an English artist and engraver who arrived in New York in 1789. See Robert W. Reid and Charles Rollinson, *William Rollinson, Engraver*; and entries 219 (1:144–45), 240 (1:160), and 292 (the Tanesse map, 1:193) in Deák, *Picturing America*. A second state of the map appeared ca. 1825 on which some engraver added the steeple on the Cathedral in the vignette at center top. Drawing the steeple at its proper size required the heavy ruled border to be changed to an arch at that point. An impression of this version is in the Louisiana State Museum.

8. At the lower right of the view of the Third Municipality the artist signed his name and dated his work 1842. The printers, Manouvrier and Chavin, are not listed as partners until 1843, and their association lasted only another year. It seems most likely that 1843 was the publication date. In Reps, *Views and Viewmakers*, where I attempted to date all views by year of publication rather than delineation, I followed the Tulane University Library in dating them 1842. Impressions of the views may be in private collections, but of the institutions surveyed only the Tulane University Library has all three, and the only recorded impressions elsewhere are those of the First and Third Municipalities at the Mariners' Museum in Newport News, Virginia. See entries 1146–48 in *Views and Viewmakers*, 311. I should note that in two of these entries I misspelled the name of the artist. It is curious that the imprint on the view of the Third Municipality gives the printer as F. Chav[in], while the other two identify the printer as J. Manouvrier and Chav[in]. It is possible that the Third Municipality print (with the artist's signature and the 1842 date signed in the stone) was printed first and in 1842 before Chavin joined with Manouvrier to form their partnership.

of prints one can observe a sail-assisted vessel with a walking-beam engine amidships, several sidewheel passenger steamers, a schooner sailing downstream under partial canvas, a small sloop beating its way upwind and upstream, and a ferry arriving at Algiers Point from the French Quarter on the other side of the river.

All the Mississippi River city views that we have examined so far came from artists who created only single prints of this type or, like Montulé or Lesueur, a limited number of images produced only as adjuncts to their main purposes for visiting these cities. It is only in St. Louis in the 1840s that we meet for the first time artists who devoted most of their time to drawing and converting to printed images the likenesses of towns along the Mississippi. These artists—John Caspar Wild and Henry Lewis—thus dominated Mississippi River urban view-making in the 1840s.

Wild (1804–1846), born in Switzerland, came to St. Louis in 1839, eight years after his arrival in America from France, where in Paris he was known as a landscape painter. First in Philadelphia, then in Cincinnati, and then in Philadelphia again, Wild left behind him an impressive number of painted and lithographed views of cities and urban buildings. A series of small prints of Philadelphia scenes and a more ambitious set of four prints depicting the city as seen looking toward the cardinal points of the compass from Independence Hall were warmly praised and were apparently financially successful as well. Nevertheless, Wild suddenly transferred his share of a business to his partner and by the end of 1838 had left for the West.[9]

The St. Louis *Daily Evening Gazette* first noted Wild's presence in St. Louis on April 29, 1839, announcing the publication of "a very neatly colored lithographic drawing of St. Louis, as seen from the opposite shore." Readers learned that while "the sketch was drawn and colored by Mr. J. C. Wild," it had been printed by "Mr. Dupré's well known establishment." In this large print Wild looked across the Mississippi from a point southeast of the town's center, framing the skyline of St. Louis

with trees on either side and adding two figures in the foreground that helped to give depth to the scene.[10]

The printer, Eugene Charles Dupré, was the city's pioneer lithographer. He apparently had little training in this craft, since he came to St. Louis from France to make his living selling women's coats and teaching his native language. In 1837 he advertised that, "having procured the necessary apparatus," he could "furnish at the shortest notice and in the neatest manner, Lithographic drawings of towns, public and private buildings, maps, charts, views of natural scenery, and drawings of machinery of every description." He then added: "A good writer on stone can find employment in the above establishment."[11]

It is possible that Dupré's efforts to find a skilled lithographer ("writer on stone") attracted Wild's attention and led him to come to St. Louis. Certainly Wild's abilities in drawing on and printing from lithographic stone vastly exceeded those of Dupré. Indeed, Dupré's work never demonstrated more than elementary knowledge of lithographic techniques. After this first venture Wild dispensed with his services and served as his own printer.

Wild lost little time in demonstrating his skills, creating a superb set of eight views of St. Louis and its most important buildings. Just a year after the newspaper first noticed Wild's appearance in St. Louis and the publication of his initial view of the city, readers of the *Missouri Republican* learned that they could see Wild's paintings of his new views. The newspaper noted that subscribers could obtain lithographic versions of the painted scenes for only four dollars for the set of eight. For those wishing hand-colored prints, the price was set at eight dollars.[12]

Folio 27 reproduces four of these now extremely rare prints as colored by Wild or under his supervision. Three display the city from the opposite side of the Mississippi. The fourth offers a lively look at the St. Louis waterfront. Other lithographs in the series illustrated the courthouse then under construction, the cathedral, and the Episcopal

9. I have devoted an entire chapter to the work of J. C. Wild, concentrating on his St. Louis views and illustrating nearly all of them, in Reps, *Saint Louis Illustrated*, 29–51. For details of his career in Philadelphia, I have depended on the excellent study by Martin Snyder, "J. C. Wild and His Philadelphia Views." Wild's work in the Mississippi valley and elsewhere is the subject of two articles by John Francis McDermott, "J. C. Wild, Western Painter and Lithographer" and "John Caspar Wild: Some New Facts and a Query." I have found no published account of Wild's Cincinnati work, although the historical society in that city has reproduced several of his views.

10. For a full-page color reproduction of this view, see Reps, *Saint Louis Illustrated*, chap. 3.

11. The notice of Dupré's new business appeared in the St. Louis *Republican*, August 22, 1837. His only city view was a clumsy rendition of St. Louis, poorly executed on stone and badly printed. It appeared in E. Dupré, *Atlas of the City and County of St. Louis*, and is reproduced in Reps, *Saint Louis Illustrated*, fig. 2–10, p. 24. See in that volume the text and notes on pp. 24–25 for what little information exists about Dupré's brief career as a lithographer from 1837 to 1840.

12. The announcement of the display of Wild's paintings appeared in the St. Louis *Missouri Republican* on April 28, 1840.

and Second Presbyterian churches. The paintings have apparently not survived, and only two complete sets of the lithographs have been recorded in institutional collections.[13]

Although their rarity suggests that Wild succeeded in selling few impressions, his announcement in December 1840 that he intended to issue a second edition with four additional views indicates his belief that enough customers could be found to justify the additional effort. However, for reasons that will probably never be known, he decided instead to broaden the scope of his pictorial efforts and to include other places along with St. Louis in a vastly expanded series of projected views.

The *Missouri Republican* on March 13, 1841, told its readers that Wild had "commenced the publication" of a work bearing the title "The Valley of the Mississippi" that would include "views of the principal cities and towns in the Great West." These were to appear monthly in groups of four views with accompanying "historical descriptions." The newspaper urged its readers to support this venture, pointing out that this publication would be appropriate "to transmit to eastern friends to give those who have never been west an idea of western science, western scenery, &c."

The first part of this ambitious publication appeared in July 1841. It contained a single view, a redrawn version of Wild's first lithograph of St. Louis in 1839. Wild reduced this to about six by eight inches to fit the size of eight and one-half by eleven inches selected for the text pages and wrapper. The text by Lewis Thomas described what Wild portrayed:

> The compact portion of the city . . . presents a beautiful view, when beheld from the opposite shore in Illinois, or from various other points in approaching it. The fleet of steam boats and other craft lining the landing for a mile—the white-fronted warehouses extending for equal length—the dense mass of buildings in the rear, seemingly mingling with the horizon in the distance, with here and there a church tower, a belfry, or a steeple looming to the skies, exhibit a panorama of exceeding beauty.[14]

Wild published several additional sections that year, adding others in the first part of 1842 and ending with the final two parts that spring. The death of his young wife that January and a possible disagreement with the editor and author of the text, Lewis Thomas, may have led Wild to terminate the series far short of its announced goal of fifty views and two hundred pages of text each year.[15]

Although Wild originally intended to depict "views of the principal cities and towns in the Great West," his *Valley of the Mississippi Illustrated* contained images only of places in Missouri and Illinois. Those of St. Louis predominated. In addition to the redrawn version of his earlier print of St. Louis in the first issue and views of several of the city's buildings, Wild included a remarkable four-sheet lithograph in the last issue showing St. Louis as the artist saw it looking to the cardinal points of the compass from the roof of a centrally located hotel.[16]

Wild's lithographic plates of Kaskaskia and Cahokia, the two early French settlements in Illinois, are particularly valuable because so few images of these places exist. Folio 24 reproduces these views, the winter scene of Cahokia being of special interest for its clear images of the characteristic French colonial houses and the winter appearance the artist chose to record. Wild depicted the appearance of several other places in Illinois: Cairo, Illinois Town (East St. Louis), Prairie du Rocher, and Alton, whose portrait appears in Folio 31. The Missouri towns that he recorded in addition to St. Louis are St. Charles, whose image is reproduced in Folio 30, and Carondelet, now part of St. Louis.[17]

Given that Wild had lived in Paris, Philadelphia, Cincinnati, Philadelphia again, and St. Louis in just over ten years, it would have been uncharacteristic for him to have settled in one place for long. Although the St. Louis city directory for 1845 lists him as "Lithographic Printer," by the time the directory appeared he may already have moved to

---

13. Although a few other collections have one or more of these lithographs, only the New-York Historical Society and the Missouri Historical Society own all eight.

14. J. C. Wild, *The Valley of the Mississippi Illustrated in a Series of Views*, 10.

15. The title page issued with the first part reads: "*The Valley of the Mississippi Illustrated: In a Series of Views embracing pictures of the Principal Cities and Towns, Public Buildings and remarkable and picturesque Scenery, on the Ohio and Mississippi Rivers.* Drawn and Lithographed by J. C. Wild. Literary Department by Lewis F. Thomas. Published in monthly numbers, each number containing four views, with an average of four pages of letter press to each view descriptive of the scenery &c. &c; making at the end of each year a volume of 200 pages with fifty views. Price $1 payable monthly. J. C. Wild. publisher at the Republican Printing Office. Saint Louis, Mo. Entered according to act of Congress by J. C. Wild in the year 1841 in the Office of the Clerk of the District Court of Mo." A facsimile edition was published in 1948 and later issued in book form by Hawthorn Publishing Company of St. Louis. Later parts add, "Chambers & Knapp, Printers."

16. A reproduction of the four sheets joined as a single panorama with text identifying important structures is in Reps, *Saint Louis Illustrated*, 39–42.

17. I have reproduced the Carondelet lithograph and the lovely watercolor on which Wild evidently based his print in *Saint Louis Illustrated*, 43–44.

Davenport, Iowa. He painted that city in 1844 for a lithograph published later that year that listed Davenport as his address. That fall Wild also visited Minnesota, where he painted the Falls of St. Anthony and Fort Snelling.[18]

Folio 43 reproduces Wild's painting of the Davenport area, a work that is signed and dated 1844. For this splendidly executed distant view the artist looked upriver to Davenport on the left side and Rock Island and Moline, Illinois, on the right. The island from which the town on the Illinois side took its name can be seen in the middle. This painting is clearly the work of an artist who had mastered the techniques of topographic and landscape art. His first four views of St. Louis just as clearly demonstrate Wild's abilities as a lithographer. This makes all the more curious the quite mediocre quality of the large lithograph of the same scene, a print that Folio 43 also presents.

Wild's other printed views of towns in this region represent a much higher degree of competence. His lithograph of Muscatine, Iowa (then named Bloomington), appears in Folio 40 and that of Galena, Illinois, in Folio 47. Both equal the early St. Louis views in the skillful treatment of sky, foliage, and dramatic lighting effects and the rendition of both landforms and water. Wild had just reached his fortieth birthday at this time and if he had lived would probably have created many more such delightful images of cities along the Mississippi and elsewhere.[19]

Wild's view of Dubuque, Iowa, reproduced in Folio 48, was apparently the first printed image of that community. From this distant perspective, however, one can tell little about the character of the place. An account written by a visitor a few years later helps to provide a more complete impression of how the new town appeared:

> She is a fair town, and in our opinion will never be less. The buildings are generally brick, the streets are regular and dry. Dubuque, we must say, looks slightly slack about the feet and ancles [*sic*].—There is about many of the houses a margin of "clutter" where all should be clean. One street, well built for a new town, extends, apparently, three fourths of a mile, leaving room for an extension on the same level beyond. We saw no hogs about town. The houses are underpinned, so we infer, the hogs are kept for service and not for society.[20]

Wild's lithograph of Dubuque and its surroundings was among the very last works that the artist produced, for by the end of the summer of 1846 he was dead. On August 13, 1846, the Davenport *Gazette* announced this event:

> We grieve to mention the death of Mr. J. C. Wild, well known for his views of Dubuque, Galena, Davenport, Rock Island, Moline, Bloomington, St. Louis, etc. He died yesterday of the dropsy after an illness of some months. At the time he was taken with his last sickness he was employed upon a most beautiful view of this place and surrounding scenery. Two or three days more of labor would have completed it. As an artist he had no superior in the west.

The artist's estate, aside from a city lot in Davenport and three lithographic presses, consisted almost entirely of unsold lithographic prints and paintings. The probate court valued the six paintings of places in Iowa and Illinois at $10.00 each and the lithographs at from $.50 to $2.00 each. Their sale probably yielded just enough to pay for a decent funeral. Wild would not have been surprised. One of his few friends described him as a man with "neither humor of his own, nor an appreciation of humor in others. He looked tragedy, thought tragedy, and his conversation outside of business and art, was never much more cheerful than tragedy."[21]

Wild had scarcely left St. Louis when another equally ambitious and somewhat more successful and less tormented artist began work on a

18. McDermott, "J. C. Wild, Western Painter," 122–23, cites newspaper accounts in the St. Louis *Daily Evening Gazette* (February 24 and 29, 1844), a letter in the estate records in the Sibley Papers at the Minnesota Historical Society, and the painting of Fort Snelling also at the Minnesota Historical Society as evidence for the Minnesota trip. For a color reproduction of Wild's painting of Fort Snelling, see pl. 8 in Rena Neumann Coen, *Painting and Sculpture in Minnesota 1820–1914.* Coen states, "His representation of the fort . . . is similar . . . to Seth Eastman's view which hangs today in the United States Capitol. Wild's picture, in water color and gouache, is essentially a picturesque and idealized view, soft in tone though precisely drawn" (p. 19).

19. There is an unexplainable error in the middle initial of Wild's name below the lower right corner of his Galena view, where the imprint reads: "DRAWN FROM NATURE AND LITHOGRAPHED BY J.G. [*sic*] WILD." It is unthinkable that Wild would have made this mistake if he had put his drawing on stone. It is equally unlikely that if someone else made this error Wild would not have seen a proof and had it corrected. This is a mystery that is not likely to be solved.

20. St. Paul *Minnesota Pioneer,* November 15, 1849, as quoted in "Steamboat Travel on the Upper Mississippi in 1849," 58.

21. [A. H. Sanders], "Artistic," in Franc B. Wilkie, *Davenport Past and Present . . . ,* 309. One poignant bit of personal information surfaced in Wild's will, which indicates that he was contemplating marriage, possibly to a relative. He specified that to "Miss Mary Jane Wild of Davenport," identified as his "intended wife," he bequeathed his "watch and chain, . . . breast pin and . . . horse." This information comes from copies of the will and probate records in the papers of John Francis McDermott in the library of Southern Illinois University, Edwardsville.

vast project that ultimately led him to produce a remarkable set of town views encompassing places from the mouth of the Mississippi almost to its headwaters. This was Henry Lewis, born in England in 1819. His widower father brought Henry and two older sons to America when Henry was ten. The family settled first in Boston, but in 1834 Henry's two brothers left for St. Louis. That February, Henry became an apprentice to a plane- and toolmaker, whose trade the young man followed for two years. In 1836 Henry convinced his father to have his articles of indenture canceled, and the two moved to St. Louis.[22]

In St. Louis, Henry, still a minor, became a U.S. citizen when his father achieved that status in 1836. It is supposed that the young man found work as a carpenter or cabinetmaker, the occupation listed after his name in a city directory in 1845. Yet on March 25 of that year the *Missouri Republican* called him "a landscape painter of more than ordinary merit." Perhaps, as some have suggested without evidence, Lewis worked as a stage carpenter and taught himself or received some instruction in the painting of stage scenery. By whatever way Lewis came to his new career, several St. Louis newspapers by 1845 had recognized his abilities as an artist.[23]

At about this time Lewis conceived the idea of creating a huge panorama of the upper Mississippi River from St. Louis to beyond Fort Snelling in Minnesota. Later he decided to include the lower river as well so that his panorama would record the appearance of the banks of the river throughout its entire length. He proposed to paint this on an enormous length of canvas that could be moved through a huge frame while a speaker described for the audience what they were seeing. Such moving panoramas were not a new idea, nor would they have been a novelty to St. Louis residents. As early as the summer of 1830 Leon Pomarede's father-in-law, Antonio Mondelli, had exhibited his moving panorama of the port of New Orleans, throwing in for good measure one depicting the eruption of Mount Vesuvius and another showing the battle of the American fleet at Tripoli. Many similar spectacles entertained and edified St. Louis audiences, including panoramas of Jerusalem, Venice, the Hudson River, the Garden of Eden, the Battle of Waterloo, and something called the "Grand Cozmorama" that took viewers around the world.[24]

Doubtless Lewis knew of the great moving panorama of the Mississippi that John Banvard began to work on after he exhibited some of his other work in St. Louis in 1841. Banvard's panorama depicted the river from the mouth of the Missouri River to New Orleans. Its initial presentation in Louisville in the fall of 1846 attracted large audiences, and Banvard soon took his panorama to Boston, New York, Washington, and then, in 1848, to Europe. Everywhere reviewers acclaimed Banvard's work, and in the national capital the House and Senate joined in a resolution that called the panorama "a truly wonderful and magnificent production."[25]

John Rowson Smith also set to work on a similar panorama and was able to exhibit it by 1848. That same year Samuel B. Stockwell showed his version of a river panorama, which was followed the next year by the one painted by Leon Pomarede. All three originated in St. Louis. Although these painted depictions of the Mississippi have not survived, printed descriptions that advertised them and contemporary newspaper accounts tell us that they featured many urban views. For example, an

22. Several letters between Henry and his brother George are in the William L. Clements Library, Ann Arbor, Michigan. The text of one from Henry to his brother in St. Louis tells how badly he wants to come to St. Louis and how he proposes to get out of his six-year indenture agreement, and it asks for George's help in convincing their father to leave Boston for the West. See the long extract in William J. Petersen, *Mississippi River Panorama: Henry Lewis Great National Work*, 14–15.

23. J. Christian Bay stated that Lewis worked at the Ben Bar opera house in St. Louis as a carpenter and painter. See his "Introduction," iii–xii. Three St. Louis newspapers in 1845 commented favorably on Lewis's work. In addition to the *Missouri Republican*, the *New Era* for March 29, 1845, noted his "very considerable skill as a landscape painter," and a writer in the *Weekly Reveille* on April 27, 1945, mentioned seeing in the studio that Lewis shared with James Wilkins, a portrait painter, "many original pictures of undoubted merit." The newspaper quotations are provided by John Francis McDermott, *The Lost Panoramas of the Mississippi*, 81–82. Many years later Lewis declared that he taught himself to paint, maintaining that "there was no one in St. Louis when I first took up art as a profession to give lessons." Lewis to Warren Upham, March 7, 1902, MS in Minnesota Historical Society, as quoted in Bertha L. Heilbron, *Making a Motion Picture in 1848: Henry Lewis' Journal of a Canoe Voyage from the Falls of St. Anthony to St. Louis*, 2.

24. These are mentioned and briefly described in McDermott, *Lost Panoramas*, 9–15. McDermott's bibliography is the most important source of references on this subject. For other treatments of panoramas and their artists, see Porter Butts, *Art in Wisconsin: The Art Experience of the Middle West Frontier*, 51–65; Coen, *Painting and Sculpture in Minnesota*, 24–31; and Heilbron, *Making a Motion Picture in 1848*.

25. Banvard's work is fully reported in McDermott, *Lost Panoramas*, 18–46. Banvard's *Self-Portrait*, an oil painting in the Minnesota Historical Society, is reproduced in Coen, *Painting and Sculpture in Minnesota*, 25. A line drawing and accompanying text explaining the mechanism used by Banvard to crank the canvas from one roll to another on the opposite side of the viewing frame appeared in *Scientific American*, December 16, 1848. For Banvard's autobiographical account of his career and the printed program identifying the features shown in the panorama, see John Banvard, "Adventures of the Artist" and "Description of Banvard's Panorama."

advertisement for Stockwell's panorama claimed that it included "every city, town, village, and 'landing' from the Gulf of Mexico to the 'Falls of St. Anthony.' "[26]

To Lewis, an artist seeking greater recognition as well as what appeared to be large and assured profits, the creation of a similar panorama that would include both the upper and lower Mississippi proved an irresistible temptation. Probably he already had the idea of a panorama in mind during the summers of 1846 and 1847 when he traveled up the Mississippi on sketching tours, later completing several oil paintings of Fort Snelling and the Falls of St. Anthony. In 1848 he embarked on a more systematic journey, a descent of the river by boat that allowed him to sketch the entire stretch of the Mississippi from Minnesota to St. Louis.[27]

Originally he planned to work with Samuel Stockwell, but the two decided to go their separate ways. Then Lewis and Leon Pomarede reached some kind of understanding about joining forces. For reasons that are far from clear but doubtless stemmed from disagreements about money or how the project should be approached, this arrangement also broke down, and Pomarede, like Stockwell, went on to create his own panorama. Lewis then obtained the services of Charles Rogers, an artist previously associated with Stockwell, whom he commissioned to sketch the river below St. Louis. He cautioned his agent in St. Louis to keep this arrangement confidential and to send Rogers north to meet him as soon as Rogers arrived in St. Louis from his sketching tour of the south.[28]

Lewis set out for St. Paul. At nearby Fort Snelling he once again saw Captain Seth Eastman, the talented soldier-artist he had first encountered on his earlier sketching visits to the area. It was more than a casual encounter, for in 1847 someone—almost certainly Lewis—asked Eastman to join him in painting "a panorama of the river from the Falls of St. Anthony to New Orleans," using sketches that Eastman had made during his present tour of duty that began in 1841 as well as even earlier work dating to 1829 when the army assigned him to the garrison at Prairie du Chien. In 1847 Eastman put Lewis off because he was then in negotiations with a potential purchaser in New York, but a year later he agreed to sell many of his sketches to Lewis.[29]

At Fort Snelling, Lewis set to work to construct the odd craft described and pictured in Folio 32. Using two fifty-foot canoes connected by planks to create a catamaran hull, Lewis built a cabin from whose roof he could sketch. A sail and oars handled by two boatman hired for the purpose provided propulsion. John S. Robb, a New Orleans journalist who by then was on the staff of the St. Louis *Weekly Reveille*, accompanied Lewis and wrote several reports of the voyage for his newspaper. At Galena they finally found Charles Rogers, his sketches of the lower river completed. Rogers was "a gentleman," Lewis wrote, "I had been anxiously looking for, to assist me in making sketches."[30]

26. St. Louis *Weekly Reveille*, October 29, 1848, and St. Louis *Missouri Republican*, October 24, 1848, as quoted in McDermott, *Lost Panoramas*, 74. A printed version of The Balize from Smith's panorama appeared in *Graham's Magazine* 35 (1849): opposite p. 304. The panorama must have also included a likeness of the Mormon town of Nauvoo, Illinois, for *Graham's* used another wood engraving of the Nauvoo Temple in the article referring to the Smith panorama. For notes on and illustrations from a panorama painted in 1850 by Dr. Montroville W. Dickeson and John J. Egan, see Rathbone, ed., *Mississippi Panorama*, 127–35.

27. Color reproductions of two Lewis paintings of the region, *The Gorge of the St. Croix* (1847) and *St. Anthony Falls as It Appeared in 1848* (1855), can be found in Coen, *Painting and Sculpture in Minnesota*, pls. 9 and 10. Both paintings are in the Minneapolis Institute of Arts.

28. McDermott says in his *Lost Panoramas*, 87, that Rogers "arrived to join the party at Galena on July 21. It is certain that, as early as June 14 when writing to Stagg about the final break with Pomarede, Lewis impressed on his partner at home that they must not lose Rogers 'on any acct as his knowledge of sket[c]hing and of the character of the river is imense.' As soon as Rogers arrived at St. Louis with the southern sketches, Stagg was to send him up river to meet Lewis. The arrangement was secret: 'don't say

a word to any one that we have engag'd him.' Apparently Rogers was being enticed away from Stockwell to whom he had been engaged. The word was to be put out casually by Stagg that Lewis had 'abandoned the idea of sending a person down south to make sketches.' "

29. The quotation is in a letter from Eastman to Charles Lanman, November 1, 1847, Charles Lanman Papers, Library of Congress, as quoted in John Francis McDermott, *Seth Eastman's Mississippi: A Lost Portfolio Recovered*, 7. This volume reproduces numerous Eastman sketches from the portfolio that Lewis eventually bought, and McDermott points out that Lewis used Eastman's work as the basis for many of his lithographs. He also quotes a letter from Lewis to his brother in 1847 stating that Eastman's works were "the very sketches we want" and that they could "render our affair of much more ease and importance than we thought." In his book Lewis acknowledges Eastman as the source of some of the views. According to McDermott, Lewis probably purchased the views in October 1848 when they may have been delivered by Mrs. Eastman to Lewis in Cincinnati where he had gone to paint his panorama. For Eastman as the source of many of the images painted by Lewis, see also Lila M. Johnson, "Found (and Purchased): Seth Eastman Water Colors."

30. This is the last sentence in the July 21, 1848, entry of a journal Lewis kept of the trip downriver. The complete text can be found in "Journal of Canoe Voyage from the Falls of St. Anthony to St. Louis." The passage quoted is on p. 301. The journal is presented as part of Bertha L. Heilbron, "Making a Motion Picture in 1848: Henry Lewis on the Upper Mississippi."

The two artists drew the towns below Galena as they moved down-river until they reached St. Louis early in August. Not long thereafter a St. Louis newspaper noted, "Mr. Lewis will shortly leave for the east to commit his labors to the canvass, and in the accomplishment of this object, he will be assisted by one or more artists of eminent reputation, and thus securing not only accuracy, but beauty and interest of a finished painting." The "east" turned out to be Cincinnati, where Lewis began work on September 20, 1848, at a task that kept him, John Leslie, a scene painter for a Cincinnati theater, and several assistants—possibly including Rogers—busy until the following May. By that time Lewis had completed the first part of his panorama, the section from the Falls of St. Anthony to St. Louis, a painting 825 yards long and 4 yards high.[31]

Although no description of Lewis's studio in Cincinnati seems to exist, conditions there must have resembled closely those observed two years earlier in Louisville by a friend of John Banvard when Banvard was at work on his own Mississippi river panorama:

> Here and there were scattered about the floor, piles of his original sketches, bales of canvas, and heaps of boxes. Paint-pots, brushes, jars and kegs were strewed about, without order or arrangement, while along one of the walls several large cases were piled, containing rolls of finished sections of the painting. On the opposite was spread a canvas, extending its whole length, upon which the artist was then at work. A portion of this canvas was wound upon an upright roller, or drum, standing at one end of the building, and as the artist completed his painting he thus disposed of it.[32]

Lewis exhibited his panorama first in Cincinnati and then in Louisville. In both places it received much acclaim from the press, but expenses proved to be high, and an outbreak of cholera reduced the size of the crowds at the performances. Returning to Cincinnati, Lewis, assisted by Leslie and Rogers, finished the lower river section and added a view of St. Louis showing the great fire that destroyed much of the central portion of the city and a large number of steamboats on May 17–18, 1849.[33]

It was thus to a ravaged city and one still mainly preoccupied with rebuilding that Lewis brought his panorama at the end of August. After a preview for the St. Louis press and other invited guests, Lewis opened the panorama to the public for its first showing in his home city on September 1. As in Cincinnati, the newspapers showered praise on Lewis and his work. Comments in the St. Louis *Union* were typical. On September 14 the paper informed its readers that "the Lewis Panorama is all the rage and this fine hall is nightly filled by the elite of the city." The next day the paper carried this appraisal:

> The editor has visited it several times, as have other citizens, and on each occasion saw some new beauty, or some rare effect of sky and water, which had escaped our previous notice. The Panorama is the most elaborate and faithful that has ever been exhibited in the country. The accumulated labor of years pass in rapid succession before the eyes of the spectator, in the compass of two hours. . . . Thus, Mr. Lewis has adopted a style peculiarly original and pleasant—stepping out, as it were, from the old routine usually pursued by artists on similar works.[34]

Approval by the critics, however, did not necessarily mean box-office profits. After leaving St. Louis, Lewis showed his panorama in Peoria, Illinois. At the end of a three-night run, Lewis reported to one of his brothers that he made "more in these three nights than we did in Cincin[nati] and St. Louis in 6 weeks." The panorama drew crowds in Chicago, although expenses exceeded Lewis's projections. Nevertheless, he told his brother that after nine showings he had "a good profit"—namely $437.76. With part of the extra cash from the Peoria and Chicago performances Lewis paid off some of the notes he had executed when borrowing money for the cost of his travels, canvas and paints, assistants, studio space in Cincinnati, and other expenses.[35]

31. St. Louis *Missouri Republican*, September 11, 1848. In Cincinnati, Lewis had the help of at least four Cincinnati artists, identified by McDermott in *Lost Panoramas*, 192, n. 70, as: "John R. Johnston, portrait painter and panoramaist, born Cincinnati, March 10, 1826, went to St. Louis in the summer of 1848 to paint on Stockwell's panorama and returned in December to paint on Lewis', doing 'figures, boats, and cities.' A bit later in Cincinnati, with Edwin F. Durang he painted a panorama of biblical scenes." "John Leslie was scenic artist at the National Theatre, Cincinnati." "Laidlaw had recently come from the Drury Lane Theatre, London, according to press references."

32. Letter from S. Woodworth to General Morris, April 13, 1846, as quoted in Banvard, "Adventures of the Artist," 120.

33. In a long letter to his brother George on July 11, 1849, Lewis detailed the business aspect of producing and showing a panorama. The text appears in Petersen, *Mississippi River Panorama*, 24–26.

34. As quoted in ibid., 30.

35. The letters to his brother are quoted in ibid., 33.

Lewis took his panorama to Milwaukee, Detroit, Rochester, and Buffalo, evidently showing the upper-river section one night and the lower-river portion the following evening. Each apparently required about two hours to present. Lewis wrote his brother from Buffalo on December 29, 1849, that he had decided to send Washington King, who was then his coproprietor, to Syracuse with the upper-river panorama while he took the one of the lower river to Rochester, a city where the other part had already been seen. In informing his brother of the progress of events, Lewis wrote:

> We are going to try how it will go to make two complete exhibitions one following the other. I am now busy getting up a new frame, proscenium and all the et ceteras ready for a start. After he has finis'd exhibiting the Upper river in a place, I come up and put the Lower one on the same frame, both frames being made the same size. We shall by this means save taking down the frames.[36]

From upstate New York, Lewis moved to Washington, avoiding New York City, where he had learned, as he reported to his brother, that there were "five panoramas exhibiting there and none of them were paying expenses. The place is overdone." In the national capital Lewis rented the Odd Fellows' Hall for his performances, and he also took the panorama to Richmond for two weeks. Then at the end of the summer of 1850 he moved on to Salem, Massachusetts, and Bangor, Maine. During the winter he visited Canada, displaying his work in Halifax, Toronto, Hamilton, Kingston, and Montreal.[37]

Around mid-October 1851 he put his panorama on a boat for England, traveled to Boston, boarded the *Daniel Webster*, and after a voyage of a little more than three weeks disembarked in Liverpool on November 25. After shows in England and the Netherlands, Lewis took the panorama to Germany, where, because of competition with another panorama of the Mississippi by one James Tosh, box-office receipts remained low. Using the arts center of Düsseldorf as a base after 1853, Lewis displayed his panorama in a few other European cities. Then, in

1857, he finally succeeded in selling it to a Dutchman who intended to take it to Java. Apparently the new owner reached Calcutta, but there the trail ends, and the ultimate fate of the panorama remains uncertain.

Although Lewis never received the full $4,000 agreed on as a purchase price, a partial payment allowed him to begin the serious study of art in Düsseldorf. There he met many artists, including Carl Wimar, George Caleb Bingham, and Albert Bierstadt, who had come to study art, and Emanuel Leutze, with whom Lewis studied for a time. When Leutze went to America in 1859 he left his studio in Lewis's care, and it was to this residence that Lewis brought his bride, Maria Jones, the English governess in the household of the purchaser of the panorama. During these first years in Düsseldorf, Lewis sent some of his paintings to St. Louis to be sold by his brother, while others went to Boston in care of his cousin Horace.

Meanwhile Lewis decided to use his extensive collection of Mississippi River sketches by himself, Eastman, and Rogers as the basis for a series of lithographs illustrating a book about the Mississippi. Probably Lewis discussed this in America in 1848 with Heinrich Arnz, a Düsseldorf publisher, and it may be that this is what brought Lewis to that city in 1853. The project called for twenty parts, each containing sixteen to twenty-four text pages and four illustrations, with one part to be issued each month beginning in the summer of 1854. For a title Lewis—or Arnz—borrowed the one used by J. C. Wild and translated it into German: *Das Illustrirte Mississippithal* (The valley of the Mississippi illustrated).[38]

In a preface Lewis declared his "intention . . . to render each single number, as far as practicable, complete in itself, with regard to the history and geography of that particular region." He included three testimonials signed by numerous persons who had seen his panorama and praised it for its accuracy and beauty. They included President Zachary Taylor, several members of congress from states along the Mississippi, Governor James Doty of Wisconsin, and Seth Eastman. Lewis stated, "In presenting this work to the public, the author hopes it will be found all it is represented, namely, a fine work of art, as well as a correct delineation of the 'Great Father of Waters.'"[39]

---

36. Quoted in ibid., 34.

37. McDermott, *Lost Panoramas,* 142, reproduces a copy of the handbill used by Lewis to advertise the Montreal showing. In addition to hearing spoken commentary at showings of the panorama, audiences could purchase written guides. What is apparently the earliest, describing only the upper river, is in the Minnesota Historical Society collections: Charles Gaylor, *Lewis' Panorama. A Description of Lewis' Mammoth Panorama of the Mississippi River, from the Falls of St. Anthony to the City of St. Louis. . . .*

38. The early meeting with Arnz is discussed in the "Editor's Introduction" by Heilbron in Lewis, *Valley of the Mississippi Illustrated,* 8–9, and McDermott, *Seth Eastman's Mississippi,* 8–9.

39. Lewis, *Valley of the Mississippi Illustrated,* 35–36.

Almost immediately everything went wrong. Heinrich Arnz died, and Lewis had difficulty getting paid for his work. Only three parts were published in 1854 and three more the following year, although eventually the remaining fourteen parts did appear. The completed work assembled in book form in 1857 was in German. An intended English edition remained incomplete after the first seventy-two pages were printed. Relatively few copies were ever distributed of the single-volume version containing all twenty parts with seventy-eight lithographs (that of New Orleans occupying two pages) and an illustrated title page.[40]

Because of their attractive appearance and their importance as both the first and the most complete pictorial record of towns along the Mississippi, many of the Lewis lithographs appear among the folios of this book. They allow the viewer to ascend the river with stops at a dozen places among the many others whose appearance Lewis and his assistants recorded in the summer of 1848. Folios 10, 15, and 19 provide glimpses of Baton Rouge, Vicksburg, and Memphis—all along the southern stretches of the river. Evidently Lewis's assistant, Charles Rogers, sketched these towns, among others in the south, before joining Lewis at Galena. Folio 32 illustrates four of the Lewis views from the central portion of the Mississippi: Port Byron and Warsaw, Illinois; Louisiana, Missouri; and Bellevue, Iowa. Folios 28 and 33 offer images of two other cities in this region: St. Louis and Hannibal, Missouri.

Although Lewis appropriated much of the text accompanying these views from previously published sources, he evidently composed the brief passage on Louisiana, Missouri, himself. He referred to it as "a busy little town in Missouri, 105 English miles above St. Louis . . . famous for its flour mills. In 1851 it had a population of about 300. The aspect of the town, which we sketched for our illustration at sunrise was one of the most charming of our entire journey."[41]

Concerning Warsaw, Lewis had this to say:

> This city is located on the east bank of the Mississippi, in Hancock County, Illinois, 175 miles above St. Louis. It is a small, vigorous, rapidly growing city, surrounded by numerous settlements and a farming population which together exert a favorable influence on the development of the community. Fort Edwards, a well-known frontier post . . . , formerly

stood on the hill on the other side of the city. In 1851 the population was about five hundred.[42]

Near Warsaw in Illinois was Nauvoo, a city planned in 1839 by Joseph Smith after religious persecutions drove him and his fellow Mormons from Missouri. In a few years it became the most populous city in the state, but when Lewis saw the place it was a ghost town, abandoned by its founders when they left to seek sanctuary in the Far West. The Lewis lithograph in Folio 37 depicts the city before vandals burned the temple whose steeple dominated the skyline. Across the river lay Keokuk, Iowa, whose view Folio 36 reproduces. Folios 53 and 58, with reproductions of the Lewis views of Prairie du Chien, Wisconsin, and St. Paul, Minnesota, complete the representative selection of his work presented in this book.[43]

In his text Lewis tells of the founding of St. Paul, a story he may have heard from the land agent, Henry H. Sibley, mentioned in this passage:

> There was a government land sale at which the site was purchased by an agent of certain associates—some 200 in number—who had, before the sale, agreed upon the ownership of the several lots, and thus rendered the business of conveying from the agent to the associates a very easy matter. . . . The price paid to the government by the town's agent was a little over $200, or $1.25 an acre. . . . The town was very fully represented at the sale, there being encamped on the ground nearly 200 *St. Paulites* who had come there *"to see justice done"*; in other words to frown indignantly on any *"outsiders"* who should presume to bid against their agent![44]

Lewis spent the rest of his life in Düsseldorf. Sales of his paintings brought him some income, but he derived much of his support by

---

40. Heilbron traces the complex printing history of *Das Illustrirte Mississippithal* in her Introduction to the modern English translation previously cited, 8–20.

41. Lewis, *Valley of the Mississippi Illustrated*, 277–78.

42. Ibid., 260. Since the Census of 1850 recorded Louisiana's population as 912 and Warsaw's as 3,000, the much lower figures given by Lewis probably date from his visits there nearly a decade before he published his book.

43. Those wishing to investigate Lewis and his art should not overlook the original drawings by Lewis and Rogers, many of which are in the Missouri Historical Society. The lithographs do not fully reflect the meticulous detail of the drawings, being much simplified and more impressionistic. Further, the printed versions exaggerate vertical elements while compressing the horizontal. McDermott reproduces the drawings for Quincy, Alton (in three sections), and Carondelet in *Lost Panoramas*, 116–17, 124–31.

44. Lewis, *Valley of the Mississippi Illustrated*, 84. Heilbron in her English edition of Lewis's work (p. 84, n. 2) points out that Sibley and Lewis knew each other well and that "there is a strong possibility that [Sibley] himself told Lewis this story, which is recorded in his 'Reminiscences of the Early Days of Minnesota,' in *Minnesota Historical Collections*, 3:244 (1880)."

taking in roomers in a comfortable house that he and his wife purchased. After 1867 he also enjoyed a small salary from the U.S. government for his services as a consular agent in Düsseldorf, which brought him about $1,000 a year until his resignation in 1884. He returned to the United States only once, in 1881, when he visited relatives and friends in New York, St. Louis, and Victor, Iowa, where his brother George then lived. Lewis died in Düsseldorf on September 16, 1904.

Although Lewis never achieved either the artistic renown or the financial rewards he sought from his panorama, his book, or his paintings, he left a precious legacy for print lovers and historians alike. His views never fail to charm those who see them, and they give us our earliest complete look at the results of the rapid progress of urbanization along the great river. In addition Lewis also depicts what

seems to be a nearly unending catalog of river craft powered by paddle wheels, oars, poles, and sails or—like the great log rafts steered by long sweeps—intended only to drift downstream.

Even while they recorded the features of towns in the valley of the Mississippi, both Wild and Lewis must have realized how rapidly their urban portraits would become out-of-date. Indeed, by the time the Lewis lithographs appeared almost a decade after his voyage in 1848, many of the towns and small cities he or Rogers had drawn bore little resemblance to their sketchbook images. It fell to a new generation of artists in the next decade to record the changed faces of the region's new and expanded urban communities. It is their work that the next chapter will explore.

III

Images of Towns in the Age of Wood Engraving

Book and Magazine Illustrations before and after the Civil War

By the middle of the nineteenth century most of the favorable locations for towns along the Mississippi had been occupied. These included the sites for places that would later grow and prosper as well as for those that did not succeed. Of the former, New Orleans and St. Louis then dominated the urban scene, and many assumed that the latter city would some day become one of the largest in the nation. On the other hand, two places destined to become major metropolitan centers—St. Paul and Minneapolis—at that time appeared to have no more of an assured future than a dozen other communities with locations that seemed just as favorable.[1]

A wave of town founding transformed the upper river in the 1830s, part of a mania for townsite speculation that swept the nation. Until the speculative bubble burst in 1837, would-be town developers platted hundreds of new communities in the still only partly settled region of the country extending from the Appalachians to the Mississippi valley. Similar speculative orgies of town platting occurred in the 1840s and again in the 1850s.

The procedure used by townsite promoters seldom varied. Land was cheap and sometimes free. No one expected to find in a newly platted town any of the urban facilities and services that we now take for granted, and the only real costs were those involved in arranging for a printed town plan and paying for newspaper advertisements and posters that announced the venture and trumpeted its certain and glorious future. If the venture succeeded, profits could be substantial; if it failed, the promoter had little to lose.

In 1838 young Henry Miller observed the consequences of this process in the mid–Mississippi valley and noted them in his journal:

> Up the different rivers and through the whole western country there have been many plans for cities laid out which were to rival everything else that was ever heard of; Ancient Babylon and Nineveh would have been no circumstance to them in extent while Athens & Rome would have been outshone in convenience and splendor. But alas, how have they passed away? Their *ruins* like those of Rome & Athens do not strike the traveler with wonder and amazement, but like Babylon & Nineveh their cities cannot be found. . . . We find that these famous cities exhisted [*sic*] only on *paper* and their future greatness in the immaginations [*sic*] of some hair brained individuals.[2]

Exactly a decade later an English observer, John Lewis Peyton, visited St. Paul, a place he felt "was distinguished for nothing but its frontier appearance." He told his readers how "a sagacious downeaster" named Cook had established a land claim, divided the site into blocks and lots, and put them up for sale "at a high price to such strangers as followed into the country." Peyton noted that Cook had

---

1. It should be noted that several towns that exist today had not yet been established, while others flourishing a century and a half ago eventually dwindled in size or disappeared altogether.

2. "Journal of Henry B. Miller," 224–25.

done almost nothing to improve the site. Instead, "Mr Cook . . . did little else than mark out and name new streets, avenues, squares and parks. These were staked out with small white billets of wood, and sold by their numbers as exhibited on a plot which he prepared with the assistance of a co-partner in his speculations. The future streets were marked simply by a plough furrow."

The promotional claims advanced by Cook and his associates struck Peyton as ludicrous. Although he could see "nothing but a wild waste," the "enterprising speculators predicted that their city would within five years be the most populous on the Upper Mississippi." He also believed them to be totally unrealistic about another matter:

> Messrs. Cook and Company had already laid out and located three railway stations on their property around the town, and were asking an additional price for lots in these favoured localities. From the constant conversation upon the subject of the steam-horse, one would have supposed that the fiery steed was in the immediate vicinity and dashing forward to take the town. Yet at this time no railway was within seven hundred miles of St. Anthony, nor did any human being contemplate constructing one to this point, short of a half century, outside of the immediate circle of Cook and Co's Real Estate Office.[3]

In the places that did attract permanent settlers, those who emerged as leaders of the community followed many of the same boosterish techniques used by the townsite promoter. All of them hoped for and worked toward an ultimate victory in what they saw as the contest for trade, industry, population, and wealth. Much of the writing about towns in this period thus comes not from disinterested observers but from persons engaged in boosting the place where they lived or had business interests. Authors of tracts, articles, and books of this type merely carried on a long American tradition that had its roots in colonial times.[4]

Many of the new towns created after 1830 could be found in Iowa, Wisconsin, and Minnesota, regions that until that time lay too far from established communities and supply points or had not yet been opened for settlement because of treaties with Indian tribes. Settlers in Illinois had long regarded the region across the river in Iowa as desirable, but it was not until the end of the Black Hawk War that land became available. Almost immediately townsite promoters surveyed promising sites into streets, blocks, and lots and began efforts to promote their new enterprises.

In 1856 when his publishers issued his *States and Territories of the Great West*, Jacob Ferris described the results of these town development efforts:

> The principal shipping ports are Keokuk, at the mouth of the Des Moines; Fort Madison, just above, on the Mississippi, two hundred and forty-eight miles from St. Louis; Muscatine City, thirty-two miles below Davenport; Davenport, one hundred miles below Galena, and three hundred and thirty-eight above St. Louis. It is situated opposite Rock Island and is connected by railroad with Chicago, and another line is projected westward to Council Bluffs. Also Lyons, Bellevue, and Dubuque.[5]

Although not mentioned by Ferris, Burlington could claim equal importance among these Iowa communities. It gained early prominence with its designation in 1837 as the temporary capital of Wisconsin Territory and in 1838, after Congress created Iowa Territory, as the first capital of that new territory. Dubuque, too, was of greater consequence than Ferris seemed to think. French settlers occupied its site late in the eighteenth century, but its modern history began in the 1830s with the formal platting of streets and lots. Rock Island, Illinois, had a similar beginning during this period.[6]

Muscatine began its existence in 1836 as Bloomington at the site of a trading post established three years before, retaining its original name

---

3. *Over the Alleghanies and across the Prairies . . .*, 241–43. Despite these criticisms, Peyton conceded that "it would be difficult to imagine a more beautiful country than that around St. Paul's [sic], or a more advantageous situation for a town. . . . At some future period the capital of Minesota [sic] will doubtless verify the prophecies of Messrs. Cook and Co. and become a proud and famous city" (244).

4. For an overview of aspects of this process following the American Revolution, see chap. 13, "Cities for Sale: Land Speculation in American Planning," in Reps, *The Making of Urban America*, 349–80.

5. *States and Territories of the Great West . . .*, 247. For a study of urban development of Davenport, Rock Island, Moline, and Bettendorf (the Quad Cities, as they are known), see Edward B. Espenshade, Jr., "Urban Development at the Upper Rapids of the Mississippi."

6. The founders of all these towns used some version of the grid street plan, although Davenport's original plat of 1836 had some unusual features. Of the forty-two blocks, three were set aside for public squares. One of these survives as Lafayette Park, another is occupied by the courthouse and jail, and the third is the site of the YMCA. That the founders intended these squares to be community focal points is indicated by the fact that, while most of the city blocks have lots facing either north or south, those blocks bordering each square are divided so that the lots on the east and west sides, as well as those on the north and south, face the square.

until 1849. Guttenberg, too, bore another name for a time. Settled as Prairie La Porte and given its plan in 1837, it changed its name after 1845 when the Western Settlement Society, an organization based in Cincinnati, brought the first of several groups of German immigrants there in 1845. Keokuk also began in 1837 as a town laid out by an agent of a New York land company on a site used earlier as a trading center by the American Fur Company. Clinton, Iowa, joined this group of new communities in 1838, being called New York for several years before assuming its present name.[7]

The expanding urban network in Iowa and elsewhere on the river attracted a new generation of artists. Railroads from the east and steamboats on the river made it easy for them to reach their subjects, and the results of their work soon appeared in a variety of forms. These included book illustrations in guides and travel accounts, pictures in magazines and newspapers, plates published in works combining pictorial and literary coverage of places throughout the world, and separately issued, single-sheet prints intended as wall decorations for home and office.

Publishers used several printmaking techniques for these views: engraving, lithography, and wood engraving. The first was most widely employed for book illustrations printed as separate plates and bound with pages printed from type. Lithography also was occasionally used for illustrations in books but proved most popular for large, separately issued views. Because wood engraving, like set type, is a relief process, it became the almost universally employed medium where the illustrations appeared on the same page as text, as was the case with pictorial newspapers and magazines and cheaper books.

Book illustrations provide some of the most interesting views of Mississippi river towns. The decade of the 1850s began with the publication in 1851 of one of the best of these sources: a volume printed in Cincinnati at the lithographic press of Otto Onken. At Onken's establishment

Adolph Forbriger put on stone the nineteen views and illustrated title page drawn by an anonymous artist for *Western Scenery; or, Land and River, Hill and Dale, in the Mississippi Valley.* William Wells wrote the text for this book—a combination of travel guide and topographic history—which because of its rarity is not as well known as it deserves to be. At the time, however, it provided images that later artists knew well enough to copy and pass off as their own work.[8]

Four of the Onken views, showing Vicksburg, Memphis, Burlington, and Galena, can be seen in Folios 15, 19, 39, and 47. One can note how the style of these views resembles that adopted by Lewis for his own more numerous lithographs of river towns. Indeed, it may be that Lewis saw a copy of the book in Düsseldorf—sent there, perhaps, by his brother in St. Louis—and decided to adopt this style instead of that used in his sketchbooks. Onken's artist and Lewis both exaggerated vertical dimensions while at the same time compressing horizontal ones. In doing so, these artists sacrificed accuracy for dramatic effect while preserving recognizable images of each city's general profile and major buildings.

Distorted or not, the views in folios 15 and 47 of Vicksburg, Mississippi, and Galena, Illinois, printed and published by Onken in 1851 seem to be the earliest printed depictions of these two places, and for this reason alone they deserve better recognition. They also represent a high level of lithographic printing. Like the Lewis lithographs, the Onken river-city views are modest in size, measuring only about six by eight inches, but each provides a clear and convincing portrayal of its subject. Unlike Lewis, Onken did not color his views, but his prints achieve much the same effect. On the Galena view, for example, Forbriger skillfully created a range of tonal values from the dark foliage in the left foreground to the faint outlines of the hills above the Fever River at the far right. This both provides effective contrast in the

7. William L. Crozier, "From Rural to Urban: Nineteenth Century Industrialization and Urbanization in the Upper Mississippi River Valley." Crozier's bibliography provides a useful guide to relevant literature. A more elaborate study is Timothy R. Mahoney, *River Towns in the Great West: The Structure of Provincial Urbanization in the American Midwest, 1820–1870,* The title is slightly misleading, since this valuable study concentrates on towns in Ohio, Illinois, and Iowa. The map on p. 105 locates thirty towns founded between 1826 and 1838 along the Great Bend of the Mississippi from Muscatine, Iowa, to Port Byron, Illinois. Mahoney provides founding dates and identifies the seventeen that did not survive. Four of these were located some distance from the Mississippi.

8. Cincinnati at this time had become a major center for lithographic printing where a large majority of the craftsmen were of German extraction. Onken produced a variety of lithographic works, and one history of the city's lithographers refers to *Western Scenery* as containing "some of the finest examples of stone lithography of the day, or of any day, by the best craftsmen operating in Cincinnati at the time" (*Lithography in Cincinnati: Presented by Young and Klein, Inc.,* pt. 1, unpaged, comment with an illustration of the book's title page). Forbriger formed his own lithographing establishment with Peter Ehrgott in premises at the southwest corner of Fourth and Main streets in Cincinnati.

play of light and shadow and establishes a sense of depth through the technique of atmospheric perspective.[9]

A few years after Onken printed the Galena view William Ferguson visited the city and "climbed the hill behind the town" after "ascending . . . a steep street, and . . . a rough wooden stair of 105 steps." From this vantage point Ferguson enjoyed "a superb view of the city and surrounding country," a scene he described in his book:

> The city is built in a small crescent-shaped hollow, amidst the hills, and is very picturesque. Manufactories and business-houses occupy the flat portion of the site; while dwelling-houses, with often little gardens attached to them, are perched on the sides of the hills, which surround it on every side. These first rise in bluffs from the river, then recede, leaving a table-land, beyond which they rise in the distance into hills.[10]

Another series of town views appears in a book by Frederick Piercy (1830–1891). Piercy drew them in 1853, and they were engraved in England for publication two years later. These views seem less dramatic than those by Onken and Lewis because the artist did not exaggerate elevations. His illustrations of such places as New Orleans, Baton Rouge, Natchez, Vicksburg, Memphis, St. Louis, and Nauvoo closely resemble what one sees now looking at places similar in size to those that Piercy sketched almost a century and a half ago: low and elongated towns with the water of the great river dominating the scene.

Piercy mentions using a camera lucida—an optical-mechanical device used as an aid to accurate drawing—for at least one of his American sketches on his trip. Whether or not he employed this instrument for all of his town views, he elected not to enhance their images with artistic distortions. Although he was only twenty-three when he came to America, Piercy had been exhibiting his work at the Royal Academy of Arts in London for five years and was thus fully qualified to record faithfully what he observed.[11]

Mormon missionaries in England commissioned Piercy to draw and write about a route that Mormon converts might take on their journey to Salt Lake City, which had been founded in 1847 as a center for the Morman Church. Arriving in New Orleans on March 21, 1853, Piercy made several stops while traveling by steamboat up the Mississippi and Missouri rivers to St. Joseph, Missouri. He then struck out overland to Kanesville (now Council Bluffs, Iowa), which he left to cross the plains and mountains to Utah. The account of his travels with engravings prepared by Harry Fenn and notes by James Linforth appeared in 1855 as *Route from Liverpool to Great Salt Lake Valley.*[12]

The Piercy views of Natchez, Memphis, and Nauvoo reproduced in Folios 13, 19, and 37 illustrate the straightforward, reportorial approach he used in recording what Mormons might encounter on their way to the Great Basin via New Orleans and the Mississippi River. As a converted Mormon, Piercy must have found his depiction of Nauvoo painful to execute, for it was here that the Mormons had created and then been forced to abandon a lively and populous city. The two snags in the foreground, the threatening sky, and the panorama of a nearly deserted site all suggest the melancholy history of this place that was so important in Mormon tradition.

Earlier, on his visit to Memphis to sketch the city for the view in Folio 19, Piercy enjoyed a much happier experience. "An old German . . . the proprietor of the Ferry-boat at Memphis" took Piercy to the west bank of the river, and Piercy tells how

> after my sketching all day within sight of the old man of course he knew that I was an artist, and when I got into the boat to return he asked me to show him my sketch, which I did with the greatest readiness. When I offered him the fare for taking me over, he drew himself up with an air of dignity, and said "No," he could not think of taking money from one who practiced so noble an art. I thought how very convenient it would be for poor students if all grim, hard-hearted tradesmen entertained the same view.[13]

9. Linear perspective creates an impression of depth when the artist renders lines that in reality are parallel as if they were converging toward a point on the horizon in the background. Atmospheric perspective suggests depth through rendering distant objects in fainter lines or tones than those in the foreground.

10. *America by River and Rail . . .*, 401.

11. Fairbanks analyzes Piercy's work and illustrates some of the artist's sketches and the engravings made from them in "The Great Platte River Trail in 1853." See his comment on Piercy's use of the camera lucida in the caption to fig. 2, p. 71.

12. The book is now rare, but a reprint exists edited by Fawn M. Brodie. As Fairbanks points out, in discussing the artist Brodie confused him with his son, the sculptor Frederick Hawkins Piercy. The only reliable account of the life of the senior Piercy seems to be Wilford Hill LeCheminant, "'Entitled to be an Artist': Landscape and Portrait Painter Frederick Piercy." The engraver, Harry Fenn (1838–1911), learned wood engraving in England under the Dalziel brothers. At nineteen he visited the United States on a vacation trip to Canada and decided to make his home there. In 1870 he began work on many of the illustrations reproduced as steel engravings in the two-volume publication edited by William Cullen Bryant, *Picturesque America, or The Land We Live In.* Fenn's illustrations appeared in many books and magazines, including *Harper's Monthly.*

13. *Route from Liverpool to Great Salt Lake Valley,* 83.

During the first half of the 1850s Americans could also find views of Mississippi River towns in a serial publication issued in parts and designed to present a pictorial record of cities, scenery, historical spots, and other features of the expanding nation. This was an offshoot of a publication issued in Germany by Joseph Meyer as *Meyer's Universum*. Meyer's son, Herrmann Julius, arranged with the managing editor of the *New York Tribune*, Charles A. Dana, to serve as the editor of an American *Universum*, whose first issue appeared in July 1851.[14]

A second series began in September 1853 under the title *The United States Illustrated*. It reprinted some of the plates that had already appeared in the *Universum* but added many new ones of American towns and scenic places, thirty-three in all. Some of these illustrations may have come from sketches made under an agreement reached in 1851 between Joseph Meyer and Conrad Witter of St. Louis. Witter in turn arranged for one Th. Anders to do the drawings for $10 each and the Reverend John Mason Peck to write the text.[15]

Anders may have provided the sketches for the engravings of Alton, Nauvoo, and Galena that the senior Meyer had printed in his shop in Hildburghausen. Folios 31, 37, and 47 reproduce these images. In the case of the Alton view, one can see how Anders or someone else copied almost all of the features of another view reproduced in the same folio: J. C. Wild's depiction drawn a decade earlier for his *Valley of the Mississippi Illustrated*. Meyer's artist simply added a number of new structures and substituted a different set of foreground boats and figures.

Many other views in Meyer's publications were also pirated versions of Wild's earlier images, including those of St. Louis and St. Charles. A recent study of Meyer's images of urban places on the Missouri River documents the source of his Jefferson City, Missouri, view as a photograph of about 1850 or a wood engraving based on the photograph published in 1852.[16]

Unfortunately, later publishers used Meyer's illustrations as models for their own, thus creating successive images that lagged even further behind reality. Already out-of-date when they first appeared in print, the Meyer images continued to mislead new and later readers who encountered them in books or periodicals. In one form or another, therefore, these little engravings must have been seen by thousands of persons. Their not infrequent appearance in the shops of print dealers today gives some indication of their popularity at the time they first appeared.

By far the most ambitious of these book illustrations was a long, folded engraving showing St. Louis in John Hogan's *Thoughts about the City of St. Louis, Her Commerce and Manufactures, Railroads, &c.* Dated 1855 but printed a year earlier by the firm of Leopold Gast & Brother, this panorama measuring seven and three-quarters by fifty-two inches and reproduced in Folio 28 displays the city's two-mile-long waterfront and skyline in splendidly detailed and spirited style. Two other features of this print make it of special interest: it was printed by a process referred to as stone engraving, and in 1868 the original publisher brought it up-to-date to show the many changes in the St. Louis skyline.[17]

Views of river towns appeared in a variety of other kinds of bound volumes. Folio 59, a view of St. Paul, Minnesota, in 1853, provides one example. John Mix Stanley (1814–1872) drew this as one of his many contributions to a twelve-volume, profusely illustrated set of

14. David Boutros, "The West Illustrated: Meyer's Views of Missouri River Towns." Boutros provides the text for Meyer's advertisement of the publication: "The object of this work is to present accurate views of the most remarkable and interesting places in all countries with accompanying descriptive and historical text. . . . A number will appear on the 1st and 15th of every month, containing four fine steel engravings, with about 20 pages of text. Twelve numbers will make a volume. Subscription price, 25 cents a number, or $3 a volume."

15. Robert Cazden documents the Meyer-Witter connection in *A Social History of the German Book Trade in America to the Civil War*, 436 and n. 28. Boutros, "The West Illustrated," 308–13, discusses this matter and also Peck's involvement with the project. Witter, German-born, came to St. Louis in the middle of the nineteenth century. He sold and published books in St. Louis between 1853 and 1866 at a book and stationery shop located at the corner of Walnut and Second streets. An unusually handsome lettersheet published by him is reproduced in Reps, *Saint Louis Illustrated*, fig. 6–4, p. 105.

16. Boutros, "The West Illustrated," 315–18.

17. The later version is reproduced in color in Reps, *Saint Louis Illustrated*, fig. 6–10, pp. 112–13; see nn. 22–23 for information about a key to the view identifying by number nearly fifty buildings. Gast, Moeller and Co. issued the revised version. Impressions can be seen in the collections of the Missouri Historical Society and A. G. Edwards Co., St. Louis. Leopold Gast, the printer and copyright holder of the view, had come to St. Louis from Germany by May 1849, for he is identified as the engraver of a plan and view of the great St. Louis fire that occurred that month. The following year Gast and the view's publisher, Julius Hutawa, formed a partnership, but by 1852 Gast and his brother had established their own shop. Leopold continued to be active in this business until 1868, when he sold his interest to his brother, August. Hutawa came to Missouri from Poland about 1832, and he is listed in a St. Louis directory for 1842 as a lithographer. He remained in business for many years, although at different addresses. Probably Gast worked for him before establishing his own printing shop. For the information about Gast that I have been able to assemble, see *Saint Louis Illustrated*, 71–73.

government documents reporting the results of surveys for several possible routes for the construction of one or more transcontinental railroads. Stanley was a sign painter in Detroit until a trained artist, James Bowman, gave him lessons and Stanley began to paint portraits for a living, working first in Chicago from 1836 to 1838.[18]

In 1839 while in Fort Snelling he began to paint portraits of Indians, and after earning money in the east by painting and as a daguerreotypist he moved to Oklahoma in 1842 to paint the Indians who had been resettled there on government reservations. Stanley first gained recognition when he exhibited his work in Cincinnati in 1846. That year he joined Colonel Stephen Kearny's troops on their march from Santa Fe to California during the Mexican War, serving as the artist for the expedition. He later visited Oregon Territory and Hawaii, where he painted portraits of the king and queen.[19]

Selected as artist for the survey of the northern railroad route, Stanley arrived in May 1853 at St. Paul, where the survey was to begin. It must have been shortly thereafter that he sketched his view of the city that seven years later was finally printed in New York by one of the city's major lithographing firms, Sarony, Major & Knapp. It is this view that Folio 59 reproduces, showing St. Paul from the opposite side of the Mississippi and upriver from the edge of the growing town.[20]

18. Two small wood engravings in Laurence Oliphant's *Minnesota and the Far West* may be the first images of St. Paul and St. Anthony to be printed, although Stanley drew his more detailed and attractive version a year earlier. Oliphant's small wood engravings seem to be little more than diagrams and show only a handful of houses. He visited these places in 1854 and claims to have sketched them himself. However, his description of St. Paul as having "four or five hotels, . . . at least half-a-dozen handsome churches . . . , and a population of seven or eight thousand" seems at odds with his illustration.

19. My main source of information about Stanley is chap. 1, "John M. Stanley and the Pacific Railroad Surveys," in *Artists and Illustrators of the Old West, 1850–1900*, 1–21. In 1852 his Indian paintings were put on display at the Smithsonian Institution, and his additions to them over the years brought their number to about two hundred by 1865 when a fire destroyed all but five.

20. For Sarony, Major and Knapp, see Peter C. Marzio, *The Democratic Art: Pictures for a 19th-Century America*, 50–51; and Harry T. Peters, *America on Stone: The Other Printmakers to the American People*, 350–57. As the next chapter will indicate, Stanley's assistant, Max Strobel, also drew St. Paul in 1853 and was able to see his printed version reach the market later that same year after the publisher sent it to Philadelphia to be lithographed in folio size. Strobel, along with twenty-five others, soon dropped out of the survey expedition and "rendered valuable service to Minnesota by his sketches of the Minnesota river from Lac qui Parle to Traverse des Sious," according to a note in

Just a year after Stanley's view was printed, a Cincinnati publisher issued a two-volume work illustrated by scores of wood engravings made from sketches by John Warner Barber and Henry Howe. The two authors and artists had already, either separately or jointly, produced similar books combining history, descriptions, and illustrations for Connecticut, Massachusetts, New York, New Jersey, Pennsylvania, Virginia, and Ohio. Their new study, *Our Whole Country*, summarized their previous work and added much new material.

Volume 2 included eighteen wood engravings of places along the Mississippi. The largest, like that of Keokuk, Iowa, in Folio 36, measure only about three by four inches. The view of Natchez in Folio 13 is not quite that size, while the smallest—like those Barber and Howe used of Helena and Napoleon, Arkansas—are about one and one-half by four inches. Barber claimed that any reader could "with the book in hand . . . place himself within a yard or two of the precise spot from whence each was drawn." He explained that "care was taken that every engraving should be truthful; and as the work intends to be one of *facts only*, fancy sketches and artistic representations merely have been avoided." The artists did not hesitate to use the work of others when it suited their purposes. They did, however, acknowledge their sources. For example, the first sentence of the caption under their view of Alton reads: "The view is from Prospect-street, taken by Mr. Roeder and designed by him for a large engraving."[21]

State atlases provided another source of urban images of towns and cities in Minnesota and Iowa. To pursue these sources we must look at publications from well after the decade leading up to the Civil War. The leading figure was Alfred T. Andreas (1839–1900), who published atlases of these states in 1874 and 1875, each with several city views. The size of these folio volumes made possible the publication of illustrations much larger than those found in books of conventional dimensions, and

the New York *Tribune*, August 3, 1853, p. 5, col. 2, as quoted by Robert Taft, *Artists and Illustrators of the Old West, 1850–1900*, n. 44, p. 273.

21. John Warner Barber and Henry Howe, *Our Whole Country. A Panorama and Encyclopedia of the United States, Historical, Geographical and Pictorial*, 1:vi. I have used the 1863 printing in the Cornell University Library. This bears a copyright date of 1861, apparently the year of first publication. This is also the date given in John T. Cunningham, "Barber and Howe: History's Camp Followers," which concentrates on their work in New Jersey. In 1860 Con[rad?] Roeder drew and published a lithographic view of Alton, doubtless the source of the image used by Barber and Howe. In Reps, *Views and Viewmakers*, this is no. 774.

the views they contained are correspondingly more detailed and easier to examine.[22]

Andreas published his Minnesota atlas in 1874 after having worked for a firm that drew and published large wall maps of counties. He then began his own business, first in Davenport, Iowa, with his father-in-law, preparing and publishing several atlases of counties in Illinois, and then, after 1873, as head of his own company in Chicago. From his Chicago office Andreas eventually issued atlases of Minnesota, Iowa, Indiana, and Dakota and histories of Milwaukee, northern Wisconsin, Nebraska, Kansas, and Cook County, Illinois.[23]

His Minnesota atlas contained three long lithographic city views that Andreas evidently arranged with their publishers to have slightly modified for his use. Both the atlas and the views came from the press of Charles Shober and Company in Chicago, and it was probably there that the top margins of the atlas versions were lowered slightly so that the height of the image would not exceed the vertical dimension of the atlas. All three presented their subjects as if seen from a slightly elevated position, a method of depicting cities that by the 1870s had almost gone out of style, as a subsequent chapter will explain.[24]

These views of St. Paul and Minneapolis appear in Folios 60 and 62, and Folio 55 reproduces a detail from the view of Winona. George Ellsbury probably drew all three, although his name is found only on that of St. Paul. Ellsbury also doubtless published these with Vernon Green,

even though no publisher's name appears in the imprint of the St. Paul view. That view, however, does identify someone named Hoffman as the lithographer. Not much else is known about those responsible for these attractive urban scenes. Ellsbury's name appears on two other lithographic views, the first being the lithograph of Winona, Minnesota, in Folio 55 that Ellsbury drew in 1866. His La Crosse, Wisconsin, scene appears in Folio 54.[25]

Whether the separately issued versions or those found in the atlas appeared first cannot be determined. Perhaps the atlas versions had priority, for in August 1874 Ellsbury and Green were still trying to secure enough orders for their lithograph of St. Paul to justify having it printed. The newspaper notice with this information also provides an additional item of interest, stating that the view was to be "lithographed in six colors, making a very handsome picture, at the very low price of $1.50."[26]

Andreas's Iowa atlas contained additional views, but none of them matched the quality and character of the three Minnesota views just discussed. The one example used in this book, reproduced in Folio 40, shows Muscatine. The parallel horizontal lines in the water and similar diagonal lines in the sky, the streets, and the buildings of the city betray the use of a mechanical ruling device responsible for the lifeless quality of the print. However, the bird's-eye perspective used by the anonymous artist allows one to see into every block of the city, and the numbered legend below identifies eighteen of the public buildings, churches, and major industrial establishments.[27]

Although the views in the Iowa atlas have no signatures, at least some of them may have been the work of William Wallace Elliott (1842–?). A brief notice in an Elkader, Iowa, newspaper documents his position as an artist for the Andreas atlas—perhaps the head of the artistic staff: "Mr. W. W. Elliott, artist of the grand State Atlas enterprize, is in town soliciting views for presentation in this work. We should be glad to see Elkader and vicinity go 'into pictures' to a

22. The development of state atlas publishing by commercial firms after the Civil War is the subject of chap. 26, "The New State of State Atlases," in Walter W. Ristow, *American Maps and Mapmakers: Commercial Cartography in the Nineteenth Century*, 427–44.

23. Born in Orange County, New York, Andreas at eighteen moved to Dubuque, Iowa, in 1857 and then to Sparta, Illinois, where he taught school before enlisting in the Union army in 1861. He rose to the rank of captain in the Quartermaster Corps and after leaving service in 1865 settled in Davenport. A skating rink venture of his failed, and in 1867 he joined Thomas H. Thompson and Louis H. Everts—both army acquaintances—in their county map business. Andreas published his first county atlases in 1871, adding others of Illinois in the next two years. By 1873 he had established his business in Chicago, where he issued three Iowa county atlases before publishing his first state atlas in 1874 containing Minnesota maps and views. See "Historical Introduction" in the 1970 reprint by the Iowa State Historical Society of *Illustrated Historical Atlas of the State of Iowa*.

24. When I compiled the catalog portion of *Views and Viewmakers* I was not aware of the differences between the vertical dimensions of the three views in the atlas and those that were separately issued. An examination of the atlas at the Minnesota Historical Society revealed these discrepancies. For example, on the St. Paul view the vertical measurement of the image, with imprint, of the separately issued version is 17 3/8 inches; the atlas version measures 16 1/2 inches.

25. These views are from *Illustrated Historical Atlas of the State of Minnesota*. A somewhat reduced facsimile of the atlas was published in 1979 by Unigraphic, Inc., at Evansville, Indiana.

26. St. Paul *Daily Pioneer*, August 8, 1874.

27. In addition to the view of Muscatine, images of Dubuque, Davenport, and Burlington were among the many Iowa cities illustrated in the atlas.

reasonable extent. Parties desiring to confer with Mr. Elliott will find his headquarters at the Boardman House."[28]

Finally, among other books providing sources of Mississippi urban views, *Picturesque America* stands out as the most important. A product in 1872–1874 of D. Appleton and Co, this massive, two-volume work under the nominal editorship of the aged William Cullen Bryant presented the contributions of twenty-eight writers and more than thirty artists and engravers. A number of these pictured and described towns along the Mississippi. The work included many full-page steel engravings, but they are outnumbered by the very large number of wood engravings printed either as full-page illustrations or on pages with some text. The view of Rock Island, Illinois, in Folio 41 is unsigned, but elsewhere the volume identifies Alfred R. Waud as the artist. His background and earlier views of river towns will be reviewed shortly.[29]

The two wood engravings of Dubuque in Folio 51 come from this same source, both also from Waud's facile pencil. Waud sketched this major industrial center from high on the bluff above town looking upriver to the northeast. He also sketched a scene showing one of the streets connecting the level river valley with the heights to the west where new neighborhoods were taking shape. In the days before power excavating equipment, construction of thoroughfares like this required laborious work by men and animals.[30]

Another example of a wood engraving from *Picturesque America* is the view in Folio 60 showing St. Paul from Dayton's Bluff, a downstream vantage point high on the right bank of the Mississippi. Waud captured the appearance of Minnesota's capital city at the end of an extraordinarily prosperous era that commenced with the completion of the Civil War and lasted until the depression that began in the fall of 1873. For the next five years or so few new buildings were erected, and this view of St. Paul—like all of the other city views in that two-volume compendium—enjoyed a somewhat longer life of accuracy than many others drawn in a different period.

Townscape artists found another outlet for their talents in America's new illustrated magazines, among them *Gleason's Pictorial*, later *Ballou's*, the first such American publication. Beginning with issues in 1855, subscribers could travel vicariously to Baton Rouge, Vicksburg, Memphis, Cairo, Nauvoo, and on to the Iowa towns of Burlington and Dubuque, to mention only those views reproduced here in Folios 10, 15, 19, 22, 37, 39, and 49. Two of these—Vicksburg and Burlington—can be traced to earlier depictions published by Otto Onken in 1851. The versions in *Ballou's* four years later differed only in their linear character, dictated by the use of wood engraving as the medium of reproduction.

The views of Baton Rouge, Cairo, Muscatine, and Dubuque, on the other hand, may have been drawn on the spot by artists sent to these places by the magazine's editor. On the other hand, Boston wood engravers may simply have copied existing printed images of these places from sources that have yet to be identified. In either case, we know

28. *Clayton County Journal,* November 26, 1874, as quoted in "Historical Introduction" to the facsimile of *Illustrated Historical Atlas of the State of Iowa.* The wording of the notice indicates that views of farms, commercial establishments, homes, and so forth, appeared in the atlas as a result of payments to the publisher by those who wished their places of residence or work depicted. As applied to separately issued lithographic views, this aspect of viewmaking is discussed in chap. 7, pp. 53–58, of Reps, *Views and Viewmakers.* That volume also documents Elliott's work in California. Beginning in 1879 in San Francisco, Elliott was responsible for nearly fifty separately issued city views, either as artist, printer, or publisher. Another who may have been involved with these views in Iowa and who later worked in California is the one artist other than Ellsbury and Green whose name appears on a view in Andreas's Minnesota atlas. This is E. S. Moore, who signed the atlas view of Preston, Minnesota. In 1886 Moore drew the first of sixteen views of places in California and three in Oregon. For such scraps of material on the viewmaking careers of Elliott and Moore, see pp. 173–74 and 192 of *Views and Viewmakers.* When that was written I was not aware of Elliott's connection with Andreas.

29. Vol. 1 of *Picturesque America* contains a chapter (pp. 262–78) titled "The Lower Mississippi," written by T. B. Thorpe with illustrations by Alfred R. Waud. This includes a steel engraving of the New Orleans waterfront as well as a wood engraving of another view of riverboat traffic at the city. An oddity: although this volume has a copyright date of 1872, the copyright date on the steel engraving is 1873. Vol. 2 has a chapter by R. E. Garczynski, pp. 318–52, "The Upper Mississippi," with illustrations by Waud. These include wood engravings of the levee at St. Louis and views of La Crosse, Wisconsin, and St. Paul and Minneapolis, Minnesota, in addition to three of Dubuque. A steel engraving of St. Louis by A. C. Warren in this chapter is reproduced from a hand-colored impression in Reps, *Saint Louis Illustrated,* 117, fig. 6–12.

30. A number of well-known artists and illustrators contributed their talents to *Picturesque America* in addition to Waud. They include Thomas Moran, Jules Tavernier, J. F. Kensett, Harry Fenn, F. O. C. Darley, and J. W. Casilear, to name just a few. Of Richardson and Filmer, whose names appear on the Dubuque views as engravers, I can find nothing except that Filmer may be John Filmer, listed in Boston directories in 1860 and after as a wood engraver. Oliver B. Bunce organized and coordinated the work of the many writers, artists, editors, and printers of this publication, and he wrote several sections of the text as well. Although the Appleton company must have incurred high initial expenses in its publication, the project surely proved to be enormously profitable as many subsequent printings were needed to satisfy the demand for this book that continued until the end of the century.

only the names of the wood engravers for some of these illustrations: Samuel Kilburn for those of Cairo and Dubuque and Asa Warren for the view of Muscatine. In the case of the Baton Rouge view only the initials *G.A.O.* are on the print.[31]

The illustrated periodical in which these views appeared began in 1851, founded by Frederick Gleason in Boston as *Gleason's Pictorial Drawing-Room Companion*. Gleason hoped to emulate the *Illustrated London News*, a highly successful, profusely illustrated English weekly first issued in 1842. Gleason hired the former head of that magazine's engraving staff, one Henry Carter, who changed his name to Frank Leslie. *Gleason's* was the first of the American illustrated magazines, although it ceased publication in 1859. From 1855 it appeared as *Ballou's Pictorial Drawing-Room Companion* following its sale to the magazine's first editor, Maturin Murray Ballou.[32]

By that time Leslie had moved to New York, going there in 1853 to work briefly at a rival publication with a very short life, the *Illustrated News*. Soon another illustrated periodical made its appearance, *Harper's Weekly*, and this may have inspired Leslie to begin his own publication. In 1856 he published the first issue of *Frank Leslie's Illustrated Newspaper*.

In one form or another and with various titles this publication, one of several that Leslie founded, continued until 1922.

An editor of one of Leslie's periodicals compared the publisher's achievements with those of his competitors at *Harper's*:

> In his immense establishment—the largest of its kind in the world—Frank Leslie was the sole originator, the sole mover, and the sole director. Unlike his greater rivals, the Harpers, who were four brothers, strong in will, energetic in action, united in purpose and native to the country, he came alone, a young man, from a foreign soil, without means and without friends, and built up a business the like of which the world had never seen.[33]

Ballou's, *Leslie's*, and *Harper's* employed or bought sketches from a number of artists, several of whom recorded the appearance of towns along the Mississippi River. These included Samuel Kilburn and Asa Warren, whose work has already been noted, and Alfred R. Waud, who drew many authentic views for two of the illustrated magazines during tours of the lower Mississippi in 1866 and 1871. Although the circulation of *Ballou's* was apparently not large enough to justify continued publication, both *Leslie's* and *Harper's Weekly* appeared in large editions for many decades. The urban images appearing in these publications must have powerfully influenced how these towns were perceived by large numbers of the American public.[34]

Certainly no one in 1856 looking at the view of Cairo from *Ballou's* (Folio 22) could have expected to find there anything more than a few scattered buildings and some wharfboats moored along the riverbank to provide a place for passengers and freight to be transferred to and from passing steamboats. A reader seeing the Baton Rouge engraving of about the same time in Folio 10 must have found it more impressive,

31. Samuel Kilburn learned wood engraving in Boston as an apprentice to Abel Bowen. Later, he and Richard P. Mallory formed a partnership extending from 1852 to 1865, the period when he produced a number of wood engravings for *Ballou's Pictorial*. His name can be found on a great many wood engravings used as illustrations for books published during the nineteenth century. Asa Coolidge Warren (1819–1904) began an apprenticeship with a Boston jeweler, then completed an apprenticeship with George Smith, a Boston engraver. Warren worked for the New England Bank Note Company and for the publishing house of Ticknor and Field. Because of poor eyesight he was forced to turn to wood engraving for five years. In 1863 he moved to New York City, where he resumed engraving on metal and produced many book plates and decorative and pictorial vignettes used on banknotes. In later life he painted portraits and landscapes.

32. A reproduction of the masthead of the first issue of the *Illustrated London News* can be found in Eric de Maré, *The Victorian Woodblock Illustrators*, 81. Although this book deals exclusively with English wood engraving and engravers, it is an excellent survey of the technique as practiced there and elsewhere in the last century. See also Mason Jackson, *The Pictorial Press: Its Origin and Progress*. Chap. 9, 315–54, is particularly good on the process of making woodcuts as well as providing information on the life of special artists and correspondents for illustrated newspapers and magazines. For the American story, see William James Linton, *The History of Wood Engraving in America*. Linton, an Englishman who came to America in 1866, had a major impact on wood engraving in his adopted country. Frank Leslie hired him as artistic director of *Frank Leslie's Illustrated Newspaper*. In 1880 he became the first wood engraver to be elected to membership in the American Academy of Arts. A biography is F. B. Smith, *Radical Artisan*.

33. As quoted from an obituary of Leslie by Richard B. Kimball that appeared in *Frank Leslie's Popular Monthly* 9 (March 1880): 260, by Budd Leslie Gambee, Jr., *Frank Leslie and His Illustrated Newspaper, 1855–1860*, 1. Gambee traces Leslie's career in England and the United States before concentrating on his first five years as publisher of *Frank Leslie's Illustrated Newspaper*, a journal that outlasted its great competitor, *Harper's Weekly*, founded in 1857 and finally halted in 1916.

34. Many artists provided sketches of other subjects for the illustrated periodicals. Two among the better known were Thomas Nast and Winslow Homer. Perhaps the most useful treatment of America's popular illustrated journals can be found in Frank Luther Mott, *A History of American Magazines*, vol. 1, 1850–1865, 43–45, 409–12 (*Ballou's*), 452–65 (*Leslie's*), 468–87 (*Harper's Weekly*); vol. 3, 1865–1885, 186–91, 357–60 (*Every Saturday*).

especially given the appearance of the strange Gothic structure at the far right that had been built as the state capitol.

The view of Dubuque from an 1857 issue of *Ballou's* in Folio 49 offered a more elevated perspective of one of the Iowa towns that had grown so remarkably during the previous decade. The artist sketched the city from a vantage point high on the bluffs overlooking the valley below. The waterfront, shown unoccupied in Wild's view a dozen years before, now encompassed an extensive industrial district served by a railroad line paralleling the river.[35]

During the Civil War the illustrated magazines naturally devoted much of their space to all aspects of the conflict. Although military camp and battle scenes, along with illustrations of political and military leaders, predominated, the editors of these publications also included a few views of cities on the Mississippi. The unsigned wood engraving of Memphis from the Arkansas side of the river that Folio 20 reproduces appeared in the May 31, 1862, issue of *Harper's Weekly*.[36]

Just as it was necessary to extend our examination of book illustrations beyond the years of the Civil War, so, too, must we look at examples of city views in illustrated periodicals from the 1860s and 1870s. The earliest postwar urban portraits can be found in *Harper's Weekly*. Not long after the war ended its editor dispatched one of its most experienced artists and correspondents to visit several important places in the South and report on the progress of Reconstruction using both sketches and words.

This was Alfred Rodolph Waud (1828–1891), who proved to be the ideal choice for this assignment. Waud had learned to draw while a student in London at the School of Design located in Somerset House. He continued his studies at the Royal Academy and then came to New York in 1850 seeking a position as a theatrical designer. For a time he made a living as a freelance artist, later joining the staff of *Harper's Weekly* in 1862 as a war correspondent and artist. From the front he

sent dozens of sketches and reports that the magazine used to inform its readers about the progress of the war.[37]

On his peacetime assignment in the spring of 1866 Waud arrived in Memphis by steamboat after traveling down the Ohio River. There he drew the scene in Folio 20 after sketching the city as he looked upriver from a point near its southern outskirts. From the steamboats at the left to the large buildings on the right, the Memphis skyline he drew gives every impression of a thriving community. Waud's description tells a different story:

> Memphis has now the unenviable reputation of being the worst behaved city in the Union. There is a floating population here, made up of the dregs of both armies, which would be a curse to any city. . . . Business is remarkably dull, and all the stores look overstocked. The hotels, lobbies, and halls are overcrowded with loungers, people doing business in the city, commercial travelers and "reconstructed" citizens.[38]

Waud returned to Memphis five years later as a special artist for an illustrated weekly that had but a short life. This was *Every Saturday*, begun in 1866 with Thomas Bailey Aldrich as editor. Its publishers, the respected Boston firm of Ticknor and Fields, transformed it into an illustrated periodical in 1870 but abandoned this format after only two years. In that brief interval the new publication attracted Waud and Winslow Homer among other artists whose work had previously appeared in *Harper's Weekly*.[39]

On his second journey to the south—this time for *Every Saturday* in 1871—Waud enjoyed the company of Ralph Keeler on an assignment similar to his earlier tour through the same region for *Harper's Weekly*. Keeler's text and Waud's sketches for the wood engravings that accompanied the printed account of their impressions provided readers of the

35. Although his name appears nowhere on the print, J. C. Wolfe drew the view of Dubuque according to information in the text accompanying this view. Cincinnati and Dayton city directories list John C. Wolfe's name between 1843 and 1851, as does a Chicago directory of 1859. He is known to have executed a panorama of *Pilgrim's Progress* and to have collaborated on one of *Paradise Lost*.

36. A few other city views from wartime issues of the magazine are reproduced—apparently from the original wood engravings—in Alfred H. Guernsey and Henry M. Alden, *Harper's Pictorial History of the Great Rebellion*, vol. 2.

37. Unlike many of the artists of Mississippi River towns, Waud has left a biographical trail. I have relied on Ray, *Alfred R. Waud*; Historic New Orleans Collection, *Alfred R. Waud*; and "The Creole Sketchbook of A. R. Waud." See also Taft, *Artists and Illustrators of the Old West*, 58–62 and notes pp. 296ff. For a photograph of Waud sketching the battlefield at Gettysburg in July 1863, see Keith F. Davis, "'A Terrible Distinctness': Photography of the Civil War Era," 150, fig. IV–13.

38. *Harper's Weekly* 10 (May 5, 1866): 286.

39. According to Mott, "most of the pictures used in *Every Saturday* in 1870, and at least half of those used in 1871 were printed from electrotypes made from wood blocks which had been cut for the new London *Graphic*, one of the best of the popular illustrated journals of England. . . . Much of the American engraving in the Boston paper, however, compared favorably with the English" (*History of American Magazines*, vol. 3, 1865–1885, 359).

new publication with an informative, lively, and attractive review of conditions along the Mississippi from New Orleans to St. Louis.[40]

Waud's new view of Memphis in Folio 21 displays the riverfront facade and skyline of a city of more than 40,000 persons, a place larger than either Nashville or Atlanta and one enjoying rapid growth from a revitalized cotton trade. The illustration also provides a revealing glimpse of the wharfboat along the Arkansas side of the river. Telegraphic lines to the shore doubtless connected with the cable that linked both sides of the Mississippi by 1860. We look at the city just two years before yellow fever killed 2,000, a tragedy followed by a much worse outbreak in 1878 when more than 5,000 died of the 17,600 who contracted the disease.[41]

On his second trip along the Mississippi, Waud paused at two places below Memphis, Helena and Napoleon, both towns on the Arkansas side of the river, whose images can be found in Folio 17. Twenty-five years earlier a traveler visiting Helena found only "a tavern and three or four small stores." It was, he concluded "a wretched-looking place." Keeler and Waud, however, stated that "Helena . . . presents, as will be seen by our picture, a thriving appearance." If not thriving today, Helena has at least survived; Napoleon, however, has vanished—washed away long ago by the floodwaters of the Mississippi combined with those of the Arkansas River, at whose mouth Napoleon enjoyed its brief existence.[42]

Below Memphis, Helena, and Napoleon lay Vicksburg, a place that had suffered terribly during the Civil War from General Grant's protracted siege. Waud produced splendid views of the city on both of his visits, as Folio 15 demonstrates. One of the passages of text in the

folio provides Waud's description of what he drew in 1866 as he looked downriver from the heights where a Spanish fort had once been located.

For his 1871 depiction Waud crossed the river to draw the city from "the neighborhood of the old Federal rifle-pits." From that point he could record almost the entire length of the town, and its steep hillside location made it possible to show the facades of most of the important buildings. Keeler and Waud provided their readers with a useful description of what they could see:

> Most of the buildings of the city are of red brick. The galleries and gingerbread ornamentation, so general in Southern architecture, are not observable here. On the river are the two wharf-boats and to the right of them is the new elevator now building. Between the wharf-boats lies the doughty little ferry-boat, which seemed always whistling but never going across the river. The court-house rises in the middle of the city and commands a fine view of the whole surrounding country.[43]

In 1866 Waud continued down the Mississippi to Natchez, where he drew another long panorama, similar to that of Vicksburg. He found that the best location to sketch was "from the cupola of the Marine Hospital" at the north end of town. He told his readers what lay before him:

> The River is a prominent as well as necessary part of the picture, as in all views of cities upon its banks. Then there is the Fort, with its inclosed buildings, surrounded by a ditch and palisade; and in front of that a knoll covered with tents, occupied, I believe, by white troops. On the left the Catholic Church is most noticeable. The Market-house, the Episcopal and other churches, can also be made out by the initiated. Natchez on the Hill . . . is clean, healthy, and pleasant, and appears to be more orderly than towns higher up the river.

Waud did notice one feature that made Natchez less impressive than it might otherwise have been: "a number of gaps . . . where houses have been burned, giving some parts . . . a ruined appearance." He concluded that these gaps were "probably the effects of private incendiarism, as Natchez has not suffered from any battles being fought near it." He admired the initiative that the city had taken in providing for a recreational feature that still charms visitors today: "Along the edge of the

---

40. Waud and Keeler apparently were to continue upriver, but while they were in St. Louis their editor assigned them to cover the great fire in Chicago in 1871, and they never completed their Mississippi River series of articles and illustrations. For Waud and Keeler in St. Louis and one of Waud's views of the city, see Reps, *Saint Louis Illustrated*, 114–15 and fig. 6–11.

41. See chap. 8, "The Sting of the Yellowjack," in Gerald M. Capers, Jr., *The Biography of a River Town, Memphis: Its Heroic Age*, 186–209. Although the city's population almost doubled between 1860 and 1870 to reach 40,226, the 1880 census revealed that by that year the population had declined to 33,592.

42. Nichols, in *Forty Years of American Life*, 1:173, describes Helena as he first saw it in 1845. According to Frederic Trautmann, "Frederick Notrebe, once a general on Napoleon Bonaparte's staff, founded Napoleon, Arkansas, in the 1820s." See n. 24, p. 95, in the volume Trautmann edited, Ernst von Hesse-Wartegg, *Travels on the Lower Mississippi, 1879–1880*.

43. "On the Mississippi, Natchez and Vicksburg," 190.

bluff—a fine cliff of about 150 feet in height—the city of Natchez has reserved a strip of land, fenced in and planted with trees—a delicious place for a walk at sundown in the fresh breeze, and affording a fine view of the river, stretching away to the right and left till it disappears in the bends."[44]

Waud's comment about the clean, healthy, and orderly character of Natchez on the Hill did not apply, of course, to the disreputable settlement wedged between the water's edge and the steep bluff that left little flat or level land on which to build. Folio 14 reproduces the artist's record of how this settlement looked to him in 1866 and 1871. On the later visit Keeler and Waud wrote that the "view was taken from the bluff where the citizens sit in the shade on public benches." In noting that the only buildings were of Natchez-under-the-Hill, they explained that "there seemed to be no spot where we could get sight of any considerable portion of Upper Natchez and of these glorious reaches of the Mississippi at the same time."[45]

In 1866 *Harper's Weekly* used two of Waud's general sketches of Baton Rouge for wood engravings printed together on a single page. The top section of his illustration reproduced in Folio 10 presents his panorama of the city where what he referred to as "the melancholy shell" of the old Capitol stood as one of the two most prominent features on the skyline. The other—the "Louisiana State Deaf and Dumb Asylum—a very pleasant and commodious building"—can be seen to the right. The view at the bottom of the illustration shows the levee with a crowd of

people present during the landing of a steamboat. In the foreground at the right we can see the unloading of a cargo of ice from another vessel. In Baton Rouge, Waud wrote, as "in all the Southern cities along the rivers the Levee is the place of first importance. If there is any life it will be seen here."[46]

Waud was not the last artist of Mississippi River towns whose work appeared in illustrated periodicals. Among other and later illustrations is the one reproduced in Folio 63. The *New York Daily Graphic* published this long, narrow wood engraving of Minneapolis in its August 17, 1878, issue. The image occupied the top of two of the folio-size pages of the journal and provided a sweeping panorama of the city as seen looking to the southwest across Nicollet Island in the foreground and one of the channels of the Mississippi spanned by a handsome suspension bridge. According to information in the imprint below the image, it had been drawn from photographs.

All of these magazine and newspaper illustrations add something to our knowledge of the appearance of river cities in the last century, and some of them are attractive compositions as well. Yet they are surpassed both in numbers and in visual appeal by the many separately issued views. The chapter to follow examines the work of the artists who created such images in the years leading up to the Civil War, while subsequent chapters follow the careers and discuss the views produced by the several itinerant artists who dominated urban viewmaking in the latter part of the century.

44. "Pictures of the South: Vicksburg."
45. "On the Mississippi," 188.

46. "Pictures of the South: Mobile . . . Baton Rouge."

IV

Townscape Views and Viewmakers at the End of the Antebellum Period, 1850–1859

During the decade of the 1850s, while the American illustrated press published their first (usually derivative) images of the cities on the Mississippi, more-capable artists living in or visiting the region created far more elaborate and much more attractive urban portraits. Often large in size and colored either by hand or through the process of multistone lithography, these single-sheet views rank with the best of their kind. Artists known to be adequately trained in conventional drawing and painting created a number of these, while others came from the hands of persons whose backgrounds remain largely unexplored but who obviously possessed considerable talent and skills in townscape rendering.

In examining this period of Mississippi city viewmaking we can take another tour of the river, beginning at New Orleans and ending at St. Paul and Minneapolis. Except for one notable example, all the views that make possible this retrospective voyage up the Mississippi came from artists, printers, and publishers using the lithographic process to create their images. It was this period leading up to the Civil War that most authorities regard as the greatest era of American lithography.[1]

This was also the period when the lithographer—the person who put the artist's drawing on stone (sometimes the artist himself)—played a vital role rivaling that of the artist. By exercising skills in drawing on stone and producing through the use of a variety of lithographic crayons, pens, or brushes the textures needed to portray convincingly sky, soil, water, smoke, vegetation, buildings, boats, vehicles, and human figures, the lithographer could convert a routine sketch into an effective composition of real beauty.

These skills and those of the printer became even more important with the development of toned or two-stone lithographs, like Henry Petit's view of Dubuque, referred to later, and especially in creating what are usually referred to as chromolithographs. In that process multiple stones, each inked with a single color, produce a fully colored image. Among the multistone prints discussed later in this chapter, Max Strobel's view of St. Paul and Edwin Whitefield's views of St. Anthony and Minneapolis offer excellent examples of how artist, lithographer, and printer could combine their separate talents and skills to yield results that are so pleasing to the eye.

New Orleans offers three superb examples of lithographic city views that can bear comparison with any published in this country. John

---

1. Subsequent chapters will show that the views created in the latter half of the century, while presenting their subjects in different ways than most of those reviewed in the present chapter, possess their own qualities that make them equally desirable. The

reader should keep in mind, however, that these later views often lack the decorative appeal that so many of the antebellum city views unquestionably possess.

Bachman created the earliest, a print published in 1851 that Folio 7 reproduces. Unlike most of the other views examined in this chapter, Bachman's view uses a high-level perspective that enabled him to display almost the entire city from a point in the air opposite what is known as the Garden District. One can see here the fanlike system of streets leading to and from the river and crossed by others that follow the curving alignment of the Mississippi responsible for the nickname *Crescent City.*

Toward the right-hand side, the spire of the cathedral on Jackson Square marks the center of the old French quarter, or Vieux Carré. A few blocks to the left of the cathedral, the dark diagonal line of Canal Street with its shops, banks, and business offices separates the Creole and American neighborhoods on either side. In the foreground and elsewhere in the river Bachman drew realistic steamboats, ferries, and sailing ships, but one wonders about his powers of observation. He shows the steamboats at the levee with their sterns angled upriver, an impossible position that would have been quickly rectified by the current if any captain had been so unwise as to attempt to land in that manner.[2]

Bachman (Bachmann on many other prints) almost certainly came from Germany, probably arriving in New York in 1848 or 1849. His skillfully drawn and beautifully lithographed views of Boston, New York, and Philadelphia produced in 1850 provide evidence of sound training and several years of experience in Europe with this kind of topographic rendering, yet nothing is known of that career. Unfortunately, his life in America also remains largely a blank. Except for the trail of views that Bachman drew and published and a few street addresses in New York and, later, in Hoboken, New Jersey, nothing has been discovered about this artist who created some of the most captivating of American city portraits.[3]

Bachman's lithograph offers only a distant glimpse of the levee through which passed so much of the city's commerce. A visitor in 1860 noted that it "extends about five miles along the river," and that during the business season extending "from November to June" one could see here "from 1,000 to 1,500 steam boats, flat boats, and foreign ships, constantly arriving, departing, or lying moored against this place." He described what greeted his eyes during his visit:

> Morning by morning this "Levee" was the most bustling scene imaginable. It was usually covered with cotton, piled up in lots, to the height of fifteen or sixteen bales, ranged like streets of houses; also with corn, sugar, port, provisions, and various other articles, in prodigious quantities. Day by day, thousands of carts and drays were loading and unloading. Before night, nearly the whole of that merchandise seen in the morning would have disappeared, and the space would again become occupied with a succession of other supplies.[4]

The artists and publishers of two of the other prints of New Orleans at this time are not so obscure. John William Hill (1812–1879) and Benjamin Franklin Smith, Jr. (1830–1927), collaborated on the pair of views illustrated in Folio 7. One provides a distant view of the city from the lower cotton press downriver from the French quarter; the other, looking downriver from the tower of St. Patrick's Church, shows details of many of the buildings stretching from the vicinity of Lafayette Square to Canal Street. Both are exceptionally large prints, each measuring over

2. The assertion in the view's imprint that Bachman drew from nature and on stone is thus difficult to believe. Often an unnamed lithographer in the office of the printer or publisher provided human figures, boats, vegetation, and so forth, on images sketched by the artist in such a way that only the major elements appeared on paper. The incorrect positioning of the boats is an oddity that I have pointed out in connection with some views of St. Louis. See Reps, *Saint Louis Illustrated,* 89–90 and figs. 5–4 and 5–5.

3. Several undated versions of his New Orleans view bear the names of printers in Paris and a publisher in that city named Wild—possibly a relative of J. C. Wild—so he may have been associated with one of those firms. For such information as I have been able to find about Bachman, see the biographical note in Reps, *Views and Viewmakers,*

160–61. See also the index of artists in Deák, *Picturing America,* vol. 1, for several views in which Bachman was involved as artist or publisher. It is possible that John Bachman was the Swiss photographer Johann Jacob Bachmann, who worked as a goldsmith in Danzig in 1843–1844 and as a daguerreotypist in northern Germany until 1847. After that date there are no records of him in Germany, so the John Bachmann whose name first appears in New York in 1849 may well be the same person. In addition to his obviously German surname, his connection with Germany is further indicated by the sale in that country of several of his American city views with German titles. These include *Ansicht von New York und Brooklyn* (1863), *Hoboken bei New York* (1874), and *New York. Totalansicht aus der Vogelschau* (1881). This information about the European Bachmann and the views with German titles comes from letters by Rudiger Articus of the Hamburger Museum fur Archaologie to Gloria Gilda Deák of September 4, 1991, and to the author on December 17, 1991. Articus called my attention to two paragraphs on Bachmann's career as a daguerreotypist in Wilhelm Weimar, *Die Daguerrotypie in Hamburg, 1839–1860,* 35.

4. Henry Ashworth, *A Tour in the United States, Cuba, and Canada,* 77.

forty inches in width, and both display a high degree of craftsmanship in drawing on and printing in color from multiple lithographic stones.[5]

The separate contributions of the two artists cannot be determined. John William Hill was certainly the better known, and—as far as can be determined—the more versatile and better trained of the two. He learned to draw and paint from his father, an established English aquatint artist who had moved to America. The younger Hill worked for the New York State Geological Survey while continuing to paint, and in 1848 he began a five-year association with the publishing venture begun by B. F. Smith and three of his brothers, all of whom had earlier served as agents for an itinerant artist-publisher of city views, Edwin Whitefield.[6]

Before coming to New Orleans, Hill had already drawn or helped to draw for the Smith brothers two views of Philadelphia and single images of St. John in New Brunswick and Charleston, South Carolina. At Philadelphia he also collaborated with one of the Smiths, doubtless Benjamin Franklin, the artist of the group, who had produced his first city view in 1846 at the age of sixteen. With his three younger brothers, Smith began to publish city views in 1849, and in the next six years the firm issued more than forty large-folio prints, nearly all in the medium of lithography but also including a few engravings.[7]

The Hill-Smith view of New Orleans from the tower of St. Patrick's Church provides the first detailed glimpse of the buildings in the American quarter upriver from Canal Street. Lafayette Square in the left foreground was one of the several civic spaces reserved for public use by plantation owners when they began to subdivide their lands for development. Its location between St. Charles and Camp streets ("rue St. Charles" and "rue du Camp") in the fourth block beyond Canal Street can be seen on the map of the city reproduced in Folio 3.

At the far left, the spire-topped building facing Lafayette Square is the Second Presbyterian Church. Beyond it stands City Hall, a structure not dedicated until 1853 but drawn by Hill and Smith as designed by James Gallier, Sr. The large building with the colonnaded dome beyond the square is one famous in New Orleans and admired by all who stopped there for so much as one night. This was the St. Charles Hotel, destroyed by fire in January 1851. The great dome that had become a city landmark vanished forever except in this image and a few earlier depictions.[8]

Hill and Smith completed their drawing sometime in 1850, as indicated by the notice about the finished lithograph in the New Orleans *Times Picayune* for April 27, 1852, stating that "it was undertaken two years ago." The date of 1852 in the title of the print thus refers to the date of publication, not the time of depiction. Whether the artists and publishers did not know about the destruction of the St. Charles hotel or knew but believed that the dome would be rebuilt is a question that can never be answered.[9]

To draw views is one thing; to sell them is another. In the late 1840s Edwin Whitefield taught the Smiths the importance of publicity in local newspapers as a way to promote sales. They and many other viewmakers who worked later in the century followed Whitefield's example. This usually began with a call on newspaper editors to announce their arrival and their intention to publish a view of the city. The artist or his

5. David William Moody put on stone the Hill-Smith drawing from the lower cotton press. Moody then worked for the firm of Sarony and Major in New York where the Smith Brothers, publishers of both views, had this lithograph printed. For the other view, Smith put on stone the drawing he and Hill created looking downriver from St. Patrick's Church. The first state of this print does not include a printer's name, but it was almost surely the printing establishment in New York owned by Francis Michelin and George E. Leefe whose name appears on the second state. For the contribution of Michelin to American color lithography, see Marzio, *The Democratic Art*, 19.

6. Whitefield's contribution to views of cities on the Mississippi with his lithographs of Galena, Illinois, and St. Anthony and Minneapolis, Minnesota, will be examined later in this chapter.

7. Hill and Smith produced two quite different portraits of Philadelphia, an approach they adopted in New Orleans. One of the Philadelphia views looked west across the Delaware River to depict the panorama of the city in the distance. The other offered an interior view of Philadelphia looking to the east with the building of Girard College in the foreground. See Reps, *Views and Viewmakers*, 183–84, 206–8, for biographical notes about the Smiths and Hill.

8. An image of the St. Charles Hotel also appears on a silver coffee and tea service produced in New York by Tiffany, Young and Ellis, a firm headed by Charles L. Tiffany. See the exhibition catalog issued by the Historic New Orleans Collection, *Crescent City Silver*. I am indebted to an anonymous reader of the manuscript of this book for calling my attention to this version of the hotel's image.

9. The Smith Brothers frequently fell behind in delivering prints to subscribers. In 1850 they exhibited a drawing of Syracuse, New York, to obtain subscriptions for a printed version. On June 25, 1851, the Syracuse *Standard* reported that delivery would be delayed "on account of the illness of Mr. Smith, the Artist." Fourteen months later the publishers mailed a notice to subscribers stating that they expected "to have [the view] finished ready for delivery some time this fall." The completed lithograph finally arrived in Syracuse in the middle of December 1852. The notice mailed to subscribers in 1851 did not mention Syracuse by name but used the phrase "your city," suggesting that subscribers in other places encountered the same delays in obtaining delivery of their prints.

agent also hoped for another newspaper notice announcing the completion of the view, its availability for inspection, and the opening of a subscription list for those wishing to purchase the view when printed. Usually the newspaper urged citizens to support the project, pointing out that unless a sufficient number of subscribers came forward the view could not be published.

Almost always the newspaper called attention to the arrival of the printed version, provided information about its distribution to subscribers, and mentioned the availability of additional copies to those who had not reserved them in advance. Newspapers also usually praised the results, as was the case when the first of the lithographs of New Orleans published by the Smith brothers reached the city in late April 1852:

> We have received from Messrs. Smith, Brothers & Co., a colored engraving [*sic*] representing a view of New Orleans taken from the tower of St. Patrick's church and looking northward. It . . . has entailed much labor on the projectors. The large size of the picture, the faithful manner in which every object has been delineated, and the superior style of the execution, render this view one of the best of the kind ever brought to completion in this country. The views for subscribers will be ready, we are informed, in the course of next week.[10]

Another New Orleans newspaper used the arrival of the second of the two views as an opportunity to commend both of the lithographs:

> We have seen the second of the two views of the Port of New Orleans. . . . These pictures are certainly the most beautiful specimens of art and give the only just and accurate views we have ever seen of our Port. These two pictures ought to be in the offices or drawing-rooms of all our citizens. Together, they afford a full picture of the city. The two pictures may be obtained at Hall's Store, No. 48 Canal Street.[11]

From these three examples of sophisticated American lithographic printing that document the urbane character of New Orleans in the 1850s we move upriver to a quite different community and its image recorded in two less well executed but rare and little known prints

reproduced in Folio 10. Both capture the appearance of Baton Rouge as one would have seen it from the west bank of the Mississippi in the period from 1853 to 1857. J. A. Maurel, the artist of what is apparently the earlier of the two views, sketched the town about 1853 and put his own drawing on stone; then either he or some anonymous publisher arranged for Louis Xavier Magny of New Orleans to print the results.[12]

Maurel's skills as artist and lithographer did not match those of Bachman, Hill, or Smith. Was it his intent to divert attention from the town itself? Certainly the viewer's eye is drawn immediately to the steamboats in the Mississippi rather than to the profile of Baton Rouge in the distant background. And what *are* the three side-wheelers steaming furiously in the center and left of the view up to? Is it some mad race to see which one can first smash its bow against the shore in the foreground? Or were passengers so rare that three ferryboats would engage in this kind of competition to pick up the couple standing on the bank at the right?

Of what we can see of the town, the most striking feature is the outline of the strange and wonderful Gothic revival Capitol that James H. Dakin of New York designed for a site conveyed for that purpose by the city to the state of Louisiana in 1847. Five years later the completed building became an object of wonder to all visitors and a symbol of civic pride to residents of Baton Rouge. And so the building stood until December 1862 when, while it was occupied by Union troops, a fire gutted its interior and overnight turned it into a ruin. This disaster led to the removal of the seat of government, and it was not until 1882 that the Capitol was finally rebuilt when Baton Rouge once again became the state capital.

It was this building that Mark Twain criticized in *Life on the Mississippi* just as it reassumed its original use. Blaming its original design on the influence of Sir Walter Scott, "for it is not conceivable that this little sham castle would ever have been built if he had not run the people mad, a couple of generations ago, with his medieval romances," Twain maintained that "the South has not yet recovered from the debilitating influence of his books." His comments continued:

---

10. New Orleans *Times Picayune,* April 27, 1852.

11. New Orleans *Daily Delta,* June 3, 1852. Chap. 5, "The Business of Viewmaking: Sales, Promotion, and Advertising," in Reps, *Views and Viewmakers,* 39–44, provides many other examples of newspaper notices.

12. Magny (1800 to 1810–1855) came to New Orleans from Avignon, France, and is known to have run a lithographic printing establishment as early as 1847. He is last recorded in this business in 1855. See Historic New Orleans Collection, *Encyclopaedia of New Orleans Artists,* 250.

It is pathetic enough that a whitewashed castle, with turrets and things—materials all ungenuine within and without, pretending to be what they are not—should ever have been built in this otherwise honorable place; but it is much more pathetic to see this architectural falsehood undergoing restoration and perpetuation in our day, when it would have been so easy to let dynamite finish what a charitable fire began, and then devote this restoration money to the building of something genuine.[13]

At the far left Maurel shows the military post, a feature that one can just make out from the cluster of barracks and other buildings and the flagstaff. Built on the site of the Spanish Fort San Carlos, this Pentagon Barracks, as it was known, was begun in 1819 in the Spanish Town section of Baton Rouge. Between Spanish Town and the Capitol lay the major buildings of a community whose population reached 3,900 in 1850 and was to grow to 5,400 during the decade. However, the city's development in the nineteenth century never matched the promise that its site appeared to offer as the first really high ground travelers encountered on the Mississippi as they moved upstream from the river's mouth.[14]

A more accomplished French-born artist, Marie Adrien Persac (1823–1873), drew and put on stone in 1855 a similar view of Baton Rouge from the opposite side of the Mississippi. Persac probably published this himself and arranged to have it printed in New Orleans by Louis Pessou and Benedict Simon, whose lithographic shop occupied premises at 161 Chartres Street and with whom Persac shortly became associated. This accomplished artist may have received his training in France, where he was born in or near Lyons. By 1851 he was in Baton Rouge, and there in the mid–1850s he seems to have earned a living as a painter and as a partner in a photographic business. Most of his later work centered in New Orleans, where he produced a variety of images.[15]

Persac surely had seen Maurel's work and must have resolved that on his version of the town's portrait no steamboats would obstruct a clear view of the buildings. Persac added two important features to the skyline that do not appear in Maurel's lithograph: the Deaf and Dumb Asylum to the right of the Capitol and—slightly to the right of the high steeple of the First Methodist Church (a landmark used by river pilots)—the Gothic Revival steeple of the Roman Catholic Church.[16]

Persac obviously worked from the architectural plans for both these structures, for the asylum was not completed until 1858, and the steeple never existed in Persac's lifetime, not being finished until around 1890. Certainly no artist had greater knowledge of Baton Rouge's appearance than Persac, who drew and painted several buildings there and elsewhere in Louisiana. Aside from these two examples of anticipatory detail, Persac's view must be regarded as a faithful record of what steamboat passengers saw when passing Baton Rouge in the years preceding the Civil War.[17]

During that decade no artists of separately published images created views of Natchez, Vicksburg, or Memphis, so for our vicarious visit to river towns in the 1850s using such images the next stop on an upriver voyage is Cape Girardeau, Missouri. There in 1858 one A. Bottger sketched the town as a whole as well as the details of a great

---

13. *Life on the Mississippi*, 291.

14. Mark T. Carleton, *River Capital: An Illustrated History of Baton Rouge,* reproduces a map of Baton Rouge in 1837 on p. 37, a map of the U.S reservation and Spanish Town in 1839 on p. 41, and a manuscript plan of Fort San Carlos on p. 73. See also the color reproduction on p. 76 of a painted view of Baton Rouge done between 1825 and 1835 from a point similar to that used by Maurel. The author describes on p. 36 the several subdivided strips of land extending back from the river that comprised the town and the nature of their inhabitants in the early part of the century. The Capitol stood in the elaborately planned Beauregard Town at the south, or downriver, end of Baton Rouge.

15. About 1855 Pessou and Simon printed a view of Jackson Square from a drawing by J. Dürler. This multistone color lithograph shows the new Pontalba Buildings built

a few years earlier on designs by James Gallier. Facing each other across the square, these three-story brick buildings with white stone trim and continuous lines of iron balconies at each of the upper levels made the square one of the most impressive civic spaces in North America. A versatile artist, Persac also worked as an architect, engineer, and cartographer. A vignette of his Baton Rouge view appears on a map titled *City of Baton Rouge the Capital of Louisiana,* surveyed and published in 1855 by Michael Gill. Persac also drew the map of part of the Mississippi published by B. M. Norman of New Orleans in 1858 as *Norman's Chart of the Lower Mississippi River by A. Persac.*

16. The date of publication is established by the address of the printers, who by 1857 had moved to 23 Royal Street. Lacking this information, I followed in my entry in Reps, *Views and Viewmakers,* the date of ca. 1857 assigned by the Anglo-American Museum, Louisiana State University (now the Louisiana State University Museum of Art), where one of the two recorded institutional impressions of this rare view can be found.

17. The highly productive career of Persac is summarized in Historic New Orleans Collection, *Encyclopaedia of New Orleans Artists,* 299–301. See also the three paragraphs of notes on Persac in *Louisiana History* 20 (Winter 1979): 427. For a color reproduction of his watercolor rendering of the Deaf and Dumb Asylum, see Carleton, *River Capital,* 6–7. Carleton also reproduces Persac's photographic portrait on p. 47 and a color photograph of a shaving mug decorated with Persac's view of Baton Rouge. This unusual piece is in the collection of the Louisiana State University Museum of Art. The museum's director, H. Parrott Bacot, kindly provided me with the information about the Catholic Church spire and other material about Persac in a letter dated August 6, 1986.

many of its important buildings. He then put his composition on stone, creating the wonderfully busy but delightful lithograph reproduced in Folio 24 that Charles Robyn of St. Louis printed in 1858. The twenty-eight vignettes surrounding the oval-framed principal view depict the town's public buildings and significant private structures as well as some whose owners doubtless paid for the privilege and honor of having images of their homes or enterprises given such prominence.

Among the vignettes is one of the courthouse built in 1854 on a site high above the water and reached by a flight of fifty-nine steps leading up the steep slope. One can also find an image of St. Vincent's Academy, which was established in 1838 but moved to its new three-and-a-half-story building in 1843. Damaged by a steamboat explosion five years later and by a tornado in 1850, the building was reconstructed and converted to a seminary for training Roman Catholic priests before Bottger recorded its likeness in the lithograph. The artist depicted the city near the end of a decade that saw its population increase from under 1,000 to 3,000.[18]

Artists in the 1850s found St. Louis an appealing subject for their work. Not only did the city provide an exciting townscape with its

18. Of Bottger nothing can be said except that he obviously possessed training or experience to enable him to produce a view of this quality. His name appears only once in connection with a similar view, a lithograph of Alton by Conrad Roeder that Bottger put on stone and that Julius Hutawa of St. Louis printed in 1860. Probably Bottger then worked for Hutawa, just as in 1858 he was probably employed by Charles Robyn or by Thomas Schrader, who purchased Robyn's business about that time. Charles and Eduard Robyn came to St. Louis in 1846 from their native Westphalia, left for Philadelphia a year later to work in graphic arts, and returned to St. Louis in 1851 or 1852 to begin a printing company. About 1857 or 1858 they sold their business to Schrader, who had worked for them since 1853. See brief notes about Eduard Robyn in Reps, *Views and Viewmakers*, 200–201; and—with additional information—Reps, *Saint Louis Illustrated*, 68–71 (fig. 4–12 reproduces in color the rare and lovely view of St. Louis that Eduard Robyn drew and lithographed and the two brothers printed and published in 1853). The Alton view by Roeder is the one mentioned in the previous chapter as the source of one of Barber and Howe's tiny wood engravings. I found few contemporary descriptions of Cape Girardeau. However, when Ralph Keeler and Alfred Waud passed by in 1871 Waud drew one of the streets of the town and Keeler recorded these impressions: "we came in sight of the old town of Cape Girardeau, and of Saint Vincent's college. The college is beautifully situated on a high bank of the river, below the town, and so embowered in shade that we could get no satisfactory picture of the quaint buildings as we steamed by. At Cape Girardeau, however, we stayed long enough to make the sketch of the street scene which will be found among our engravings. Standing at the head of the street in that picture is the old town-hall, formerly I believe, the court-house of the county. The cupola of the St. Charles Hotel is recognizable in its venerable place on the second corner from the river" ("From Memphis to St. Louis," 333).

many spires and domes furnishing vertical accents that artists could exaggerate for dramatic effect, but the rapidly growing population of the city and the prosperity that prevailed in this Western boomtown offered opportunities for selling many copies of printed views. Even the great fire that in 1849 destroyed a substantial portion of the commercial center of St. Louis did not long hinder the city's development. In 1850 the census reported the city's population at 77,860 persons, and many thousand more lived outside the municipal boundaries.

The engraved plate from a St. Louis city directory for 1848 reproduced in Folio 28 provides the best record of the city at this time. The view at the top offers convincing evidence of how St. Louis had transformed itself from a frontier village to a major urban center in a few decades. The map below displays the vastly expanded street pattern created by private landowners seeking to profit from the demand for housing and commercial space by subdividing what had once been farms or estates well beyond the limits of the built-up area. The vignettes around the borders parade before the viewer the impressive buildings that public bodies, churches, fire companies, and commercial enterprises had built to house their many activities.

Another page of Folio 28 reproduces an extraordinarily beautiful engraved view showing St. Louis from an elevated vantage point much like the approach Bachman used for his lithograph of New Orleans. Published in 1854 by the artist of the view, George Hofmann, its engraver, Emil B. Krausse, and a St. Louis businessman, Charles A. Cuno, this large (twenty-five-by-thirty-six-inch) steel engraving was printed in New York by William Pate. According to information in the imprint, the artist based his work partly on a daguerreotype of St. Louis by Thomas Easterly, incorrectly spelled *Aesterly* on the print.[19]

Since photographs from the air were not then possible, this probably meant only that an Easterly photograph of the waterfront from across the river served as a guide in drawing the facades of buildings facing the levee in the foreground. Hofmann probably did not need Easterly's

19. Born in Vermont in 1809, Thomas Easterly came to St. Louis in 1847 or 1848 to begin a long career as a daguerreotypist who in addition to individual portraiture steadfastly recorded the changing face of the city during the next quarter of a century. For a brief comment on and several examples of his pictorial work, see Martha A. Sandweiss, "Undecisive Moments: The Narrative Tradition in Western Photography," 108–11, and sources cited in her n. 28. The author reproduces Easterly's daguerreotype of 1850, which seems to be taken from a viewpoint on Chouteau's Lake similar to that used a decade earlier by J. C. Wild for the view reproduced in Folio 27.

photograph, for although his background is not known, in 1854 the St. Louis city directory identified him as a "portraitpainter," so he must have already achieved some kind of recognition as an artist.[20]

It now seems likely that Krausse, listed as the engraver, actively participated in drawing at least some details of the view. A few surviving sketches by him in a private collection indicate that he had both a perceptive eye and a deft hand in sketching steamboats. As a portrait painter Hofmann may have had less experience in this kind of drawing than Krausse, and it is possible that the latter may have thus played a double role as coartist and as engraver, a craft in which he had been engaged in Germany.[21]

The view shows the city in 1852, and it remains one of the liveliest of all Mississippi River city portraits. Better than any other view of St. Louis, it recalls the once-seen-never-forgotten (but now long-vanished) bustle and excitement of the broad levee sloping down to the steamboat landing along the great river. It was this busy waterfront that so impressed Charles Mackay in 1858 when he first glimpsed the

levee extending "along the right bank of the Mississippi for nearly six miles, about half of which length is densely built upon." He felt that no "city in the world offers to the gaze of the spectators such a vast assemblage of river steam-boats," noting that "as many as one hundred and seventy, loading and unloading, have been counted along the levee at one time."[22]

Thomas L. Rodgers remembered additional details of the levee as it looked when he arrived in St. Louis in 1857:

> The old levee was . . . the most inspiring sight on this continent. For more than a mile it was thickly lined with steamers loading and unloading the products of the West and East, and for all that distance one could walk over the piles of produce and not set foot on the ground. There were bales of hemp, hogsheads of tobacco, piles of bacon, huge piles of grain in bags, and boxes, bales &c. of merchandise from eastern points for consumption in the city, and to be forwarded to the far West.[23]

The Hofmann-Krausse view also reminds us that by midcentury St. Louis no longer occupied only a narrow strip of land paralleling the river but extended westward many blocks into recently subdivided land where builders struggled to keep pace with the city's burgeoning population. It was doubtless the growing reputation of St. Louis as the future metropolis of the region that attracted James T. Palmatary to the city to prepare his remarkable view of it, a huge lithograph reproduced in Folio 28 together with a detail from it of the business district, the wholesale section, and the waterfront.

This is the first true bird's-eye view of a Mississippi River city in that the artist selected a viewpoint high enough to allow him to show the pattern of all the city's streets and all the building facades that would have been visible from such a height. Although Hofmann and Krausse in St. Louis and Bachman in New Orleans created elevated perspectives, neither of their views could be used to obtain a reliable and detailed idea of the basic pattern of streets, blocks, open spaces, and public building sites. It was this bird's-eye approach that dominated viewmaking in the Mississippi valley following the Civil War. Palmatary, therefore, must be regarded as one of the pioneers of his craft.

The artist of this view probably acted as his own publisher, as he had for many earlier lithographs of other places. Like so many others

---

20. Since the very word *daguerreotype* had a magic quality suggesting precise accuracy and an absence of artistic exaggeration, the publishers may have added the note about Easterly to help sales of the view.

21. Although it is far from conclusive on this point, a newspaper notice early in 1854 announcing the forthcoming publication of the print stated that the writer had been shown a proof and noted that "the artists are Mr. Hoffman portrait painter, and Mr. Krausse, engraver." Here, on the print, and in city directories the name of the portrait painter is variously spelled Hofmann, Hoffman, and Hoffmann. Emil Bernard Krausse (1827–1886) came to St. Louis in 1851, arriving from Leipzig, where his brother, Alfred, had taught him to engrave and where he worked for the firm of Brockhaus. The Belcher Sugar Refining Company in St. Louis asked Brockhaus to send someone to engrave a view of the city that would advertise its steamboats. Emil Krausse volunteered, intending to return to Germany on the completion of his assignment. How Cuno became involved in this project and why he, the artist, and the engraver became the view's publishers rather than the Sugar Company remains a mystery. Belcher's original sponsorship is reflected only in the depiction on the river of the steamboat *Charles Belcher*. Material on Krausse's life previously unknown to me has been kindly provided by his great-granddaughter, Alberta Schlesinger, and by James W. Devitt. In my *Saint Louis Illustrated* I erroneously rendered Krausse's first name as Emille. In a letter to me of May 1, 1990, Schlesinger included electrostatic copies of a photographic portrait of Emil and his brother, Alfred, and some of Krausse's pencil sketches of steamboats. After finishing the large engraving, Krausse decided to abandon that craft, apparently because of vision difficulties. As a student he learned some aspects of chemistry, and from his father, who was a foreman in a large dye factory in Germany, he knew something of that industry. He purchased Cuno's interest in the Western Color Works, a color and dye company, and began a successful business career in St. Louis that ended only with his death. His obituary appeared in the *Westliche Post* for June 25, 1886.

22. *Life and Liberty in America; or, Sketches of a Tour in the United States and Canada in 1857–8*, 144.

23. "Recollections of St. Louis—1857–1860," 116–17.

of his calling, however, he remains a shadowy figure whose outlines can be traced only by appearances of his name on views and in city directories, the earliest being listings in a Philadelphia directory as an "agent" from 1845 through 1851. These are followed by his identification as publisher in 1853 of a view of Lancaster, Pennsylvania, drawn by Charles Parsons and printed in New York by Endicott and Co.[24]

In April 1850 Edwin Whitefield hired Palmatary as a sales agent, a position he held at least until May 1852. Possibly he assisted Whitefield in sketching views, since he later claimed responsibility for four of them. In 1853 he began an association with Edward Sachse, an accomplished artist, lithographer, and printer whose firm in Baltimore produced some outstanding examples of multistone color lithographs. Although several views of midwestern cities printed by Sachse in the next two years identify Sachse as the artist, contemporary newspaper accounts reveal that Palmatary drew them.[25]

Thus when he struck out on his own as artist-publisher after he and Sachse parted company, Palmatary had a great deal of experience behind him both as artist and as sales agent. He evidently determined to set himself apart from competitors by producing views of enormous size. His lithograph of Louisville in 1855 measured thirty-three by fifty-two inches, "the largest view of this kind ever engraved [*sic*] in the United States," according to a local newspaper, and one to be printed "with ten different colors in oil." Perhaps its very size inhibited large sales, for it is known only from a single impression. Palmatary followed this in 1856 with a Milwaukee view of about the same dimensions. This, too, is extremely rare.[26]

By the end of August 1856, Palmatary was completing an even larger view of Chicago that the local firm of Braunhold and Sonne published the following year. Because of the view's heroic size the Philadelphia printer had to use four sheets that when assembled as one formed a perspective of the city measuring forty-five by eighty-two inches. Subscribers paid ten dollars for it, while the publishers charged twelve dollars for copies not ordered in advance. After Palmatary exhibited portions of his drawing, Chicago newspapers urged readers to subscribe, and five months before the artist completed his work the Chicago *Daily Democratic Press* reported that he had "over a hundred" names on his subscription list. Newspapers also praised the results when the lithograph became available, and many additional copies must have been sold as a result.[27]

Palmatary surely arrived in St. Louis sometime in 1857 with every expectation that newspapers as well as customers would reward his efforts as well as they had been rewarded in Chicago. He decided to make his St. Louis view larger than the one he had just completed, again using four sheets to create an image of St. Louis that is four and one-half feet high by not quite eight feet in width. Unfortunately for Palmatary, just about the time he probably received the first proofs from his Cincinnati printer the severe depression of 1857 began. The lithograph remained unfinished, lacking printed street names and—possibly—any additions or corrections that the artist intended to make before the final printing. Because only a single proof impression exists —one difficult to display or examine owing to its size—Palmatary's gigantic portrait of St. Louis may be one of the least known and used of the country's major urban views.[28]

24. His name first appears as "Palmatray [*sic*], James T., Agent" in *McElroy's Philadelphia Directory* for 1846, a listing that continues annually through 1851 with the spelling changed to Palmatary after 1848. At the same address one finds only "Susan B. Palmatary, Agent" in 1852, her occupation changed to tailoress in 1854 and 1855 and again in 1860, while in the years 1857–1859 she is identified as "gentw.," or gentlewoman.

25. Whitefield's diaries in the Boston Public Library mention Palmatary only as a canvasser; however, in 1851 he aided Whitefield in selecting the best site for a view of Newark, suggesting he already was involved in drawing. Three years later he listed among the views he had drawn four signed by Whitefield: Jersey City, Wilmington, Montreal, and Quebec. See *Alexandria Gazette and Virginia Advertiser*, August 24, 1853. Because, in Virginia, Palmatary also claimed credit for the Lancaster, Pennsylvania, view, his statements about the Whitefield views may be exaggerated or completely false. For biographical notes on Palmatary see Reps, *Views and Viewmakers*, 194–96. An unpublished conference paper by me on the work of Edward Sachse contains additional material on Palmatary, whose trail is so tantalizingly elusive.

26. Louisville *Daily Journal*, August 5, 1855.

27. *Daily Democratic Press*, March 20, 1856. This account states Palmatary's intention to print the view in eight colors and also mentions his claim that this was the "fifty-third city which he has sketched and lithographed in the same style." On August 28 of that year the same source noted that the "work . . . is now rapidly approaching completion." The view "will be printed with oil colors in the latest style of the art, and with a naturalness of color second only to painting." The notice concluded by advising that "all who can derive advantages from the possession of so fine a view . . . should lose no time in subscribing." In its issue of November 4, 1856, a writer for the paper reported seeing "a proof impression" of one of the sheets that "shows the section of the city north of Lake street, east of Clark." A month later, on December 5, another section had arrived, and the paper urged, "Those wishing copies had better subscribe early." Professor Gerald Danzer, University of Illinois at Chicago, who has studied this view in detail, was kind enough to provide transcriptions of these newspaper accounts.

28. For my arguments supporting the conclusion that the unique impression in the Missouri Historical Society is a proof and that the view was never published, see Reps,

Near the upper left corner of the detail from the view one can see the station of the new Pacific Railroad at the end of its tracks, which head westward up the valley of Mill Creek. Construction began on this line in 1851 from a temporary terminus at Fifteenth Street. The new station on Seventh Street shown in Palmatary's view replaced the temporary one a few years later after an intervening pond had been drained. While St. Louis greeted this new means of transportation enthusiastically, its residents could not have foreseen that eventually rail transportation would replace almost entirely the passenger and freight shipments by riverboat that had brought the city such prosperity.

Not far away from St. Louis lay St. Charles, Missouri, an early settlement that had been overshadowed by its metropolitan neighbor. In 1850 a St. Louis publisher issued the lithograph in Folio 30, the work of an anonymous artist who portrayed St. Charles as he saw it from the south side of the Missouri River. At this time German immigrants were coming in large numbers to live there and in communities farther up the Missouri River. St. Charles also profited from business generated by persons passing through en route to the California gold fields, some of whom stopped long enough to equip themselves for the venture.[29]

Above St. Charles on the Mississippi other places developed more rapidly as new waves of settlers moved into and beyond the Midwest and created markets for mercantile and manufacturing centers along the great river. Such a place was Quincy, Illinois, which at midcentury was the second most populous city in the state. Five steamboats stopped each day, and manufacturing plants turned out a variety of agricultural implements and vehicles, shoes, tobacco, lumber, and other products. Hog growers in the vicinity brought their animals to Quincy for shipment to St. Louis: 20,000 in 1847; 70,000 a year in later years.[30]

In these boom years of growth—interrupted after a cholera epidemic in 1832 only by national depressions—Quincy sat for its portrait by lithographic artists several times. Two of these views from about 1859 and 1860 appear in Folio 34. P. S. Duval and Son of Philadelphia printed what is presumed to be the earlier of the two of these undated views. The imprint tells us nothing about artist, lithographer, or publisher. The other is the work of H. G. Haerting, who had put on stone and may have drawn the St. Charles view of 1850. Haerting published the Quincy print with the publisher of the St. Charles view, identified only as Ortloff.

The artists of both of the Quincy views chose the same high-level perspective that Palmatary used in St. Louis, giving us an unrestricted look at the entire street pattern of the city as well as opportunities to examine the facades of all the buildings of the town. Near the center of each print one can see the block-square expanse of the central square that the original settlers included in their town plat. Along its right, or south, side and leading at right angles from the levee to the western horizon is Maine Street, along whose path wealthy residents built great mansions of imposing size standing in spacious grounds. Many of these handsome structures still exist as impressive reminders of the wealth generated in this busy river port during much of the nineteenth century.

Across from Quincy in Missouri and some miles to the north, near the Iowa border, Alexandria occupied a site at the mouth of the Des Moines River. Today a tiny village, in the years from 1848 to 1872 this place was a center of pork meatpacking surpassed in volume only by Chicago and St. Louis. This explains why artist J. B. Miller recorded its appearance, an image reproduced in Folio 36 that a lithographer identified in the print only as J. B. put on stone some time after 1850 for the Pittsburgh lithographer William Schuchman. Perhaps one of the meatpackers whose plants are identified by the smoking chimneys

---

Saint Louis Illustrated, 94. Contemporary newspaper notices about Palmatary in St. Louis or the view he created may exist, but they have eluded my searches and those of an assistant as we scrolled through microfilm editions of several of the city's newspapers. Palmatary's name is not associated with any other city view until 1864, when he began drawing a view of Syracuse, another four-sheet production that when issued in 1868 did not have his name in the imprint. For more on this and Palmatary's initial involvement in its preparation, see John W. Reps, "Upstate Cities on Paper and Stone: Urban Lithographs of Nineteenth-Century New York." By 1867 Palmatary was in Baltimore as an employee of E. Sachse and Co., and he almost certainly participated in preparing that firm's twelve-sheet view of the city published in 1869.

29. A. Janicke and Co. printed the view, which was put on stone by H. G. Haerting and published by Ortloff. Haerting may have been the artist as well, since he is so identified on a few later views of other places. The Janicke firm did competent lithographic work. See the view of St. Louis in 1859 printed by them in fig. 5–6, p. 91, of Reps, *Saint Louis Illustrated.*

30. Urban growth often took place where rail lines could be easily extended from the east or where lines might conveniently be thrust westward to tap the agricultural produce of the ever-moving frontier.

commissioned the artist to create this peaceful scene, although not one hog can be found.[31]

Now that Iowa towns had passed through their fledgling years and were sprouting economic wings, artists began to draw their images as well. Folio 39 reproduces two of these showing Burlington. Father Berchem Lucrode drew the first, a lithograph printed in 1850 in St. Louis by Julius Hutawa and Leopold Gast during their brief partnership. The only recorded impression in the state historical society shows evidence of a hard life, but some of its drab qualities probably stem from the lack of experience by midwestern printers and lithographers. The style of execution is certainly unusual, with only the foreground strongly printed. Perhaps this was someone's not altogether successful attempt at atmospheric perspective.

The contrast between this crude effort and the elegantly drawn, printed, and colored view of 1858 from a drawing by William Bourne could scarcely be greater. Bourne, who also published this view, had it printed by the old and highly respected lithograph printing firm in New York headed by William Endicott. Whether crude or sophisticated, both views provide a sense of how these Iowa towns had developed within two decades from nothing more than seemingly promising sites to places whose buildings seemed little different from those in far older towns in the more settled East. Already Burlington had outgrown the restricted level land along the river and had climbed the steep bluffs to more spacious sites to the west.[32]

Farther upriver, Davenport had also grown substantially, and here, also, two artists created images of the city during the 1850s. Both are reproduced in Folio 43, the earlier by E. P. Gillett as printed in Boston at the shop of John Henry Bufford about 1855 and the other drawn and published by Rufus Wright in 1858. Of Gillett [or Gillet] we know only that an Indianapolis newspaper referred to him in 1852 as having "a striking propensity for art" and predicted that he would "become one

of the state's best artists." Why he came to draw Davenport and what he accomplished after that does not seem to have been recorded.[33]

Wright, born in 1832, studied in New York at the National Academy of Design. By early February 1858 he had exhibited his painting of Davenport, and in the *Daily Iowa State Democrat* for February 9 he told prospective customers that "it will soon be lithographed and fully colored in the best possible style, at the famous establishment of Messrs. Sarony & Major, of New York City." Wright was also involved in a much larger artistic endeavor, painting what the same newspaper on April 22, 1959, identified as "A Panorama of the Mormons . . . with a beautiful sketch of Davenport." The announcement claimed that this work required "14,000 feet of canvass, and will be a painting worthy of the artist."[34]

Notices in the *Daily Iowa State Democrat* for May 19, 1858, alerted residents to the publication of Wright's view of the city. The newspaper reported that a proof had just arrived from the New York printer and called it "by far the best representation of our city ever produced." The paper urged its readers to subscribe now "as there will be no extra numbers struck off for subsequent sale." Citizens wishing "to preserve the landmarks of the onward progress" of the city should "subscribe for

---

31. Droves of a thousand hogs from Iowa and Missouri hog farms as far away as a hundred miles were not uncommon, according to Federal Writers' Program, Work Projects Administration, *Missouri: A Guide to the "Show Me" State.*

32. As Deák notes in *Picturing America,* 1:417, the firm that William Endicott and his brother, George, headed "was twice cited for excellence by the American Institute of the City of New York, an organization that monitored technological progress in manufactures, agriculture, and the arts."

33. My information on Gillett comes from entry 715 in Deák, *Picturing America,* 1:486–87. She cites the *Indiana Journal* for October 18, 1852, as quoted in Wilbur D. Peat, *Pioneer Painters of Indiana* (Indianapolis: Art Association of Indianapolis, Indiana, 1954), 61–62. Her note on the content of the view follows I. N. Phelps Stokes: "The large house at the extreme right of the view is the residence of Antoine le Claire, the first settler of Davenport. . . . The spire seen behind the steamer *Ben Bolt* belongs to the Baptist Church. The large building at the top of the hill, on the opposite side of the same street, is the old District Number 2 School. . . . It was built in 1853–1854 at a cost of $8,000 and was then considered a triumph of architecture." For Bufford's career, see David Tatham, "John Henry Bufford, American Lithographer," and the note on Bufford in Sally Pierce and Catharina Slautterback, *Boston Lithography, 1825–1880: The Boston Athenaeum Collection,* 130–32.

34. During the Civil War, Wright painted a number of portraits of public figures, and he spent most of his professional life in Washington, New York City, and Brooklyn. Probably his stay in Iowa was brief. See the short notes in Perry Rathbone, ed., *Westward the Way: The Character and Development of the Louisiana Territory as Seen by Artists and Writers of the Nineteenth Century,* 279; and *Appletons' Cyclopedia of American Biography,* 1:626–27. A smaller version of Wright's view of Davenport that omits the train in the foreground and shows fewer river craft became the frontispiece in Wilkie, *Davenport Past and Present.* Measuring 6 1/4 x 10 1/2 inches, this print included the name of both artist and lithographic printer, so presumably it was not simply a pirated version. I do not know if the Mormon panorama was designed as a moving or a stationary painting or, indeed, if it was ever completed.

this work of art, have it put in a frame and suspended upon the walls of your parlors and offices as a memento of the past."[35]

Ten days later, on May 29, Wright addressed the people of Davenport in the same newspaper, claiming that the view had cost him "much time and trouble" and "without previous assurances in the shape of subscriptions . . . with a few generous exceptions." He told of going to New York "at a very large additional expense" to engage the best firm in the country to print the view. "Owing to ill health," he felt unable to solicit subscriptions, delegating that task to a "Mr. H. Eastman." He advised prospective purchasers that the final view would look like the proof "with the exception of a few errors which I have ordered corrected, and the census table, since 1830 to the present time, to go upon the lower margin."[36]

For foreground interest Gillett and Wright selected what were then complimentary means of transportation. Gillett shows us a sturdy ferry powerfully churning its way across the Mississippi to a landing on the Illinois shore. Wright also presents a spirited image of a river vessel, but he provides as well a lively, smoke-chuffing locomotive. It symbolizes the conflict between river and rails that in the coming decades would see increasing numbers of passengers and ever-greater amounts of freight traffic captured by the railroad with a resulting weakening of the north-south linkages along the river that the steamboat had made possible and the strengthening of economic ties between East and West.

Gillett in 1855 and even Wright in 1858 drew Davenport before the city began to feel the full effect of the national depression. Its population by 1858 had reached about 11,000, and it had enjoyed a five-

year building boom that from 1853 through 1857 saw more than 2,600 buildings erected, perhaps half of those in 1857 alone. Builders provided another 1,100 in 1858 to bring the total to about 5,000. It was the promise of rail connections to the East with the incorporation of the Rock Island Railroad Company in 1852 that began the boom. That promise was fulfilled when the line reached Rock Island, Illinois, across the river in 1854, and two years later came to Davenport itself on the first bridge to link the two sides of the Mississippi.[37]

Dubuque, farther up the Mississippi, was not so fortunate, for although the Illinois Central Railroad reached the Mississippi shore opposite Dubuque in 1855, an event celebrated by cannon shots, bands, a parade, and a speech by Senator Stephen A. Douglas, citizens had to wait eleven long years for the construction of a bridge across the Mississippi. Even so, the city's population quadrupled during the decade, growing from only 3,108 in 1850 to 13,000 ten years later.

It is Dubuque near the beginning of this period of rapid growth that one of the views in Folio 49 displays. The artist, Miss Lucinda Farnham, as her name can be found in the imprint of this large lithograph, seemingly is the only woman to have drawn a published Mississippi River print of this type. Sometime between 1852 and 1855 John Cameron of New York put Farnham's drawing on stone and doubtless printed the view as well. No biographical information has come to light about the artist, not even a listing in Dubuque city directories. Cameron is known from his lithographs used as book illustrations, a number of separate prints, and many of the Currier and Ives comic prints and caricatures. The two combined their talents to produce an interesting close-up view of the oldest settlement in Iowa just as it, like Davenport, enjoyed the economically beneficial effect of rail transportation. The artist drew one

35. When printed, Wright's view included these words under the title: "From the Original Picture in the Possession of Geo. Davenport." Thus, the artist either gave or sold the painting to George Davenport before a New York lithographer put the design on stone.

36. I believe the view of Davenport by Wright numbered 1015 in Reps, *Views and Viewmakers,* and dated there 1856 is the proof state of the 1858 view with the population table before Wright brought it up-to-date. The other change was the addition of the address of the printers. In Wright's notice he states that there had been *three previous failures* in this same enterprise" of Davenport viewmaking. One of these must have been what the *Daily Iowa Democrat* for February 13, 1858, identified as "Mrs. Codding's picture of the City of Davenport," then on exhibition with her agent "receiving subscriptions for the lithographic copies to be made therefrom." Despite the paper's assertion that "the numerous visitors who examine this painting, are unanimous in its praise," Codding does not seem to have obtained sufficient backing to justify having her depiction of Davenport printed. Wright's view was also then on exhibition and was evidently regarded as superior.

37. Construction data are from Timothy R. Mahoney, "Down in Davenport: The Social Response of Antebellum Elites to Regional Urbanization." In the first part of this study, "Down in Davenport: A Regional Perspective on Antebellum Town Economic Development," 471, Mahoney summarizes the effect of the railroad on the local economy: "The economic orientation of the town shifted dramatically to the East. Within eighteen months, two-thirds of the produce once sent from Davenport to St. Louis was diverted by rail to Chicago. . . . Old Mercantile arrangements with St. Louis were thrown over for new ones with Chicago and New York." The populations of Illinois and Iowa river towns cited in this chapter can be found in appendix C of Mahoney's fine *River Towns in the Great West,* 285–89.

of the Illinois Central trains in the left foreground as it steamed away from the ferry stop on the Illinois side.[38]

It is Dubuque on the eve of the Civil War that Henry W. Petit drew in 1860 for a view published by a Dubuque bookstore proprietor, W. J. Gilbert. This unusual lithograph consists of a distant prospect of the city framed within an ellipse. Sixteen vignettes of buildings surround it, and in the final state of the print the seal of the city appears at the top center. Petit may have designed the decorative, lacelike background on which the vignettes appear, or this could have been added at the Endicott shop in New York, where Gilbert sent it to be printed.[39]

Petit shows near the center of his view and also in one of the vignettes a new landmark built in 1855 on the island in front of the town. This is the Shot Tower, a structure still standing and now proudly regarded as a valued symbol of Dubuque's history. One can also see a number of buildings located atop the bluff above the older part of the town on the river terrace. Here Dubuque's schools and colleges found suitable uncrowded locations amid the spacious grounds of new mansions.[40]

Several newspaper notices in the Dubuque *Herald* tell us something about the artist and the way the view was sold. On February 24, 1860, the paper noted that Henry Petit, a former resident and the author of "a series of illustrated papers published in the Great Republic Monthly," had returned to Dubuque "with a view to a permanent residence." A month later, on March 22, the paper told its readers that Petit had been placed in "charge of the Local Department of the *Herald*" and requested "friends in all parts of the city . . . [to] . . . render him all the assistance they can."

In the interim, on March 16, the paper announced that Petit had "just completed a drawing of Dubuque . . . for W. J. Gilbert" that was to be "lithographed immediately," and "sold at the low figure of $1." The writer declared Petit's drawing "not only perfect in its artistic character, but as a likeness." Artist and publisher intended "to surround the lithograph with views of the finest houses in Dubuque, in case the owners are willing to pay the bare expenses of the lithographing." Persons interested were told they could inspect the drawing "for a few days at Gilbert's book store."

The March 23 issue of the *Herald* carried this notice about the view:

> Mr. W. J. Gilbert . . . desires us to say that his new view of Dubuque will remain on exhibition for a few days longer . . . after which it will be sent to N.Y. to the engraver. Those who wish to have views of their residences or places of business engraved upon the margin of the picture, should improve this opportunity without delay, as the number is limited to ten or twelve. The expense will be only the extra amount of cost in the engraving.

Readers found additional information about the view and what they might expect of the finished lithograph:

> The picture is to be retouched by the artist, a mistake or two corrected, and then the thing is ready to be sent away. For the information of those who are unacquainted with such matters, we would say that the engraving will have a much finer appearance than the drawing. The lines will be more distinct, the shades much darker, and a better relief will be given to the lights than it is possible to produce with the common lead pencil.

Perhaps Edwin Whitefield, one of the most prolific city-view artists of the time, also intended to portray Dubuque. However, his experience in Galena, Illinois—across the Mississippi from Dubuque and a short distance up the Fever River—may have changed his mind. In 1855 Whitefield visited and chose Galena as the subject for one of his lithographs, and Folio 47 reproduces the print that Whitefield issued a year later. The artist selected a viewpoint similar to that used by Wild more than ten years before, and a comparison of the two shows how Galena had grown during the intervening years. As was his normal procedure, the artist acted as publisher, and he probably put his drawing on stone as well.

38. Peters, *America on Stone,* 130–31, provides the information that Cameron was at 208 Broadway, the address on the print, in the years 1852–1855 and in 1862. The latter date can almost certainly be ignored in dating the Dubuque print. I have located only three impressions, in the Iowa Historical Society, the Dubuque County Historical Society, and the Chicago Historical Society.

39. State I of the print is in the Iowa State Historical Society. It lacks the seal but at the bottom of the ellipse identifies Endicott as the printer. State II is in the Stokes Collection of the New York Public Library. It includes the seal and has Gilbert's name as publisher substituted for Endicott as printer. State III is in the collection of the Mariners' Museum at Newport News, Virginia. It adds Petit's name as artist and has the names of both Gilbert and Endicott. This information supersedes my entries for what were then the two known states in Reps, *Views and Viewmakers,* 303, entries 1036–37. The existence of what are obviously two proof states of this view suggests that Gilbert may have taken an unusual amount of care to make certain that the final product was correct in every detail.

40. The absence of the Shot Tower in Miss Farnham's view probably indicates that she drew it no later than 1854. Following material first provided by I. N. Phelps Stokes, Deák identifies some of the buildings in Petit's view of Dubuque in entry 748, 1:507–8, of *Picturing America.*

The Endicott firm in New York had printed earlier views by White-field, and it was to this lithographic shop that he again turned for his Galena view. Whitefield's confidence proved well placed, for the resulting lithograph is one of his most successful compositions. Although not exactly unprejudiced in the matter, Whitefield asserted, "I believe I might say without fear of contradiction that a better specimen of the Fine Arts of a similar character has not been produced in this country."

In canvassing the town for subscriptions, Whitefield claimed that he obtained only "a number barely sufficient to pay all the expenses necessarily attendant upon such a work." If that statement is accurate, he must have been elated to obtain from the City Council an order for ten copies at eight dollars each. He could not have foreseen the difficulties he would encounter in collecting payment when it came time to deliver the finished lithograph to a newly elected council.

To his dismay, Whitefield received payment not in U.S. currency but in what the artist in a complaining letter referred to as "scrip," doubtless payable only in discounted notes issued by a local bank. Whitefield complained to the council because he found that instead of the eighty dollars he anticipated he could only realize "about two-thirds" of that amount if he exchanged the scrip. He asked for either payment in full or that the council increase the number of views subscribed for "sufficiently to enable me to realize the original amount, say five or six copies extra." The council rebuffed the artist on both points and wrote him a blunt letter setting forth its position:

> The committee to whom was refered [sic] the written communication touching the views of the city with ten copies of said views for the sum of $80—which sum is now drawn in his favor but in consequence of the discount the amt. has not been accepted or the views delivered. They find further that the price of these views from the stores vary from 4 to 5 [dollars each]—they would therefore report that the 80—already appropriated is a sufficient sum which he can receive or retain his views.[41]

Whether or not Whitefield swallowed his pride and delivered the ten views in exchange for the discounted scrip does not appear on the record of the council. If these prints existed today, they would be worth a small fortune, for all of Whitefield's lithographs are eagerly pursued by collectors, and that of Galena is a particularly striking depiction of one of the Mississippi's most unusual places. Here entire streets of fine nineteenth-century buildings still exist, not just isolated architectural remnants of the past as in many other towns, so the Galena of Whitefield's era and that of our own seem much alike.

The opposite condition prevails in the case of views published in 1853 and 1856 of St. Paul, a city now so thoroughly changed as to make it difficult to believe these early prints once fairly represented its appearance. Reproduced in Folio 59, these lithographs display the skyline of St. Paul as seen from across the Mississippi, both using nearly the same viewpoint. Max Strobel, who served for a short time as Seth Eastman's assistant in 1853 but who is otherwise undocumented, drew the earlier of the two for its publisher, Thompson Ritchie. James Fuller Queen put this on stone in Philadelphia, where he worked for Peter S. Duval, one of the innovators in American lithography.[42]

S. Holmes Andrews in 1855 painted the scene of St. Paul that the next year Endicott and Co. printed and C. Hamilton and Co. published. Andrews is yet another of the many artists of Mississippi River city views who has eluded efforts of scholars to uncover biographical information. He is known to have exhibited his work at the National Academy of Design when he lived in New York in 1845, and it is possible that he is the Andrews who in the year his lithograph appeared was showing to eastern viewers a panorama of the American West. Perhaps his painting was a study for that larger work.[43]

Both Strobel and Andrews placed Indians as foreground figures near the lower right corners of their compositions. The natives in the Andrews view of 1856 may be less amazed by the white man's city than transfixed by the sight of the great river that the artist depicted apparently swooping downhill at the right like a roller coaster. Andrews also

---

41. For the full text of Whitefield's letter and the reply dated December 16, 1856, see Betty I. Madden, *Art, Crafts, and Architecture in Early Illinois*, 215–16. Madden does not give the date of Whitefield's letter in the Galena Public Library.

42. Queen (1820 or 1821–1886) in 1835 began an apprenticeship to the early Philadelphia lithographers George Lehman and Peter S. Duval. In "James Queen Philadelphia Lithographer," 141, Carl M. Cochran remarks on Queen's versatility: "Queen will be remembered for the infinite variety of the lithographs which he drew for the large printing houses of Wagner & McGuigan, Thomas Sinclair, and Duval. Never a specialist in any one kind of work, he drew views of buildings, and cities, and scenic attractions; he made prints of newsworthy events; he drew portraits, sheet music covers, certificates and diplomas, advertisements, illustrations for magazines, books, and government reports, and finally, he became an outstanding chromolithographer."

43. My information on Andrews comes entirely from Coen, *Painting and Sculpture in Minnesota*, 48. Andrews's painting is in the collection of the Minnesota Historical Society, which has produced a fine color facsimile.

appears to have exaggerated the height of the hills in the background; in reality they were far from the almost alpine character he delineated.

Both artists, however, give one a good sense of the problems encountered at St. Paul in gaining access to the river due to the steep bluff at this otherwise admirable site for a town. When these views appeared most steamboats landed at the foot of Jackson Street, where the topography made it less difficult for persons and vehicles to make their way to the level land above. In each of the views the landing area can be seen at the far right—in the case of the one by Andrews, it is almost invisible at the bottom of the curiously drawn water slope that makes this view both fascinating and unfathomable.[44]

The tall spire at the center of Strobel's view of 1853 and to right of center in Andrews's depiction of the city belonged to the First Presbyterian Church built in 1850 at the corner of Third and St. Peter streets, a site later occupied by the Women's City Club. The large building with the cupola seen to the left of the church and farther back from the river is the Territorial Capitol on Tenth and Cedar streets, a structure begun in 1851 and completed in 1853 when Strobel's view was published. It became the State Capitol after 1858 with Minnesota's change in status.[45]

The city grew substantially between the dates of the two views, and it was in the summer of 1856, about the time that the Andrews view was published, that a *Harper's Magazine* writer visited St. Paul and reported these impressions:

> St. Paul . . . in 1846 . . . contained ten inhabitants; in 1856 it contained ten thousand; in June and July of that year . . . steamers were coming and going—drays and teams and loads of emigrants were driving hither and thither and away. Carpenters and masons were hard at work . . . , shops and dwellings were starting out of the ground as if magicians were busy; and all was life, and energy, and hope. The Court-house, Presbyterian Church, Baldwin School-house, State House, hotels, the new Cathedral, Masonic Hall, theatres, and Odd Fellows' Hall, adorn the city and tell the story of wealth and work.[46]

One final lithograph remains to be examined on this voyage up the Mississippi in the 1850s. This is an 1857 work by Edwin Whitefield, reproduced in Folio 62. In the view Whitefield depicts his graphic impressions of St. Anthony, at the right, and—across the river at the other end of the distinctive suspension bridge—the smaller and younger town of Minneapolis. Whitefield looked upriver to the Falls of St. Anthony, where a drop of some eighty feet furnished an abundant source of power and attracted milling industries here to process the grain of the upper Great Plains.[47]

St. Anthony then had a population of about 3,600, while Minneapolis, which had achieved legal status only in 1855, could claim less than half that number. The important buildings of the falls settlements all could be found in St. Anthony. The large building at the far right housed the infant University of Minnesota established in 1851. On the skyline, the other large structure is the New Hotel, one of several hotels that were prospering from early tourists attracted by the beauty and majesty of the falls. Its companion with the tall spire is the Methodist Church. Whitefield's legend identifies other buildings in St. Anthony and in Minneapolis, where the principal structure was the courthouse.[48]

In this decade before the Civil War American lithographic viewmaking reached its heights of artistic achievement. If one can find no genuine masterpieces of art among these views, neither does one encounter more than one or two notable failures. Those responsible for their creation surely strove to produce beautiful prints that anyone would be proud to own and display in a home or office. Most artists followed the canons of landscape depiction; that is, they delineated a town or city from an identifiable point and showed only what an observer could see if he or she stood at the same spot selected by the artist.

After the Civil War viewmakers produced far fewer compositions of this type. A new generation of urban artists came to this peculiar aspect of American art with less training in or inclination to follow the

---

44. In another view of St. Paul published in 1853 a lithographer in New York at the Endicott shop used a daguerreotype by Joel Whitney to create an image of the city showing it from a point similar to that used by Seth Eastman the same year and reproduced in Folio 59. For information on Whitney's career as a photographer in St. Paul, a note on this lithograph, and a reproduction of the view, see Deák, *Picturing America,* entry 656, 1:445–46, and 2:656.

45. For a note on Strobel's view see ibid., entry 655, 1:444–45.

46. "The Upper Mississippi," 446.

47. The largest of these was the famous Pillsbury "A" Mill that consolidated parts of older structures with new facilities soaring six stories above the river. The mill occupied a site a short distance below the falls and, in the view, approximately halfway between the left and right margins.

48. Deák's note on the view in *Picturing America* is entry 730, 1:496. Whitefield produced few views of inferior quality, but perhaps he took extra care with this one of St. Anthony and Minneapolis. At this time he was deeply involved with a land development venture in Minnesota and in promoting the Kandiyohi Town Site Company in which he had invested. This episode in his life, which resulted in several views of Minnesota scenery, is recounted in Norton, *Edwin Whitefield,* 22–27.

traditions of pictorial townscape drawing. Instead, most of them elected to portray towns and cities in the style that Bachman, Hofmann, and especially Palmatary had pioneered in the Mississippi valley. If this era of viewmaking produced few prints comparable in quality to those of J. C. Wild, J. W. Hill, or Edwin Whitefield, the bird's-eye perspective that became so popular with artists, publishers, and customers provides far better opportunities for understanding the structure and character of the places depicted than do the prewar views. It is this era of Mississippi city viewmaking that the next chapter will explore.

V

Bird's-eye Views of the Upper River by Albert Ruger and His Followers, 1867–1879

The economic panic that began in 1857 affected urban viewmaking no less than it did other business enterprises. What in the best of times probably yielded no more than a modest income must have seemed an even less attractive field of endeavor when consumers worried about being able to purchase just the necessities of life. Most artists in this specialized profession turned to other pursuits. Even before the depression began, the Smith brothers evidently decided that their viewmaking activities held little promise, and they produced no more of their large and elaborate views after 1855.

Then, just as economic conditions began to improve, the Civil War turned the nation upside down and diverted the attention and energies of everyone to other matters. Depression and war thus explain the scarcity of city views issued between 1858 and 1866. Almost the only exceptions were images of Washington, where artists like Edward Sachse and John Bachman produced several views of a city that overnight became the center of all eyes.

Once the country began to adjust to peacetime conditions and resumed its growth and economic development, a new generation of urban viewmakers began to record the appearance of towns and cities throughout the country. From 1866 to the beginning of the early 1890s artists and publishers created far more of these images than before the war. They did not neglect places on the Mississippi River, and it

is their efforts that provide us with such a complete record of how these cities looked. For many towns and cities two or more images are available, making it possible either to see clearly the changes that occurred or to realize that not every river town prospered and grew during this period.

During these years of American viewmaking most artists of separately issued prints adopted the high-level, bird's-eye perspective that Palmatary had used at St. Louis in 1857. Of those active in the Mississippi valley during the decade following the Civil War, Albert Ruger was by far the most prolific. During a four-year period of work in this region beginning in 1867, Ruger created eighteen city views. He returned in 1879 to draw a second view of Minneapolis.

Several other artists also found the towns of the Mississippi River attractive subjects for their work at this time. Augustus Hageboeck produced several images of Davenport as well as of other places to the north. George Ellsbury, whose atlas views of the Twin Cities were described in Chapter III, also prepared two portraits of Winona, Minnesota, among other work. Augustus Koch produced views of Dubuque and Muscatine. Clemens J. Pauli drew and published views of La Crosse, Wisconsin, and Davenport, Iowa. Charles Vogt also drew Davenport in 1865 and added another view showing Dubuque a year later.

Camille N. Dry delineated the appearance of St. Louis on a view requiring no fewer than 110 sheets just a year after Charles Parsons and Lyman S. Atwater drew that city in 1874 for the firm of Currier and Ives. That company's smaller view of New Orleans and a near-duplicate issued in Germany both appeared about 1873. Artists represented only by single views of places on the river include George Richards, Frank Jervis, Augustus Lambrecht, and Herman Brosius. Clearly, there was no shortage of artists. Indeed, there are almost more of them than there are documented facts about their lives, for most of them remain biographical ghosts.

Of Ruger, however, we do have some information. Like most of his contemporaries responsible for a smaller number of Mississippi River city views, he followed a career as an itinerant artist. Ruger and his contemporaries often acted as their own publishers as well. These artists or their agents selected cities to be depicted, sought newspaper publicity to announce their arrival in town, attempted to obtain further public notice when they had completed a preliminary drawing and exhibited the results, and solicited subscriptions for the lithographic version that would be printed and distributed several months later.

As was the case with Henry Petit's 1860 view of Dubuque, discussed in the previous chapter, artists, agents, or publishers also attempted to secure payment from individuals wishing to have their buildings given prominence by display in a border vignette. Public exhibition of the artist's drawing also provided opportunities for residents to call the artist's attention to mistakes or omissions that could be corrected before the drawing went to a lithographer to be put on stone for printing. In following these practices, postwar artists of bird's-eye views simply built on the sales methods that earlier viewmakers such as Whitefield and the Smiths had helped to perfect.[1]

A few artists during this period still clung to a more conventional method of portraying cities, drawing them from a point on the ground, perhaps high enough so that the resulting image offered some feeling of depth but rarely showing clearly the details of buildings and other elements of the townscape beyond those in the foreground. In the Mississippi valley such views came mainly from local artists like Alex Simplot, who drew only his hometown of Dubuque, rather than from itinerants such as Ruger and Henry Wellge, whose career will be examined in greater detail in the next chapter. Only George Ellsbury and Augustus Hageboeck, among those who favored skyline rather than bird's-eye depictions, ventured into places other than the cities in which they lived or worked.

Ruger and virtually all the others whose activities this and the following chapter will explore got their start in the upper Midwest. Lithographic presses in Chicago and Milwaukee, located close to raw materials for manufacturing paper, offered convenient and inexpensive facilities for printing city views. Skilled craftsmen, many of them from Germany, trained and experienced in lithographic printing, eliminated the need for artists and publishers to send their work east to be printed in Cincinnati, Philadelphia, New York, or Boston.[2]

It was in the Midwest and beyond that publishers also found a new market for city views in the scores of towns springing up along the transcontinental railroads thrusting their way across the Great Plains to the Pacific Coast. Civic and business leaders in these places welcomed the creation of city views as an effective device to help promote settlement and stimulate land sales. Residents of towns on the Mississippi settled earlier than these Western prairie and plains communities pursued urban expansion policies with no less intensity. They seldom failed to greet warmly a new view of their town, copies of which they might send to distant friends, relatives, or prospective businessmen and investors as visual proof of the progressive community in which they lived.[3]

In the immediate postwar years Albert Ruger emerged as the key figure. A German stonemason who came to America about 1850 and settled somewhere in or near Akron, Ohio, Ruger at the age of thirty-six and just as the Civil War was coming to an end enlisted as a Union soldier. He is known to have completed drawings of several military camps, so he obviously possessed some skills in sketching before entering service. In 1865 he produced a bird's-eye lithograph showing the Ohio capitol at Columbus as the body of Abraham Lincoln passed among a throng of mourners. Although no artistic triumph, it evidently sold well enough to suggest to Ruger that when he was mustered out

---

1. For a fuller treatment of the business practices of American view artists and publishers, see chaps. 5–7 in Reps, *Views and Viewmakers*, 39–58.

2. For the important role played by Milwaukee lithographers, see Thomas Beckman, *Milwaukee Illustrated: Panoramic and Bird's-eye Views of a Midwestern Metropolis, 1844–1908.*

3. Viewmakers consciously played on rivalries among towns in the same region by pointing out in each new place visited that views of their competitors had been subscribed to and were in the process of publication. Local newspapers never failed to urge citizens to support the creation of a new view lest some other town gain a step in the race for urban supremacy.

he could make a living as an artist rather than resuming his occupation as a stonemason.[4]

Beginning in 1866 from his headquarters in Battle Creek, Michigan, Ruger visited, and drew lithographs of, several places in southern Michigan and northern Indiana. The style of depiction he then selected remained virtually unchanged during the remaining twenty-five years he spent as an itinerant artist drawing more than two hundred and fifty city views in twenty-four states and three Canadian provinces. In his early years as a viewmaker Ruger acted as his own publisher, employing Eli S. Glover—later an artist of city views himself—as his agent. Glover was only the first of several persons who worked for or with Ruger as agent, assistant, or publisher.[5]

In 1867 Ruger selected cities farther west and produced seven views of towns on the Mississippi from Cairo to Minneapolis. Two more appeared the following year, followed by seven others in 1869 and two in 1870—one of the latter being Memphis, the only place on the river below Cairo that Ruger depicted. Ruger then shifted his attention to other parts of the country, returning only once to the Mississippi to create at the end of the 1870s a new image of a Minneapolis that had enlarged considerably since he first depicted it a dozen years earlier.[6]

With a few exceptions, Ruger avoided towns with previously published views, perhaps feeling that the fabric of those places had not changed sufficiently to motivate residents to buy another lithographic view. This did not concern Henry Wellge. In 1883 he drew St. Paul for a view published in Madison by Joseph J. Stoner, a former associate of Ruger's. Like Ruger's view of that city in 1867, this also displayed the city as if seen from on high with the river in the foreground. Several folios in this book contain images of towns as drawn by both Ruger and Wellge, usually about two decades apart. These make it possible to see the changes that had occurred during a comparatively short period of time and allow one to examine the effects of population growth, increased demand for housing, industrialization, improvements in rail transportation, and other forces that at this time reshaped patterns of living as towns and cities expanded.[7]

Ruger's views—and those of several of his contemporaries—provide the vehicle for yet another vicarious voyage on the Mississippi, visiting its towns and cities in the decade following the Civil War. This time we will move downstream from St. Cloud, Minnesota, whose view can be found in Folio 65. Ruger visited and drew this city more than 120 miles upriver from Minneapolis in October 1869. On October 30, the St. Cloud *Times* identified the artist as "Prof. Ruger, of Chicago," and told its readers that his sketch "shows every residence and building in the city almost as distinctly as if you were looking at the building itself. Streets and alleys are shown with the same accuracy."

The style and nearly square format of this print are typical of Ruger's work. He normally included only two vignettes, usually—as here—two public buildings placed at opposite corners flanking a decorative title block. He usually divided his legends as he did here also, and he often limited the numbered items to a dozen or so references to public buildings, schools, churches, and the railroad station. Ruger selected a very high-level viewpoint that allowed him to present street patterns quite clearly and to draw the complete facades of all buildings facing him.

4. There are two versions of this lithograph bearing Ruger's name. Both are in the collection of the Ohio Historical Society in Columbus.

5. Glover's name also appears as publisher on a few of the views drawn by Ruger and published in 1868. Thereafter until his shop was destroyed by fire in 1871, Glover printed a number of the Ruger views. By 1869, and probably at least part of the previous year, Ruger employed another agent, Thaddeus M. Fowler, who in turn also became an itinerant artist. Both Glover and Fowler must have helped Ruger in his sketching, for it would have been impossible for one person to produce the sixty-two views bearing Ruger's name that were published in 1869. Fowler became the most prolific of all city view artists. In what are surely incomplete tabulations, I have found his name on 426 views published from 1870 through 1922. Ruger had the services of at least one other figure important in the field of city viewmaking. This was Joseph J. Stoner, whose name appears as the artist's agent for an 1868 view of Oberlin, Ohio. Stoner later published many of Ruger's views, jointly published others, and acted as publisher for several other artists from his home and office in Madison, Wisconsin. Stoner's name can be found on 314 city views. See my biographical notes on Fowler, Glover, and Stoner in Reps, *Views and Viewmakers*, 174–77, 201–4, and 209–12. For Stoner, see also Michael J. Fox, "Joseph John Stoner, 1829–1918"; for Fowler, see James Raymond Warren, "Thaddeus Mortimer Fowler, Bird's-eye-View Artist."

6. My note on Ruger in *Views and Viewmakers* contains information of his later activities. Some of the material therein comes from John Cumming, "Albert Ruger and His Views." It may be helpful to an understanding of how Ruger and several of the other itinerant artists concentrated their activities to examine the maps in *Views and*

Viewmakers, 9–14. Fig. 1 in that series locates the cities drawn by Ruger in each of the first six years of his viewmaking career, beginning in 1866.

7. Many of the folios also contain photographs from the air taken just a century after Wellge or one of his contemporaries recorded the appearance of the important towns of the Mississippi. These photographs closely approximate the perspectives created by Ruger, Wellge, or one of their contemporaries who painstakingly constructed aerial perspectives from their ground-level sketches.

The St. Cloud view illustrates another aspect of Ruger's approach to viewmaking, one used with variations by almost all other bird's-eye-view artists. For his Mississippi River views he consistently used a two-point perspective system, with lines parallel on the ground drawn as converging toward one of two vanishing points. Instead of locating both vanishing points on the horizon and within the picture's borders, as called for by the conventions of perspective drawing, Ruger always placed one vanishing point well beyond one side of the picture and the other inside the picture's borders but located far above the horizon.

Such a treatment did not arise from ignorance of the rules of linear perspective; instead, Ruger and his fellows understood that artistic conventions had to be stretched in the interests of commerce. Mass sales required that every person's property be delineated legibly and accurately in order to attract as many subscribers as possible to the finished lithograph. Therefore, images of buildings in the background needed to be nearly as large as those of similar dimensions in the foreground. Perspective points located on the horizon and within the picture border would produce lines converging so sharply that images of buildings beyond the foreground would be so small as to be unrecognizable.[8]

Ruger's approach offered a compromise that preserved enough reality to make his views fairly convincing while allowing him enough scope to delineate almost all of the buildings of the town with sufficient detail to capture the attention of their owners—all of whom he looked on as prospective customers. This explains why so many views of this type and time give the impression that the cities have been built on tilted plains that slope upward from the foreground, so that if a

person took one careless step beyond the horizon it would be a very long one indeed.[9]

The St. Cloud that Ruger drew in 1869 was only fifteen years old, but it had prospered earlier as an important shipping point in the fur trade, found a new function after 1858 as the site of a government land office that attracted many immigrants, and from 1868 had its economy fed by the development of quarries producing granite building stones and monuments. The original town plat of 1854 soon proved too restrictive, and adjoining land was laid out in two grid systems, each oriented to the river as it curved around the town.

Just above and slightly to the left of the sailboat in the Mississippi is the State Normal School, opened only the month before Ruger finished his view. This eventually became St. Cloud University, an institution that has gradually absorbed much of the street grid in the left half of the view. The air photo in the same folio looks down on St. Cloud from a nearly identical viewpoint, making it easy to trace in the visage of the modern city many of the features that Ruger saw and drew well over a century earlier. Chapter VIII will comment further on this and the other modern air photos that many of these folios include.

Two years before the publication of Ruger's view of St. Cloud, he produced the first bird's-eye depiction of Minneapolis and St. Anthony, a lithograph reproduced in Folio 62. In that year—1867—Minneapolis obtained its charter as a city, and it became apparent that it was going to exceed the older St. Anthony in size and importance. Indeed, five years later the two became a single municipality under the name of Minneapolis.

Ruger looked down from his imaginary position on the two towns divided by the river and linked at that time not only by the distinctive suspension bridge but by the St. Paul and Pacific Railroad bridge leading to a depot in St. Anthony where the first train arrived in 1862. Across the Mississippi near the complex of mill buildings at the falls stood the larger station, engine roundhouse, and yards of the Minnesota Central line, a route that linked Minneapolis with Chicago via St. Paul. Ruger's view makes clear that within a few short years this center of urban development had experienced rapid growth and was filling up

---

8. Because the street pattern of St. Cloud is divided into two grid systems each, with its own orientation, Ruger's approach to perspective drawing may not be so evident as with other of his views. An examination of the view of Winona in Folio 55 may help. Straight edges (two sheets of paper will do nicely) placed along the center lines of any two streets running back from the river will meet only a substantial distance above the horizon. Straight edges so placed on the streets paralleling the river will meet at a point far beyond the left-hand edge of the view. Moving the straight edges to converge at the horizon or within the picture will demonstrate how images of buildings in the distance would need to be much smaller than Ruger was able to draw them here.

9. This is even more apparent in views with only a single vanishing point located beyond the horizon. Palmatary's view of St. Louis in Folio 28 is a good example. So is the view of Muscatine by August Koch, reproduced in Folio 40.

the blocks of its grid street pattern, which landowners had surveyed roughly parallel and perpendicular to the course of the Mississippi.[10]

For St. Paul, Ruger created a similar image in 1867, one reproduced in Folio 60 and the earliest view to display the city from an aerial perspective. It was steamboat travel that made St. Paul accessible and stimulated its early development, and Ruger shows us a variety of river craft. He drew them arriving, departing, or tied up along the landing below the bridge crossing the Mississippi where it reaches its northernmost point in the city.

The artist surely found gratifying the long notice of his work that the St. Paul *Minnesota Pioneer* printed on August 20, 1867:

> We have been shown a bird's eye sketch of . . . our . . . city, taken from the bluff above West St. Paul, by the Chicago artist A. Ruger. It takes in the entire circle of the city, from Dayton's Bluff and Summit Avenue, as far West as the Stewart residence, showing at a single glance all the public and private residences in the city proper. The Merchant's International, Capitol, Opera House and city buildings give it a decidedly metropolitan appearance.

The article noted that Ruger showed "the steamboat landing . . . lined with steamboats discharging their cargoes, and railroad trains on the St. Paul & Pacific Railroad and Minnesota Valley Railroad . . . arriving and departing." The paper informed its readers that Ruger intended to have his drawing lithographed and that he was "in the city for the purpose of canvassing for subscribers." The writer asserted that the view "will, when completed, give a much better general idea of St. Paul than any picture hitherto published."

Ruger's portrait of the city certainly shows at an early date the results of completely unregulated land development. However unimaginative a critic might find the repetitive grid of the original town plat extending back from the river at center right, it is far superior to the chaotic pattern of streets that emerged elsewhere as owners of adjoining land divided their property as they pleased. The bewildering, wasteful, and unattractive development one sees at the left gave St. Paul a set of dangerous street intersections and building sites of inefficient shape that have made this district a problem area to which there are no fully satisfactory solutions.

10. Although Minneapolis and St. Anthony possessed almost unlimited waterpower resources, the rapids and falls in the Mississippi River above St. Paul prevented steamboats from reaching them. Railroad transportation thus became even more important than for other towns along the river.

Between 1867 and 1870 Ruger also drew several other cities in this region of the upper river: Hastings, Red Wing, and Winona in Minnesota; Alma, La Crosse, and Prairie du Chien in Wisconsin; and McGregor and Guttenberg in northern Iowa. The reader will find their images in Folios 52–57. Ruger's depiction of Winona in Folio 55 reinforces the description of the site a decade earlier by a visitor who noted enthusiastically that here "the prairie is some ten miles in length, and three in width, and so level as not to require the grading of a single street."[11]

In La Crosse, depicted by Ruger in the view in Folio 54, as in many other places on the river above St. Louis, sawmills and lumberyards played important roles in supporting the local economy. Great log rafts guided by steering sweeps at front and rear moved downriver from the forests of Wisconsin and Minnesota to supply the mills with logs. Boards from the mills moved to local construction sites or were shipped by rail to help build the prairie towns springing up along the railroads thrusting westward.[12]

A lithograph by George Ellsbury half a dozen years later, also reproduced in Folio 54, shows one of these rafts as well as a boat towing two barges loaded with railroad boxcars. This is how much of the freight crossed the Mississippi before the construction of railroad bridges linking rail lines on opposite sides of the river. In this view of La Crosse in 1873 Ellsbury anticipated by nearly twenty years the construction of the bridge he shows in the distance. He also took some liberties with

11. Harriet E. Bishop, *Floral Home or, First Years of Minnesota . . .*, 227. Anyone would have found it easy to draw Winona's surroundings, but Ruger's view of McGregor demonstrates his considerable skill in rendering topography, something that was far from easy in such a restricted site and in days before topographic maps became available. The Guttenberg view demonstrates some of the limitations in another area of rendering. No one can tell from Ruger's depictions of buildings that a great many were splendid examples of stone construction, the work of German artisans who settled here and gave the town its name.

12. Many of the places shown on Ruger's lithograph of La Crosse and on three other views of the city were identified and analyzed by Albert H. Sanford in "Four Pictures Portray La Crosse of Early Day," which illustrates all four views. Copies were kindly furnished me by Anita Taylor Doering, archivist, La Crosse Public Library. Much of this material appeared later in Albert H. Sanford and H. J. Hirshheimer, *A History of La Crosse, Wisconsin 1841–1900*, 118–25. In this view Ruger provides another image of the steamboat *Phil Sheridan*, a vessel also appearing in his lithograph of St. Paul. It seems to me likely that artists received fees for including an image of a steamboat in their views, as it is known they did for incorporating images of private buildings.

reality in bringing within the left edge of his view the station of the Milwaukee Railroad.[13]

The view in the same folio by Clemens J. Pauli in 1876 looks at the city from still another viewpoint, one typical of the lithographs produced by this artist, printer, and publisher who often placed his imaginary easel high in the air, locating it so that the river forms one side of the print. In the distance one can see the railroad bridge over the Mississippi and the Black rivers, a structure completed the year Pauli drew La Crosse. Across the bottom of the view, Pauli provided a legend of forty-two items, each corresponding to a number in the view itself. Pauli drew three or perhaps four other views of Mississippi River towns: Davenport, Iowa, in 1876 (Folio 45 and discussed below); Moline, Illinois, in 1877 (not illustrated); Vicksburg, Mississippi, in 1891 (discussed in Chapter VII and illustrated in Folio 16); and, perhaps, Quincy, Illinois, in 1878 (see Folio 35).[14]

Pauli (1835–1896) came from a prominent family in Lübeck, Germany. He began but did not complete the study of agriculture at the University of Jena and came to America in 1863 to pursue the same subject. By 1867, however, he was living in Burlington, identified in the city directory the following year as a draftsman working for the U.S. Army Engineer Corps, a position he seems to have held until 1875. How Pauli decided to begin drawing city views is not likely ever to be known, but possibly he had seen one or more of the eight views that Augustus Hageboeck drew and printed between 1866 and 1874 or knew about those created by Charles H. Vogt, also of Burlington.

Pauli moved to Milwaukee about 1875 and promptly set to work on a view of that city that he published the following year. During the next two years he lived the life of an itinerant view artist, drawing and publishing lithographs of at least eight cities, as well as drawing one or more views published by Charles Vogt. In 1878 he formed a partnership with Adam Beck, and their firm, the Beck and Pauli Lithographing Company, soon attracted business from many artists and publishers of city views. During their partnership, which lasted until 1886, Beck and Pauli printed hundreds of city views, mainly for Joseph J. Stoner, Ruger and Stoner, Norris Wellge and Co., and Henry Wellge.[15]

After passing a number of small towns below La Crosse, a Mississippi traveler in the late 1860s would have come to Dubuque. That city's population grew from a little over 3,000 in 1850 to over 13,000 in 1860 to make it Iowa's most populous city. Ruger did not do a view of Dubuque, probably because he learned that Charles Vogt had done so in 1866 and judged that there would be only a limited demand for another printed image only a year or so later.

Vogt's lithograph is reproduced in Folio 50, a view from the north that looks down on the city's grid of streets tightly restricted by the bluffs on one side and the floodplain of the Mississippi on the other. At the center right the artist includes a portion of the town struggling to find expansion room by pushing its way up a partial break in the wall of the bluff and spreading out along the flat land beyond. The effect of this expansion, duplicated in several other places along the western edge of the older town, inspired an author in 1872 to this description of Dubuque: "There is an absolute confusion of lines. Here is a wall, there a stairway. Above that wall is a house, with more stairways. Then

13. Ellsbury is identified and his work briefly discussed in Chapter III. Of the buildings in the city appearing in Ellsbury's print of La Crosse, Sanford observes in "Four Pictures": "One cannot tell much from this picture about the streets and buildings of La Crosse. At the left we see the spires of the Congregational Church and the Cathedral. The square building next is doubtless the old court house. Near them a slender tower is shown, with a flag staff above it. This was the fire station . . . just east of the State Bank Building. . . . The large mansard roof next to the right belongs to the Pomeroy Opera House, at the corner of Fourth and Main streets."

14. In his "Four Pictures," Sanford comments about Pauli's delineation of topography: "A glance at the area east of the city, extending to the bluffs, shows clearly that those who think of the original site of La Crosse as a level plain are quite mistaken. It was a region of hummocks and hollows, such as may still [1938] be seen beyond the eastern limits of the city. Much leveling had to be done as new streets were opened." The Quincy view was printed in Milwaukee in 1878 by a firm that Pauli established that year with another German lithographer, Adam Beck. Further search of Quincy newspapers will probably reveal the name of Pauli as the artist.

15. Nearly all Beck and Pauli lithographs used a tone stone to add cloud and shadow features to the basic black and white of the underlying image. In addition to Stoner and Wellge, Lucien R. Burleigh sent several of his views to be printed by Beck and Pauli before he established his own press in Troy, New York. Beck was himself a skilled lithographer, having served his apprenticeship in Nuremberg. Two years after coming to America in 1866 he went to work for the Chicago Lithographing Company directed by Louis Kurz, and Beck may have followed Kurz to Milwaukee after the Chicago fire of 1871 destroyed that company. If they did not know one another before, Pauli probably met Beck at Kurz's American Oleograph Company, the Milwaukee company that printed Pauli's Milwaukee, La Crosse, Moline, and Davenport lithographs. Kurz's decision to return to Chicago may have led Beck and Pauli to form their own company in Milwaukee. My debt to Thomas Beckman for his research on Pauli and Beck is enormous. Most of the material on these two artists and lithographers that Beckman kindly shared with me in the late 1970s while he prepared his *Milwaukee Illustrated* is incorporated in his "The Beck & Pauli Lithographing Company."

comes another wall, and perhaps another house, or a castellated mass of limestone, overlooking the architectural muddle. It is as quaint as any of the scenes in the old cities of Lombardy upon the slopes of any mountains, among the terraces cultivated with the grape, the olive and the fig."[16]

Vogt, born in Germany like so many other artists and lithographers of the Mississippi, was in Davenport by 1864. Possibly he, like Pauli, worked for the army engineers, and he, too, moved to Milwaukee, where he appears in city directories through 1878. There he operated a lithographic printing business that, like Beck and Pauli, printed many city views. He drew or collaborated with others in drawing some of these himself, but he seems to have relied on other artists for the views he published under his own name.

Vogt and his anonymous artist surrounded the Dubuque view with a frieze of vignettes. For these images the publisher almost surely collected some payment. He pictured only two public structures among two dozen vignettes: the custom house and post office and the city hall and market. Eight business buildings and four banks are memorialized in this fashion, and the elaborate residences of what must have been ten of the most wealthy Dubuque families are pictured, each image set in its own circular, leafy frame.

Alex Simplot (1837–1914), a native of Dubuque, provided another view of Dubuque in 1870, a lithograph also reproduced in Folio 50. The artist looked from the opposite shore near the Illinois end of the great bridge that had been completed shortly after Vogt issued his view. From this distance, Dubuque looks far less impressive than in Vogt's image, and the artist obviously made no attempt to render the view except as honestly and as directly as possible. At the left in the river he shows a towboat with a barge on either side that has evidently just passed through the swing bridge whose pivot rests on the elongated pier just to the right of center.

Simplot enjoyed an unusually full education, beginning at the parochial school attached to the cathedral at Dubuque and then pursuing two years of college studies in Mount Morris, Illinois. He then transferred to Union College in Schenectady, New York, where he studied law and graduated in 1858. Law, however, held little interest for him, and on his return to Dubuque he taught school for a time before

deciding to pursue a career using the talents as an artist that he had displayed in childhood.

In 1861 Simplot sent a sketch of Iowa volunteers in the Civil War to *Harper's Weekly*, where it was not only accepted for publication but brought an offer for Simplot to serve this illustrated journal as a war correspondent. The view of the levee at Memphis in 1862 that Folio 20 reproduces is an example of the several wood engravings made from his sketches that *Harper's* used in its wartime issues.[17]

An illness brought Simplot back to Dubuque before the end of the Civil War, where he lived for the rest of his life. He engaged in several enterprises including a grain business and a retail dry-goods establishment at First and Main streets that he ran with two brothers. He also used his legal training, practicing as a patent attorney. His main interests may have been in the operation of a printing and engraving company whose output included several views of Dubuque, even though he himself took his first view of Dubuque in 1870 to be printed in Chicago, the place misleadingly stated in the imprint as his address.[18]

16. R. E. Garczynski, "The Upper Mississippi, from St. Louis to St. Anthony's Falls," 333.

17. Simplot's parents settled in Dubuque a year before he was born, after residing first in Chicago and then in Nauvoo, Illinois, following their emigration from France. His father, Henry, became a successful businessman and served as a member of the board of aldermen. At about the same time that Simplot joined *Harper's* he secured an appointment as assistant engineer in the War Department and in both capacities accompanied Union troops to several battles and on a number of campaigns. His notebooks indicate that as an artist he did not receive a salary; instead the magazine paid him from ten to twenty-five dollars for each sketch accepted for publication. Fifty of these have been identified, although he may have produced others that were unsigned or otherwise not attributed to his pencil.

18. Perhaps Simplot also issued another separate view in 1872. A small engraved version that may have been copied from a larger original appears in two county histories. In the earlier volume it bears the title *View of Dubuque in 1872*. The later one identifies it only as *Dubuque in Early Days*. The artist looked down on the city from a bluff near the lower end of the settled portion of Dubuque. See *The History of Dubuque County, Iowa, Containing a History of the County, Its Cities, Towns, &c. . . .* , frontispiece opposite title page; and Franklin T. Oldt, ed., *History of Dubuque County Iowa*, opposite p. 33. The latter volume also has opposite p. 65 another view of Dubuque drawn by Simplot and copyrighted by him in 1907. This is an extremely close copy of a view drawn by John Caspar Wild ca. 1844. In the book this has a title lettered in the body of the print: "Dubuque, Iowa. 1846." In addition to his signature as artist in the plate at lower left, there is a lettered inscription outside the neat line at lower right: "Alex. Simplot - Patents - Engravings." Below that in the margin in set type appears the following: "(Daily Telegraph Print)." A version of this, matted and framed, is in the collection of Loras College, Dubuque. In 1897 Simplot drew, engraved, published, and copyrighted a fine view of Dubuque looking toward the Mississippi. The imprint of this advertises the artist's business and professional activities. After his name appears: "Solicitor of

A more accomplished and productive artist of city views, Augustus Koch (1840–1899), drew Dubuque for a lithograph that appeared in 1872, an image that Koch may also have published, as he did many of his other works. Folio 50 reproduces this first true bird's-eye view of the entire city as this itinerant artist of American cities visualized its appearance from high in the air over the Mississippi. The artist provided an unusually complete legend, identifying with numbers fifty-four of the city's buildings and places of importance.

Koch's view clearly shows how roads had been driven up the few clefts in the otherwise unbroken wall of bluffs facing the river. Expensive to construct and maintain, these connected the older town below with new neighborhoods then developing on land at the western fringe of the expanding city. The eastern edge of Dubuque also had a ragged boundary, for flood-prone land along the Mississippi had not yet been made safe for building, and the lines and causeways of several railroads and wagon roads crisscrossed the waterfront and separated the city from the very river that had been responsible for its initial growth and prosperity. Koch visited Dubuque not long after the railroads had begun to supplant steamboat transportation as the chief means of moving freight and passengers to and from the city. In his view he looked down on the city at such a steep angle that only a narrow strip of sky appears above the horizon, a style he used in many of his city views elsewhere in the country. This approach continues the cartographic approach to viewmaking that Ruger introduced to the region after the Civil War.

Koch, like Ruger, came from Germany and served in the Civil War after enlisting in the Wisconsin Infantry as a private in the fall of 1861. After serving as a clerk and draftsman with the topographical engineers in St. Louis, he was recommended for and received a commission as second lieutenant in April 1864. He was then assigned as an engineering officer with the Fifty-first U.S. Infantry, one of the black regiments on duty in the lower Mississippi. Receiving a discharge in 1865, he doubtless returned to his parent's home in Manitowoc, Wisconsin, and probably sought employment as a draftsman or artist in Milwaukee or Chicago.

By 1868 he had established himself as an itinerant city-view artist, drawing several towns in the interior of Iowa that year and in 1869 before venturing into Utah, Wyoming, and California in 1870 and 1871. He returned to the Midwest in 1872 and not long thereafter began to draw views published by or with Joseph J. Stoner, the Madison, Wisconsin, publisher with whom Ruger had also been associated. That is one reason for suspecting that Koch may have begun his career as one of Ruger's assistants.[19]

Leaving Dubuque and moving downriver some 130 miles, a traveler would reach its great Iowa rival, Davenport, along with the adjoining cities of Rock Island and Moline, across the Mississippi in Illinois. By 1860 Davenport's population was slightly over 11,000, a figure that almost doubled to 20,038 in 1870; Rock Island counted 5,130 persons in 1860 and 7,890 in 1870; and Moline grew from 3,273 to 5,754 in those years. This multicentered little metropolis attracted a great deal of favorable attention, and it is little wonder that several artists found this an advantageous place to practice their craft.

Ruger visited this area to draw Rock Island and Moline for views published in 1869. His lithograph of Moline in Folio 42 emphasizes

Patents - Photo, Brush and Half-Tone Engravings - Dubuque, Iowa." As early as 1880 one of his biographical sketches stated, "Mr. Simplot has had a large experience as an artist in sketching and engraving, and has an extended reputation; he works by the new photo engraving process, and with excellent success, and has all he can do with his other business" (*The History of Dubuque County*, 882). The entire entry is on pp. 881–82. Other information on Simplot's life and career comes from Oldt, ed., *History of Dubuque County*, 690–91; "Simplot Comes Home to Dubuque," Dubuque *Telegraph-Herald*, April 5, 1964, 23 (with Simplot's sketches of the family dry-goods store and newspaper correspondents in a log schoolhouse in Warsaw, Missouri, a photographic portrait of Simplot and his wife, and reproductions of Simplot's paintings of a river steamer and Galena, Illinois, on the occasion of General Grant's return); and "Dubuque Loses an Early Settler," Dubuque *Telegraph-Herald*, October 22, 1914, 14.

19. In Reps, *Views and Viewmakers*, my biographical note on Koch (pp. 184–86) includes this observation: "Both Ruger and Koch were active in Iowa in 1868, and views by both were printed at [Eli S.] Glover's press [in Chicago]. These views lack a publisher's name, and it would be no surprise to find that Glover acted in this capacity as well as printer and that all three men were thus involved in the same enterprise. It may have been Ruger who introduced Koch to Joseph J. Stoner of Madison, who at this time was publishing some of Ruger's views either alone or as copublisher with the artist." Koch's association with Stoner continued only through 1873. During his career Koch visited twenty-three states to draw well over one hundred city views. More than half of them were done after Koch and his family had moved to Kansas City, Missouri, where in 1880 his name appears in the city directory as an artist and thereafter until 1895 as a lithographer. From Kansas City he traveled in search of subjects for his views, although for at least part of the time in 1887–1888 he was employed by one of the city's most important lithographic and printing firms, Ramsey, Millett and Hudson. That company had printed sixteen of Koch's views of Colorado, Kansas, and Nebraska in the early 1880s. I am grateful to David Boutros of the Kansas City public library for searching city directories to verify my hunch that Koch may have lived in Kansas City.

the importance of waterpower in the industrial development of this community. At the end of the bridge one can see a tight concentration of factory buildings facing the river. Several of them belonged to the company John Deere established in Moline in 1847 to manufacture the plows he had devised to cut cleanly through the heavy prairie soil. Deere expanded his business to include the manufacture of wagons and other agricultural implements, and Moline prospered along with the town's best-known entrepreneur.

Deere and Co. was not the only successful industry. Ruger's legend identifies a total of sixteen manufacturing concerns in Moline whose factories produced paper, flour, woolens, iron products, beer, and lumber, among other items. A secondary industrial cluster of buildings on the river at the left belonged to the Dimmock, Gould and Company's tub and pail works. The logs in the river, the factory's piles of lumber, and the log raft being broken up downstream at Keator's sawmill remind us of the continuing importance of the Wisconsin and Minnesota timberlands and the essential link the river provided between the suppliers of timber and the manufacturers of wood products in dozens of river towns along the Mississippi.

Ruger also portrayed Moline's neighbor, Rock Island, in 1869. The town occupied a site on the Illinois shore just below the lower end of the island from which the town took its name. Here a railroad bridged the Mississippi for the first time in 1855, but the view, reproduced in Folio 41, shows no great concentration of industry as one might expect for a place so strategically located. Instead, Rock Island seems to consist only of a substantial business district midway along a linear grid otherwise devoted to residential use.[20]

Only the large building seen at the lower left hints at what brought people and commerce to this location. The building stands at one end of Rock Island, where it divides the Mississippi into two channels. It is one of the many structures comprising the federal arsenal that the U.S. government decided to place here in 1862. The Civil War delayed this intended use for a few years, while the army used the island as a camp for Confederate prisoners. Eventually rows of stone buildings were built where residents of Rock Island, Moline, or Davenport

were employed in producing, storing, and shipping a variety of military weapons.

Almost certainly Ruger intended to add a view of Davenport, but on his arrival he must have learned that only three and four years earlier two local viewmakers had each produced large lithographic portraits of the place. Their existence doubtless convinced Ruger that the local market might not yet be ready for another such print. Moreover, the size of Davenport may have dissuaded him from any such attempt, since the far greater number of buildings would have required a great deal more time than he needed to spend in drawing Rock Island and Moline.

Charles Vogt published the earlier of the two postwar views of Davenport in 1865, a lithograph illustrated in Folio 44. Vogt put this on stone from a drawing done by some anonymous artist. He then sent it to St. Louis to be printed. Although it is certainly no masterpiece, Vogt's view clearly displays all the features of the city and its street plan while providing more detailed information about the appearance of selected residences and business and civic buildings in the border vignettes.

The same folio contains the companion view that Augustus Hageboeck issued the following year, five years after he moved to Davenport in 1861. He came from St. Louis, where city directories for 1859 and 1860 listed him as a lithographer and his brother, John, as a lithographic printer. Probably the Hageboecks worked for a St. Louis firm like that headed by Leopold Gast before deciding to open their own business away from established competition.

As a growing community with a substantial German population, Davenport offered opportunities for the two brothers. In 1861 the city directory carried a full-page advertisement for "Hageboeck & Bro. Practical Lithographers, Engravers and Printers." The advertisement listed some of the types of printing they were prepared to carry out at their establishment located at 29 Main Street: "commercial blanks of every description, maps, plans, views, diplomas, show-cards, circulars, frontispieces, drawings of machinery . . . drafts, notes, checks, landscapes, letterheads, billheads, business and visiting cards, liquor, tobacco, segar and fancy labels, &c. &c."[21]

In his Davenport view, his first recorded effort at depicting a city, Hageboeck rejected the bird's-eye style that Ruger and most of the

---

20. When Mark Twain reached this area on his Mississippi River tour in 1882, the Rock Island railroad bridge was no longer a novelty. Calling Rock Island "a flourishing town . . . which lies at the foot of the Upper Rapids," he noted that the bridge was but "one of . . . thirteen which fret the Mississippi and the pilots, between St. Louis and St. Paul" (*Life on the Mississippi*, 566).

21. The two brothers lived on Brown Street between Fourth and Fifth.

other view artists of the time had adopted. Instead, he portrayed Davenport as one would have seen it from a slightly elevated position on the opposite side of the river. Because Davenport occupies a ramplike site with a substantial slope toward the river, the view happily lacks the artificial stage-set quality of most of Hageboeck's other work, which tends to show the skylines of river towns with only the buildings in the immediate foreground delineated with any conviction.

No fewer than forty-nine vignettes surround the main center element of the lithograph. They constitute a veritable catalog of the architectural styles that a visitor at the time would have encountered. If Hageboeck followed the usual practice of charging owners for the privilege of having their buildings singled out in this manner, he must have enjoyed a substantial return even before he put copies of the work up for sale or delivered them to subscribers. Thus, it seems strange that vignettes do not appear on any of his other lithographs.[22]

These later works include three other printed images of Davenport, one being the image of 1874 or thereabouts that Folio 44 also reproduces. This is signed in the image by Aug.[ustus?] Lambrecht, possibly an employee of Hageboeck's and conceivably the artist of the publisher's several other unsigned views. This view of Davenport, one published in 1874 of Rock Island (Folio 41), and Hageboeck's view of Minneapolis a year earlier in Folio 63 illustrate the long, narrow profiles of cities that Hageboeck specialized in.[23]

Hageboeck was not the only viewmaker partial to the older panoramic townscape style. In 1875 one Frank Jervis drew and, with an associate named Wolfe, published another lithograph of Davenport illustrated in Folio 44. According to the imprint, Jervis climbed the tower of the Rock Island Arsenal to look across at Davenport, which in the view sits just above the railroad bridge. The text below the title of this attractive print appears in both English and German, an obvious attempt to appeal to the large number of German-speaking residents in Davenport and the surrounding area.[24]

Folio 45 reproduces another view of Davenport in this period, one drawn by C. J. Pauli showing the city in 1876. Because in these early years of his career Pauli always selected viewpoints that differed substantially from those used by other artists, his images often reveal elements of his subjects not discernible elsewhere. His Davenport lithograph shows a site less confined by steep bluffs than that at Dubuque, and the city here was able to expand away from the river with less expense and with fewer disjunctions in the street pattern than occurred at its upstream rival.

Muscatine, forty miles or so downstream, enjoyed some of these same site advantages. Augustus Koch's view of 1874, reproduced in Folio 40, reveals a nearly unbroken grid of streets continuing the pattern established when the original, much smaller townsite was first surveyed. Here, too, one finds evidence of the importance of the lumber trade. On the left, at the mouth of the Muscatine River, a boom encloses the floating logs that the Hershey and Irvine sawmill on the bank converted to lumber.[25]

As with Koch's view of Dubuque, his Muscatine view shows a city in a state of transition between railway and steamboat transportation. This lithograph includes an amusing mistake, probably one committed by an anonymous lithographer where Koch's drawing was put on stone rather than by the artist himself. In the river one sees the wakes of the steamboats moving up- or downstream. But the log raft also has a wake extending to its left—the downstream end. Unless the crew using the steering sweeps at what would be the stern were working at an inhuman pace, it would have been impossible to move the great log raft upstream at any speed, let alone at a pace fast enough to generate a perceptible wake.[26]

---

22. In his view of Davenport published in 1881 Hageboeck festooned the borders with dozens of advertisements much like the unillustrated commercial notices published in newspapers.

23. Some of Hageboeck's skyline scenes state that they were engraved, printed, and published by him; others substitute "drawn" for "engraved." The latter term almost certainly refers to engraving on stone, since none of his prints have a plate mark to indicate they came from a copper or steel plate. Stone engraving is a variation of lithographic printing in which the basic design is created by drawing fine lines with an etching needle through a thin coating of dried varnish on the stone. These lines are then inked, the varnish "resist" removed, and the stone rolled with lithographic printer's ink and printed in the normal manner.

24. Of Jervis and Wolfe nothing is known. The imprint gives Davenport as their address. Because a Chicago firm printed the lithograph, it is safe to assume that the publishers were not printers.

25. According to one source, "in 1870 a single order of 400,000 feet of lumber, lath, shingles, and pickets was shipped to a firm in Omaha, Neb." (Federal Writers' Project, Works Projects Administration, *Iowa: A Guide to the Hawkeye State*, 290).

26. Koch also drew a view of Louisiana, Missouri, dated 1876. I have not had an opportunity to see this lithograph. It is possible that he is also the artist of a view of Keokuk in 1878, another print that I have not been able to see or to obtain a photographic copy of.

It seems odd that neither Ruger, Koch, nor Pauli visited and recorded the appearance of Burlington, a town that in 1870 had nearly 15,000 inhabitants and was more than twice the size of Muscatine. It was not until many years later that the last of the Mississippi River itinerant view artists, Henry Wellge, came here to produce one of his large lithographs, a view referred to in Chapter VII.

Pauli did go to Quincy, Illinois, the largest of all the river towns north of St. Louis with 24,052 residents in 1870. An unsigned view of Quincy in 1878 so closely resembles Pauli's other views of this period that it can reasonably be attributed to him; in addition, it was printed by his new Milwaukee firm of Beck and Pauli founded that same year. Reproduced in Folio 35, Pauli's lithograph looks down on Quincy from a point above the downriver end of this prosperous community. In the foreground Pauli identifies several industries suggesting Quincy's diversified economic base. These firms engaged in pork packing and making furniture, stoves, tobacco products, boilers, and many other commodities.

To the left of center one can see the well-developed business district extending along Maine Street to the right of the building-lined, wooded town square. Few topographic barriers existed to prevent Quincy's easy expansion to the east and north, and owners of what had once been farms at the outskirts of the town divided their property into building sites along streets that continued Quincy's original grid design. Willard Glazier stopped there in 1881 and reported his impressions of what was then the second most populous city in Illinois:

> The city has an extensive river traffic; a splendid railroad bridge across the Mississippi; four well proportioned parks, providing convenient breathing-places for the citizens, who crowd them in warm summer evenings; a fine fair-ground, covering about eighty acres; many elegant public and private edifices; numerous manufactories, employing about four thousand operatives, and producing annually $10,000,000 worth of goods. Lines of horse-cars traverse the leading thoroughfares. Many of the private residences are spacious, elegantly and tastefully planned, and surrounded by well-kept and very beautiful grounds.[27]

We can conclude this downstream tour of upper Mississippi River cities as we began, with the views of Albert Ruger. In 1869 he prepared views for both Hannibal and St. Charles, Missouri. Two years earlier he

27. *Down the Great River . . . ,* 300–301.

visited Alton, Illinois. These three lithographs can be found in Folios 33, 30, and 31, each one similar in style to those he drew of places farther up the great river. And, as he did occasionally elsewhere, in his St. Charles view he turned ahead a few pages of the calendar by showing as if completed the great bridge across the Missouri River, a structure that did not open until 1871 following a series of construction disasters.

Ruger's image of Hannibal must surely rank among the most attractive he created during his long career. It is also appealing because it shows a place made memorable by Mark Twain, who as Samuel Clemens spent his boyhood in Hannibal and lived on Hill Street just two blocks from the mighty river and the steamboat landing. It was there—not many years before Ruger drew the city's portrait—that Clemens contracted his case of steamboat fever from which he never really recovered.

Holliday's Hill, rising from the end of North Main Street on the right, became the Cardiff Hill of *Tom Sawyer* and *Huckleberry Finn*. Near the public square stood the school that the real Sam and the fictional Tom attended. The island at the far left may have been remembered by Twain in devising the setting for several of the adventures in his two books set in this locale. But in addition to recognizing these literary associations and using the view to gain a greater understanding of Twain and the life about which he wrote, one can delight in some of the decorative elements of this print.

Note in the foreground the evocative scene along the river. There, horse-drawn coaches await passengers disembarking from the train at the waterside station of the Hannibal and Naples Railroad or from the steam ferry that has just arrived from Hannibal. On the Hannibal side stands the station of the Hannibal and St. Joseph Railroad, one of the several lines expected to benefit from the completion of the Union Pacific–Central Pacific transcontinental route in the year Ruger published this view.

The Hannibal and St. Joe line led westward up the valley of Bear Creek (seen at left center), and between it and the creek Ruger shows the very extensive lumberyards of John J. Cruikshank, one of the merchants filling the demands of farmers and town builders out on the Great Plains where timber was scarce or nonexistent. Ruger's legend identifies the locations of the several other lumber dealers and planing mills who were then the town's chief industrial employers.

Below Hannibal lies St. Louis, the starting point for the second leg of our journey down the river in the years immediately following the Civil

War. The next chapter describes some of the post–Civil War views of that city and examines in more detail the largest and most remarkable of all Mississippi River urban portraits. From St. Louis we continue downstream to Cairo, Memphis, Vicksburg, and New Orleans on the trail of Ruger and other urban viewmakers who pursued their artistic craft in these years following the Civil War.

VI

Bird's-eye Views of St. Louis and the Lower River, 1867–1879

Although St. Louis suffered economically during the Civil War from the interruption of steamboat traffic to and from the South, it suffered no wartime destruction like Vicksburg nor had to endure, as did Memphis and New Orleans, the painful effects of military occupation. Several views of the late 1860s documented its appearance as a city that, while not growing as rapidly as in the previous decades, still clearly retained its dominant position as the metropolis of the mid-Mississippi valley.[1]

Business leaders felt confident that the construction of a railroad and vehicular bridge across the Mississippi would enable St. Louis to regain at least some of the ground it had lost to Chicago. That city's unrivaled rail connections allowed it to serve markets in the upper river towns that St. Louis merchants had once supplied. To improve St. Louis's competitive position the Eads Bridge, designed by and named for James Buchanan Eads, was begun in 1867. It stands as one of the great engineering achievements of the nineteenth century.[2]

Alfred Falk, an Australian traveler and author who visited St. Louis in 1876, called the bridge "the pride of St. Louis" and described it for his readers:

This bridge . . . is constructed in three cast-steel spans, (two of which are each 500 feet wide, the centre one being 520 feet), supported upon four granite piers, sunk over 100 feet through the sandy bed of the river, until they rest upon the solid rock. These spans or arches are sixty feet above the water-level, and therefore do not impede the navigation of the river; and the bridge itself consists of two roadways, an upper one for carriages and pedestrians, and a lower one for railway trains.[3]

The completion of the Eads Bridge in 1874 and its formal opening on July 4 of that year inspired many artists to produce drawings of the bridge and the city that now could boast at last of an uninterrupted transportation link to the East. Folio 29 reproduces the best known of these images, a large lithograph published by the New York firm of Currier and Ives. The firm's proprietors, Nathaniel Currier and James Ives, assigned the task of drawing the city to two artists who specialized in city views, Charles R. Parsons and Lyman Atwater.[4]

---

1. The two most important images of this period are a lithograph of ca. 1865 that Edward Sachse printed in Baltimore and may have drawn and a substantially revised version issued in 1867 of the long skyline depiction of St. Louis that Folio 28 reproduces. Both of these are reproduced in color in Reps, *Saint Louis Illustrated,* figs. 6–9 and 6–10, pp. 110 and 112–13.

2. A wood engraving from a drawing by Alfred Waud shows the partly finished structure in 1871 when it consisted only of the two unfinished piers in midstream and the abutments on either bank of the river. This wood engraving from *Every Saturday,* with later hand coloring, is reproduced in Reps, *Saint Louis Illustrated,* fig. 6–11, p. 115.

3. *Trans-Pacific Sketches: A Tour through the United States and Canada,* 246.

4. Among the other views of St. Louis at this time showing the bridge were those by George Degan (published in 1873 and thus anticipating its opening by a year); a curiously stylized image that Augustus Hageboeck engraved, printed, and published in 1874; a lithograph issued ca. 1874 by the *Saint Louis Times;* and a wood engraving from a drawing by Charles A. Vanderhoof that appeared in *Harper's Weekly* in 1876. For

In its very high-level perspective, bright colors, and unnumbered legend in the lower margin, this St. Louis view closely resembled views the two artists drew of Boston in 1873, of Chicago in 1874, and of Philadelphia in 1875, all for Currier and Ives. It was a style that Parsons also used for subsequent lithographs he did alone of such cities as San Francisco, Brooklyn, Washington, Baltimore, and New York.

Although nothing is known of Atwater, a few biographical facts about Parsons have emerged. His father, Charles Parsons, came from England in 1833 and at the age of twelve began an apprenticeship with George Endicott, one of the pioneer lithographers of New York City. The senior Parsons put on stone several views of New York City and in 1853 drew a view of Lancaster, Pennsylvania, that James T. Palmatary published. Parsons also drew or lithographed several views published by the Smith brothers before beginning in 1855 an association with Nathaniel Currier. By 1868—perhaps before—Charles R. Parsons, the son, began to do work with Atwater for what was then the firm of Currier and Ives. The father, although still occasionally producing drawings for that firm, had become head of the art department of the Harper's publishing company.[5]

A guide to American cities published in 1877 described in glowing terms the St. Louis that Parsons and Atwater drew:

> As the natural commercial entrepot of the vast Mississippi Valley, the commerce of St. Louis is immense; the chief articles of receipt and shipment being breadstuffs, live-stock, provisions, cotton, lead (from the Missouri mines), hay, salt, wool, hides and pelts, lumber, tobacco, and groceries. There are, including those in East St. Louis, 6 grain elevators and warehouses, 5 establishments for storing and compressing cotton, and 2 stock-yards.[6]

In portraying very large cities like St. Louis, Parsons and Atwater, as did many other artists, devoted most of their attention to important and easily recognizable structures in the foreground and middle distance. For example, their delineation of the Eads Bridge with its vehicular lanes on the top and the railroad tracks below is substantially accurate. So is their image of the domed courthouse at the center of the print. At first glance, then, views like this seem to reflect reality with considerable accuracy and to be as detailed as one of Ruger's small-town lithographs.

However, closer examination reveals that except for most of the buildings in the foreground and for large and important buildings elsewhere, the artists drew the structures of St. Louis in a highly stylized manner without distinguishing recognizable features. When viewed from a moderate distance, the lithograph conveys a fairly good sense of the city's size, structure, and density. Through a magnifying glass, however, the Currier and Ives print of St. Louis provides little information about any architectural details other than the most general and obvious.

The reasons for this are readily understandable. In most of the towns along the Mississippi an experienced city-view artist could look at and draw virtually every building during a visit that could be as brief as a few days and that would rarely require more than two weeks. Recording all the corresponding images in cities like St. Louis or New Orleans with their thousands of structures, many neighborhoods, and vast networks of streets would obviously require far more time.

Indeed, the daunting task of drawing every structure in St. Louis with easily recognizable features would seem to have been insurmountable. Nevertheless, in 1874, the year Currier and Ives published their view, Camille N. Dry and a team of assistants set out to accomplish just such a goal. Richard J. Compton, a lithographic printer and publisher who had moved to St. Louis from Buffalo sometime prior to 1863, distributed a specimen page (reproduced in Folio 29) to advertise the enterprise. He issued the results late in 1875.[7]

reproductions of these, see Reps, *Saint Louis Illustrated*, figs. 6–13, 6–14, 6–15, and 7–1, pp. 118–19, 121, and 127.

5. My biographical note on Charles Parsons and Charles R. Parsons can be found in Reps, *Views and Viewmakers*, 196–98. It is unclear which Parsons was responsible for a number of lithographs signed "C. Parsons." It seems likely that at least some were the work of the son.

6. *Appletons' Illustrated Hand-Book of American Cities* . . . , 112, also pointed out that "St. Louis is the first city of the Union in manufacture of flour," with "24 mills in operation in 1874." That season, too, St. Louis packinghouses processed 463,793 hogs. Yet "vast as are its commercial interests . . . the prosperity of the city is chiefly due to its manufactures, in which it is surpassed only by New York and Philadelphia." According to this guide, more than 4,500 manufacturing plants existed in 1870 employing nearly

41,000 persons and producing goods that in 1874 had a value of nearly a quarter of a billion dollars.

7. Compton's career in Buffalo is briefly noted in Marzio, *The Democratic Art*, 188. Compton is first listed in St. Louis directories in 1863 as an engraver. He was in business as a music publisher by 1865 and, somewhat later, as a manufacturer of pianos. In 1873 he was president of the Democrat Lith. and Printing Co. of St. Louis but resided in Alton, Illinois. In 1875 he managed the St. Louis Lithographing Co. and also headed Richard J. Compton and Co. He continued to own or manage successor companies until

Compton titled this elaborate publication *Pictorial St. Louis: The Great Metropolis of the Mississippi Valley*. It was a bound volume priced at $25.00 whose 222 pages began with a frontispiece view of the Eads Bridge, a title page with a map of the city, and a diagram of the perspective grid used by the artist. This diagram also served as an index map for the 110 folio-sized sheets, each depicting in elaborate detail a rectangular section of the city. Compton filled the other pages with his historic and descriptive text and detailed descriptions about important business enterprises of the city.

The artist of this remarkable work, Camille N. Dry, has left little more than his lithographic city views as clues to his background. Before 1875 Dry spelled his name Drie. In that form it appeared on several lithographic town views, beginning in 1871 with those of Galveston, Texas, and Columbus and Vicksburg, Mississippi, the latter being an image that will be discussed later in this chapter. He then produced views in 1872 of Augusta and Macon, Georgia; Charleston and Columbia, South Carolina; and Raleigh, North Carolina; and in 1873 of Norfolk, Virginia.

These views demonstrate an increasing sophistication in their approach, progressing from simple axonometric projections with no vanishing points in his earliest recorded work to a much more convincing style for his view of Norfolk—his last such effort before he arrived in St. Louis. This improvement in his technique suggests that he may have received instruction from more experienced viewmakers, most likely Joseph J. Stoner and Albert Ruger, who in the early 1870s were also active in the Southeast. Stoner published Drie's view of Augusta, and Albert Ruger served in a similar capacity for his Macon lithograph.[8]

The change in spelling from *Drie* to *Dry* to make clear that when sounded the name would rhyme with *cry* indicates that despite his French-sounding first name of Camille, this viewmaker was probably of German origin. It is the latter spelling that the St. Louis city directories use in listing him for the years 1875–1878, with his occupation as "draughtsman." Aside from these listings he vanishes from sight

until 1903 and 1904, when he produced views of Anniston and Birmingham, Alabama.[9]

The Dry and Compton portrait of St. Louis far surpassed in both size and complexity anything that Dry attempted before or after. Its 110 sheets created a gigantic image measuring about eight by twenty-two feet. The images on each sheet overlapped slightly those on adjoining sheets, so it was impossible to mount them as a single view without trimming the overlapped portions. Even then, the sheets did not join properly because Dry drew his perspective by treating each sheet as if it were a separate view, moving his perspective point so that it remained the same distance from the center of each sheet.

The inability to join the sheets is an obvious drawback, and it explains why in Folio 29 the four adjacent sheets of this part of the view are slightly separated to minimize the disjunctions at their edges. Dry's technique, however, has a compensating advantage. He was able to draw places on the outskirts of the metropolis with the same fidelity as those in the immediate foreground. For example, a comparison of the sheet used by Compton in 1874 to publicize his forthcoming publication—a section of industrial St. Louis in the foreground of the view—with one on the opposite page in the folio depicting the most distant section in the far southwest reveals that the wealth of architectural and topographic detail is exactly the same.

It was that portion of St. Louis shown on the four combined sheets in Folio 29 that Ralph Keeler and Alfred Waud described in such detail in one of their several articles on cities along the Mississippi that appeared in *Every Saturday* during the summer and fall of 1871. In one passage of their long account of St. Louis they mention "wandering up and down Fourth or Fifth Street," from near the courthouse, which these thoroughfares bound on the east and the west. Here, they wrote,

> great blocks of stone and iron and brick buildings rise . . . on every hand, in all stages of tall splendor, dinginess, and newness, with processions of shops in which even the trivialist articles of our every-day needs, to say nothing of our red-letter luxuries, are encased in a sheen so regal and so very republican. . . . Magnificent stores, however, are no more peculiar to St. Louis than are the attractive offices—realized dreams of glazing and upholstery—with which they are sandwiched.[10]

---

at least 1896. See Reps, *Saint Louis Illustrated*, 130 and nn. 5–7, for additional information about Compton's career in St. Louis.

8. This conclusive evidence that Ruger and Drie were more than casually acquainted is one reason for believing Ruger may have been connected with the preparation of the multisheet view of St. Louis that bears only Dry's name as artist. This point will be developed shortly.

9. My biographical note on Dry in Reps, *Views and Viewmakers*, 172, contains little additional information.

10. "St. Louis. II. Rambling about the City," 412. Keeler and Waud noted that streets running back from the river, crossing Fourth and Fifth streets at right angles, and con-

Dry not only delineated every building in St. Louis with remarkable detail, he also identified in legends at the bottom of each sheet more than one thousand places of business, residence, industry, worship, education, and transportation. This feature makes his view an unrivaled guide not only to the appearance of the city and all of its building but also to the exact uses and occupants of its major structures. And, of course, these identifications doubtless helped Compton sell copies of the view to merchants of downtown St. Louis and elsewhere whose stores and offices Dry drew with such fidelity.

Clearly no single artist could have accomplished this task, and Dry must have had a staff of assistants to prepare the hundreds of field sketches that would have been needed to construct this splendidly conceived and executed city view. Their names probably are among the lists of those who, like Dry, had studios or were employed in the Insurance Exchange Building at the southeast corner of Olive and Fifth streets during the period the view was in preparation. There Dry presumably directed the work of his helpers in sketching in the field, assembling the drawings they brought back into a preliminary perspective, revising and correcting this first draft, and preparing the lithographic stones or zinc plates for the printer.[11]

Noting the publication of his extraordinary work, a St. Louis newspaper explained to its readers how the view had been prepared:

> The preliminary drawings for the work were made early in the spring of 1874. After a careful consideration of the subject, it was determined to locate the point of view so that the city would be seen from the southeast, believing that to be the most advantageous in all respects. Accordingly the point of sight was established on the Illinois side of the river, looking to the northwest, and at sufficient altitude to overlook the roofs of ordinary houses into the streets.

According to this account, Dry used a survey of the city to construct a "careful perspective" that "required a surface of 300 square feet" to include a distance measured along the river of some ten miles. The report stated,

> Every foot of the vast territory . . . has been carefully examined and topographically drawn in perspective by C. N. Dry and his assistants, and the faithfulness and accuracy with which this work has been done an examination of its pages will attest. Absolute truth and accuracy . . . has been the standard, and in no case have additions or alterations been made unless the same were actually in course of construction. In a few cases important public and private edifices that are not yet finished, are shown completed, and as they will appear when done.[12]

There is at least the possibility that Albert Ruger may have been among the "assistants" who played a role in the creation of this heroic urban portrait. His views of Savannah and Atlanta, Georgia, in 1871 (and three others at this same time) identify him as the publisher with St. Louis as his address. More evidence of his involvement, admittedly circumstantial, is his curious record of production. It shows that from 1872 through 1876 Ruger virtually ceased creating city views, although in the years immediately before and after that period he proved highly prolific.[13]

Whether or not the more experienced Ruger assisted Dry in preparing his St. Louis view will probably never be known. In any event, the creation of such a magnificently detailed and elaborate portrait of a

---

11. For the artists and craftsmen recorded in city directories as working in the building, see Reps, *Saint Louis Illustrated*, 136–37.

tinuing westward led "past fine residences miles away into the suburbs." In the other direction, a wanderer "can turn eastward" and "pass Second Street and the crowded, solid regions of the wholesale merchants, before he comes upon the dust and smoke of the levee." There he could watch "barges and stern-wheelers shambling up and down the current, and the ferry-boats weaving Missouri into Illinois, or Illinois into Missouri."

12. St. Louis *Globe-Democrat*, January 2, 1876. The date of this account indicates that the view was not published until very late in 1875. It concludes with this passage of praise: "The engravings [*sic*] excite wonder by their number and accuracy. An index gives the key to the whole. The magnitude of the work surpasses comprehension. Nothing of the kind was ever before attempted, but the success has been in all respects complete and unparalleled." The survey that Dry used was almost certainly one published in nine sheets by a St. Louis firm in 1874, *Map of the City of St. Louis. 1874*. The names of both E. A. Garvey and Edward Charles Schultse, engineers and surveyors, appear in the imprint as having contributed to its preparation. The outer limits of this map and those of the Dry perspective coincide. The impression of the map I examined is in the Geography and Maps Division, Library of Congress.

13. In 1872 only three views with Ruger's name in the imprint were published, in 1873 there were no Ruger views whatsoever, and there were only two in 1874, none in 1875, and two in 1876. Yet in 1870–1871 he did forty-four views, and in 1877–1878, twenty-nine. Ruger would hardly have given St. Louis as his address unless he had established some connection with the city. Certainly he was familiar with the city, probably using St. Louis as his base when preparing his lithographs of Hannibal and several other cities of Missouri in 1869. We know as well that two years earlier he was in the vicinity to prepare the view of Alton, Illinois, mentioned in the previous chapter, as well as one of Cairo, Illinois, to be described shortly.

very large city remains one of the great achievements in this specialized form of artistic endeavor. Whatever help he may have received from others, the ultimate credit belongs to Dry—doubtless encouraged by Compton, whose investment in this enterprise must have been substantial, although evidently not financially rewarding.[14]

In one respect, at least, Dry failed to portray an important but unattractive feature of St. Louis. In common with other cities having many industries, railroads, and coal-burning domestic heating systems, St. Louis was blanketed by heavy clouds of smoke and soot a great part of the time. In 1862 Edward Dicey, an English war correspondent, correctly noted that it was the burning of soft, bituminous coal by "the great factories by the riverside" that "covered the lower part of St. Louis with an English-looking haze of smoke."[15]

Two decades later a writer for a major American periodical told its readers that from the Eads Bridge "the city itself is barely visible." Looming out of the billowing smoke one could see only "a dome or two, or the outlines of a shot-tower or an elevator." The author considered mounting the courthouse dome to obtain a panoramic view but explained why the notion had been rejected: "The photographers take their pictures on Sundays when the chimneys have stopped streaming for the time being, and then some partial prospects are to be had; but, as a rule, St. Louis is as invisible as London. When it is old and as large it is likely to be at least as sooty."[16]

It was the smoke of St. Louis that many visitors remembered vividly. As he set out for New Orleans in 1879 for a tour of the lower Mississippi that would provide the material for his perceptive book on the region, Ernst von Hesse-Wartegg, an Austro-German traveler and writer, had his last glimpse of St. Louis from a steamboat at night. He recorded that "black smoke cloaks the city to the last precinct, wrapping everything in a gloom of profound depths." He passed Carondelet, once a sleepy French suburb, now the site of iron furnaces, smelters, and foundries. There, he observed that "every flue, every door, every window, every last crack radiates incandescence. Cones of fire reach for the heavens."[17]

Hesse-Wartegg explored Cape Girardeau while his steamboat discharged and loaded cargo and passengers. It is disappointing to learn that neither Ruger nor any other of the single-sheet, lithographic viewmakers drew this town during the postwar years, but the author's description helps us to visualize its appearance. He first encountered "a row of substantial houses" facing the river, looking "down from steep banks . . . , melting like sugar into the river," from which extended a stone wharf, "the only stone wharf on the 1,250 miles between St. Louis and New Orleans." Ascending the bank and walking into the upper town, he found

> in Cape Girardeau . . . little more than a settlement, in other words a large village in its tenderest years: streets unpaved and muddy, cut and furrowed by creeks that form in the rain, and houses not in rows but scattered sporadically to either side of a street. An occasional house of brick interjects luxury amid a picturesque array and disarray of wood houses. Brick or wood, all hug the ground as if the earnest builders feared earthquakes at any moment.[18]

Below Cape Girardeau and on the Illinois side of the Mississippi lay Cairo, which Ruger visited and drew for the lithograph published in 1867 that Folio 23 reproduces. During the Civil War, Cairo's strategic location at the junction of two major waterways brought the city momentary prosperity when it served as a supply base and shipping point for Union military action against the Confederate forces in the lower Mississippi valley. Willard Glazier recalled that "for a time it rose into comparative importance and seemed to realize in a degree the dreams of its youth. But with the close of the war came the close of

14. In 1878 a report by an agent for R. G. Dun Co., a credit-rating agency, noted that Compton had "an old debt hanging over him in the shape of a stock note for [$5,000] while a member of the Democrat Job Printing Co. a few years ago." A subsequent report in 1882 stated, "Rich J. Compton has been sued in the Circuit Court by the Globe Printing Co. for $4,832.84. This is an old matter." The Globe Printing Co. printed the 110-sheet view of 1875. The records cited here and others on Compton's business activities can be found in the Dun records in the library of the Harvard Business School, St. Louis vols. 38, p. 4106.1; 40, p. 298; and 44, p. 395.

15. *Six Months in the Federal States*, 2:99

16. *Harper's New Monthly Magazine* 68 (March 1884): 497–98. This writer explained that conditions elsewhere in the region resembled those of St. Louis: "These Western cities exhale a tainted breath, stifle themselves in the fumes of their own prosperity. They burn a soft and inferior coal, yielded them by the region round about, and all are more or less enveloped in smoke. While the sun is shining on the Eastern sea-board . . . these cities of the plain, artificers in iron and brass and every useful work, are pouring forth vapors as if they were but the mouthpieces of some fiery subterranean activity."

17. *Travels*, 29. Hesse-Wartegg evidently made several trips through the Mississippi valley, and his book reflects composite treatment of his experiences.

18. Ibid., 31.

its prosperous times. The streets were again empty and comparatively silent, and the town lapsed into decadence."[19]

Ruger's portrait of Cairo shows that buildings had scarcely begun to fill the irregular grid of streets that developers and promoters had platted within the restricted confines of the low-lying and unhealthy site. A good part of the city's economy depended on the steamboat trade. Here passengers and freight transported along the Ohio or the Mississippi river routes could be transferred to boats plying the other stream or to the Illinois Central Railroad, whose line, depots, and engine house can be seen located along the Ohio River frontage in the foreground of Ruger's view.[20]

On his visit a few years later Hesse-Wartegg found Cairo no more attractive than had earlier travelers:

> We could not have stopped anywhere more miserable, more desolate, more wretched on the Mississippi. Zealous boosters of America predict a bright future for Cairo because of its uniquely favorable position at the juncture of the country's chief rivers. But he who has seen Cairo will blink at such stargazing. . . . Cairo . . . presents one of the gloomiest and most deplorable aspects of any city on earth, if it can be said to be on earth.[21]

Although Cairo had remained firmly in Union control throughout the Civil War while Memphis suffered through a military occupation after its capture in June 1862, it was the latter city that prospered and grew after hostilities ceased. Further, unlike Vicksburg, Atlanta, and Richmond, Memphis suffered no devastation when Union forces assumed control. When Ruger drew the view of 1870 illustrated in Folio 20, the city's population numbered more than 40,000—nearly double what it had been only ten years earlier and exceeding in size both Nashville with its 25,000 residents or Atlanta with its population of only 21,700.

19. *Down the Great River*, 341.

20. Two other railroads reached Cairo a bit later: the Mobile and Ohio and the Cleveland, Cincinnati, Chicago and St. Louis.

21. *Travels*, 33. Not long after Ruger drew the city, a writer for *Harper's New Monthly Magazine* recorded his impressions: "A more disheartening place I never beheld. . . . I would not like to prophesy as to its future beyond that of a third-class graveyard, but to-day it is the vilest hole above-ground, if the streets formed by introducing foreign soil can be said to be above-ground; for the open lots formed by the streets were partially filled with water covered with green scum, and which was also the receptacle for offal, dead animals, and other offensive refuse. Turn which way you would the sight was unspeakably disgusting. The streets were knee-deep in mud, and it seemed impossible to transact business upon them when horses and wagons were required" (George Ward Nichols, "Down the Mississippi," 839).

At the time Ruger visited Memphis its cotton trade was once again thriving as cotton presses kept busy compressing ginned cotton into bales for shipment by one of the eleven steamboat lines or the four railroads then serving the city. In his view Ruger includes images of two of the most famous steamboats on the Mississippi, the *Natchez* (second from the right) and the *Robert E. Lee* (the larger of the two vessels seen near the left side). Their race from New Orleans to St. Louis in July 1870 caused enormous excitement along the lower river. Ruger exercised artistic license in showing them both, for the *Lee* reached Memphis shortly before 11:00 P.M. the night of July 2 and had unloaded, refueled, and was gone by the time the *Natchez* arrived an hour and three minutes later.[22]

When Ruger sketched Memphis he found a building boom underway. New hotels provided modern accommodations for the business community and other travelers. The year before Ruger's lithograph appeared Robert Campbell Brinkley proudly opened his elegant, five-story Peabody House, a hotel whose reputation soon extended far beyond the city. This building with its short mansard-roof tower stood at the corner of Main and Monroe until its demolition in 1923. The old name remains on its replacement, a recently renovated Memphis hotel fondly regarded by residents and travelers alike.[23]

Memphis had expanded well beyond its original platted limits. One can easily distinguish the first streets of the linear grid that its founders had surveyed parallel to the river and the public square they had provided near the grid's center between Main and Second streets. North, east, and south, however, the whims of other landowners had prevailed, resulting in many jogs, offsets, and angled intersections across the boundaries of adjoining tracts. Even those newly platted lands some distance from the town's historic center were already partially built up. New and extended horsecar lines, whose routes Ruger shows, reduced the time required to move between outlying neighborhoods and the business and office district nearer the river.

Many visitors complained about the muddy streets of the city, a condition that no city view ever managed to convey. Hesse-Wartegg wrote of "foot-deep mire . . . like a polypous creature with tentacles,

22. Fredrick Lee Coulter, *Memphis, 1800–1900,* 2:114–16, describes this event. Much of my treatment here of Memphis at the time of the Ruger view comes from this source, one of three volumes on the city sponsored by the city's Pink Palace Museum.

23. A wood engraving of the Peabody House is reproduced in ibid., 2:111.

threatening to pull our overshoes off" and "horrible mud" combined with "mire upon muck, and offal upon excrement" in which "people sink to the knees . . . every day." City officials did pave some of the streets of the business district with treated wood blocks, a method widely used in the United States at the time and then believed to be a fully acceptable solution to the problem. In most places, as in Memphis, these blocks soon decayed, and had to be either replaced or removed.[24]

However, Hesse-Wartegg called the two-mile-long extent of "the wide Main Street of imposing buildings" with its "grand public edifices and rows of pretty houses—the most beautiful street between St. Louis and New Orleans," adding:

> At the midpoint of those two miles, the shady Magnolia Square, or so-called City Park, asserts itself and with it the city's largest buildings: Oddfellows Hall and the Peabody Hotel. The *haut monde* has settled away from the principal streets, away from Main, Front, and Second: in and around Vance Street. Front, perpendicular to Main, follows the riverbank and provides the city its chief emporium for cotton, fruit, and other foodstuffs.[25]

Another Memphis visitor, J. T. Trowbridge, recorded what could be seen from "the brow of the bluff, with the city behind you, and the river below." From this vantage point Trowbridge looked down "upon a superb array of steamers, lying along the shore," much as Ruger drew them in his view. Trowbridge described the scene for his readers:

> The levee is crowded with casks and cotton bales, covering acres of ground. Up and down the steep way cut through the brow of the bluff, affording access to the landing from the town, a stream of drays is passing and repassing. . . . Bales of cotton and hay, casks, boxes, sacks of grain, lumber, household furniture, supplies for plantations, mules, ploughs, wagons, are tumbled, rolled, carried, tossed, driven, pushed, and dragged, by an army of laborers from the levee along the broad wooden stages to the steamers' decks.[26]

Nightfall brought no end to the activity, for, as Trowbridge noted, "the levee is lighted by great smoking and flaring flambeaux," each made from coal, wood, and "flakes of oil-soaked cotton" burning in a grate mounted on the end of a pole. Workers toiled well into the night loading and unloading the many steamboats arriving with cargo or carrying to other markets the products manufactured in Memphis or passing through its warehouses and cotton presses. The view that Ruger drew reflects this economic vitality that Memphis enjoyed in the immediate postwar years.

Probably Ruger doubted that there would be sufficient demand for a view of Vicksburg, a place that had suffered severely during the Union siege and that was slow to recover after the war. Or, in visiting Memphis in 1870, he may have learned that Camille Drie (as he then styled himself) had begun work on such a view—a lithograph published in 1871 and reproduced in Folio 16. Although the imprint does not identify Drie as the artist, he almost surely drew this view on which his name appears only as the publisher, with New Orleans as his address.[27]

In 1860, 4,591 persons lived in Vicksburg. During the war the population was believed to have soared to as high as 50,000 before declining with almost equal rapidity to around 12,000 in 1866. All this reflected the effects of the siege of Vicksburg as well as the influx of freed slaves to the city after the war, a phenomenon that occurred in virtually every city of the Confederacy. A year before Drie's view appeared, the census of 1870 counted 12,443 residents of Vicksburg.

An observer from the North in 1866 reported seeing little evidence of the siege and the extensive damage that resulted:

> Vicksburg, city of hills and caves, had already lost most of the traces of the siege, that for a year blocked the progress of our arms in the West, and concentrated the gaze of the continent. Few of the houses showed much serious damage. The hiding-holes dug in the hill-sides for security against the shells, had been filled up again; stores had been reopened; ox-teams, bringing in cotton, filled the streets; returned Rebel soldiers were looking after their abandoned property, and receiving the heartiest welcomes from their old friends and neighbors.[28]

---

24. The Austro-German observer reported the consequences: "You cannot imagine the mountains, ravines, and craters brought about by the so-called Nicholson wooden pavement. Poor mules and miserable horses sink knee-deep in mire and ruts. Cotton wagons would be stuck in a trice, and break wheels and axles" (*Travels*, 49). It is not flattering to cities of "Missouri, Kansas, or Illinois" to learn that Hesse-Wartegg thought Memphis similar to them in its "layout and architecture" and in "the same life in the streets and the inns." *Travels*, 46, describes the Memphis mud. Street paving in downtown Memphis is mentioned briefly in Capers, *Biography of a River Town*, 180. The author states, "The expense entailed was no small factor in the city's ultimate bankruptcy."

25. *Travels*, 48.

26. *The South: A Tour of Its Battle-Fields and Ruined Cities*, 334.

27. A year after the publication of the Vicksburg lithograph, Drie drew a view of Macon, Georgia, that Ruger published. It is possible that the two met at the Chicago Lithographing Company. This firm printed many of Ruger's views, and Drie sent or brought his Vicksburg drawing and one of Galveston, Texas, in 1871 there as well.

28. Whitelaw Reid, *After the War: A Tour of the Southern States 1865–1866*, 289.

Drie provided no legend for his view, but his depiction tells us much about this place nonetheless. Smokestacks attached to some of the larger buildings locate the principal industries of Vicksburg, and from other sources we know that two dozen of them in 1860 produced agricultural implements, metal and leather products, lumber, carriages, and clothing, among other enterprises. Toward the right-hand side of the view and within the curve made by the rail line one can see the remains of the earthworks thrown up by the Confederate forces in 1863 to defend the city from General Grant's troops.

John Richard Dennett visited Vicksburg in 1866 while writing about the South after the Civil War for the *Nation*, and he commented about how this event had affected the townscape.

> I walked about the place, observing with curiosity the singular bluff on which the town stands and overlooks many miles of the surrounding lowlands and saw the semi-circular sweep of the Federal earthworks. In the streets there are still vestiges of the innermost lines of the besieged, and also of the caves or burrows in which people hid themselves from Grant's shot and shell. Not much, I suppose, has been done to remove the traces of the siege.[29]

Drie did provide the names of the city streets as well as that of the Vicksburg and Meridian Railroad. That line ended on relatively level land between Washington and Mulberry streets, but near it to the right one can see the deep cut made in the hillside that was necessary to provide a suitable grade for the tracks. They lead up the steep hill in a great curve to the semicircular engine house and what must be the passenger and freight depot on the opposite side of the tracks.

Washington Street between Jackson and South streets stands out as the location for what are obviously the major retail and office buildings of Vicksburg. Occupying an entire block between Jackson and Grove and bounded on the east and west by Cherry and Monroe streets is a porticoed building topped with a lofty tower or lantern. This is the courthouse, completed in 1858. A few church spires also add vertical elements to the skyline, but elsewhere Vicksburg consisted of neighborhoods of one-, two-, and three-story houses occupying lots that stairstepped up the steep slope on which the town had been located.

Visiting Vicksburg in 1865, Trowbridge noted how "the hills are cut through, and their sides sliced off, by the deeply indented streets of the upper portion of the city." In some places he saw "crests completely cut around, isolated, and left standing like yellowish square sugar-loaves with irregular tops." This topography made it difficult to maintain the streets serving Vicksburg's factories, stores, houses, and public buildings. A newspaper in 1869 recorded the complaint about street conditions made by one resident of the town: "Awful ravines have been washed into the middle of . . . [Crawford] street, rendering it entirely unfit for use, and every succeeding rain washes them still deeper. A perfect 'Niagara' of water rushes down the street, and [it is even worse] when we consider that this street is the principal thoroughfare to and from the river—nearly all the heavy hauling being done upon it."[30]

Fifteen years before Drie drew his view, Frederick Law Olmsted stopped briefly in Vicksburg. For his readers he explained a feature of the city that can be clearly seen in Drie's lithograph:

> There are no wharves on the Mississippi, or any of the southern rivers. The wharf-boat is an old steamboat, with her paddle boxes and machinery removed and otherwise dismantled, on which steamboats discharge passengers and freight. The main deck is used as a warehouse, and, in place of the furnace, has in this case a dramshop, a chandler's shop, a forwarding agency, and a telegraph office. Overhead, the saloon and state-rooms remain, and with the bar-room and clerk's office, kitchen, and barber's shop, constitute a stationary though floating hostelry.[31]

No bird's-eye-view artist produced a lithograph of Helena, Arkansas, although Hesse-Wartegg called it "a lively commercial center of 6,000 people." Nor did any artist leave an aerial portrait of Napoleon, located at the mouth of the Arkansas River. Hesse-Wartegg told his readers of the town's rise and fall:

> Years ago a fairly big town was there, ominously named Napoleon. The Napoleonic dynasty and Napoleon, Arkansas, disappeared together. During the Civil War, Napoleon was an important rendezvous for gunboats and other warships. . . . Then Napoleon's fortune sank. . . . The river itself, in one of its evil tempers, steadily undercut its bank at Napoleon. Every day a foot of land washed away. . . . Seeing that Napoleon was not to be saved, people

---

29. *The South as It Is: 1865–1866*, 349. Dennett did not admire Vicksburg, referring to the "repulsiveness of the place" in his brief treatment of the physical city.

30. Trowbridge, *The South*, 356–57. Vicksburg *Daily Times*, April 30, 1869, as quoted on p. 208 in a work from which much of my information about Vicksburg in this period has been found: James T. Currie, *Enclave: Vicksburg and Her Plantations, 1863–1870*.

31. *A Journey in the Back Country*, 125.

left. Only the riffraff remained . . . until Napoleon would be afloat on its own deluge.[32]

Perhaps Drie considered drawing Baton Rouge, and possibly other artists who specialized in similar single-sheet, separately issued urban portraits may have done so as well. However, no such view is known to exist, although by 1870 Baton Rouge exceeded in population several other places on the upper river where artists-publishers apparently found a market for their products. At the beginning of the Civil War the town had about 5,500 residents. Occupied by Union troops in the spring of 1862, it suffered damage from a fierce but unsuccessful attack by the Confederates a few months later. Later that year a fire gutted the state Capitol where Federal troops were quartered.

Long before that the Confederate state of Louisiana had moved its seat of government from the city—first to Opelousas, then to Alexandria, and eventually to Shreveport. After the war, with Louisiana united as a state once again, it was New Orleans that housed the legislature and state administrative and judicial officials. Not until 1882 did Baton Rouge once again became the capital city; until then it remained, as Alfred Falk, an Australian traveler, remarked after visiting Baton Rouge in 1876, "a dull and sleepy place."[33]

Although other cities of the South increased in size and importance as rail transportation helped them capture markets and increase their trade, New Orleans—while perhaps relatively less dominant than in former times—retained its position as the great metropolis of the region. It seems strange, therefore, that neither Ruger, Dry, Koch, nor one of the other viewmakers active in this field after the Civil War came to New Orleans to depict it in the 1870s or earlier for the kind of detailed image they produced elsewhere.

Instead, we have only the two lithographs reproduced in Folio 8, one published by Currier and Ives and the other printed and published by F. C. Wentzel of Weissenburg, Germany. Both are of only modest size, and neither is dated or bears an artist's name. They probably appeared in 1873 or 1874. Although similar, they differ enough to suggest that one was not a copy of the other. The Currier and Ives view, for example, encompasses more of the city, extending downriver a few blocks beyond Jackson Square and the cathedral and including on the

left more of the Garden District and the newer neighborhoods that lay farther upriver.

The artists of both lithographs resorted to shortcuts by delineating the majority of the buildings in a stylized manner with occasional images of larger structures displaying details that residents and others familiar with the city might be expected to recognize. The Currier and Ives print seems far more successful in conveying some semblance of reality, and this lithograph also demonstrates a far more sensitive use of color, some of which may have been added by hand to improve the appearance of prints made from multiple stones or zinc plates.

The legend of the Currier and Ives print identifies only a few places. These include the St. Charles Hotel, located on the street of that name between Common and Gravier streets. The view shows the second building by that name on the site, one constructed after a fire destroyed the first in 1851. A northern visitor in 1865 noted that it had been "famous before the war as a hotel, and during the war as the headquarters of General Butler." He described it as "a conspicuous edifice, with white-pillared porticos, and a spacious Rotunda, thronged nightly with a crowd which strikes a stranger with astonishment."[34]

During its days as a luxurious hotel the St. Charles was rivaled only by the St. Louis, whose building stood on the northeast side of St. Louis between Royal and Chartres streets. Edward King in 1875 referred to it as "one of the most imposing monuments of the French quarter, as well as one of the finest hotels in the United States." King noted that originally it had combined "a city exchange, hotel, bank, ball-rooms, and private stores," but that "the rotunda, metamorphosed into a dining-hall," became "one of the most beautiful in this country." Another feature caught his eye: "The great inner circle of the dome is richly frescoed with allegorical scenes and busts of eminent Americans." By the end of the 1870s, as Hesse-Wartegg records, the building no longer housed a hotel but instead contained the executive offices and legislative chambers for the State of Louisiana:

The kitchens have become the state archives. Junoesque beauties, the bloom of Creole society, dwelt and slept in rooms that accommodate whisky drinking, tobacco chewing—and statecraft. . . . In a few years the hotel became a dingy, unkempt, ruinous pile—and so it looks to the astonished tourist. . . . This building—doors sprung, banisters wrecked, many windows

32. *Travels*, 95–96.
33. *Trans-Pacific Sketches*, 357.

34. Trowbridge, *The South*, 399.

broken—houses the offices of governor, cabinet (including the secretary of state), and the chambers of the senate and the house of representatives![35]

Both views show Canal Street extending back from the levee, although the heavily colored trees in Wentzel's view make the thoroughfare's location and alignment far easier to discern. Earlier visitors seldom failed to comment about this major artery of both commerce and transportation, and postwar visitors continued to follow this tradition. In their series of descriptions and drawings of southern cities for *Every Saturday* in 1871, Keeler and Waud in their first article described and drew what they saw: "Canal Street is about twice as wide as Broadway [in New York City]. . . . All the street-railways of the city centre here. They have an elevated space apart to themselves for several tracks abreast, running along the middle of the broad thoroughfare. Two rows of small trees shade the foot-way which extends the whole length of this elevated space."[36]

At this time, of course, the "street-railways" were horse-drawn, and as a journalist for *Appleton's Journal* told his readers in 1870, "their jingling bells sending a merry peal of Yankee progress defiantly athwart the mediaeval atmosphere of Old Town." The writer tells of his excursion from Canal Street through the newer neighborhoods upriver:

> Jumping on one of the many horse-cars, you pass rapidly up-town through wider streets, where the hand of progress has given more modern shape and fresher aspect to the buildings. The names on the signs are more American, and the exteriors of the houses show the national tendency for smart paint, rather than the Spanish one for parrots and singing-birds, or the French one for flowers. [One passes] many churches and some imposing buildings, and threading streets that run round corners and are bifurcated by open plats.[37]

Hesse-Wartegg might have been looking at one of the views in this folio when he composed his description of the city's street pattern, pointing out that "the streets of New Orleans do not follow the checkerboard of most American cities." Noting the effects of the natural

conditions of the site and of the ancient plantation boundaries, he remarked that, although individual quarters might have an orthogonal design, "their relation to one another conforms in part to the bends of the Mississippi, in part to the shape of large areas once privately owned." He explained that this is why "a number of straight avenues, miles long, crisscross the residential districts, converge and diverge, and lead at last to some destination on the river or lake, without so much as having touched an important place. Of hundreds of streets, not a dozen go in the same direction." Adding to this apparent lack of order were "a number of bayous and ship canals [that] cross the city in various directions."[38]

Hesse-Wartegg found Canal Street a fascinating sight as he encountered it in 1879 and 1880, calling it "the most beautiful [street] here if not in all America." He described this 170-foot-wide thoroughfare as "dead straight" and offering the visitor "miles of big stores, shops of splendid elegance under the arcades, large restaurants, French cafes, oyster bars, [and] billiard halls." He admired the "wide sidewalks, laid with big, beautiful slabs of stone," the "long double rows of trees . . . and well-sanded footpaths," and the "narrow, open drainage" ditches located between the sidewalks and the shaded paths near the center of the thoroughfare.

He explained how this thoroughfare divided the two cultures and ways of life that he observed during his stay in the city:

> Canal Street divides New Orleans as the Straits of Dover do England from France. Indeed, English culture and French—better called Anglo-Germanic and Latin—could not be more precisely and more surely set at intervals than here. . . . From the Mississippi inland, everything to the left is Anglo-Saxon, and to the right it is Spanish, Italian, and French. . . . Ask directions in public and get the answer in English to the left, in French to the right. Each nation dwells as a separate society, isolated from one another, not mingling.[39]

Off Canal Street in what we know as the Garden District he encountered "superb gardens and majestic villas," although in looking at the streets of this quarter he noted that "instead of opulence we see filth" and roadways where "piles of rock alternate with sinkholes and heaps of filth. Rocks occupy the ditches, water takes to the streets." Hesse-Wartegg also explored poorer neighborhoods "of narrow streets, tall,

35. Edward King, *The Great South*, 1:37; Hesse-Wartegg, *Travels*, 165–67.
36. "New Orleans. I.—The Heart of the City."
37. T. C. De Leon, "New Orleans," 451–52. In his *Travels*, 157, Hesse-Wartegg notes that at the time of his visit there were "streetcars, horse-drawn and steam-powered." He describes a "network of streetcars, probably covering more than 100 miles" that served "every part of the city with Canal Street as the hub."

38. *Travels*, 154.
39. Ibid., 156–57, 162–63.

over-crowded *'tenements'* and boardinghouses—much dirt, many children at the doors: home to the Negro, the semiskilled, and the laborer."

Hesse-Wartegg admired Rampart Street, the inland border of the old French town, as "a street beautifully sunny and lined with fine buildings," but he also thought New Orleans a city of "gross contrasts," listing a number of examples:

Plush palaces and newly built homes beside old Spanish churches and cloisters. Broad canals versus stagnant water unused by any boat. Squares of small, intimate gardens opposed to the strange, polyglot life of bustling market halls and tropical products for sale. Streets without end are home to the petite bourgeoisie in little one-story houses with the obligatory balcony and flower pots at the windows. Streetcars roll and bump along, amid chime and clank of rolling stock on bad rails.[40]

Reaching the riverfront, he visited Jackson Square, where the cathedral faced the river and the equestrian statue of the general stood in the center. He enjoyed the quiet of the square and its "tropical luxury shielded from the river by tall orange trees and magnolias along the edge." Nearby, a "step between the trees and onto the levees," he came to the bustling and noisy French market that reminded him of "bazaars in Constantinople and Tunis." Here he browsed at "hundreds of small counters and stalls, row upon row," where one could buy "clothing, knitted goods, furniture, silverware, and especially food: meat, fruits, vegetables."[41]

A decade earlier the reporter for *Appleton's Journal* found that "all round this part of the city, with the busy wharf-men on the levee, the noisy rattle of the horse-cars, and the puffing of manufactories, the American life comes strongly out." Keeler and Waud also commented on conditions along the levee, which appears so prominently in each of the views in the folio. Demonstrating their ignorance of such matters, the artist of each view—one in New York and the other in Germany— drew steamboats with sterns impossibly angled upstream—an error that has been noted previously on other views.[42]

Waud would not have made a mistake of this kind, and it is a pity that he did not try his hand at creating a bird's-eye portrait of New

Orleans. Instead, we must rely on the description he and Keeler provided to the readers of *Every Saturday:*

The steamboat landing may be said to centre at the foot of Canal Street and extend a mile or more from there both up and down the river. The ocean ships have their wharves both above and below the landing for the river craft. Goods . . . are landed on the open levee or wharves, where they lie some time before they are put under the sheds; and in consequence of this practice, it is said, some of the most scientific thieving of which the country can boast is done here.[43]

Hesse-Wartegg describes the appearance of the levee as he saw it eight or nine years later:

Warehouses, railway stations, roofs without walls of giant proportions, and of course the mountains of boards and beams, baled cotton, barrels of sugar, and barrels of petroleum—each occupies occasional portions of this vast space; none comes at all near filling it anywhere. Railroad cars, dozens of horse-drawn wagons, and hundreds of heavy-duty carts, full and empty, go to and fro in unbroken lines. Thousands of people—officials, merchants, sailors, policemen, passengers, fruit and vegetable handlers, and inevitably dockworkers—hurry among baled cotton, agricultural implements, and every other product imaginable.[44]

The two views showing New Orleans in this period are not very impressive, either as examples of good printmaking or as reliable and useful graphic evidence in documenting the growth and development of the city. In the 1880s, however, Currier and Ives issued a much larger view than the one just discussed, although it, too, is flawed. More important, although not well known because of its relative rarity, is another more detailed and reliable depiction of New Orleans. It is particularly valuable because it looks down on the city from a point of view not previously used by other artists. It is with that portrait of New Orleans that we can begin our final nineteenth-century expedition along the Mississippi, a journey that will be the subject of the next chapter.

---

40. Ibid., 158–60.
41. Ibid., 163.
42. The quotation is from De Leon, "New Orleans," 451–52.

43. "New Orleans. III. On the Levee," 92.
44. *Travels*, 139.

VII

River City Views at the End of an Era

The Work of Henry Wellge and His Fellow Urban Artists, 1880–1900

This final vicarious voyage to the cities of the Mississippi through the images of the region's nineteenth-century view-makers begins in New Orleans in 1883. In that year Gustave Koeckert published and Theodore Pohlmann copyrighted a splendidly detailed lithographic view of New Orleans using a high-level vantage point different from any previous perspective. Folio 9 illustrates this large print measuring more than two feet by nearly three and one-half feet. Near the lower left corner the signature "Geo. J. Kerth" appears.

All three men worked as lithographers. Koeckert, born in Leipzig around 1842, had come to New Orleans by 1871, when the city directory identified him as a lithographer. Later listings also record his occupation as map engraver or engraver. In 1880 he became treasurer of the New Orleans Lithographing and Engraving Company, a firm founded by him and three partners. In March 1883 he, one of his partners, and George J. Kerth established the New Orleans Lithographing Company. That fall another partner was added, and in February 1884 the company merged with the Southern Lithographic Company, with Theodore Pohlmann, who had worked as a lithographer in New Orleans only since 1882, as president.[1]

Despite the absence of recognizable features and the use of generalized building forms in the more distant portions of the view, it provides a remarkably detailed and accurate delineation on a single sheet of what had by this time become a major metropolitan center. The broad swath of Canal Street running diagonally from the river toward the upper right attracts one's attention immediately. The artist pictured numerous horsecars on the tracks running down the center, tree-shaded lanes of this thoroughfare. Ten years later the street would display its first electric lights, and electric trolleys would replace the older type of vehicles.

A short distance downriver from Canal Street one can see three low buildings on the levee, each with six pitched sections forming their roofs. The view's helpful legend identifies these as sugar sheds, essential storage facilities for the Louisiana Sugar Refinery, the multistory structure with the smoking chimney beyond the sheds. The second building downriver from the refinery housed the Sugar Exchange, the

---

1. The ambiguous signature in the stone could, of course, mean that Kerth only drew the view, that he only put it on stone, or that he did both. His background and experience in this kind of art remain unknown. The record shows only that from 1880 to 1884 the city directory lists him as a lithographer, as directories do for the years 1886–

1890, 1893–1896, and 1898–1902. It is the single identification as "artist" for the Southern Lithographic Company in 1885 that suggests Kerth may have created the image for this view rather than putting on stone the work of some anonymous artist. My information on the directory listings of the three persons named on this print comes entirely from the entries in Historic New Orleans Collection, *Encyclopaedia of New Orleans Artists,* 213 (Kerth), 216 (Koeckert), 281 (New Orleans Lithographing and Engraving Co. and New Orleans Lithographing Company), 309 (Pohlmann), and 362 (Southern Lithographic Company).

financial heart of an industry based on sugarcane from Louisiana plantations, a product that had become one of the city's principal exports.

Further to the right of these structures one can see how other buildings had cut off Jackson Square, St. Louis Cathedral, the Cabildo, and the Presbytère from the Mississippi. Although doubtless not drawn with surveyed accuracy, the artist's depiction of closely packed city blocks in this oldest part of New Orleans offers a realistic impression of conditions as they then existed. In the years to follow efforts to realize higher returns on real estate would create even greater pressures and result in ever more intensive use of property.

Near the lower right corner the trees down the center of a broad street identify Esplanade Avenue, the downriver end of the old French Quarter. Not far away and diverging at an angle from Esplanade is Elysian Fields Avenue. This leads toward Lake Pontchartrain, a portion of which can be seen near the upper right corner of the view. On the levee at Esplanade the artist drew the image of the U.S. Mint, a building designed in 1835 by William Strickland to occupy the site of Fort St. Charles. Fronting the river opposite the levee end of Esplanade once stood the mansion of Bernard Marigny, from which John L. Boqueta de Woiseri drew the view of New Orleans in 1803 that Folio 2 reproduces.

Six blocks beyond Rampart Street, the other tree-planted street bordering the French Quarter, the view shows the St. Louis Cemetery No. 2 occupying the three blocks bounded by Claiborn, Robertson, St. Louis, and Iberville streets. Together with the smaller Cemetery No. 1 one block north of Rampart, this is perhaps the most famous of the many aboveground "burial" sites in the city—a place containing the tombs of a great many older New Orleans families.[2]

A short distance toward the Mississippi from St. Louis Cemetery No. 2, the spire of Christ Church rose above Canal Street after its completion on a site selected in 1845. Near it in the center of Canal Street and circled by trolley tracks stood the statue of Henry Clay begun in

1856, completed four years later, and a city landmark on that site until 1901. Then, to expedite the flow of traffic on this major commercial artery, the statue was moved to Lafayette Square, the counterpart in the American quarter to the Place d'Armes (now Jackson Square) of the Creole community.

One could reach this important civic open space from Canal Street by following St. Charles Avenue from its beginning directly opposite the Clay Monument. In the second block from Canal Street the impressive bulk of the St. Charles Hotel occupied the block between Common and Gravier streets. A traveler continuing three blocks farther on St. Charles would enter Lafayette Square at the corner by the Greek Revival city hall that James Gallier designed in 1850. Diagonally across the square stood a building housing the courts, while facing the square on the side away from Canal Street the First Presbyterian Church added its English Gothic style to the eclectic architecture of the square.

Continuing upriver, the visitor would next come to Lee Circle at the intersection of St. Charles and Howard Street. There in 1876 work began on the white marble shaft topped by a bronze statue of Robert E. Lee, a memorial dedicated before a large crowd in 1884. Enough progress had been made by 1883 that the artist of the view felt confident in showing it as if fully completed. It is at this point that St. Charles bends somewhat to follow an alignment more nearly parallel to the river—one of several such changes that can be seen in the view.

Another project that had not been completely realized in 1883 but that the artist drew nonetheless appears near the upper left where the Mississippi curves away to the right. This is the World's Industrial and Cotton Exposition, an international fair and exhibition held in 1884–1885 that its organizers erected in Audubon Park, a former plantation purchased by the city for a recreational ground in 1871. The artist portrayed the buildings of the Cotton Centennial as if they had been completed, although it would be another year before the fair opened its doors to the public.[3]

On the other side of St. Charles Avenue one can see another roughly rectangular site. Here Tulane University erected its first building in 1894. Ten years later Loyola Academy (later Loyola University) became

---

2. Virtually every visitor who recorded impressions of New Orleans commented about the peculiar character of these burial places. Thus, in writing about his visit in 1881, Captain Glazier merely followed a long tradition in telling his readers, "The cemeteries of New Orleans are most peculiar. The ground is so low that water is reached at a depth of two or three feet, so that the tombs are all placed above ground. Some of them are very handsome structures of marble, granite or iron. Others are mere cells placed in tiers, one above another. These cells look like ovens, and when one receives a coffin it is hermetically sealed, and usually a marble tablet is placed over the brickwork. There are no less than thirty-three cemeteries in and near the city" (Glazier, *Down the Great River*, 425).

3. The exposition marked "the one hundredth anniversary of the first shipment of cotton from Louisiana to a foreign port. A striking feature for that day was the illumination of the building and grounds by electricity" (Federal Writers' Project, Works Projects Administration, *New Orleans City Guide*, 331).

Tulane's neighbor, and both institutions stimulated the further development of this part of an ever-expanding New Orleans. Here, too, land developers repeated the fanlike street pattern that had characterized the earlier enlargements of the city beyond the original French grid.

Although the lithograph that Kerth, Pohlmann, and Koeckert created in 1883 uses arbitrary shapes for buildings in the background and doubtless does not reproduce with complete accuracy even major details of many other structures, it remains a notable achievement in urban iconography for a city of this size and complexity. Certainly it is far superior in almost every respect to the much better known image of similar dimensions that Folio 9 also presents. Currier and Ives published this lithograph in 1885, doubtless timing it to coincide with the Cotton Centennial, whose buildings the anonymous artist depicts at the far left.

A cursory examination of this view and a brief comparison with the one just discussed disclose how the artist for Currier and Ives drastically shortened St. Charles Avenue to omit several miles of development between the Centennial grounds and the neighborhoods centering around Lee Circle and Lafayette Square. Further, even the closely packed city blocks in the foreground contain few buildings of recognizable character. Only church towers and spires and a few major buildings seem to represent real buildings to the left, or upriver side, of Canal Street.

The artist exaggerated the size and height of all these structures, distortions that are present to an even greater degree for that part of the view representing the French quarter. The cathedral, a building of quite modest size, appears much like one of the great ecclesiastical monuments of Europe. Aside from a few other buildings on or near Jackson Square, the majority of those within the boundaries of the old town dissolve into a jumble of roofs, each indistinguishable from all the rest. Nevertheless, despite these all too obvious flaws, the view possesses a sense of vitality that conveys something of the distinctive character of this, one of America's most captivating cities.[4]

Throughout these last two decades of the century artists of city views passed by both Baton Rouge and Natchez, evidently either judging them not sufficiently attractive subjects for their work or feeling that

selling views of these places would not prove financially rewarding. Vicksburg thus becomes our next stop on this late nineteenth-century tour of Mississippi River cities, a visit made possible by a portrait drawn by Clemens J. Pauli, which was published in 1891 and is reproduced in Folio 16.[5]

An observer who described Vicksburg during the twenty-year period separating the views of Camille Drie and Clemens Pauli noted in 1880 that no fewer than "nineteen steamboat lines maintain wharves and anchorages." Pauli's view shows that by 1891 the Louisville, New Orleans and Texas Railroad also served the city, preempting much of the waterfront for its car and locomotive shops, tracks, yards, and freight and passenger stations.[6]

Industrial plants—far more than those shown in Drie's lithograph from twenty years earlier—occupy prime sites along the river, allowing them to use either rail or water transportation to receive raw materials or to ship finished products to their customers. Pauli identifies most of them in the extensive legend below the image of the city. Nevertheless, Vicksburg had not expanded or changed during the quarter century following the end of the Civil War to the same extent as had New Orleans or Memphis. The city that Drie visited and sketched in 1871 and that several visitors described at that time still made up most of the town's urban fabric. In the perpetual contest for urban supremacy and commercial success, Vicksburg had failed to keep pace with its larger

---

4. The definitive study of the evolution of New Orleans from the perspective of a perceptive geographer is Peirce F. Lewis, *New Orleans—The Making of an Urban Landscape.*

5. Chapter 5 discussed Pauli's views of La Crosse, Davenport, and Moline in 1876 and 1877, as well as one of Quincy, Illinois, in 1878 that also may be his. Pauli then abruptly abandoned the life of a traveling artist to join with Adam Beck in founding the Beck and Pauli printing firm in Milwaukee. Two years after Beck and Pauli dissolved their partnership in 1886, Pauli resumed his career as an artist of city views. From 1888 through 1896 he produced forty-six urban lithographs, most of them of places in Wisconsin and Michigan, but including the one of Vicksburg.

6. Ten years before Pauli arrived to draw Vicksburg, Hesse-Wartegg described it for his German readers. He admired "the beautiful courthouse" and the "large and handsome hotels and stores" on Washington Street, "Vicksburg's thoroughfare." He noted how "the many short, narrow streets . . . plunge from there to the river, to the many massive warehouses and magazines along its banks." The slopes of these streets he found so steep that "people pant and wheeze" to mount them, "wheeled vehicles cannot use them," and "to walk is to sink into a foot of debris" because "the streets are not paved." Moreover, he criticized the city for the conduct of some of its inhabitants: "Vicksburg has meant *infamy* since the war. Multifarious riffraff, found in every port city, assert themselves with exceptional energy here. People carry revolvers as a matter of habit, as they might pencils or toothpicks. Lynching, murder, gunplay occurred almost weekly for years. If things have improved in latter days, have the rowdies become as meek as lambs? Not at all!" (*Travels,* 76–77).

rivals, although it retained its role as the preeminent metropolis of its largely rural state.

Doubtless its leaders looked with envy on its upstream rival, Memphis, whose substantial growth in less than twenty years can be appreciated by comparing Ruger's earlier view in Folio 20 with the view of 1887 reproduced in Folio 21. This later view is the work of Henry Wellge, whose many highly detailed portraits allow us to examine the appearance and urban patterns of several communities on the Mississippi River from Memphis to St. Paul.

Among the most prolific of the bird's-eye-view artists-publishers of the last century with at least 152 views bearing his name in some capacity, Wellge was also among the last to practice this craft before photography and halftone printing brought the era of hand-drawn stone and zinc lithographs to an end. And, like so many of his colleagues, he remains a figure about whose life little can be said except to list the images he left behind.

Wellge was born in Germany in 1850. Of his early life and training, possibly in Prussia, we have nothing other than fragmentary and partially conflicting statements by him or his agents used by local newspapers in noting the artist's presence in their cities. Was he a "captain in the engineer corps of the Russian Army," as three Nebraska newspapers told their readers in 1889? Or, as a Rock Island, Illinois, paper stated that same year, had he served as "a staff artist of the Prussian army with the rank of Captain, during the Franco-German war," an officer "intrusted with the work of drawing some of the most important plans of that wonderful campaign?"[7]

About all that can be documented is that by 1878 Wellge's name had made its appearance in Milwaukee, whose city directories listed him then as a lithographer, in 1879 as an artist, and in 1881 as an architect.

His American career as a viewmaker apparently began with his arrival in Milwaukee, for in 1878 and 1879 in association with one J. Bach he published four views of towns in Wisconsin. In 1880 he began a series of some forty views drawn for and published by Joseph J. Stoner over a five-year period, including one of St. Paul in 1883.

Following Stoner's retirement as a view publisher in 1884, Wellge formed a partnership with George E. Norris in Brockton, Massachusetts, a business that the two moved to Milwaukee the next year. Wellge roamed the country for subjects, traveling at that time to Florida, Georgia, Alabama, Texas, and Tennessee, as well as drawing cities closer to home in Michigan and Wisconsin. Norris soon withdrew from the business, and in 1887 Wellge became both artist and publisher, doing business as Henry Wellge and Co. and then, in 1888 and thereafter, as the American Publishing Company. It was during this period in his career that Wellge drew and published views of Memphis and eight other places from Cairo to La Crosse.[8]

Like Ruger, Wellge also concentrated his efforts, working in 1887, 1888, and 1889 to draw his ten river-city views and focusing on towns of the upper Mississippi—Memphis and Cairo being the only exceptions. The Memphis view in Folio 21 is typical of his highly competent style of delineation in its very detailed legend using both numbers and letters and in the vignettes at both the top and the bottom. Wellge also used the phrase *Perspective Map* to categorize his product, employed outline lettering for the main title, and added a single tone stone to provide the cloud and shadow features that heighten the sense of realism of the print.

Characteristic, also, is the format of his Memphis view with a strong emphasis on the horizontal dimension, a feature that is all the more obvious if one disregards the vignettes and concentrates only on the principal image in the center. And, as a local newspaper pointed out in its notice calling attention to the completion of Wellge's drawing, the view is packed with persuasive detail that does not seem to diminish from foreground to background.[9]

7. The three Nebraska newspaper stories were in the Lincoln *Daily Nebraska State Journal*, June 2, 1889; Norfolk *Daily News*, June 15, 1889; and Fremont *Weekly Herald*, July 4, 1889. His identification with the Prussian (and not the Russian) army and his association with the Franco-German war appeared in the Rock Island *Daily Union* for January 15, 1889. All of these notices refer to orders for views of 20,000 copies, a figure that stretches credulity to the breaking point. That the same number is mentioned in all four notices (in one case it is given as 10,000 to 20,000) surely points to its origin in some kind of press release passed out by Wellge's agent, Charles J. Smith (identified as H. G. Smith by the Rock Island paper). An affiliation as a military artist and an officer might well have been an invention aimed at stimulating sales of the view. It does seem highly unlikely that Wellge would have attained the rank of captain at the age of twenty.

8. For Wellge's work after leaving the Mississippi valley in search of other subjects, see the biographical note in Reps, *Views and Viewmakers*, 213–15. As noted there, I relied for material about his life on Beckman, *Milwaukee Illustrated*, note for exhibit item 48, and on an unpublished conference paper Beckman kindly made available to me.

9. The Memphis *Avalanche* in its May 10, 1887, issue informed its readers, "Mr. Henry Wellge of Milwaukee, who has been in the city about six weeks, has just finished one of the most admirable perspective maps of the city yet published. Every street and alley

Shortly after Wellge completed this view, J. H. Beale described some of the city's outstanding features. A passage in his book provides a helpful explanation for the image that Wellge produced:

> Memphis . . . has fine public buildings, hotels, and theatres, 50 churches, 3 colleges, 100 schools, railways connecting it with New Orleans, Charleston, Louisville, Little Rock, and all parts of the country; with several foundries; 10 of the largest oil-mills in the United States, producing vast quantities of cotton-seed oil and oil cake, in the production of which is consumed 500,000 sacks of cotton seen annually; manufactories of boilers, machinery, etc. . . . There is a Cotton Exchange, a Custom-house, a Chamber of Commerce, and a Board of Health.

Adding that "the city is very picturesque when viewed from the river," Beale also observed that "the large warehouses along the bluff present a fine appearance," found "the streets . . . regular and broad," and admired the "numerous handsome residences, with fine lawns and gardens." Like authors of other encyclopedic guides and similar works of the time, he rarely used a critical word about any place mentioned; nevertheless, this description of Memphis contained more truth than hyperbole.[10]

Wellge's only other lithograph of a city on the lower Mississippi captures the image of Cairo, a city with a quite different history. While a comparison of this 1888 view, reproduced in Folio 23, with the one Ruger drew two decades earlier reveals some changes, Wellge's portrait indicates that what its founders hoped would become a great metropolis still had not fulfilled such expectations. Rail lines completely encircled the city, whose business district occupied the blocks lining Commercial Avenue. This thoroughfare began at the six-story Halliday Hotel overlooking the Ohio River near its mouth. Behind the hotel stood the grandly named Cairo Union Depot.

At the point of land where the two rivers join Wellge drew a ferry loading or unloading railroad cars by way of the railway incline. This led upward to a rail line atop the dike that parallels the Mississippi. Another rail incline appears to the right of center. This connected another railroad ferry landing with the tracks leading along the Ohio River frontage and past the Illinois Central Railroad bridge spanning the river at the outer limits of Cairo. Clearly, the economy of the city depended almost entirely on its role as a place where freight and passengers moved among steamboat and rail lines.

St. Louis, too, depended on the many railroads leading to it from all directions, but unlike Cairo the city had a highly diversified economy. Although the railroads employed thousands of workers, they were but one segment of a much larger and quite varied labor force. In its extensive zone of economic influence St. Louis enjoyed an unrivaled position as a major manufacturing, wholesaling, and distribution center. It also offered its burgeoning population and its many visitors opportunities to shop at its vast and varied retail establishments.

Wellge omitted St. Louis from his series of Mississippi River views, but a local artist produced an informative image of this visibly prosperous city as the century neared its end. A lithographer, engraver, and artist named Charles Juehne drew, printed, and published in 1896 the last and best of three views he produced in 1894–1896. Juehne came from Albany, where he was a lithographer, arriving in St. Louis in 1874 to work for a publisher as an engraver.

The St. Louis city directory for the following year lists him as a lithographer with an office in room 42 of the Insurance Exchange Building—the same building where Camille N. Dry then occupied room 48. If Juehne did not help in drawing Dry's great multisheet view, he would at least have become familiar with how one went about preparing such a perspective. A little over twenty years later Juehne produced his own version of St. Louis as seen from the air. It is probably no coincidence that he selected a perspective point seemingly identical to that used by Dry.[11]

---

and every building in the city, no matter how small, can be readily pointed out. It is an admirable piece of work in every respect." This is of considerable interest in indicating the time needed by an experienced artist of city views in drawing a city of this size.

10. *Picturesque Sketches of American Progress . . .*, 135. As Capers points out in *Biography of a River Town*, 214, it was after 1880 that Memphis overcame its twin problems of poor public health and excessive debt and emerged as a symbol of what was then referred to as the New South. Changes in the city reflected what occurred in the region as, in Capers's words, "in the eighties the Land of Cotton began to enjoy the commercial and industrial prosperity which the fifties had promised. . . . A section rich in mineral deposits, water power, timber, and fertility of the soil, but lacking the capital necessary for their development, aroused the cupidity of enterprising Yankees, and the South became popular as a field for investment."

11. I have not been able to find out anything concerning Juehne except through his city directory listings. Albany, New York, directories list him in that city as a lithographer in 1872 and 1873. He is not listed there for the years 1868–1871, so he either came to Albany about 1872 or came of age then and began to work. The St. Louis directory in 1874 lists him as an engraver working for Robert A. Campbell, a publisher. There are frequent listings of him through 1911. At that time and for the previous decade he is identified as an artist. In 1882 he lived at 2718 Gamble Avenue. This was next door

The result appears on the next-to-last page of Folio 29, a view showing at its center the new and imposing Union Station, the terminus of many rail lines that brought passengers into the heart of the city. Above and slightly to the right one can see the image of the new city hall, a huge structure occupying an entire city block—unhappily, the site of the former Washington Park, one of the few open spaces available in the central portion of the city. The view identifies two important parks in the southern section of St. Louis: Tower Grove Park and the adjoining Shaw's Garden near the upper left. The far larger Forest Park can be seen on the horizon to the left of center.[12]

To the right of the station and beginning near the Missouri end of the Eads Bridge, Juehne's view shows the dense business district. This was then expanding both outward and upward as residential buildings at its edges fell to make way for new stores, office buildings, or hotels and as ever taller buildings replaced older structures at the district's core. The depression of 1893 slowed such growth and expansion, but as one anonymous observer remarked in 1896:

> The unmistakable air of prosperity that St. Louis wears, is in marked contrast with the ill-concealed signs of distress which many of the smaller cities of the West are evincing in consequence of the frightfully depressed business conditions of the past three or four years. In times like these, the larger centres usually prosper at the expense of their lesser rivals. It must be remembered that St. Louis is at the centre of a greater mileage of railways than any other city in the world. . . . Thus, considered as an industrial community, St. Louis has at length reached the point where its own momentum makes certain a large future growth.[13]

The same author noted an important change in the structure of this metropolis, one that Juehne's view helps us appreciate. He noted that St. Louis had been transformed "within the past five or six years" from what "was until lately an exceptionally compact city." He explained how this had come about: "The old horse-car lines have all been made

over into electric trolley roads, which have been extended until the entire system now comprises nearly three hundred street-miles of electric lines, all radiating from the central district." He summarized the results:

> The consequence has been an almost magical development of a great residential zone, three or four miles wide, the outer edge of which lies upon the average about six miles from the centre of the city. Within this belt are thousands of attractive new homes, the typical St. Louis residence being a square, detached, red brick house, standing within a small plot of well-kept ground. . . .
> The passage by swift trolley car makes it feasible for a large proportion of the men of small incomes to own their own homes somewhere in the zone of outer wards.[14]

Cities to the north of St. Louis also felt the effects of better public transportation, as what was once farmland well beyond the older urban areas came into the hands of land developers eager to profit from the demand for housing in growing communities. Burlington, Iowa, offers an excellent example, as Wellge's view of 1889 in Folio 39 suggests. The town that had once occupied only the valley and hillsides within a few blocks of the river now stretched out westward on land easier to develop and build on.

A close examination of Wellge's view reveals a number of trolley lines running through new neighborhoods that were then only partly built up or were nearly vacant. These lines reached the business and industrial districts near the river via Angular and Division streets, whose steep slopes must have made it difficult for cars to climb and both dangerous and thrilling for them to descend. Obviously many persons still walked to work or to shop, but the transportation revolution in Burlington had changed forever the nature of the original compact community.

Burlington could boast of many industries. In addition to those located along the river and thus able to use both rail and water transportation, a major industrial corridor then lined the curving tracks of the Burlington Railroad. They followed a valley extending back from the Mississippi and led to the industrial community of West Burlington, whose smoking factories and locomotive shops can be seen on the horizon toward the upper right corner. This area is apparently the subject of the untitled vignette at the lower right.

---

to the residence of Theodore Schrader, a lithographer who had printed and published several views of cities in Missouri and Illinois before the Civil War.

12. Henry Shaw gave the Missouri Botanical Garden (almost always called Shaw's Garden) to the public in 1859. Ten years later he offered the city a larger tract that became Tower Grove Park when it opened in 1870. On the north side of the city O'Fallon Park occupied 159 acres that the city acquired in 1876. The 1,400-acre tract for Forest Park was transferred to public hands in 1874 and 1875. The 180 acres of Carondelet Park are too far south to appear on Juehne's view.

13. "St. Louis: This Year's Convention City," 675–76.

14. Ibid., 674–75, 677–78.

Davenport provides another example of growth, one better documented by city views. The lithographs of the city in 1881 by Hageboeck and in 1888 by Wellge in Folio 46 reveal how much the city had expanded since Pauli drew it in 1876 for the view that has been examined previously. Both Hageboeck and Wellge show trolley lines. These are easiest to see in the 1881 almost maplike, very high level depiction by Hageboeck, where he identifies them with heavy black lines. Clearly, the extension of these lines to serve the flat, easily developed prairie beyond the steep river bluffs contributed substantially to this early manifestation of what a later generation would label as urban sprawl.

On Mark Twain's nostalgic visit to the Mississippi in 1882, he described for his readers Rock Island, which sits in the river between Davenport and the city of Rock Island on the Illinois side:

> The charming island of Rock Island, three miles long and half a mile wide belongs to the United States, and the Government has turned it into a wonderful park, enhancing its natural attractions by art, and threading its fine forests with many miles of drives. Near the centre of the island one catches glimpses, through the trees, of ten vast stone four-story buildings, each of which covers an acre of ground. These are the government workshops; for the Rock Island establishment is a national armory and arsenal.[15]

The lower end of the island appears at the left in Wellge's view of the city of Rock Island in Folio 41. Wellge published this in 1889 imagining himself above Davenport looking east. The Rock Island *Daily Union* on January 15 of that year declared the result "the handsomest and most effective thing yet devised for giving people a comprehensive idea of Rock Island." After identifying Wellge as a former "staff artist of the Prussian army . . . during the Franco-German war," the writer claimed that Wellge's American Publishing Company had received "an order for 20,000 lithographed reproductions of this view" from the "Advertising Committee of the Citizens' Improvement Association," which expected "to be largely reimbursed by orders received from some of our large manufacturers and by a general sale." The paper announced that single copies would cost two dollars, but that "there will be considerable reductions on large orders."

It seems highly doubtful that Wellge's company printed even one-tenth of the obviously inflated number mentioned in this account. Still,

15. *Life on the Mississippi*, 566–67.

the skillfully drawn and printed lithograph must have appealed to many who lived there, and multiple copies may well have been used by manufacturers seeking to publicize their businesses and promote their community. The newspaper report described what recipients of the view would see:

> The chart shows the Rock Island bridges and something of the Arsenal buildings on the left foreground, and stretches down the city front with the turn of the river on the right, while the background shows the bold bluffs on the left and the plain through which the roads from the city reach Milan, with the Watch Tower, the Rock river water power, mills and bridges, and the confluence of the Rock with the Mississippi.

Wellge also drew Rock Island's neighboring city, Moline—a view that can be found in Folio 42. Twenty years earlier Ruger produced his own images of the two places, and these pairs of images of the two cities make abundantly clear how swift had been the pace of industrialization and urbanization at this source of almost unlimited waterpower. In the case of Moline one can see how the waterfront with its handful of industrial plants in 1869 had been transformed into a concentrated belt of factories that preempted the entire shoreline from one end to the other.

Dubuque provides another example of rapid urban development—experienced in this case at a place with far older roots than either Rock Island or Moline. And although Ruger skipped Dubuque on his visits to the Mississippi valley, the 1872 view by Augustus Koch in Folio 50 captured the image of the city before it began a period of massive industrial growth and change. Wellge's lithograph in Folio 51 is another of the several his company issued in 1889 and reveals what had occurred in the intervening seventeen years. In comparing the two urban portraits one is immediately struck by the changes in the shoreline. At the bottom center of his view Koch shows the mudflats that then existed. By the time of Wellge's visit this area had been transformed into the tidy industrial district that Wellge depicted linked to the Illinois shore by the two bridges in the foreground. Additional filled and platted sites to the left and right of this central quasi-peninsula can also be seen. Huge stacks of sawed lumber fill many blocks in the vicinity of the Standard Lumber Company mills and yards in the center and the C. W. Robinson Company at the far left.

While Dubuque supplied lumber to builders in Iowa towns west of the river, some of the city's important industrial concerns used much of the lumber mills' production. In the extensive legend that is typical of Wellge's views, he lists companies manufacturing furniture, coffins, hardwood plows, shingles, wagons, carriages, buggies, and sleighs. Many other factories produced pumps, steam engines, mill machinery, boots and shoes, clothing, food and tobacco products, and a variety of other goods. Dubuque's population registered steady gains, growing from 18,434 in 1870 to 22,254 ten years later and reaching 30,311 in 1890, the year after Wellge's view appeared.

Lumber also loomed large in the economy of La Crosse, Wisconsin, when Wellge arrived to draw that city for his view published in 1887. In Ruger's view in Folio 54, issued just twenty years earlier, one looks in vain for signs of this industry. It existed, but on a small scale that Ruger evidently felt did not need to be emphasized. By contrast, the Wellge view, also in Folio 54, looks down on great stacks of milled lumber on the river on either side of Cass Street, the principal thoroughfare leading inland. No trace of these lumberyards and mills remains in the modern city.[16]

In the legend Wellge used the letter *D* to identify electric-light towers. Several appear in the view; perhaps the easiest to make out stands in the middle of Cass Street at Tenth. Such towers were used for a time in many cities in the United States to light the streets at night instead of the lights at each street corner that became the norm. Some referred to these powerful lights atop their towers as "artificial moons." Moonlike or not, this system of night lighting fell from popularity, and images like those in Wellge's view provide virtually the only evidence of how these devices appeared.

In 1889 Clemens J. Pauli came to Winona, Minnesota, a short distance upriver and on the opposite bank from La Crosse. Folio 55 shows the results of his work in what must be a proof impression of the lithograph since the image contains numbers on many buildings but lacks the corresponding printed legend. No legend is needed, however, to recognize the many lumberyards and—nearby—what are obviously the

mills where logs from the forests of Minnesota and Wisconsin had been converted to boards, laths, shingles, and other building products.

We have now arrived at St. Paul on this journey that began in New Orleans. Two splendid views of the city in the 1880s illustrate how the Minnesota capital appeared after many years of nearly continuous expansion, slowed only by national depressions. Both lithographs appear in Folio 61, the earlier being published in 1883 by J. J. Stoner from a drawing by Henry Wellge before the artist founded his own publishing concern in Milwaukee. One hundred and fifteen numbered and three lettered references in the legend locate virtually every point of interest in St. Paul, and vignettes of many buildings provide additional information about this community.

Stoner chose an excellent time to issue a view of St. Paul. As a special report of the 1880 census stated, following the recovery from the depression of 1873, "the growth of the city has been remarkable. Its increase of population, business, capital, etc. has been unprecedented." In addition, in the year the view appeared St. Paul had gained rail access via Duluth to the Pacific Coast with the completion of the Northern Pacific Railroad. The union depot that line served occupied a site near the river six blocks to the right of the bridge crossing the Mississippi.[17]

Immediately beyond the station one can see the extensive railroad yards, freight stations, and other buildings of this and other rail lines that brought raw materials and foodstuffs into St. Paul and provided its manufacturers and merchants ready access to markets both east and west. Rail transportation continued to improve after James J. Hill of St. Paul gained full control over the St. Paul and Pacific Railroad in 1883. Hill renamed it the Great Northern and a decade later finished the last segment of this direct link between St. Paul and Seattle.

It was the completion of the Northern Pacific line in 1883 that brought Nicolaus Mohr, a German journalist and Bremen newspaper publisher, to St. Paul as the guest of Henry Villard, the president of the railroad. Mohr's impressions of the city appeared in a book published in Berlin the following year in which he commented on the changes taking place in St. Paul:

> The wooden structures have disappeared from the center of the city. Many of the buildings that were first erected to replace them are quite modest, but just as the city is growing the style of building is also taking on a new

---

16. In one of his extremely helpful notes on the views of La Crosse in "Four Pictures," Sanford identifies the mills: "Beginning at the north is Sawyer and Austin's, then the McDonald mill. These are north of the Clinton street bridge. Next, between that bridge and the Milwaukee R.R. tracks, is the La Crosse Lumber company. . . . This was the 'big mill,' on the present site of Copeland park. Next, Davidson's (the 'Packet Mill') and Holways. Below the tracks is Trow's and across the Black [River] is the Polleys' mill. These mills and those farther down were the main support of La Crosse industry for many years. There is no visible sign of any of them left."

17. The quotation is from U.S. Census Office, *Report on the Social Statistics of Cities,* 2:697.

character. Some of the business blocks have brick buildings rising six stories and although they are simple, they look functional.

Store after store lines the streets. But brick apparently is not adequate because they are now using sandstone as the building material for the very newest structures. Everybody in St. Paul has the wildest dreams and expectations for a continuing boom.

After visiting some of the outlying neighborhoods, Mohr noted, "The roads leading out of the city are lined with many beautiful houses which are surrounded by gardens and beautiful shade trees. In these areas the wooden structures have by no means been done away with, but they are no longer the only construction material in use." He professed astonishment at "the number of vehicles constantly out and about in every city," and concluded, "The American of the West is a born rider and driver. Whenever conditions permit, he takes a buggy with one horse or a team to get wherever he wants to go."

Although apparently favorably impressed generally by St. Paul, Mohr vigorously criticized the condition of its thoroughfares:

The streets, the streets! The streets are a sore point in every American city. Dirty, muddy, or dusty, it all depends on the weather. Rough, full of holes, hilly, in every city almost without exception they are the object of cursing and swearing. But in spite of all the complaining, it seems that nothing can be done to improve them.

In St. Paul the sidewalks are entirely made of wood. So long as the planks are nailed down, the understructure solid, and the holes not too large or too frequent, then it goes all right. They say these are only temporary until they can lay a sidewalk of stone slabs or cinders.[18]

The amount of land occupied by St. Paul's railroads and their shops and yards suggests how important employment was in that segment of the local economy. The city also enjoyed its role as the state capital, an advantage brought home to the city's residents by the construction of a new Capitol (the second such structure) on Wabasha and Tenth streets. An image of this building appears in the center of the vignettes along the top of the Wellge-Stoner view. It housed the Minnesota legislature and other public offices until lawmakers occupied the third and present Capitol some distance to the north in 1905.

18. *Excursion through America*, 276–78, 281.

Many of the other vignettes emphasize a vital aspect of St. Paul's existence—its role as a major center of wholesaling. Among the vignettes are images of wholesale enterprises that distributed throughout a wide region such products as medicines, stationary, hardware, dry goods, groceries, and books. Some of these goods came from St. Paul factories that, in addition, produced agricultural implements, buggies and wagons, beer, leather products, boilers, furniture, and other merchandise. The city also enjoyed a reputation as the banking center of the upper Midwest.[19]

Wellge's depiction of St. Paul caught the city just as it emerged fully from its initial stages of development and well before the depression of 1893 halted for a time significant further change. The other view of St. Paul in this folio is similar in character. It bears the date of January 1888 at the bottom and in some of its impressions includes at the top a lengthy advertisement for the publisher of the view, the J. H. Mahler Company, manufacturers of "Daisy" buggies, wagons, carriages, sleighs, and equipment associated with these vehicles. Another bit of advertising fills the space at the top of the lithograph: "THE MOST EXTENSIVE CARRIAGE AND HARNESS HOUSE IN THE WORLD." Even on those impressions lacking the advertisements at the top, the name of the company and its principal product also appears in two places within the view as if painted on the face of the bluff. Finally, to make certain that no one owning a copy of the view could possibly mistake its source, in the legend that identifies 347 buildings or places, the company's name appears in two listings in large boldface type.[20]

At first glance this view appears to have come from the same stone or plate as the Wellge-Stoner view of 1883. The two differ in many ways, however, although the anonymous artist of the later lithograph doubtless based its perspective on the one Wellge created and undoubtedly found Wellge's drawings of individual buildings a useful guide in providing convincing and accurate details. One obvious difference is in the additional bridges shown on the lithograph of 1888. The view's artist must have relied on engineering drawings of the high bridge near

19. Ronald Abler, John S. Adams, and John R. Borchert, "The Twin Cities of St. Paul and Minneapolis."

20. The Mahler Company's warehouse and salesrooms could be found on East Third and East Fifth streets. The impression of the lithograph in the Ramsey County Historical Society shows the advertisement in the sky. Otherwise, it and the version reproduced in Folio 61 from the Minnesota Historical Society appear to be identical. Both identify the printer as the Orcutt Litho. Co. of Chicago.

the bottom left, for it was begun in the year the view appeared and did not open until 1889.

Another clearly discernible difference appears in the foreground in the images of buildings lining what is now Wabasha Avenue south of the single bridge shown in the 1883 view. Less easily seen are the changes along Summit Avenue. This thoroughfare followed the crest of the steep bluff located half a dozen blocks north of the river and seen in the view at the left side about halfway between the river and the horizon. There the manufacturing, financial, and professional tycoons of St. Paul erected great mansions. The legend identifies many of them, including the splendid thirty-two-room house of red stone that James J. Hill built in 1887 at 240 Summit Avenue.[21]

Minneapolis, too, was prospering. Indeed, by 1880 it had overtaken St. Paul in population and by the end of the decade would even surpass its older rival as a center of wholesaling. Several factors contributed to this shift in position: the decline in the importance of river transportation that reduced St. Paul's advantage as a better location for steamboat landings; the superb waterpower resources provided by the Falls of St. Anthony, which attracted industry; and the growth of wheat farming in the seemingly endless prairie country of western Minnesota and the Dakota Territory.

At first the milling of lumber was the most important industry in Minneapolis, and as early as 1869 fifteen sawmills occupied sites near the falls. Production continued to increase until 1900 and remained high for another decade before exhaustion of local timber supplies closed the mills. Flour milling also began at a fairly early date, for thirteen mills existed in 1870. At first the mills mainly filled local demand, but with better rail connections to both the East and the West and quickly rising wheat production, the mills of Minneapolis began to supply other regions as well.

The economies of larger-scale production and the ambitions of certain mill owners led to rapid consolidation. Where once seventeen firms owned the twenty mills operating in 1876, a decade and a half later four firms controlled virtually all flour production, with Pillsbury and Company and what became General Mills as the two largest of these

enterprises. Around the mills other industries grew up making such things as the bags and barrels needed to ship flour to markets, machinery used in the mills, and livestock feed and other food products. Grain elevators for storage vied with the towering mill buildings as the dominant structures of the city's skyline. They could be found along the tracks of railroads bringing grain to Minneapolis from the west and hauling flour to the Midwest and East.[22]

The lithograph of 1885 in Folio 63 and the two views in Folio 64 showing important portions of the city in 1886 and 1891 reveal much about the character of Minneapolis at this time. It was during this period that Nicolaus Mohr visited Minneapolis and marveled at the great mills converting wheat to flour, "among them some whose sizes outstrip anything of their kind in the world." He wrote about his visit to one of the most impressive of these buildings:

> One of the huge mills, the Pillsbury, was shown to us in every detail. We started at the lowest level where a large shaft of water is brought in through a special channel. . . .
>
> We climbed from floor to floor until at last we stood high on the roof and enjoyed the panoramic view of the city and its countryside, including the towers of St. Paul off in the distance. The Pillsbury mill turns out five thousand barrels of flour every day but it has rivals for this record on the other side of the river.[23]

In the view of 1885 we can see most of the city as William Valentine Herancourt drew it, the last such work he produced. Herancourt's name joins the list of artists responsible for Mississippi River city views who seem to be known only by the views they created. His works include depictions of Cedar Rapids, Iowa, in 1881, eight views of places in South Dakota in the years 1882–1884, and this Minneapolis print. One South Dakota view of 1882 gives his address as Dubuque, Iowa, and the Minneapolis directory for 1885–1886 identifies him as an

---

21. Summit Avenue remains one of the great residential streets of America, although many of the mansions now provide quarters for nonprofit organizations or other businesses. The Hill mansion is owned by the Minnesota Historical Society and operated as a museum house.

22. Writing about Minneapolis in 1882, Mark Twain listed some of the city's industrial and commercial accomplishments: "Thirty flouring mills turn out two million barrels of the very choicest of flour every year; twenty sawmills produce two hundred million feet of lumber annually; then there are woolen mills, cotton mills, paper and oil mills; and sash, nail, furniture, barrel, and other factories, without number, so to speak. . . . Sixteen railroads meet in Minneapolis, and sixty-five passenger trains arrive and depart daily" (*Life on the Mississippi*, 448). In summarizing the industrial growth of Minneapolis during this period, I have followed closely the treatment of the subject by Abler, Adams, and Borchert in "Twin Cities of St. Paul and Minneapolis," 373–74.

23. *Excursion through America*, 71–73.

artist, boarding at 424 South Seventh. In 1889 he drew several scenes of the Oklahoma land rush that *Harper's Weekly* published as wood engravings.[24]

Augustus Hageboeck in 1886 drew, printed, and published the first of the two views of Minneapolis reproduced in Folio 64. It is a curious image in which the artist looks directly upriver with the Tenth Avenue Bridge in the immediate foreground. The train crossing the river just beyond that bridge is on what is known as the Stone Arch Bridge of the Great Northern Railroad, erected in 1881 and called then by some Hill's Folly. On the right side of the Mississippi is that portion of the city that began its existence as St. Anthony. Lining the river on both sides are the great flour mills. A comparison of the waterfront portion of Ruger's view of 1867 in Folio 62 with this scene of industrial concentration emphasizes the enormous changes that Minneapolis underwent in less than two decades.

True, Hageboeck seems to have exaggerated somewhat the bulk of the buildings and their density in much the same way that would a modern photograph taken with a powerful telephoto lens. And it is impossible to identify the great domed and turreted structure with what appears to be a bell tower at one corner that Hageboeck placed near the upper right corner of his print. Nevertheless, his view conveys better than any other the waterpower resources of the site and the development that they stimulated.[25]

24. Herancourt may have sought work as a magazine illustrator after finding that his separately issued city views did not provide a living. That only three impressions of this view can be found in institutional collections suggests it failed to attract many purchasers at the time of publication. The rarity of this large lithograph, measuring more than two feet by nearly three and one-half feet, seems to have limited its use by urban geographers, architectural historians, or others concerned with the structure of the city and the appearance of its buildings at this critical period of its development. My brief biographical note on Herancourt in Reps, *Views and Viewmakers,* 182–83, contains no more relevant information about this biographical ghost than his Minneapolis address. At the time I compiled my entry (#1926) for this view in my book I could list only the impression in the Geography and Map Division of the Library of Congress. That has since been misplaced and cannot be found. The Hennepin County Historical Society has one impression, and in 1991 the Minnesota Historical Society acquired a third.

25. Federal Writers' Project, Works Projects Administration, *Minnesota: A State Guide,* 189, contains this description, which corresponds closely to what Hageboeck's view displays: "The Tenth Avenue Bridge . . . is one of the finest vantage points in the city. Some distance above the bridge, the upper dam diverts water to the mills whose windowless walls tower above the riverbanks—a massive stone front that dwarfs the river-drop, where the once raging cataract is now an ordered flow of harnessed waters over man-made spillways. On the left bank, looking upstream, are the huge Washburn Crosby

Finally, to end this last tour of Mississippi River cities with the viewmakers of the last century, we can examine the other Minneapolis view in Folio 64. Frank Pezolt drew this very high level view, and its publisher, A. M. Smith, a food and wine merchant, had it printed in Chicago by the F. G. Christoph Lithographing Company. Its vivid, bold colors and heroic size (twenty-nine by forty-one inches) make it one of the most striking (if not particularly attractive) of all American city views.[26]

If Pezolt drew other views, his work has gone unrecorded. Nor was Smith a publisher of other city views. Apparently he arranged for this one to be drawn only as a device to advertise his business and to promote sales of wine and other food products. Two buildings occupied by his enterprise—a "wine depot" and his "California wine vault"—are identified among the fifty-three numbered and lettered items in the legend at the bottom left. A building with the name of Smith's wine vault on the roof can be seen near the lower right corner and immediately above the bottom border line.

Smith had Pezolt add additional words to the roofs of the two long, low buildings across the tracks from the Chicago, Milwaukee, and St. Paul Railroad station, whose image appears near the center of the lithograph. The words on the two roofs read "Go to A. M. Smith's and by [*sic*] this picture. 249 Hennepin Ave." Lettering of the company name on the building's roof also identified the Smith premises on Hennepin between Washington and Third.

Near Smith's business several tall structures in the office and retail district had begun to change the appearance of this part of the city. The prevailing horizontal character that had marked downtown Minneapolis until a few years earlier was coming to an end. Two concentrations of tall structures emerged, one in the business district, where lower

mills and elevators, grouped with the King Midas, Russell-Miller, Northwestern, and older structures. On the right is Pillsbury's long row of interconnected silos—a magnificent architectural mass. Upstream is the graceful curve of old Stone Arch Bridge, and beyond are the Third Avenue and Hennepin Avenue bridges."

26. Smith also issued a smaller version of this image, with a panel of text claiming that the full-size lithograph had been printed in seven colors and that it had cost Smith $4,000 to publish. The publisher offered this "Large Chromo Lithograph . . . FREE to any person buying Two Dollar's ($2) worth at one time, Alcohol excepted. This offer is only good to December 26th, 1892." Smith probably sold copies of the print to others, although there is no information about what price he charged. An impression of the smaller (15 1/2 x 21 1/2 inches) lithograph is in the Hennepin County Historical Society.

buildings and streets somewhat separated the taller ones, and the other along the river, where the closely packed mills and elevators formed a compact mass of masonry.

The city's residential neighborhoods offered a strong contrast, as a writer for the *New England Magazine* noted in 1890:

> It has been the Minneapolis fashion and ambition to secure at least one full lot for a citizen's home. This separation of the dwellings gives an effect of space and largeness hardly known in older American cities, and in strong contrast with some younger ones. . . .
>
> Thanks to the taste and enterprise of a number of young architects, who have brought the best ideas and projects of American and foreign schools of architecture, the dwellings of the city are generally tasteful in design, and the instances of decided beauty are numerous.[27]

Presiding over this changing scene of urban design, the new city and county building asserted its own place among these tall structures. Its great clock tower thrust some four hundred feet above the entrance on Fourth Street of this massive red granite home of local government. This replaced an older and much smaller city hall that stood where

Hennepin and Nicollet avenues converged on the bridge crossing the tracks of the Great Northern Railroad and leading across the Mississippi River to that part of the city originally founded as St. Anthony.

Minneapolis and St. Paul, like the other cities both great and small along the Mississippi, would experience further changes in the century that followed the publication of this view. Some cities grew rapidly, others expanded at a more moderate pace, and several found themselves declining in population and saw their older buildings deteriorate or vanish. Yet, however different they might now appear to a resident of the past century miraculously transported to the present by some time machine, the original urban structure still shapes every modern community.

One can appreciate this best from the air. Just as the nineteenth-century bird's-eye-view artists found their elevated perspectives the most effective way to display the features of the places they depicted, so now can aerial photography be used to reveal the appearance of contemporary communities. In a brief reprise using this medium of urban exploration, the concluding chapter of this book will take the reader-viewer on yet another expedition along the Mississippi.

27. W. W. Folwell, "Minneapolis in 1890," 97.

VIII

After the Viewmakers Left

A Centennial Portrait of the Urban Mississippi

Henry Wellge was the last of the urban viewmakers to visit and draw images of several towns along the Mississippi. His appearance in the region in the early years of the last decade of the century marked the beginning of the end for the printed bird's-eye depictions of cities. Although Wellge produced a handful of views of cities elsewhere in the nation after the end of the century, and although two long-lived artists—Thaddeus M. Fowler and Oakley Hoopes Bailey—continued their careers until the 1920s, by the 1900s mechanically reproduced photographic images had largely replaced the hand-drawn lithographs that had once been so popular and numerous.[1]

Here and there along the Mississippi a local artist like Frederick Graf in St. Louis might produce a portrait of his own city for some special event in the twentieth century, but for the overwhelming majority of Mississippi towns the close of the nineteenth century marked the close of an era of urban viewmaking as well. Persons who may have wanted a view of an entire community had to be content for many years with photographs taken from some tower or hill. Yet virtually none of the towns along the Mississippi could be photographed from a high enough natural or man-made elevation to display the street

pattern in a manner comparable to that used in the lithographs of Wellge, Ruger, or the many other bird's-eye-view artists active in the nineteenth century.

It was not until the development of aerial photography that the images of cities could once again be captured from on high. Almost all of these photographic images, however, showed their subjects from directly overhead and resembled maps more than views. These vertical photographs—produced on a large scale in the 1930s as part of a nationwide project by the federal government—had none of the decorative appeal of the earlier lithographic views, however valuable they might be for scientific purposes.

More recently, occasional pilot photographers began to photograph individual cities for a variety of clients who used the images they took for advertising, for publicity, as subjects for postcards or posters, or for other purposes. Most persons found these photographs taken from an angle rather from directly overhead much easier to understand. The development of color film with faster emulsions than were first available made possible color photographs from the air. Further improvements in film, greater understanding of the importance of filters, better cameras, and the use of gyro-stabilizers all led to substantial improvements in the quality of aerial color photography.

A century after Wellge last sketched a Mississippi River city and roughly 120 years from the time Ruger produced his even more extensive series of river-city views, a new set of urban images was produced through color photography from the air. Taken by Alex S. MacLean,

---

1. For a chart showing the years of activity of America's forty-seven most active viewmakers, see Reps, *Views and Viewmakers*, 5. More detailed information for each artist or publisher can be found in the biographical notes, 159–217. The chart for each viewmaker shows the states in which he produced views in each active year and the number for which he was responsible.

these photographs show river cities from St. Cloud, Minnesota, at the north to New Orleans, Louisiana, at the southern end of Mississippi River urbanization.[2]

These views present their subjects in modern images that almost exactly duplicate the horizontal and vertical angles of the perspectives drawn by nineteenth-century view artists. Thus, although MacLean's photographs can be enjoyed by themselves, they are best appreciated and understood when examined side-by-side with their counterparts of a century or more ago. The reader will find these photographs as the concluding illustrations in many of the folios of this book. We shall use these aerial photographs—as we did the printed images of the nineteenth century—in making our final tour of the river cities.[3]

Sadly, one must point out that the photographs are valuable in a way not contemplated when arrangements were made for them to be taken. The devastating and tragic floods in the upper river during the summer of 1993 damaged severely or destroyed altogether the waterfront portions of many of the communities photographed for this book. These aerial portraits, therefore, record the appearance of towns and cities whose architectural heritage may have suffered—perhaps substantially—as a consequence of this natural disaster. Rebuilding and reconstruction may further alter their physical fabric, although the original two-dimensional plans of streets and blocks will probably remain much as before.

In this respect, however, each of MacLean's photographs follows in the same tradition as its nineteenth-century counterpart. Both document the form, character, and architecture of a town or city at a single point in time. These "new" images by MacLean thus become—far sooner than anticipated—part of the historical record of urban growth, decay,

abandonment, or transformation, the process of change that has always characterized the world of towns and cities. Eventually, even more recent images will portray the new faces of these places as they emerge from the destruction that always threatens river towns and that from time to time overwhelms them.

Along the northern stretches of the Mississippi, flood damage was not severe. We begin our journey there at St. Cloud, the northernmost town on the Mississippi depicted by any of the artists whose work this book has explored. Folio 65 presents this photograph of 1989 together with the equivalent view, in this case one by Ruger from 1869. Ruger elected to emphasize what was then referred to as "Lower Town," laid out to the south of the original settlement of 1853. At the time of Ruger's visit few houses occupied the dozens of blocks in this extensive grid addition to St. Cloud. By the river at the foot of Washington Street stood the Normal School, the institution that opened its doors in the year Ruger sketched the nascent city. That institution became the St. Cloud State Teachers' College and grew to an enrollment of about eight hundred students at the end of the 1930s. Today it is St. Cloud State University, with a student body of over thirteen thousand. Its buildings occupy many blocks along the river south of its first location as well as extending several blocks inland and are the most prominent features to be seen in MacLean's aerial photograph.[4]

To the right, in the original town grid, the photograph shows the business district leading back from the Mississippi, a river now spanned by two highway structures and a railroad bridge. Like many other small-city downtowns, that of St. Cloud appears to have more space devoted to automobile parking than to buildings housing its retail, office, and banking activities. Beyond the university toward the horizon stretches St. Cloud's "strip," the ubiquitous highway commercial complex of fast-food establishments, motels, automobile agencies, and a variety of service and sales enterprises.

Notwithstanding all the changes that have taken place, Ruger would have little difficulty in recognizing the St. Cloud he drew 120 years before MacLean recorded its modern appearance. Despite a modest amount of suburban sprawl, most of the city's buildings stand within the frame Ruger used for his pictorial representation. Nor has the plan

2. MacLean's work, commissioned by the author, was made possible through the generosity of a grant to the author by The Graham Foundation.

3. To guide MacLean in attempting to match the perspective of each nineteenth-century bird's-eye view, I provided him with a map of each city marked with the central axis of the view. This was prepared by drawing a vertical line down the center of a photograph of each view and plotting that line on modern government topographic quadrangles using buildings and other landmarks common to both the old view and the modern map. Using this line as a guide down which to aim the camera and referring to a copy of the bird's-eye view, Maclean then used his long experience in aerial photography—aided by a computer program—in selecting the altitude to fly and the focal length to use for his lens. MacLean used a variety of medium-format cameras, each gyro-stabilized, to photograph the cities through the opening of the pilot's window in the standard single-engine, fixed-wing aircraft that he flies.

4. According to the note in Federal Writers' Project, *Minnesota*, 259, classes began in a large residence previously owned by the Stearns family. It is this structure that Ruger's view shows standing near the river in the left foreground.

of the city's streets changed substantially. The most obvious alterations are those within the university campus, where several nineteenth-century streets have been closed to provide additional land and to reduce the dangers and distractions of through traffic.

A comparison of the nineteenth-century images with the modern air photographs tells a far different story about Minneapolis and St. Paul. Although as in nearly all the places we shall visit on this last Mississippi River journey the basic street system of Minneapolis remains virtually unchanged, the city wears quite a different face in MacLean's photograph of 1989 from that recorded by Pezolt not quite a century earlier in 1891. Folio 64 reproduces these two images on facing pages.

Pezolt correctly rendered the massive cluster of flour mills and related buildings on the left as the most impressive feature of Minneapolis. To the right in the business district only a few structures rivaled the mills in height or bulk, and these stood on widely separated sites. In that part of the city the tallest object was the tower of the new city hall. This appears near the center of both portraits of Minneapolis, although in the oblique photograph it is almost lost among the soaring skyscrapers housing the business and financial premises of what had become one of the nation's major metropolitan centers. Even less conspicuous are the few churches remaining in the central district, while in Pezolt's view their spires provided important landmarks to the city's neighborhoods.

Much the same is true for St. Paul, as can be seen by looking at the view of the city in 1888 found in Folio 61 alongside MacLean's aerial photograph of 1989. The anonymous artist of the lithograph clearly copied the underlying perspective of Wellge's lithograph from five years earlier, adding the new bridges and a number of buildings that had been constructed during the intervening period. The image taken by MacLean's camera reproduces almost exactly the views that Wellge and his imitator drew in the 1880s. The photograph records the same chaotic jumble of parquetlike grids extending back from the river to the left of the business district. Efforts through the years to bring more order to this portion of the city have not been entirely successful, although some notable buildings occupy sites in this area. The most recent major addition in this section—the new, spacious quarters of the Minnesota Historical Society—was begun shortly after MacLean photographed the city for this book and therefore does not appear in the folio image.

Downriver from the metropolitan sprawl of the Twin Cities the modern visitor will come to three much smaller Minnesota towns that Ruger

drew in 1867 and 1868 and that MacLean photographed from the same perspectives just over 120 years later. These most recent aerial images of Hastings, Red Wing, and Winona will be found in Folios 57, 56, and 55, where they can be seen in conjunction with the equivalent views by Ruger. In the case of Winona, Pauli's view also appears—the only one of the three towns that this artist elected to depict on his sketching trip to the area in the late 1880s.[5]

The photographs convey much of the attractive character of these cities, whose patterns have not changed substantially since itinerant artists found them suitable subjects for their artistic efforts. As the largest of the three, Winona has undergone the greatest changes. Even so, today's visitor armed with Ruger's view would still find it useful in locating the major elements of the community. The admiring description of Winona that a tourist of 1938 would have found in the state guidebook produced by the Federal Writers' Project of the Works Projects Administration still seems appropriate:

> In spite of its two modern banks and its skyscraper tower, Winona's business streets, like most of its residences, are more suggestive of the nineteenth than of the twentieth century. . . .
>
> The visitor who comes in the summer will find it difficult to believe that this city could ever have been without trees, for its many steeples and towers rise above a sea of green. All of its broad residence streets are lined with double rows of elms and maples; the grounds of its colleges and religious institutions are landscaped; trees crowd to the foot of the granite bluffs and up the ravines to the prairies.[6]

In our own day some visitors find the small towns of this part of the river something less than completely charming. Jonathan Raban, an English visitor who traveled the Mississippi in 1980 in a small outboard-powered boat, visually dissected Wabasha, Minnesota, located between Red Wing and Winona, in one of his distinctively penetrating descriptions. Noting that "up and down the Mississippi there were hundreds of places like Wabasha which had grown up at the same date in the same way," he proceeded to guide his readers through this town:

> First there was the river. Then, standing on the levee between the wharves and the railroad track, there was a line of grain elevators. The words BIG JO

5. For an aerial photograph of Hastings "in the 1940s from the Northwest," see Lucille Hammargren Doffing, *Hastings on the Mississippi,* 31. The author reproduces an early plat of Hastings on pp. x–xi.

6. *Minnesota,* 263

FLOUR stood out in the sky over Wabasha's head like a flag. . . . I picked my way . . . on Front Street, a stretch of low white clapboard, with a muddy pickup parked in every drive and a chained dog grumbling at me from every shaven lawn.

Raban concluded that "until lately, no one of consequence would have lived on Front," because "its old shacks had been swept away by floods, and their smart successors had been built only after the levee had been made high enough to keep the river from turning up as an unexpected guest in their living rooms."

On Main Street, a block further from the river, he encountered buildings of brick, a material that "meant substance, importance, civic pride." Raban came to a "Gothic monster" of a city hall built in 1894 "which might have accommodated enough people to keep Chicago going." Across the wide Main Street he saw several older brick structures dating from the 1870s and 1880s, "each . . . a chunk of fancy architectural confectionery." He commented that while "the European origins of Wabasha showed in its German-Dutch gables . . . their facades had gone Ancient Greek, with dadoes, porticos, friezes and lots of Doric columns." Raban believed that "the constant toing-and-froing between South and North on the river had brought about a curious intermixture of taste" that included "even up here in Minnesota . . . shadows of cotton planter's Hellenism."

As in so many other towns along the Mississippi, Wabasha's founders had provided ample room for expansion if their venture in urban development met with substantial success. Raban found that these expectations "that the town, like the rest of the nation, could move indefinitely westward" had been dashed:

I went to see how far it had gone. Just two blocks on, Wabasha petered out. There were a row of wooden bungalows, a stretch of dingy grass, Highway 61, a creek, another railroad, and then nothing more than a few hundred miles of corn stubble. In whatever lottery it was that decided which American villages were going to turn into megacities, Wabasha had clearly drawn a dud ticket.[7]

On the Wisconsin side of the Mississippi, La Crosse occupies a site near the mouth of the Black River. MacLean's photograph taken in 1989 and reproduced in Folio 54 closely matches the perspective used by

7. *Old Glory: An American Voyage*, 85–87.

Henry Wellge 102 years before. Many changes occurred in the intervening years. The mills with their great piles of sawed timber are no more; instead, one sees business structures and grain elevators. At the left, where Wellge drew the locomotive roundhouse between the river and a residential quarter of modest buildings, there are now dozens of light industries and an oil tank farm. The island at the right in Wellge's view that he showed stacked with lumber now provides the site for the city's modern wastewater treatment system. Throughout the central part of the city high-rise buildings provide a distinct contrast to the still prevailingly horizontal character of the prosperous community.

Down the Mississippi at the mouth of the Wisconsin River is one of the oldest settlements on the upper river: Prairie du Chien. Folio 53 includes an aerial photograph of this place in 1988, while Folio 52 reproduces similar present-day depictions of McGregor, Iowa, its neighbor across the river, and Guttenberg, Iowa, a few miles downstream from McGregor. Were Ruger to return today, he would be able to use his views of the three places published in 1869 and 1870 as guides to the modest-size towns they have remained.

All three retain the dominant features that Ruger recorded more than a century ago. Prairie du Chien still seems to consist of three sections, although the two neighborhoods beyond the Wisconsin River have come together while the settlement along the Mississippi in the foreground appears to have declined in importance. The dramatic site of McGregor in its narrow slot between the high hills on either side still confines that town to a single street leading to and from the Mississippi. Guttenberg, occupying a more favorable site, still maintains its linear configuration with no house more than a few hundred feet from the high bank along the river. The dam and lock at the upriver end of town, with their commercial and recreational river traffic, provide a constant reminder that inland water transportation still plays an important role in the life of those who live along the Mississippi.

On the Illinois shore and downriver from Guttenberg, Galena is now a much-visited tourist attraction. The author and former towboat deckhand and pilot Richard Bissell visited this old mining town in the 1960s. He described it for his readers as "nestled down between steep hills" where "you can enter a house by the front door on one street, climb three flights of stairs, and leave by the back door which opens onto the next street up the hillside." He noted Galena's changing character:

It is a very small town and a great deal of it looks like a stage set for *King's Row, Tom Sawyer,* or even *Gone with the Wind,* for there is a strong suth'n flavor to many of the houses with their white-pillared fronts. There is no suth'n flavor around the score or so of dandy saloons, however, and the talk is corn and hogs, not cotton or who gets to vote and why not.

Bissell told his readers that "big steamboats used to come winding up the little valley from the Mississippi . . . and tie up right here at the levee a block away, sometimes in rows," but that the river had become "silted in and not wide enough for a water bug to get his proper exercise." Now, he observed, "not a trace remains of the golden age of steamboating." The only signs he found of Galena's former place as an important river port were "four aluminum outboard boats from Sears Roebuck tied to car axles driven into the bank. And one home-made skiff."[8]

Twenty years after Bissell offered his characterization of Galena, Jonathan Raban visited and described the tourist center the city had become:

> Galena's latest boom had been caused by an enterprising group of Chicago decorators and architects. They had restored the town and turned it into a museum piece for Tourists, a handsomely painted exhibition of Illinois–Queen Anne, Illinois–Romanesque, Illinois–Second Empire, Illinois–Italian Villa, Illinois–Gothic and Illinois–Doric. For just a year or two Galena had been rich again. Then the oil crisis hit the place. It was barely possible to get to Galena and back from Chicago on one tank of gas. "No one's traveling anymore," said a disconsolate clerk. . . . Now Galena looked like a movie set recently abandoned by the production crew. Even on this sunny Saturday there were few tourists about. The paint on the restored houses was beginning to crack; the short-order restaurants, done up in "historical" ticky-tacky, were mainly just short of customers. The only place in town that looked as if it were still in business in a big way was the Steinke Funeral Home, a gigantic piece of cake icing with steamboat decks and balustrades and columns. It looked as if, bit by bit, the Steinke Funeral Home were finally taking care of Galena.[9]

Continuing southward, one comes to Dubuque, now a major Iowa city with a population of 57,546. Wellge and MacLean produced their portraits of this diversified community just ninety-nine years apart in

8. *How Many Miles to Galena?,* 303–4.
9. *Old Glory,* 157–58.

1889 and 1988. Folio 51 provides the comparison of conditions near the end of the nineteenth century and in our own era. At an early stage in its development Dubuque allowed its waterfront to be monopolized by industries and the railroads. The modern photograph shows how little this has changed and that public and recreational access to the Mississippi is virtually nonexistent.

Dubuque's central business and civic district still occupies the restricted area of flat land extending back from the cluttered industrial precinct along the river to the steep bluff on the west. The beginning of suburbanization that Wellge recorded has continued, and MacLean's oblique photograph shows clearly the extensive residential growth on the higher flat land west of the original settled area. In addition, one can see a number of reminders of Dubuque's past. The Shot Tower erected in 1855 still stands and appears in the photograph near the river not far from the end of the railroad swing bridge. To the left in the smaller of the harbor indentations stands the Riverboat Museum, which celebrates Dubuque's long association with commercial and passenger riverboat traffic. Here and there throughout the lower town a number of nineteenth-century buildings have found new lives, and, on the bluff above, most of the great mansions of the past century still enjoy an unrivaled view of the river.

Davenport, Iowa, and Rock Island, Illinois, also have experienced substantial growth and have undergone many changes between the time of Wellge's visit and that of MacLean's photographs. At Davenport, as the modern view in Folio 46 shows, many blocks near the river that were once solidly occupied by industrial concerns now lie vacant. Narrow bands of land along the river in public use are being expanded, and the introduction of riverboat gambling here and at other river towns may change the character of the waterfront and focus attention once again on the Mississippi River.

Davenport and its sister communities did not impress Raban on his visit there in 1980. He recorded his impression that "the Quad Cities were a queer agglomeration. Their suburbs had leaked and dribbled into each other, and finally the whole mess had loosely congealed." He described the result:

> Rock Island and Moline, on the east bank of the river, were in Illinois: Davenport and Bettendorf were in Iowa. They hadn't come together to make a metropolis, but they had lost their identities as individual towns. For twelve miles, they straggled lumpishly along the wharves, the hard angles of their warehouses, steel tanks and factories hemming in the river. Everything

was too low, too spread out, to make much more than a cheeky gesture of encroachment on the Mississippi, like a line of children's sand castles on a seashore.[10]

Perhaps Raban would have been helped in his appraisal by seeing an air photo of this budding metropolis. In Rock Island, most of the land near the river is still devoted to industrial uses, as MacLean's photograph of 1988 in Folio 41 reveals. While the railroad lines remain, they are far less obvious than Wellge found them when he created his own image of the city in 1889. One great industry making mechanized farm and industrial vehicles—the John Deere Company—is responsible for many of the new buildings that can be seen. At the far left is the downriver tip of Rock Island, where the erection of Fort Armstrong in 1816 marked the beginning of white settlement in the area.

Ninety-nine years also separate the two images of Burlington in Folio 39. Here, as in several other river towns, efforts to open up the riverfront to nonindustrial uses have partly succeeded. The marina to the left of the bridge reflects concern for tourism and recreation. The left half of MacLean's photograph, however, clearly shows the multiple tracks of the railroad that effectively seal off the river in that part of the city. Burlington has managed to retain some vitality in its central business district, where a few new buildings can be seen. Less obvious in the photograph are some successful attempts to save and rehabilitate older structures.

The Iowa city that seems to have been most successful in linking the town to the river is Fort Madison. MacLean's photograph of 1988 in Folio 38 shows the long park that stretches from the Marina at the upriver end of town to well past the midpoint of the more densely developed portions of this little city. Wellge's view of 1889 reveals that most of the town's industries occupied sites downriver from the center and never dominated the townscape as at other Iowa cities.

Apparently neither Wellge nor Ruger visited Quincy, or if they did they must have decided that other artists had preempted the market for city views. Folio 34 pairs the photograph that MacLean took in 1988 with the bird's-eye lithograph published about 1860. In both cases we are looking directly on the orderly if somewhat unimaginative street grid whose original portion was enlivened only by the public park occupying the block not far from the river and near the center of both

images. This attractive and industrially diversified city now extends many blocks beyond the confines of the 1860 view, and, as in most American towns, businesses, offices, and light industry can now be found more at the outskirts than in the center.

Not far below Quincy on the Missouri side of the Mississippi, Hannibal from the air today closely resembles its appearance as drawn by Ruger in 1869. Both images can be found in Folio 33. At the right the Cardiff Hill of Tom Sawyer rises abruptly above the town and the river. At its foot one can see the highway bridge that now takes the place of the steam ferry that Ruger drew. River tows and barges still come to the landing, but now only to load grain from the elevator or to discharge sight-seeing tourists from one of the two vessels still regularly carrying passengers on extended river trips. The old part of town nearby trades largely on the reputations of Twain, Sawyer, and Huck Finn, as do motels, restaurants, and souvenir shops elsewhere.

Hannibal's grain elevator is an impressive structure, but it is figuratively overshadowed by the concentration of such structures along the waterfront of Alton, Illinois. Folio 31 looks down on this old settlement as MacLean saw it in 1987—an image that can be compared with Ruger's lithograph of 1867. In the lower right of the photograph we see another symbol of the continuing importance of water transportation to the towns that cling to the shore of the Mississippi. This is lock and dam number 26—the most southerly of the series of such structures that make the upper Mississippi navigable for commercial traffic. The long lakes created by the dams are intended to help prevent floods during the rainy season and to provide a sufficient flow of water during drier weather for the great tows of river barges carrying bulky commodities like grain. In MacLean's photograph one can see a tow consisting of nine barges in one of Alton's twin locks. Below Alton the tows are typically much longer since the river is free-flowing and the tows are not limited to the length of the locks.[11]

Along with the other great cities of the Mississippi, St. Louis presents a far different face to the world than it did in the nineteenth century. To see the changes that have occurred, one has only to turn to Folio 29 and compare the composite view formed by four adjoining plates of the massive Compton-Dry view of 1875 with MacLean's photograph taken

10. Ibid., 174.

11. At Alton the very long tows used on the lower river are broken into smaller units for destinations upriver. Similarly, tows heading downriver are combined into longer ones for destinations as far distant as New Orleans.

in 1987. At the lower right of both images one can see the renowned Eads Bridge—new when Dry drew his view and still serving today as an important east-west thoroughfare across the Mississippi as well as a significant landmark in the St. Louis townscape.

The elongated rectangle along the river is part of the Jefferson National Expansion Memorial National Historic Site. In the 1930s the federal government cleared forty blocks in what was the oldest and most historic part of the city, demolishing hundreds of structures with cast-iron facades—believed to be the largest concentration of such buildings in the country. The remnants of these and somewhat later structures now can be found only in a small area north of the Eads Bridge, a tourist-oriented section known as Laclede's Landing. In the center of the now parklike open space along the river stands the soaring, shining arch completed in 1965. This spectacular monument symbolizes the role St. Louis played as the gateway to the American West. Between the arch and the freeway forming the western edge of the park one can see the Old Cathedral, a Greek Revival building modeled on a temple at Paestum and the only surviving architectural legacy of the French period of St. Louis.

A short distance to the northwest is one of the glories of St. Louis architecture. This is the splendid Old Courthouse, another Greek Revival structure whose plan is in the shape of a Greek cross, each arm of which ends in a portico of Doric columns. In the photograph its green dome makes it is easy to locate this building, which occupies a site on the east-west axis of the arch.

Virtually nothing else that can be seen in the photograph existed at the time Dry drew his marvelously detailed view of St. Louis. All that remains of early St. Louis is the pattern of grid streets that continued and extended the original street plan platted by the city's French founders in the eighteenth century. One superb building of the nineteenth century—a structure built two decades after Dry completed his view—occupies a special place in St. Louis. This is the great Union Station, whose tower, head house, and covered train shed can be seen several blocks west of the Old Courthouse. Remodeled as a hotel-restaurant-shopping center, it provides a firm link with the past while serving well and prospering in its new role as a commercial focal point.

Below St. Louis at the mouth of the Ohio lies Cairo, a city whose recent history continues its long, sad, and unfortunate record of unsuccessful efforts to do more than barely survive. Now reduced in population to fewer than 5,000 persons, it has become almost an archeological site. The air photograph in Folio 23 reveals its shattered appearance in 1988, just a century after Wellge visited and drew the place when it seemed finally almost to be poised on the verge of modest prosperity and stability.

Although Cairo clings to activities generated by barge shipping on the inland waterways, the two images strongly suggest the extent to which that role diminished during the century that separates them. While in the 1888 view railroad lines ring the town and engine roundhouses and freight and passenger stations occupy prominent locations, in the photograph one must look closely to find the single railroad right-of-way extending off to the right from its beginning some distance up the Ohio River levee. Perhaps the most orderly feature of modern Cairo is the sewage treatment plant at the left near the point of land where the Ohio River meets the Mississippi.

While Cairo clings to what seems to be a declining existence, Memphis appears to be thriving. The largest city in Tennessee with a population of over 600,000, Memphis now extends many miles beyond the outer limits of the city that Wellge recorded in his lithograph of 1887. MacLean's oblique photograph in Folio 21 is somewhat deceptive in this respect, for what appears in the background to be undeveloped land in reality consists of pleasantly tree-shaded neighborhoods extending far to the east of downtown.

Although Memphis has more nineteenth-century buildings than St. Louis, few of them are obvious in the air view, hidden as they are by the modern structures rising from the business and financial district in the foreground. Ruger's view of 1870 in the previous folio shows that at that time most major business blocks faced the river. By 1887, as Wellge's portrait reveals, this was no longer true. Now we see in MacLean's photograph another stage of the cycle of change.

The inelegantly named Mud Island, created to improve navigation and port facilities for Memphis, is formed by the Mississippi in the foreground and the Wolf River, the narrower channel along the foot of the Memphis levee. The island itself was developed as an elaborate commercial park with many unusual features, but this eventually failed, and the city is now planning its future. What this photograph does not show is the enormous pyramid that, after MacLean's visit, has been erected by the water north of the business district to house an arena and other facilities.

Unlike Memphis, Vicksburg retains many features of the nineteenth century, as can be seen from MacLean's photograph in Folio 16.

Although the courthouse (several blocks left of center) is no longer the most prominent structure in the city, its site at some distance from newer and larger buildings still makes it a prominent landmark—especially as seen from the river. Several other historic buildings have been preserved or restored, and Vicksburg depends successfully on these and its National Military Park to attract the thousands of tourists who come to the city each year.

It is this aspect of Vicksburg that Tony Dunbar noted in his recent study, *Delta Time.* Dunbar found that "Vicksburg is full of beautiful places: cobblestoned streets, fine views of the rivers, the National Military Park, exquisite flower gardens, and grand old houses landscaped into the sides of the bluffs on streets running nearly vertical down to the riverbank. It is the only Delta city that qualifies as a major tourist attraction."[12]

The two-dimensional pattern of the nineteenth century as well as many buildings from that time or only slightly later are what one finds so obvious in the dramatically lit aerial photograph reproduced in the folio along with Drie's and Pauli's views of 1871 and 1891, respectively. Because many of the structures still standing existed in 1891, and some of them had been built by 1871, the photograph by Alex MacLean is of particular interest. In comparing the lithographic views with the modern image from the air, note how both of the views convey the distinctive topography of Vicksburg with far greater clarity than does the air photograph. Although an example of artistic license, the omission of trees that would otherwise have obscured details of buildings allowed the nineteenth-century artist more freedom of expression than is available to the modern photographer. Similarly, the bird's-eye-view artists of the last century could delineate without interruption by vegetation the full extent of streets, railway lines, streams, and other linear elements of the community.

MacLean's photograph records one major change that for a time threatened the economic life of Vicksburg. During a major flood the Mississippi cut a new channel and left the city without water transportation. Eventually engineers rerouted the Yazoo River from its normal mouth above Vicksburg to flow into the old and abandoned channel of the Mississippi. This explains why in the photograph one sees only a stream of modest size instead of the broad Mississippi of the earlier views.

12. *Delta Time: A Journey through Mississippi,* 221.

Finally, we come to New Orleans and the photograph in Folio 9. In taking this, MacLean has duplicated the perspective used by the artist for the splendid lithograph of New Orleans published in 1883 by Gustave Koeckert. Below and to the right of center one can easily trace the boundaries of the old French town grid. The downriver side is marked by tree-lined Esplanade Avenue, which begins at the Old U.S. Mint, whose red bulk occupies an entire block. The wide swath of Canal Street follows the upriver side of the old town. Rampart Street is not quite so obvious as it defines the inland side of the Vieux Carré. It can be seen leading diagonally up and to the left from Esplanade Avenue a few blocks more than halfway from the Mississippi to the elevated lanes of Interstate 10 cutting through the network of older thoroughfares.

At the lower right one can see the beginning of the former Third Municipality, occupying its distinct portion of the fan-shaped grid system of New Orleans. The green path of Elysian Fields Avenue is responsible for the pronounced *V* that is here so apparent. Between Elysian Fields Avenue and Esplanade Avenue the photograph shows several examples of how nearly two centuries ago persons planning street connections between these two sections of the city provided smooth links that avoided jogs and dead-ends.

Opening to the Mississippi in the old town, Jackson Square stands out clearly with the Pontalba Buildings on either side and with the cathedral and its flanking structures facing the water. Following the axis of Jackson Square away from the river, one finds just beyond Rampart Street the Municipal Auditorium and Concert Hall occupying sites in Louis Armstrong Park. To the left, the large cluster of red-roofed buildings is a public housing project bordered on one side and part of another by St. Louis Cemeteries No. 1 and No. 2. It is their typical aboveground burial vaults that appear almost like residences in a miniature city.

The photograph reveals that the French Quarter—already tightly built up in 1883, as Koeckert's view demonstrates—is now even more densely developed. Maclean's modern image nevertheless suggests that this part of the city has not entirely lost the distinctive character noted with pleasure or shock by so many visitors of the last century. Persistent and skilful efforts by preservation groups and many individuals to protect this old part of New Orleans, although not entirely successful, can be credited for saving major elements of what is one of America's most distinctive townscapes.

Across the river from Jackson Square one can see on a small part of the pointed shore the original modest grid of Algiers, once a separate community but now part of the city of New Orleans. Beyond this small part of present-day Algiers and beyond the lower margin of the photograph sprawls a huge area of suburban development. Residents of this area who work in New Orleans reach the city either by the Greater New Orleans Bridge carrying the traffic of U.S. 90 or, at least for a few, by ferry. This photograph captures the image of one of the ferries that connects Algiers with New Orleans at midriver as it churns its way toward its Canal Street landing.

Modern office and hotel towers that appear in the photograph along and particularly just beyond Canal Street testify to the general economic vitality of New Orleans since the end of World War II. Certain other landmarks stand out: the new aquarium at the foot of Canal Street and the huge Superdome looming at one corner of the intersection of Interstate 10 and U.S. 80. Between it and the river are the skyscrapers of the city's office, banking, municipal, hotel, and business center.

The waterfront has undergone many changes. A massive brewery diagonally upriver from Jackson Square has been converted to a shopping, souvenir, and restaurant center. Beyond it on the river is a new landing where excursion boats can be boarded. What the photograph does not make clear is that the levee blocks the view of the river from Jackson Square and vicinity, and one must use bridges to reach a promenade along the water. The tall, cruciform-shaped structure at the foot of Canal Street is the International Trade Building. Beyond it, a major hotel and a riverside shopping mall form what appears to be a series of joined warehouses. This is the New Orleans Convention and Exhibition Center, built, as were the many other new buildings in this district, at the time of the New Orleans World's Fair of 1984.

The photograph also looks further upriver beyond the central business district to the neighborhoods that developed in the nineteenth century as the city expanded. It shows, as did Koeckert, the distinctive crescent or fanlike pattern of these successive additions to New Orleans. This, it will be recalled, came about as landowners subdivided their holdings by creating streets parallel and perpendicular to the continually curving course of the Mississippi.

This last photograph in the MacLean series concludes our final tour of cities of the Mississippi. These and the many images produced by nineteenth-century urban viewmakers provide revealing glimpses of past conditions of the river's many towns as well as records of how they appear in our own era. The future of these river towns lies ahead, uncertain except for the inevitable changes that time always brings. One can hope only that new generations of viewmakers and observers will leave behind graphic and written evidence of urban evolution as complete and as absorbing as the materials presented in this volume.

Sixty-five City Tours on an Upstream Voyage
Guided by Artists and Authors of the Last Century

Folio 1.   The Balize, or Pilot's Station, near the Mouth of the Mississippi Is Admired by No One

Benjamin Henry Latrobe provides an early description of the place in 1819

We landed first at the Balize. A more wretched village, for it is a sort of a village, cannot be conceived. It consists of a tavern, a wretched habitation for the revenue officer U.S. & three or four other wooden buildings, belonging to the pilots, besides the blockhouse. The whole population consists of 90 men & 11 women, & an internal feud breaks up this little society into parties who are at war with each other. . . . One of the pilots keeps a tavern & a billiard room, which, it is supposed, absorbs the principal part of the wages of their underlings. There is however, some useful industry here also. Two coasting vessels were here for repair, & several boats were building.

The village consists . . . of two two-story wooden houses, habitations of pilots, a miserable one-story hovel, the floors of which are several inches under water when the wind blows high, a roomy one-story tavern with a billiard room attached to it, & the Spanish timber blockhouse, on which is a timber tower, in which the present light is kept. A wooden tower or lookout was built a year ago by the pilot, who keeps the tavern as a speculation on the Government, under the expectation that he would be appointed keeper of the light. But he was disappointed, for the Collector had the present tower repaired as part of a very strong & permanent building.

(Benjamin Henry Boneval Latrobe, *Impressions Respecting New Orleans: Diary and Sketches, 1818–1820*, 125–26)

The English traveler Basil Hall is equally critical of the Balize a decade after Latrobe's visit

We went down the South-east Pass to the dreary abode of the Pilots, called the Balize—from the Spanish word Valiza, a beacon. . . . From this wretched place—planted in the midst of a boundless swamp or morass—no firm land is in sight, or is within fifty or sixty miles of it. There are about twenty buildings in all, six of which are dwelling-houses. The intercourse between them is carried on exclusively along paths made of planks and trunks of trees laid over the slime and water. It is impossible, indeed, to walk ten yards in any direction, without sinking up to the neck in a mud-hole or a quicksand; so that, for all the usual purpose of location, the inhabitants might just as well be at sea.

In the middle of this half-drowned village, there stands a rickety sort of look-out house, to the top of which we managed to climb with some difficulty. The extensive field of view which this commanded was flat and dreary, beyond any imagination to conceive but still it was not without variety and interest.

(Basil Hall, *Travels in North America, in the Years 1827 and 1828*, 3:337–38)

A Yankee visitor in 1834 find conditions little better than did Latrobe and Hall

During the first part of our sail up the river, there was nothing sufficiently interesting in the way of incident or variety of scenery, to merit the trouble either of narration or perusal. . . . With the exception of two or three "pilot stations," near its mouth, I do not recollect that we passed any dwelling. These "stations" are situated within a few miles of the mouth of the river, and are the residences of the pilots. The one on the left bank of the river, which I had an opportunity of visiting, contained about sixteen or eighteen houses, built upon piles, in the midst of the morass, which is the only apology for land within twenty leagues. One third of these are dwelling houses, connected with each other for the purpose of intercourse, by raised walks or bridges, laid upon the surface of the mud, and constructed of timber, logs, and wrecks of vessels. Were a hapless wight to lose his footing, he would descend as easily and gracefully into the bosom of the yielding loam, as into a barrel of soft soap. The intercourse with the shore, near which this miserable, isolated congregation of shanties is imbedded, is also kept up by a causeway of similar construction and materials.

([Joseph Holt Ingraham], *The South-West. By a Yankee*, 1:74–75)

In the 1850s Henry Lewis writes of the flood problems here

The Pilots' houses are built on the highest points that can be found in the surrounding marshlands. Nevertheless the entire area is subject to floods, particularly during the prevailing northeast wind, even though the river does not rise much here at flood time, because of the numerous outlets which drain the water into the gulf. There are few trees here. . . .

The high tower built of framework . . . is the observatory from the top of which the pilots can distinguish a vessel with their glasses long before those on board can see land.

(Henry Lewis, *The Valley of the Mississippi Illustrated*, 411)

An eastern journal illustrates the place in 1856 and calls the buildings in the vicinity "picturesque"

The . . . picture . . . is an accurate view of the Belize [sic], one of the mouths by which the "Father of Waters" seeks an outlet to the Gulf. . . . The scene we . . . present is a rendezvous for pilots, and on the low shore to the right a lofty look-out is erected for their use, from which they can descry vessels at a great distance. The buildings all along the pass are picturesque, and the trees planted at intervals impart a very pleasing aspect to the scene. Many of the little houses sketched in our view, are occupied by pilots.

("The Belize" [sic], 133)

Die Balize an der Mündung des Missisippi. Drawn by Herzog Paul von Württemberg. Printed by der Künig, Anstalt, [1828–1835]. Lithograph, 11 3/4 x 16 5/8 in. (29.9 x 42.2 cm).

Stokes Collection, New York Public Library

Folio 2.   Observers Provide Details about the New Orleans Town Plan and the City's Public Buildings

Francis Baily describes the town plan as he saw it in 1797

New Orleans is laid out . . . with the streets, (which are rather narrow) crossing each other at right angles: it contains fifteen rows of streets from north-east to south-west, and seven rows in the opposite direction; and the whole area of the city may be about three hundred acres. Owing to the irregularity of the fortification which surrounds this city, all the streets are not of an equal length. The whole area is not entirely built over, as many squares on the northwest end of the town are void of houses. The principal site for buildings is as near the water as possible, as being more convenient for trade, &c.; and houses on this spot will let for more money than those farther back from the Mississippi. Fronting the river, and at an equal distance from each end of the town, there is a public square, which is left vacant, as well for the purpose of beauty and ornament, as to expose to view a church which stands at the farther end of it.
(Francis Baily, *Journal of a Tour in Unsettled Parts of North America in 1796 & 1797*, 163)

The commanding American officer at the transfer of New Orleans to American rule in 1804 lists the city's important buildings

The cathedral stands at the head of a spacious open square, about four hundred feet from the river. This building is of brick, extending about ninety feet on the street, and one hundred and twenty back of it. The roof is covered with flat and hollow tile, supported by ten large brick columns, which are plastered, and afford an agreeable appearance. Each front corner has a tower considerably elevated, and the southerly one contains two small bells. . . .

The town house is rather an elegant building, two stories high, and about ninety feet long, with an arched portico, both above and below, along its whole front. . . .

In the rear of the town house, and adjoining to it, is the prison. . . .

The public barracks are situated at the lower end of the front street. They are accommodated with a spacious area, surrounded by a brick wall, as also an extensive parade ground between them and the river. The buildings are of brick, and one story high, covered with shingles, and calculated to receive about fifteen hundred men. They were built by the French, and have a spacious arcade in front and rear.

The building denominated the king's hospital, is on the same line, but higher up. It was originally intended as a receptacle for the sick and diseased belonging to the army and navy. It will accommodate about one hundred and fifty patients, and affords to the miserable a tolerable asylum.

The convent of the Ursuline nuns is situated on the upper side of the barracks, and beyond the hospital, which stands nearer the line of the street. This was likewise built by the French: It is of brick, and spacious; covered with shingles, and two stories high. An extensive garden is attached to it. . . . Attached to the convent is a small house containing three rooms, divided longitudinally from each other by double gratings about six inches asunder, with apertures about two inches square, where strangers may see and converse with the nuns and boarders on particular business. Near to the main building, and on the street, stands an old school house, where the female children of the citizens appear at certain fixed hours to be gratuitously instructed in writing, reading, and arithmetic. . . .

The charity hospital stands on the westerly or back part of the city. Poor Spanish subjects, and sometimes strangers (provided they paid half a dollar per day) were admitted into this asylum. Those entirely destitute were admitted gratis. . . .

The government house stands on the front street, and on the fifth square, reckoning from the upper side, and one hundred feet from the river. It is an ancient building, erected by the French, and two stories high, with galleries or arcades round the whole of it. The lower front was formerly occupied by the governmental secretary, and the clerks of offices. This structure is indifferent, both as to architecture and convenience.

On the southwesterly part of the same square were the lodges and stables of the regular dragoons; which, with the garden belonging to the government house, occupy about four fifths of the square.

On the corners of the second and third squares, lower down, are the public stores, built of brick, extending about thirty five feet on front street, and about two hundred feet on a cross street. They are one story high, and were built by the French.

On the opposite, or southerly side of the stores, is the artillery yard, or ordnance depot.

Opposite to this, on the very bank of the river, is the market house, which is usually furnished with beef, pork, some mullard and veal, fish of several sorts in abundance, and cheap; wild ducks and other game in season, tame turkies [*sic*], fowls, ducks, and geese; and vegetables of all kinds during the whole year. . . .

The grand power magazine of the French and Spaniards, is situated over against the government house, on the opposite side of the river, where a guard was always stationed, and generally relieved weekly.
(Amos Stoddard, *Sketches, Historical and Descriptive, of Louisiana*, 153–55)

A View of New Orleans Taken from the Plantation of Marigny. Drawn by [John L.] Boquet[a] de Woiseri, November 1803. Aquatint with etching, 12 (matted) x 21 1/2 in. (30.5 x 54.7 cm).

Historic New Orleans Collection

Folio 3.   Visitors Tell Us More about the Private Buildings of New Orleans

Francis Baily writes of the houses of New Orleans

The houses are generally framed buildings, and are raised about seven or eight feet from the ground, in order to make room for the cellars, which are on *a level* with the ground, as no buildings can be carried on below its surface on account of the height of the surrounding water. The upper part is sometimes furnished with an open gallery, which surrounds the whole building, though in the streets this is often dispensed with. It affords an agreeable retreat in the cool of the evening in this warm climate, and is much more refreshing than within doors. The house in which I boarded had one of these galleries, which was shaded by some trees growing in the garden, and under cover of these we used to take our tea in the evening.

New Orleans may contain about a thousand houses.
(Baily, *Journal of a Tour in Unsettled Parts of North America in 1796 & 1797,* 167, 175)

Amos Stoddard provides more information about the appearance of buildings

Nearly the whole of the old houses are of wood, one story high, and make an ordinary appearance. The suburbs on the upper or north end of the city, have been built since the fire in 1794, and contain about two hundred and fifteen houses, most composed of cypress wood, and generally covered with shingles or clapboards. Among them is one elegant brick house covered with tile. Several of them are two stories high, and two in the same quarter three stories high. . . . They are plastered on the outside with white or colored mortar; this, as frosts are seldom severe in the climate, lasts many years; it beautifies the buildings, and preserves the bricks, which from the negligence or parsimony of the manufacturers, are usually too soft to resist the weather.

Stoddard also describes the city's walls, gates, and fortifications

During the administration of the baron Carondelet, between 1791, and 1796, a ditch was extended round the city, of about eighteen feet in width, with ramparts of earth, and palisades nearly six feet high along the interior or inner side of them. Five large bastions were erected at proper distances, and likewise five intervening redoubts. . . .

The inhabitants and others passed in and out of the city by means of four gates. The two next the river were the most considerable, and they were situated sixteen hundred and twenty yards from each other. The two in the rear, or on the back part of the city, were of much less note; one of them was placed on the road leading to lake Pontchartraine [*sic*].
(Stoddard, *Sketches, Historical and Descriptive, of Louisiana,* 152, 156, 157)

An architect looks at the city's buildings

New Orleans, beyond royal street, towards the swamp, retains its old character without variation. The houses are, with hardly a dozen exceptions among many hundred, one-story houses. The roofs are high, covered with tiles or shingles, & project five feet over the footway, which is also five feet wide. The eaves therefore discharge the water into the gutters. The height of the stories is hardly ten feet, the elevation above the pavement not more than a foot & a half; & therefore the eaves are not often more than 8 feet from the ground. However different this mode is from the American manner of building, it has a very great advantage both with regard to the interior of the dwelling & to the street. In the summer the walls are perfectly shaded from the sun & the house kept cool, while the passengers are also shaded from the sun & protected from the rain. . . .

In the Fauxbourg St. Mary & wherever the Americans build, they exhibit their flat brick fronts with a sufficient number of holes for light & entrance. The only French circumstance which they retain is the balcony in the upper story, which altho' generally too elevated for the protection of the passenger is still a means of shade as far as it goes. The French stucco the fronts of their buildings and often color them; the Americans exhibit their red staring brickwork, imbibing heat thro' the whole unshaded substance of the wall. . . .

I have no doubt but that the American style will ultimately be that of the whole city, especially as carpenters from the eastern border of the union are the architects, &, of course, work on in their old habits for men accustomed to these very sort of houses. But altho' room may be thereby gained, the convenience of the houses will by no means be promoted—nor the health of the city improved.

He notes details of the street plan

The streets are, in the city, all of them 36 French feet, about 38'–6" English, wide; & the squares (islets) 300 French, or about 320 English feet, square. The old lots are 60 French feet front by 120 deep. In the Fauxbourg St. Mary the streets are wider, but in that of Marigny, the same as in the city. Provision is made for several public squares, an ornament & convenience in which our other cities are most remarkably deficient. In this respect New Orleans will always maintain its superiority.
(Latrobe, *Impressions Respecting New Orleans,* 105–7)

Plan of the City and Suburbs of New Orleans. Drawn by I [i.e. Jacques] Tanesse. Engraved by [William] Rollinson. Published by Charles del Vecchio, New York, and P. Maspero, New Orleans, 1817. Engraving, 18 11/16 x 30 9/16 in. (47.5 x 77.6 cm).

Geography and Map Division, Library of Congress

Folio 4.   Timothy Flint in 1823 and Charles Joseph Latrobe a Decade Later Suggest Some of the Charms of the City

Flint notes the city's growth and the differing character of newer parts of an expanded New Orleans

When I visit the city, after the absence of a season, I discover an obvious change. New buildings have sprung up, and new improvements are going on. Its regular winter population, between forty and fifty thousand inhabitants, is five times the amount which it had, when it came under the American government. The external form of the city on the river side is graduated in some measure to the curve of the river. The street that passes along the leveé [*sic*], and conforms to the course of the river is called Leveé street, and is the one in which the greatest and most active business of the city is transacted. The upper part of the city is principally built and inhabited by Americans, and is called the "fauxbourg St. Mary." The greater number of the houses in this fauxbourg are of brick, and built in the American style. In this quarter are the Presbyterian church and the new theatre. The ancient part of the city, as you pass down Leveé street towards the Cathedral, has in one of the clear, bright January mornings, that are so common at that season, an imposing and brilliant aspect. There is something fantastic and unique in the appearance, I am told, far more resembling European cities, than any other in the United States. The houses are stuccoed externally, and this stucco is white or yellow, and strikes the eye more pleasantly than the dull and somber red of brick. There can be no question, but the American mode of building is at once more commodious, and more solid and durable, than the French and Spanish; but I think the latter have the preference in the general effect upon the eye. Young as the city is, the effect of this humid climate, operating upon the mouldering materials, of which the buildings are composed, has already given it the aspect of age, and to the eye, it would seem the most ancient city in the United States. The streets are broad, and the plan of the city is perfectly rectangular and uniform. There are in the limits of the city three malls, or parade grounds, of no great extent, and not yet sufficiently shaded, though young trees are growing in them. They serve as parade grounds, and in the winter have a beautiful carpet of clover, of a most brilliant green. Royal and Charter [*sic*] streets are the most fashionable and splendid in the city. The parade ground, near the basin, which is a harbour, dug out to receive the lake vessels, is the most beautiful of the parades.

Its most conspicuous public buildings, are the cathedral, the Presbyterian church, the charity hospital, and the New Orleans college. . . . The jail and the French theatre are very large, and, externally disagreeable buildings. . . .

There are sometimes fifty steam-boats lying in the harbour. A clergyman from the North made with me the best enumeration that we could, and we calculated that there were from twelve to fifteen hundred flat boats lying along the river. They would average from forty to sixty tons burden. . . .

At the north part of the city is the basin, a harbour which has been dug to admit vessels from the lake. There is a canal perfectly straight, which leads from this basin to the *Bayou* St. John, a sluggish stream flowing from the swamps above into lake Pontchartrain.
(Timothy Flint, *Recollections of the Last Ten Years in the Valley of the Mississippi*, 218–19, 222, 226)

The son of Benjamin Latrobe leaves a poetic impression of New Orleans as he saw it in 1832–1833

What would you have me describe?—the ancient part of the city, its narrow streets, French and Spanish-built houses, with their showy coloured stuccoes, and iron balconies,—or the numerous Faubourgs, with their spacious pavements and tall ranges of handsome buildings? Would you look upon the square of the Cathedral, whitewashed and weather-stained without, and dusty within; the public edifices; the immense buildings erected by private companies for the pressing and warehousing of the produce of the cotton plantations? Or would you peep in upon the varieties of the human race which crowd every avenue, and swarm along the levees? Were I to make choice of a spot, from the scenes passing upon or within sight of which you would glean the most vivid idea of the characteristic features of this strange city, I should lead you to the levee in front of the square of the Cathedral, and bid you post yourself for an hour in the vicinity of the markets. . . .

The lower end of the square is open to the levee and the river, whose margin appears lined for upwards of two miles with ships and boats of every size as close as they can float. Highest up the stream lie the flats, arks, and barges, and below them the tier of steam-boats, fifty of which may be seen lying here at one time. Then comes the brigs ranged in rows, with their bows against the breast of the levee; these are succeeded by the three-masters, lying in tiers of two or three deep, with their broadside to the shore, and the scene presented by the whole margin of the river as you look down upon it from the levee, or from the roof of Bishop's Hotel in a sunny morning after a night of storm, when the sails of the whole are exposed to the air, and their signals or national flags abroad, is one of the most singularly beautiful you can conceive.
(Charles Joseph Latrobe, *The Rambler in North America: MDCCCXXXII.—MDCCCXXXIII.*, 2:331–32)

NOUVELLE ORLÉANS

Nouvelle Orléans. Drawn by [Ambroise Louis] Garnerai [i.e. Garneray]. Engraved by [Sigismond] Himely. Printed or published chez Hocquart Succr de Mr. Basset rue St. Jacques, Paris. From *Vues des Côtes de France dans l'Océan et dans la Méditerranée* (Paris, ca. 1830–1835), vol. 5. Aquatint, 14 1/8 x 17 7/8 in. (35.9 x 45.5 cm).

Historic New Orleans Collection

Folio 5.   In the Mid–1830s New Orleans Continues to Impress Its Visitors with Its Vitality

Robert Baird includes information about changes in housing and the increase in population

In the central part of the city the houses are contiguous; but in the sub-urbs, or Fauxbourgs, they are separated generally by intervening gardens, of orange, olive, fig, and lemon trees, &c. The wooden buildings are giving place gradually to those of brick; and great efforts are making to improve the streets with good pavements, stone, sewers, &c. . . .

The population has increased rapidly. In 1810, it was 17,242; in 1820, it was 27,156; and in 1830, it was 46,310. This is the stationary or fixed popu-lation. In the season of business, that is, the winter, 20 or 25,000 more may be added.

He takes his readers for a tour of the levee

As far as he can see almost, up and down, the margin is lined with flat-boats, come from above, from every part of the Valley of the Mississippi. Some are laden with flour, others with corn, others with meat of various kinds, others with live stock, cattle, hogs, horses, or mules. Some have travel-ling stores: occasionally, some are to be found which are full of negroes; and some full of what is infinitely worse, "Old Monongahela" whiskey. Along the lower part, he will see a forest of masts; higher up, he may see 20 or 30 steam-boats, with their bows up against the levee, or else projecting over an "up-country" flat-boat. Every day some come from above and others de-part, on excursions of one or two thousand miles, to St. Louis, or Louisville, or Nashville, or Pittsburg, or hundreds of other places. For distance is no longer thought of in this region—it is almost annihilated by steam. And if he casts his eye down the river, he may see a whole fleet, sometimes, coming up without a sail stretched, or an oar manned—all carried along, and that not at a slow rate, by a *steam* tow-boat, of tremendous power. I was per-fectly amazed the first time I saw this spectacle. It was the Grampus tow-boat, marching up, having two large ships grappled to her sides, two or three brigs at a cable's length behind, and still further in the rear, one or two schooners and two or three sloops! all moving along very reluctantly, and not unlike a number of rogues escorted . . . to a court of Justice, who march along, because they cannot help it.

([Robert Baird], *View of the Valley of the Mississippi, or the Emigrant's and Trav-eller's Guide to the West . . . ,* 278–81)

A visitor from the North adds his comments about the city and some of its features

After passing the market on our right, a massive colonnade, about two hundred and fifty feet in length, we left the Levée, and its endless tier of shipping which had bordered one side of our walk all the way, and passing under the China-trees, that still preserved their unbroken line along the river, we crossed Levée-street, a broad, spacious esplanade, running along the front of the main body or block of the city, separating it from the Levée, and forming a magnificent thoroughfare along the whole extensive river-line. From this highway streets shoot off at right angles, till they terminate in the swamp somewhat less than a league back from the river. . . . Though the water, or shore-line, is very nearly semi-circular, the Levée-street, above mentioned, does not closely follow the shore, but is broken into two angles, from which the streets diverge as before mentioned. These streets are again intersected by others running parallel with the Levée-street, dividing the city into squares, except where the perpendicular streets meet the angles, where necessarily the "squares" are lessened in breadth at the extremity nearest the river, and occasionally form pentagons and parallelograms, with *oblique* sides, if I may so express it.

After crossing Levée-street, we entered Rue St. Pierre, which issues from it south of the grand square. This square is an open green, surrounded by a lofty iron railing, within which troops of boys . . . were playing, shouting and merry making. . . . The front of this extensive square was open to the river, bordered with its dark line of ships; on each side were blocks of rusty looking brick buildings of Spanish and French construction, with projecting balconies, heavy cornices, and lofty jalousies or barricaded windows. The lower stories of these buildings were occupied by retailers of fancy wares, vintners, segar manufacturers, dried fruit sellers, and all the other members of the innumerable occupations to which the volatile, ever ready Frenchman can always turn himself and a *sous* into the bargain. . . .

On the remaining side of this square stood the cathedral, its dark moorish-looking towers flinging their vast shadows far over the water. The whole front of the large edifice was thrown into deep shade, so that when we ap-proached, it presented one black mingled mass, frowning in stern and majes-tic silence upon the surrounding scene.

Leaving this venerable building at the right, we turned into Chartres-street, the second parallel with the Levée and the most fashionable, as well as great-est business street in the city. As we proceeded, *cafés,* confectioners, fancy stores, millineries, parfumeurs, &c. &c., were passed in rapid succession; each one of them presenting something new, and always something to strike the attention of strangers, like ourselves, for the first time in the only "for-eign" city in the United States.

([Ingraham], *The South-West. By a Yankee,* 1:90–93)

New Orleans, Taken from the Opposite Side a Short Distance above the Middle or Picayune Ferry. Sketched by A[ntoine] Mondelli and painted by W[illiam] J[ames] Bennett. Engraved by W[illiam] J[ames] Bennett. Published by Henry I. Megarey, New York, 1841. Aquatint, 16 7/8 x 25 1/8 in. (42.9 x 63.7 cm).

Stokes Collection, New York Public Library

Folio 6.   A Scottish Journalist Leaves a Splendidly Detailed Description of New Orleans in 1847

Alex Mackay paints a word picture of the city's busy harbor

Nothing can be more imposing than [New Orleans] as you approach it by the stream. Almost the entire length of the noble amphitheatric front which it presents to you is in view; the rows of warehouses and other commercial establishments, which follow each other in rapid succession, extending for nearly three miles along the margin of the river. In front of these, and close to the quays . . . are numerous vessels of all kinds, and bearing the flags of almost all nations. Opposite the upper portion of the town, the river is chiefly occupied by the barges and keel-boats which ascend and descend the river for short distances . . . and which are also extensively used for the purpose of loading and unloading the vessels in the harbour. A little below, you discern a multitude of square-rigged vessels of almost every variety of tonnage, lying moored abreast of each other. . . . Below them again are scores of steamers, built in the most fantastic manner, and painted of the most gaudy colours, most of them river boats, but some plying between New Orleans and Texas. There are also tug-boats and ferry-boats to communicate with Algiers, a small town directly opposite New Orleans, to give still greater variety to this motley group of wood, paint, paddle-boxes and funnels. Still further down, and near the lower end of the harbour, are brigs, schooners, and sloops, and other craft of a smaller size, designed for, and used chiefly in the coasting trade of the Gulf. . . . Mid-stream is crowded as well as the quays, some vessels dropping down with the current, and others being tugged up against it—some steamers arriving from above and some from below, and others departing upwards and downwards—ferry-boats crossing and re-crossing at short intervals—small boats shooting in different directions; and barges, some full, some empty, floating lazily on the current. On a fine morning, with the sun shining brightly on town and river, the scene is one of the most lively description.

He tells his readers about the old part of the city

The length of the city is parallel to the river—its width, which averages about a mile; being in the direction back from the stream. The city proper, or the old portion of New Orleans, occupies the centre of its position upon the river, and extends back to the outskirts of the town, upon the swamps behind it. Here the streets are both narrow and dirty, but straight and otherwise regularly planned. The houses on either side combine to some extent the more prominent features of modern French and Spanish architecture, and are almost all covered with stucco, and painted of some lively colour, generally white, yellow, or ochre.

Mackay helps his readers understand the contrast between the old town and the newer extensions beyond Canal Street

No one can enter Edinburgh for the first time without being at once struck by the decided contrast presented between the old town and the new. . . . A contrast resembling this, but neither so striking nor complete, the tourist may witness in New Orleans. This contrast is between the old town and the American quarter. The dividing line between them is Canal-street, a broad and spacious thoroughfare, lined throughout with trees, dividing the two quarters from each other. . . . You not only, in crossing Canal-street, seem to bound from one century into another, but you might also fancy that you had crossed the boundary line between two conterminous nations. On the American side the streets are wider, better paved, better lighted, and better cleaned; the architecture is of the most modern style; the shops are large, showy, and elegant.

He is not impressed by the public buildings of New Orleans, but he admires the residences on the outskirts of the city

New Orleans does not present much that is striking in the way of public buildings. Being the capital of the State, all the public officers are of course here; but they are almost all accommodated, as are the two branches of the legislature, in a large building, neither elegant nor imposing, which was once a charity hospital. It has for some time been intended to errect [*sic*] a capitol more in keeping with the importance of the city and the dignity of the State; but as yet that intention has, in being postponed, but shared the fate of the great bulk of commendable resolutions. Some of the municipal buildings, though not very extensive, are not without merit, and the same may be said of a few of those dedicated to commerce and its exigencies. Decidedly one of the finest structures in New Orleans is the St. Charles Hotel, situated in the American quarter, and surpassing in extent and good management, though not in exterior elegance, the famous Astor House in New York. . . . It may consequently be said to be without its equal anywhere else. . . .

There are some very elegant and attractive looking residences in the immediate vicinity of the town. They are surrounded, for the most part, by gardens, rich with the perfume of the magnolia, and shaded with orange groves and a great variety of other trees. These houses are generally inhabited by the permanent residents of the place, either those who have been born in Louisiana or immigrants into the State, who have been long enough within the sedgy limits of the Delta to be thoroughly acclimated.

(Alex Mackay, *The Western World; or, Travels in the United States in 1846–47 . . .* , 2:79–83)

VUE DE LA NOUVELLE ORLEANS

DEUXIEME MUNICIPALITE

VIEW OF NEW ORLEANS

SECOND MUNICIPALITY

Vue de la Nouvelle Orleans Deuxieme Municipalite. View of New Orleans Second Municipality. Lithographed by P[aul] Cavailler. Printed by J[ules] Manouvrier & [François] Chav[in], [1843?]. Lithograph, 14 3/16 x 18 5/8 in. (36.1 x 47.4 cm).

Special Collections, Howard-Tilton Memorial Library, Tulane University

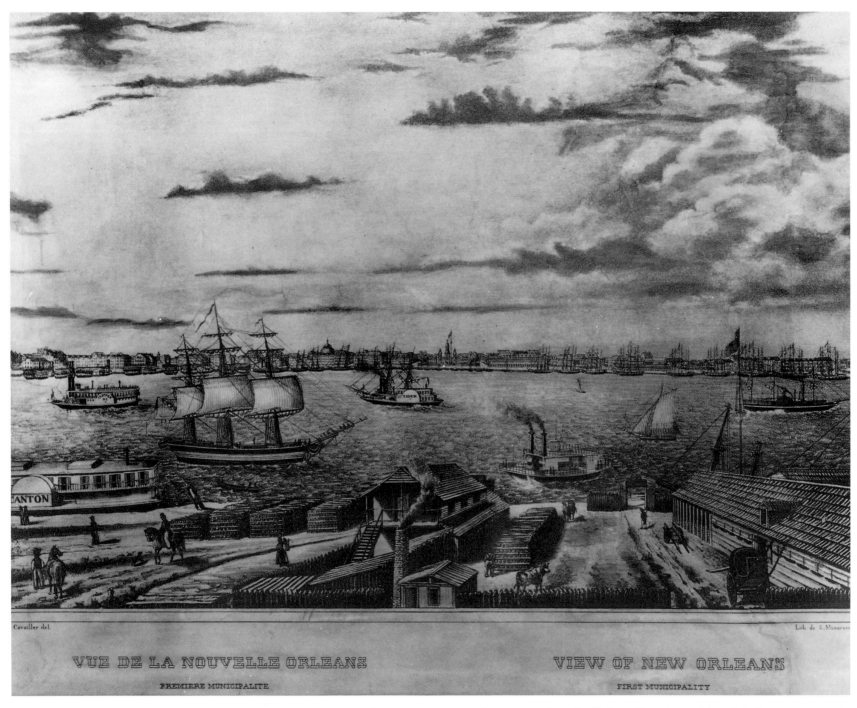

Vue de la Nouvelle Orleans Premiere Municipalite. View of New Orleans First Municipality. Drawn by P[aul] Cavailler. Printed by J[ules] Manouvrier & [François] Chav[in], [1843?]. Lithograph, 14 3/16 x 18 11/16 in. (36.1 x 47.6 cm).

Special Collections, Howard-Tilton Memorial Library, Tulane University

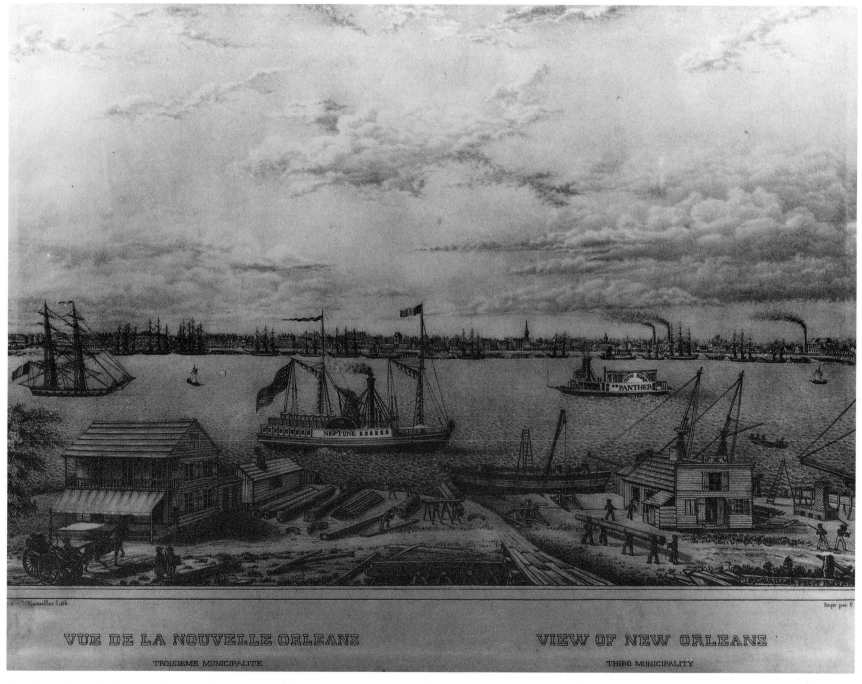

Vue de la Nouvelle Orleans Troisieme Municipalite. View of New Orleans Third Municipality. Lithographed by P[aul] Cavailler. Printed by F[rançois] Chav[in], [1843?]. Lithograph, 14 1/8 x 18 9/16 in. (36 x 47.3 cm).

Special Collections, Howard-Tilton Memorial Library, Tulane University

Folio 7.   Observers before and after the Civil War Find New Orleans a City of Contrasts

A Canadian author in 1857 encounters the differences between the old and new portions of the city

The first feeling on entering New Orleans is, that you are in a city differing from all others in the Union. Even the American quarter has borrowed and adopted the old French architecture, although now and then you come upon one of those enormities in the shape of a porticoed dwelling-house peculiar to New England. Buildings worthy of note, as models of architecture, there are none. The St. Charles Hotel is the only striking edifice in the city. Even the old Cathedral, with its *place d'armes,* is not a fine building, and the two Spanish structures by its side are striking only because they differ from the established system of edifices. The new Custom House, however, promises to be an exception. It is surrounded by scaffolding, and is now undergoing construction, the granite being brought from Boston, for there is no out-crop of rock near New Orleans—hence no building stone. Consequently the houses, even the public buildings, are built of brick, and are covered with composition, which soon looks dingy. Hence, even the best buildings have an air of dilapidation; not the wear of age, but a species of architectural shabby gentility, arising from the discolored weathering of the outside. The city may be said to be divided into two parts, Canal Street being the boundary. In one the language—the mode of doing business—the articles sold, are French. In the other quarter, we have all the bustle and stir of any other large American city. Not that the French portion is quiet; on the contrary, Chartres and Royal Streets constitute, with the northeastern side of Canal Street, the fashionable promenade. They are narrow thoroughfares, each house with its balcony and its paved arched gateway, through the latter of which can be seen the courtyard, paved with brick or flagged. Now and then you come to the heavy cornices of an old Spanish house, while beside it is a shop with its quaint French dormer windows, rising up from the tiled roof.

He looks at Jackson Square

The old *place d'armes* in front [of the Cathedral] is now laid out into a garden with walks, in which stands the equestrian figure of Jackson. As a composition, it struck me that everything is sacrificed to the position of the horse. . . . One, however, can forgive any fault, for the place would be incomplete without the statue. But certainly it wants repose, and has a clumsy look. . . . The gardens . . . are but shabbily laid out, which is inexcusable when the resources of the climate are considered.

And he ponders the choice of the city's site and visits the cemeteries

As one looks upon the Mississippi, which curves and winds round New Orleans, as it does in every part of its course, and from which the title of the Crescent City is derived, we look in vain for the reasons which prompted the choice of the site. So far as the river is concerned, the city might have been a hundred miles higher or fifty lower, the distance from the mouth of the Mississippi being one hundred miles, and the ground is so low that the drainage runs away from the river. Immediately behind the city is a low swamp, which generates fever and disease, and which is the secret of the unhealthy condition of the place. On such low ground the city is built. Indeed it is impossible to dig a grave, for water is immediately met with, and consequently the cemeteries of New Orleans differ from other spots where the dead rest, in the peculiarity that the latter are all above ground. For tombs in the literal sense of the word receive them. In some instances, these are merely brick receptacles admitting a single coffin; in others, they are large structures rising thirty and forty feet from the ground, formed into compartments, and frequently decorated with much architectural embellishment. . . . The appearance of a cemetery is therefore striking in the extreme. As you walk among these last homes of your fellows, you feel indeed that you are in the company of their remains. When beneath the sod, you forget the few feet between you and them. . . . There are several such cemeteries in New Orleans, one I believe in each ward. They are constantly open, and are visited by nearly every stranger.

([William Kingsford], *Impressions of the West and South, during a Six Weeks' Holiday,* 54–59)

Alfred Waud, an artist for Harper's Weekly, *looks at other features of New Orleans in 1867*

To an artist New Orleans is the most characteristic of all the cities of the United States. It abounds in the picturesque, especially in the French quarter, where some of the buildings are very old. Many of these are only one story high, moss-grown and weather-stained, with tiled roofs overhanging the streets, and the beams and scantling visible in the plastered walls. Catholic churches and monastic institutions overlook the smaller buildings, the institutions most withdrawn in the bosom of dreamy gardens, which sleep all day in the rays of the torrid sun, but at night rustle merrily to the cool seabreeze which evening brings to fan the heated populace, who incontinently people the door-steps and side-walks to enjoy it.

Of the better class of houses the principal peculiarity is the veranda, or gallery, not seldom projecting from several stories of the same building and mostly of graceful iron-work.

(A[lfred R.] Waud, "Sketches of New Orleans")

Bird's Eye View of New-Orleans. Drawn, lithographed, and printed by J[ohn] Bachman. Published by the Agents A. Guerber & Co. 160 Pearl St. New York, 1851. Lithograph, 24 1/4 x 31 1/2 in. (61.7 x 80.1 cm).

Prints and Photographs, Library of Congress

New Orleans from the Lower Cotton Press 1852. Drawn by [John] W[illiam] Hill and [Benjamin Franklin?] Smith. Lithographed by D[avid] W[illiam] Moody. Printed by Sarony & Major. Published by Smith Brothers & Co., 225 Fulton St., New York. Lithograph, 25 11/16 x 41 7/16 (65.2 x 105.3 cm).

Prints and Photographs, Library of Congress

New Orleans from St. Patricks. Church 1852. Drawn by J[ohn] W[illiam] Hill and [Benjamin Franklin?] Smith. Lithographed by B. F. Smith Jr. Printed by F[rancis] Michelin & Geo. E. Leefe 225 Fulton St. N.Y. New York. Published by Smith Brothers & Co. 225 Fulton St. Lithograph, 25 11/16 x 40 5/16 in. (65.2 x 102.4 cm).

Prints and Photographs, Library of Congress

Folio 8.   As New Orleans Grows, the Contrasts between Old and New Become Even Greater

Edward King in 1873 compares the French and American quarters

Step off from Canal street, that avenue of compromises which separates the French and the American quarters . . . and you will at once find yourself in a foreign atmosphere. A walk into the French section enchants you; the characteristics of an American city vanish; this might be Toulouse, or Bordeaux, or Marseilles! The houses are all of stone or brick, stuccoed or painted, the windows of each story descend to the floors, opening, like doors, upon airy, pretty balconies, protected by iron railings; quaint dormer windows peer from the great roofs; the street doors are massive, and large enough to admit carriages into the stone-paved court-yards, from which stairways communicate with the upper apartments. . . .

On the eastern and western sides of Jackson Square are the Pontalba buildings, large and not especially handsome brick structures, erected by the Countess Pontalba, many years ago. Chartres street, and all the avenues contributing to it, are thoroughly French in character; cafés, wholesale stores, pharmacies, shops for articles of luxury, all bear evidence of Gallic taste.

The American quarter of New Orleans is superior to the French in width of avenue, in beauty of garden and foliage; but to-day many streets there are grass-grown, and filled with ruts and hollows. In that section, not inaptly designated the "Garden City," there are many spacious houses surrounded by gardens, parks and orchards; orange-trees grow in the yards, and roses clamber in at the windows. The homes of well-to-do Americans . . . are found mostly on Louisiana and Napoleon avenues and on Prytania, Plaquemine, Chestnut, Camp, Jena, Cadiz, Valence, Bordeaux, and St. Charles streets. Along St. Charles street, near Canal, are the famous St. Charles Hotel; the Academy of Music, and the St. Charles Theatre, both well appointed theatrical edifices; and the Masonic, City, and Exposition Halls. Opposite the City Hall—one of the noblest public buildings in New Orleans, built of granite and white marble, in Grecian Ionic style—is Lafayette Square. On its southwestern side is the First Presbyterian Church; and at its southern extremity the Odd Fellows' Hall.

He describes Canal Street

Canal street is bordered by shops of no mean pretensions, and by many handsome residences . . . ; it boasts of Christ Church, the Varieties Theatre, the noted restaurant of Moreau, the statue of Henry Clay, a handsome fountain, and the new Custom-House. The buildings are not crowded together, as in New York and Paris; they are usually two or three stories high, and along the first story runs a porch which serves as a balcony to those dwelling above, and as protection from sun and rain to promenaders below. The

banks, insurance offices, and wholesale stores fronting on Canal street are elegant and modern, an improvement in the general tone of business architecture having taken place since the war.
(Edward King, *The Great South: A Record of Journeys* . . . , 1:28, 61–62)

An Australian visitor finds much to like as well as some things to criticize on his trip in 1876

Though large [New Orleans] is anything but a fine city, being built on the alluvial banks of the river, on ground lower than the high-water level, and only protected from inundations by a levee or embankment of earth, four feet high and fifteen feet wide. . . . The water that percolates through this embankment and the natural drainage is conducted by open gutters, which run through the streets, into a swamp that lies between the city and Lake Pontchartrain, three miles distant. . . .

The streets of New Orleans are very wide and handsome in appearance, though only the principal of them are paved. . . . The streets that are not paved, are simply quagmires: in winter they are not practicable at all, and even in summer the dust makes them almost impassable. The open gutters form a bad feature of the streets of New Orleans; these have very steep sides, and are crossed at street corners by small bridges, consisting of single stones, and allowing two persons only to cross at a time.

Canal street is the main business thoroughfare, and promenade; and may be said to divide the city into two pretty equal parts. It is nearly 200 feet wide, and has a grass-plot twenty-five feet wide, and bordered with two rows of trees in the centre, extending its whole length. Claiborne, Rampart, St. Charles, and Esplanade streets are embellished in the same manner. . . .

The churches of New Orleans are numerous and handsome. The most famous is the Roman Catholic Cathedral of St. Louis, which has an imposing façade, surmounted by a lofty blue-slated steeple and flanked by two towers, each capped by a smaller blue-slated spire. . . . The finest Episcopal Church is St. Peter's, which is a handsome specimen of Gothic architecture, and has a very rich interior. The Presbyterian Church is a fine structure in Greco-Doric style, and is much admired for its fine steeple. The Temple Sinai, the principal Jewish place of worship, has a light and elegant appearance; it is built of parti-coloured bricks, and has a handsome portico flanked by two towers, surmounted by tinted cupolas. Its Gothic windows are filled with beautifully stained glass, and the interior is remarkably rich and beautiful.
(Alfred Falk, *Trans-Pacific Sketches: A Tour through the United States and Canada*, 259, 261–62)

New-Orléans. New-Orlins. Unsigned. Printed and published by F. C. Wentzel, Weissenburg (Elsass.), [ca. 1873?]. Lithograph, 10 15/16 x 14 11/16 in. (27.9 x 37.3 cm).

Preston Player Collection, Knox College Library, Galesburg, Ill.

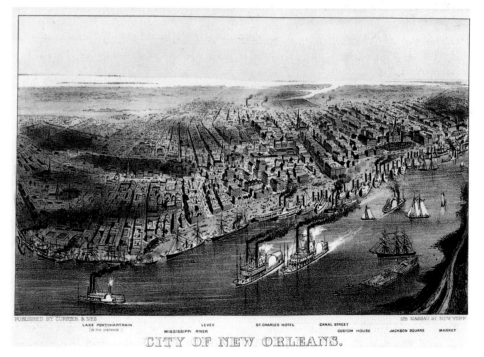

City of New Orleans. Published by Currier & Ives, New York, [ca. 1873]. Lithograph, 8 13/16 x 12 5/8 in. (22.4 x 32.1 cm).

Preston Player Collection, Knox College Library, Galesburg, Ill.

Folio 9.   Mark Twain and Charles Dudley Warner Give Their Impressions of New Orleans in the 1880s

Mark Twain returns to the city in 1882 after a long absence

The city itself had not changed—to the eye. It had greatly increased in spread and population, but the look of the town was not altered. The dust, waste-paper-littered, was still deep in the streets; the deep, trough-like gutters alongside the curb-stones were still half full of reposeful water with a dusty surface; the sidewalks were still—in the sugar and bacon region—incumbered by casks and barrels and hogsheads; the great blocks of austerely plain commercial houses were as dusty-looking as ever.

Canal Street was finer, and more attractive and stirring than formerly, with its drifting crowds of people, its several processions of hurrying street-cars, and—toward evening—its broad second-story verandas crowded with gentlemen and ladies clothed according to the latest mode.

Not that there is any "architecture" in Canal Street: to speak in broad, general terms, there is no architecture in New Orleans, except in the cemeteries. It seems a strange thing to say of a wealthy, far-seeing, and energetic city of a quarter of a million inhabitants, but it is true. There is a huge granite U.S. Custom-house—costly enough, genuine enough, but as a decoration it is inferior to a gasometer. It looks like a state prison. But it was built before the war. Architecture in America may be said to have been born since the war. New Orleans, I believe, has had the good luck—and in a sense the bad luck—to have had no great fire in late years. It must be so. If the opposite had been the case, I think one would be able to tell the "burnt district" by the radical improvement in its architecture over the old forms. . . .

However, New Orleans has begun—just this moment, as one may say. When completed, the new Cotton Exchange will be a stately and beautiful building; massive, substantial, full of architectural graces; no shams or false pretences or uglinesses about it anywhere. To the city, it will be worth many times its cost, for it will breed its species. What has been lacking hitherto, was a model to build toward; something to educate eye and taste.

I have been speaking of public architecture only. The domestic article in New Orleans is reproachless, notwithstanding it remains as it always was. All the dwellings are of wood—in the American part of the town, I mean—and all have a comfortable look. Those in the wealthy quarter are spacious; painted snow-white usually and generally have wide verandas, or double verandas, supported by ornamental columns. These mansions stand in the centre of large grounds, and rise, garlanded with roses, out of the midst of swelling masses of shining green foliage and many-colored blossoms.
(Mark Twain, *Life on the Mississippi*, 424, 427–28)

Charles Dudley Warner falls in love with New Orleans in 1885 despite—or because of—its shabbiness

The first time I saw New Orleans was on a Sunday morning in the month of March. We alighted from the train at the foot of Esplanade Street, and walked along through the French Market, and by Jackson Square to the Hotel Royal. The morning, after rain, was charming; there was a fresh breeze from the river; the foliage was a tender green; in the balconies and on the mouldering window-ledges flowers bloomed, and in the decaying courts climbing-roses mingled their perfume with the orange. . . . Nothing could be more shabby than the streets, ill-paved, with undulating sidewalks and open gutters green with slime, and both stealing and giving odor; little canals in which the cat, become the companion of the crawfish, and the vegetable in decay sought in vain a current to oblivion; the streets with rows of one-story houses, wooden, with green doors and batten window-shutters, or brick, with the painted stucco peeling off, the line broken often by an edifice of two stories, with galleries and delicate tracery of wrought-iron, houses pink and yellow and brown and gray—colors all blending and harmonious when we get a long vista of them and lose the details of view in the broad artistic effect. Nothing could be shabbier than the streets, unless it is the tumble-down, picturesque old market, bright with flowers and vegetables. . . . I liked it all from the first; I lingered long in that morning walk, liking it more and more, in spite of its shabbiness, but utterly unable to say then or ever since wherein its charm lies. I suppose we are all wrongly made up and have a fallen nature; else why is it that while the most thrifty and neat and orderly city only wins our approval, and perhaps gratifies us intellectually, such a thriftless, battered and stained, and lazy old place as the French quarter of New Orleans takes our hearts? . . .

The new residence portion of the American quarter [that] occupies the vast area in the bend of the river west of the business blocks . . . is in character a great village rather than a city. Not all its broad avenues and handsome streets are paved (and those that are not are in some seasons impassable), its houses are nearly all of wood, most of them detached, with plots of ground and gardens, and as the quarter is very well shaded, the effect is bright and agreeable. In it are many stately residences, occupying a square or half a square, and embowered in foliage and flowers.
(Charles Dudley Warner, *Studies in the South and West with Comments on Canada*, 38, 40, 43)

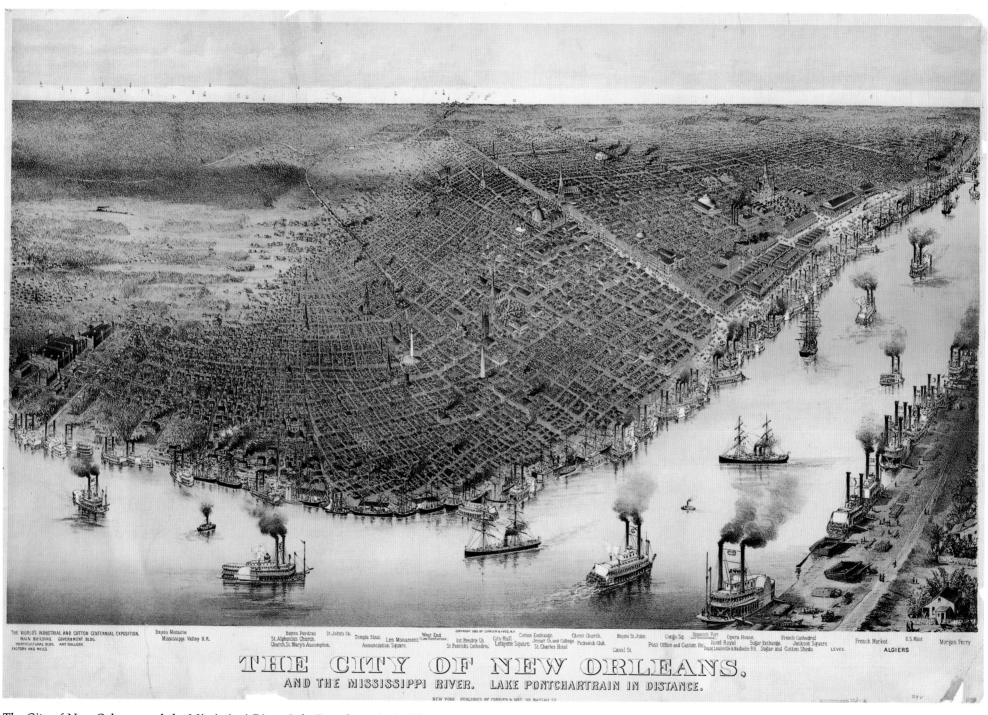

THE CITY OF NEW ORLEANS,
AND THE MISSISSIPPI RIVER. LAKE PONTCHARTRAIN IN DISTANCE.

The City of New Orleans, and the Mississippi River. Lake Pontchartrain in Distance. Unsigned. Published by Currier & Ives, New York, 1885. Lithograph, 23 7/8 x 35 in. (60.8 x 89 cm).

Prints and Photographs, Library of Congress

Published by GUSTAVE KOECKERT. 3. ANNUNCIATION SQUARE. 5. MARGARETS PLACE. 7. SHOT TOWER. 9. COURT BUILDING. 11. CITY HALL. 13 CANAL ST FERRY. 15. U.S. CUSTOM HOUSE. 16. LA. SUGAR REFINERY. 17. SUGAR EX. **BIRDS EYE VIEW OF THE** 21. CHRIST CHURCH. 22. 2ND DISTRICT FERRY. 23. JACKSON SQUARE. 25. CONGO SQUARE. 27. ESPLANADE FERRY. 29. U.S. MINT. 31. LAKE PONTCHARTRAIN. Copyright Secured 1883 Thea POHLMANN & Co.

1. JACKSON ST FERRY. 2. EXPOSITION PARK. 4. COLISEUM SQUARE. 6. LEE CIRCLE. 8. ST PATRICK'S CHURCH. 10 LAFAYETTE SQUARE. 12. PRODUCE EX. 14. COTTON EX. **CITY OF NEW ORLEANS.** 24. ST LOUIS CATHEDRAL. 26. FRENCH MARKET. 28. LOWER CITY PARK. 30. WEST END.

18. PICKWICK CLUB. 19. CLAY STATUE. 20. SUGAR SHEDS. **AND SUBURBS.**

Birds Eye View of the City of New Orleans. And Suburbs. Unsigned. Published by Gustave Koeckert. Copyright 1883 by Thea Pohlmann & Co. Lithograph, 24 7/8 x 40 1/4 in. (63.3 x 102.4 cm).

The New-York Historical Society

New Orleans, Louisiana, from the air, April 15, 1992.

Alex MacLean

Folio 10.   As the Second Most Important River Town in Louisiana, Baton Rouge Attracts Many Visitors Who Describe Its Features

Timothy Flint sees the place in 1823 and sets down his impressions

Baton Rouge is a village charmingly situated on the eastern bank of the Mississippi, one hundred and fifty miles above New Orleans. . . . The United States barracks are built in a fine style, and are, I should suppose, among the most commodious works of that class. From the esplanade, the prospect is most delightful, including a great extent of the coast, with its handsome houses and rich cultivation below, and commanding an extensive view into the back country at the east. . . . On the parade stands a beautiful monument of white marble consecrated to the memory of some officers of the garrison, who deceased here. It is not an expensive, but a very striking monument.

In the winter of 1823, in January, I ascended the Mississippi. The verdure of the country about this town, as seen from the steam-boat was brilliant; and the town itself, rising with such a fine swell from the river, with its singularly shaped French and Spanish houses, and green squares, looked in the distance like a fine landscape painting. The village is compact, and probably contains two or three thousand inhabitants.

(Flint, *Recollections of the Last Ten Years in the Valley of the Mississippi*, 215–16)

A Yankee traveler in 1834 provides a longer description of a place he found attractive

Baton Rouge is now in sight, a few miles above. As we approach it the character of the scene changes. Hills once more relieve the eye, so long wearied with gazing upon a flat yet beautiful country. These are the first hills that gladden the sight of the traveller as he ascends the river. They are to the northerner like oases in a desert. How vividly and how agreeably does the sight of their green slopes, and graceful undulations, conjure up the loved and heart-cherished scenes of home!

We are now nearly opposite the town, which is pleasantly situated upon the declivity of the hill, retreating over its brow and spreading out on a plain in the rear, where the private dwellings are placed, shaded and half embowered in the rich foliage of that loveliest of all shade-trees, "the pride of China." The stores and other places of business are upon the front street, which runs parallel with the river. The site of the town is about forty feet above the highest flood, and rises by an easy and gentle swell from the water. The barracks, a short distance from the village, are handsome and commodious, constructed around a pentagonal area—four noble buildings forming four sides, while the fifth is open, fronting upon the river. The buildings are brick, with lofty colonnades and double galleries running along the whole front. The columns are yellow-stuccoed, striking the eye with a more pleasing effect, than the red glare of brick. The view of these noble structures from the river, as we passed, was very fine. From the esplanade there is an extensive and commanding prospect of the inland country—the extended shores, stretching out north and south, dotted with elegant villas, and richly enamelled by their high state of cultivation. . . . The town, from the hasty survey which I was enabled to make of it, must be a delightful residence. It is neat and well built; the French and Spanish style of architecture prevails. The view of the town from the deck of the steamer is highly beautiful. The rich, green swells rising gradually from the water—its pleasant streets, bordered with the umbrageous China tree—its colonnaded dwellings—its mingled town and rural scenery, and its pleasant suburbs, give it an air of quiet and novel beauty, such as one loves to gaze upon in old landscapes which the imagination fills with ideal images of its own.

([Ingraham], *The South-West. By a Yankee*, 1:251–53)

An 1850 guidebook to places along the Mississippi notes Baton Rouge's new status as state capital and lists the main public buildings

Baton Rouge . . . is the capital of Louisiana. It is handsomely situated on the last bluff that is seen, in descending the river. The site is thirty or forty feet above the highest overflow of the river. The bluff rises from the river by a gentle and gradual swell, and the town, as seen from the river, in the months when the greatest verdure prevails, rising so regularly and beautifully from the banks, with its singularly shaped french and spanish houses, and its green squares, looks like a finely painted landscape. It is one of the most beautiful and pleasantly situated places on the lower Mississippi.

The U.S. Government has here an extensive arsenal, with barracks for four hundred soldiers, and a fine hospital. The barracks are built in fine style, and present a handsome appearance from the river. From the esplanade, the prospect is delightful, commanding a great extent of the coast, with its handsome houses and rich cultivation below, and an extensive view of the back country at the east.

There is here, also, a land office of the United States, a court house, the Penitentiary of the State, four churches, an academy and college, and a splendid building is now in course of erection, for a State House. The population is about three thousand.

(*Conclins' New River Guide, or A Gazetteer of all the Towns on the Western Waters*, 112–13)

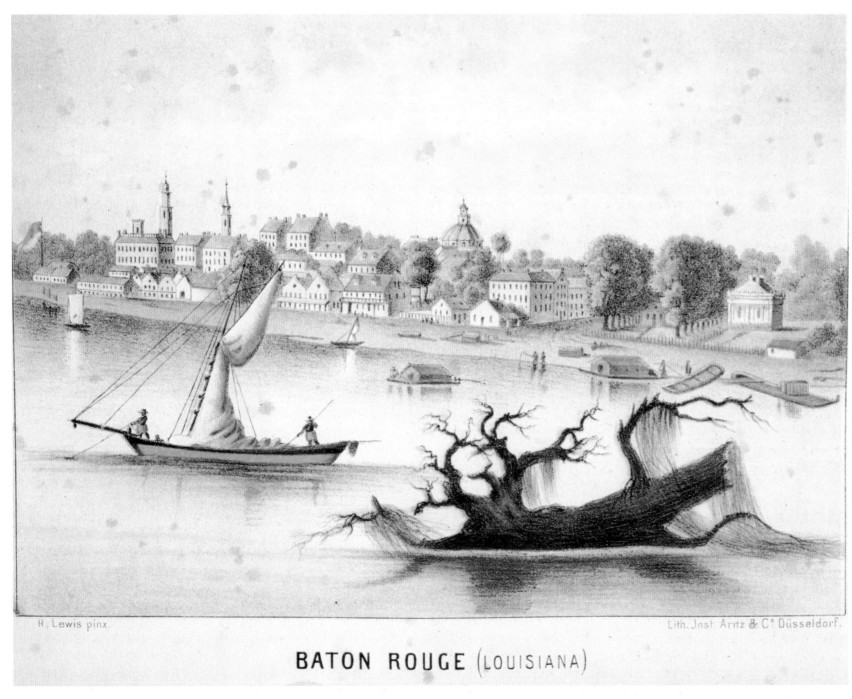

H. Lewis pinx.   Lith. Jnst. Arntz & Cᵒ Düsseldorf.

BATON ROUGE (LOUISIANA)

Baton Rouge (Louisiana). Drawn by H[enry] Lewis. [Printed by C. H. Muller, Aachen.] Published by Arnz & Co., Düsseldorf, [1854–1857].
Lithograph, 5 7/8 x 7 11/16 in. (14.9 x 19.5 cm).
Minnesota Historical Society

View of Baton Rouge Capital of Louisiana. Drawn and Litho by J. A. Maurel of B[aton] R[ouge]. Printed by X. Magny, Lithor. Exchange Alley N[ew] Or[leans], ca. 1853. Lithograph, 14 3/4 x 25 7/8 in. (37.7 x 65.9 cm).

Special Collections, Howard-Tilton Memorial Library, Tulane University

Drawn by A.Persac.

Lith: by Pessou & Simon, 161 Chartres Str. N.Orls

BATON ROUGE

(Capital of Louisiana)

Baton Rouge (Capital of Louisiana). Drawn and lithographed by [Marie] A[drien] Persac. Printed by Pessou & Simon, 161 Chartres St. N[ew] Orl[ean]s, [1855–1856]. Lithograph, 14 7/8 x 20 5/16 in. (37.9 x 51.8 cm).

Louisiana State University Museum of Art, Gift of James H. Huguet

VIEW OF BATON ROUGE, LOUISIANA.

View of Baton Rouge, Louisiana. Unsigned. From *Ballou's Pictorial Drawing-Room Companion* 8 (May 12, 1855): 304. Wood engraving, 5 1/8 x 9 3/8 in. (13 x 23.8 cm).
John W. Reps

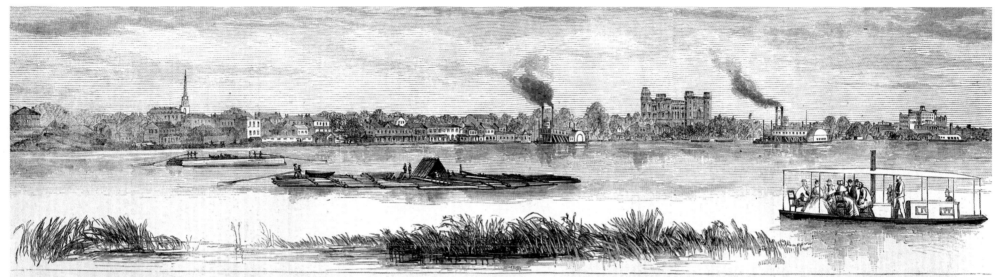

BATON ROUGE, LOUISIANA.

Baton Rouge, Louisiana. Drawn by A[lfred] R. Waud. From *Harper's Weekly* 10 (September 8, 1866): 564. Wood engraving, 9 1/8 x 13 13/16 in. (23.1 x 35 cm).

Olin Library, Cornell University

Folio 11.   Early Travelers on the Lower Mississippi Find Natchez One of the Few Settled Places

Francis Baily writes about a primitive Natchez in 1797

The houses are chiefly framed buildings; but, though this country has been settled so long, there is all that inattention to neatness, cleanliness, and the comforts attending thereon, that there is in a country just cleared. I have seen houses in this place (and those possessed by persons assuming a degree of consequence in the country) scarcely furnished beyond the first stage of civilization, when a few boards nailed together have served for a bedstead, and a mattress covered with a few blankets for a bed, when there has been scarcely a chair to sit down upon, or a table to place anything on, but everything in the greatest confusion and disorder about the room. This, to be sure, is not universally so: on the contrary, I have seen others fitted up in the neatest manner possible; but then in the greatest plainness, without any of those luxuries which decorate even the cottages of our English farmers.
(Baily, *Journal of a Tour in Unsettled Parts of North America in 1796 & 1797*, 151)

A decade later Thomas Ashe is more favorably impressed by what he sees

This city . . . contains about three hundred houses, and two thousand five hundred inhabitants, including blacks, who are very numerous. There is a printing-office and several very extensive mercantile stores. There is also a Roman Catholic Church, but the Americans have stripped it of its Spanish possessions, shut up the church, and have not yet erected one of their own. There is a great number of mechanics in the city, whose wages are very high, as is labour of every kind. The market is proportionably extravagant. Every article, except venison and game, is as dear as in London. The citizens, however, are enabled to endure the high price of provisions, by their trade between New Orleans and the back and upper country. . . .

There is an academy here, but it is much neglected. Gambling and horse-racing are the prevailing amusements. In winter there are balls and concerts—I cannot say how elegant or chaste, not having seen many of the ladies by whom they are frequented, they, for the most part, being at their summer residences, scattered around the city. The men drink profusely. It is difficult to escape from their parties under three bottles of wine a man.
(Thomas Ashe, *Travels in America, Performed in 1806 . . .* , 316–17)

A French artist and writer records his observations of the city

The city of *Natchez* is a mile in the interior, and behind an eminence, I was going to say mountain, so elevated did this acclivity of about one hundred feet appear to me, after the low country of Southern Louisiana. Having ascended the Spanish fort, a more expanded and superb prospect presented itself, on account of the varied windings which the Mississippi presented to my view. I then visited the city, containing about three hundred houses; it is as yet in its infancy, but buildings are erecting in all directions. It is as well arranged as the inequality of the soil upon which it stands will admit; since it occupies the summits of several small hills, which give it a very picturesque effect. . . . The population consists for the most part of Anglo Americans, although some Germans and French are to be found.
(E[douard] de Montulé, *A Voyage to North America, and the West Indies, in 1817*, 63)

A British traveler in 1830 admires Natchez for its attractive houses and beautiful trees

Natchez . . . is very beautifully situated on high grounds on the east side of the river, at the distance of about three-quarters of a mile from the shore, and is the largest town of the State of Mississippi, containing a population of 5000 or 6000 people. . . . One of the passengers, with whom I had got well acquainted, agreed to walk with me to the town, which is well laid out, containing many handsome houses, and which commands delightful views. Indeed, this is one of the most beautiful towns in the United States, but occasionally very unhealthy. The pride of India tree, shading the streets, was in blossom, and the odour charming. The top of this tree is full of blossoms, having a greater resemblance to the lilac than to any other of the flowering shrubs.
(James Stuart, *Three Years in North America*, 2:296–97)

The author of a travel guide published in 1834 extols the beauty and prosperity of the town

Natchez is the most important town in this state. . . . It is a place of great wealth and business. The society is good. Here are churches of Episcopalians, Presbyterians, Methodists, Baptists, and Catholics. Along the margin of the river and below the bluff upon which the principal town stands, is what is called *Natchez-below-the-hill,*—a collection of warehouses, boat stores, grog-shops, &c. . . .

The city of Natchez is one of the most beautiful places in the Valley of the Mississippi. . . . The streets are wide, and adorned with the China tree. The houses of the wealthier inhabitants are widely separated, each seeming to occupy a square, surrounded with orange trees, palmetto, and other beautiful shrubbery. The public buildings are, the court-house, churches, academy, &c. The inhabitants are distinguished for their intelligence, refinement and hospitality.
([Baird], *View of the Valley of the Mississippi*, 267)

Town and Fort of Natchez. [Drawn by Georges Bois St. Lys?] Engraved by Tardieu l'aíné. From the atlas volume of Georges Henri Victor Collot, *A Journey in North America, Containing a Survey of the Countries Watered by the Mississippi, Ohio, Missouri, and Other Affluing Rivers . . .* (1826), pl. 34. Lithograph facsimile of engraving, 7 3/4 x 10 3/4 in. (19.6 x 27.2 cm).

Olin Library, Cornell University

View of the fort of the Natchez. Engraved by Tardieu l'aíné. From Collot, *A Journey in North America,* pl. 13. Lithograph facsimile of engraving, 5 7/8 x 7 5/8 in. (14.9 x 19.3 cm).

Olin Library, Cornell University

Natchez. [Drawn by Charles-Alexandre Lesueur, ca. 1828. Printed in France before 1846.] Lithograph, 5 3/8 x 7 5/8 in. (13.7 x 19.3 cm).

Edward Caldwell Collection, Knox College Library, Galesburg, Ill.

Vue d'un village à un mille des Natchez. Drawn and lithographed by Ed[ouard] de Montulé. From Montulé, *Voyage en Amérique, en Italie, en Siciel et en Egypte, Pendant les Anées 1816, 1817, 1818, et 1819* (Paris: Dalaunay, 1821). Lithograph, 4 7/16 x 6 3/16 in. (11.3 x 15.8 cm).

Historic New Orleans Collection

Folio 12.   In the Mid–1830s Natchez Attracts Admiring Comments from a Discerning Yankee Visitor

Joseph Holt Ingraham describes the town for his readers

Natchez, mantled with rich green foliage like a garment, with its handsome structures and fine avenues, here a dome and there a tower, lies immediately before me. It is the very contrast to its straggling namesake below. The city proper consists of six streets, at right angles with the river, intersected by seven others of the same length, parallel with the stream. The front, or first parallel street, is laid out about one hundred yards back from the verge of the bluff, leaving a noble green esplanade along the front of the city, which not only adds to its beauty, but is highly useful as a promenade and parade ground. Shade trees are planted along the border, near the verge of the precipice, beneath which are placed benches, for the comfort of the lounger. . . .

The buildings on the front street face the river, and, with the exception of one or two private houses, with galleries and shrubbery . . . possess no peculiar interest. The town is entered from the parade by rude bridges at the termination of each street, spanning a dry, dilapidated brick aqueduct of large dimensions. . . .

I entered at once into the body of the city, which is built as compactly within itself and aloof from the suburbs as though it were separated from them by a wall; and in a few moments, after traversing two sides of a well-built square on fine side walks, I arrived at the "Mansion house," an extensive and commodious brick edifice said to be one of the best hotels in the south west.

The author writes of the business quarter of Natchez and its aristocratic patrons

Main-street is the "Broadway" of Natchez. It extends from the river to the eastern extremity of the city, about half a mile in length, dividing the town into nearly equal portions, north and south. . . . Here are all the banks and most of the dry goods and fancy stores. Here, consequently, is the centre of business, and, to the ladies, that of attraction. . . . In passing up this street, which is compactly built with handsome brick blocks, generally but two stories in height, the stranger is struck with the extraordinary number of private carriages, clustered before the doors of the most fashionable stores, or millineries, rolling through the street, or crossing and recrossing it from those by which it is intersected, nearly every moment, from eleven till two on each fair day. But few of these equipages are of the city: they are from the plantations in the neighbourhood, which spread out from the town over richly cultivated "hill and dale,"—a pleasant and fertile landscape—far into the interior.

He identifies the major public buildings

Natchez, like most of the minor cities of this country, cannot boast of any public buildings remarkable for harmonious conformity to the rules or orders of architecture. They are, nevertheless, well deserving of notice, highly ornamental to the city, and reflect honour upon the public spirit of its citizens. The Agricultural bank is unquestionably the finest structure in the city. It has been erected very recently on the south side of Main-street, presenting a noble colonnaded front, of the modernized Grecian style; being built somewhat after the model of the United States bank at Philadelphia; though brick and stucco are here substituted for marble, and heavy pillars for the graceful column. . . . The other banks, of which there are, in all, three, . . . are plain brick buildings, undistinguished from the adjoining stores, except by a colder and more unfurnished appearance, and the absence of signs. A short distance above this fine building is the Masonic Hall; a large square edifice, two lofty stories in height. Its front is beautifully stuccoed, and ornamented with white pilasters. . . .

On the south side of the next square is an old "burying-ground," crowning an eminence whose surface is covered with fragments of grave-stones and dismantled tombs. . . . Adjoining it, on the eastern side, and nearly at the extremity of the street and also of the city, stands the theatre; a large, commodious building, constructed of brick, with arched entrances and perfectly plain exterior. . . . Of the other public buildings of Natchez, the Presbyterian church is the finest and most imposing. It stands on a commanding site, overlooking a public square, a pleasant green flat, in the centre of which is the court-house. . . .

The court-house is a fine, large square building, opposite to the church, surmounted by a cupola. It is surrounded by a beautiful, though not spacious, green. On the streets which bound the four sides of it are situated the lawyers' and public offices, which are generally plain, neat, wooden buildings, from one to two stories in height. . . . Opposite to the south side of the square is the county prison; a handsome two story brick building, resembling, save in its grated tier of windows in the upper story, a gentleman's private dwelling. There is a fine Episcopalian church in the south-east part of the town, adding much to its beauty. It is built of brick, and surmounted by a vast dome, which has a rather heavy, overgrown appearance, and is evidently too large for the building. It has a neat front, adorned with a portico of the usual brick pillars.

([Ingraham], *The South-West. By a Yankee*, 2:22, 24, 27, 29, 37–38, 41–42)

Natchez. On the Hill, from the Old Fort. Drawn by James Tooley. Printed by [Charles] Risso & [William R.] Browne. N.Y., ca. 1835. Lithograph, 14 5/8 x 21 3/16 (37.2 x 53.9 cm).

Stokes Collection, New York Public Library

Folio 13.   The "Other" Natchez—Natchez-under-the-Hill—Provides a Bawdy Contrast to the Sedate Town Above

A young John Quitman notes the character of the community at the river

"Under the hill," in this city (a straggling town at the base of the bluff, consisting of warehouses, low taverns, groggeries, dens of prostitution, and gaming-houses), vice and infamy are rampant and glaring, and the law almost powerless. Day and night the orgies of blackguardism and depravity are enacted without shame and restraint. The Sabbath is there particularly a day of profanation and debauchery. The gambler, the bully, and the harlot reign triumphant, and little jurisdiction is taken over their atrocities. (John A. Quitman to his father, January 16, 1822, in J[ohn] F[rancis] H[amtramck] Claiborne, *Life and Correspondence of John A. Quitman*, 1:71–72)

A northern visitor in 1834 is appalled by what he sees in the lower town

On looking round me for a moment, on landing, I was far from agreeably impressed with the general appearance of the buildings. This part of the town is not properly Natchez—and strangers passing up and down the river, who have had the opportunity of seeing only this place, have, without dreaming of the beautiful city over their heads, gone on their way, with impressions very inaccurate and unfavourable.... The principal street, which terminates at the ascent of the hill, runs parallel with the river, and is lined on either side with a row of old wooden houses; which are alternately gambling-houses, brothels, and bar-rooms: a fair assemblage! As we passed through the street—which we gained with difficulty from the boat, picking our way to it as we could, through a filthy alley—the low, broken, half-sunken side-walks, were blocked up with fashionably-dressed young men, smoking or lounging, tawdrily arrayed, highly rouged females, sailors, Kentucky boatmen, negroes, negresses, mulattoes, pigs, dogs, and dirty children. The sounds of profanity and Bacchanalian revels, well harmonizing with the scene, assailed our ears as we passed hastily along, through an atmosphere of tobacco smoke and other equally fragrant odours. After a short walk we emerged into a purer air, and in front of a very neat and well-conducted hotel. From near this place, extending along the Levée to the north, commences the mercantile part of the "landing," lined with stores and extensive warehouses, in which is transacted a very heavy business. The whole of this lower town is built upon a reclaimed flat, from one to two hundred yards broad, and half a mile in length; bounded upon one side by the river, and on the other by the cliff or bluff, upon which Natchez stands, and which rises abruptly from the Batture to the height of one hundred and sixty feet. ([Ingraham], *The South-West. By a Yankee*, 2:18–20)

Another traveler confirms this description of Natchez-under-the-Hill and tells of efforts to change conditions

The lower town, containing little more than the buildings which necessarily grow up in the neighbourhood of a harbour where much shipping business is done, was considered a few years ago as the most abandoned sink of iniquity in the whole western country. It was the resort of the lowest and most profligate wretches of both sexes; and gambling, drinking, robbery, and murder, were the daily occupations of its population. But the respectable inhabitants of the upper town assembled last summer in considerable force, and under the authority of Judge Lynch, and with threats of his summary justice (which they doubtless would have fulfilled), compelled some hundreds of the most notorious characters to leave the place at a few hours' notice. Their memory is not yet dead, nor has the lower town, though much improved, been able yet to acquire a very respectable name. (Charles Augustus Murray, *Travels in North America during the Years 1834, 1835, & 1836 . . .*, 2:124)

In 1838 a visitor from Missouri finds the reforms had been short-lived

[The lower town] consists mostly of several rows of houses, mostly small and trifling, and all of frame. There are some very fine store houses & two midling Hotels with a number of smaller taverns, Groceries, Groggeries, Doggeries, Dance Houses, &c. The rest God knows; so does the Devil; the whole being too frequently the resort of low company and a place of Rendavous [*sic*] for boatmen and other river characters, and is sometimes the scene of riot and disorder, for which it has been famed in former times.... Nathez [*sic*] under the Hill has been known far and wide as a place of "High life below stairs"; this is, however, the place where all the shipping and the trade of the place must pass through. There are several Cotton Presses here and several Saw Mills, with some Lumber yards, from which it might be properly called the port of Natchez. The landing or levee extends for upwards of one mile along the shore; the principal Steam Boat Landing is down at the lower end.... The Ships generally load their cotton here. The Cotton is brought in from the country in Bales that are Pressed out on the Plantations by presses of ordinary power, but not small enough for shipping; at the Cotton Press they are all pressed over again by a steam Press of great Power, & reduced to less than half the former size, when they are ready for shipping. (Henry B. Miller, "The Journal of Henry B. Miller," 280)

Natchez, Mississippi. Drawn by H[enry] Lewis. [Printed by C. H. Muller, Aachen.] Published by Arnz & Co., Düsseldorf, [1854–1857]. Lithograph, 6 3/8 x 8 5/16 in. (16.2 x 21.9 cm).
Historic New Orleans Collection

Natchez Under the Hill. Drawn by F[rederick] Piercy. Engraved by C[harles] Fenn. From Piercy, *Route from Liverpool to Great Salt Lake Valley* (1855). Steel engraving, 6 1/2 x 10 1/2 in. (16.5 x 26.6 cm).
Mercantile Library, St. Louis

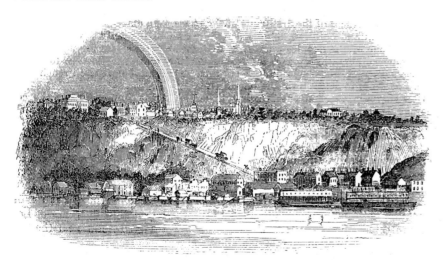

Western View of Natchez. [Drawn by John Warner Barber or Henry Howe.] From Barber and Howe, *Our Whole Country. A Panorama and Encyclopedia of the United States, Historical, Geographical and Pictorial* (1863), 2:829. Wood engraving, 2 3/4 x 4 in. (7 x 10.1 cm).
Olin Library, Cornell University

Natchez. Drawn by F[rederick] Piercy. Engraved by C[harles] Fenn. From Piercy, *Route from Liverpool to Great Salt Lake Valley.* Steel engraving, 4 7/8 x 6 1/2 in. (12.5 x 16.5 cm).
John W. Reps

Folio 14.   Its Commercial Importance Diminished, Natchez Gains Renown as a Place of Beauty and Culture

An 1863 history and guide to the western states and territories mentions Natchez favorably

Natchez is usually considered the principal city of the state, its importance arising from its being the depot of cotton, the product of the lands around it, and from being also one of the main entrepots of the internal commerce of Mississippi. The principal part of the city is built on a clayey bluff, about 150 feet high. *Natchez under the Hill,* as it is called, is that part of the city which lies upon the margin of the river, consisting of warehouses, stores, shops, etc., for the accommodation of the landing.

On the elevated ground the city is regularly laid out with broad streets, adorned with trees. Generally the style of building is plain, but many of the dwellings are elegant, and their grounds beautifully ornamented with trees and shrubbery. The surface of the ground, on which Natchez stands, and of the whole adjacent country, is uneven, undulating like the rolling of the sea in a storm, presenting a strong contrast to the low and level surface of the vast cypress swamps of Louisiana seen on the opposite side of the river. The city contains a court house, five churches, several literary institutions, three banks, a hospital, orphan asylum, etc., and about 7,000 inhabitants.
(Barber and Howe, *Our Whole Country,* 2:829)

In 1873 a visiting author notes the effects of the Civil War on the city

Natchez, like Vicksburg, lies on a line of bluffs which rear their bold heads from the water in an imposing manner. He who sees only Natchez-under-the Hill from a steamboat's deck gets an impression of a few prosaic houses huddled together not far from a wharf-boat, a road leading up a steep and high hill, and here and there a mass of foliage. Let him wander ashore, and scale the cliff, and he will find himself in a quiet unostentatious, beautifully shaded town. . . . Natchez has an impressive cathedral, a fine court-house, a handsome Masonic temple, and hosts of pretty houses. You walk beneath the shade of the China-tree and the water oak, the cedar and the laurimunda. Nowhere is there glare of sun on the pavement; nothing more clamorous than the galloping of a horse stirs the blood of the nine thousand inhabitants.

There were, before the war, great numbers of planters' residences in the suburbs,—beautiful houses, with colonnades and verandahs, with rich drawing and dining-rooms, furnished in heavy antique style, and gardens modeled after the finest in Europe. Many of these homes have been destroyed. We visited one or two whose owners have been fortunate enough to keep them. The lawns and gardens are luxurious. . . . I remember no palace garden in Europe which impressed me so powerfully with the sense of richness and exquisite profusion of costly and delicate blooms as Browns's at

Natchez, which a wealthy Scotchman cultivated for a quarter of a century, and handed down to his family, with injunctions to maintain its splendor.

On the bluffs, some three miles from the town, is a national cemetery, beautifully planned and decorated, and between it and Natchez stands the dilapidated United States Marine Hospital, and the grass-grown ramparts of Fort McPherson mark the site of a beautiful mansion which was razed for military purposes.
(King, *The Great South,* 1:292–94)

Willard Glazier tells his readers of the Natchez he saw in 1881

Few towns or cities of the Mississippi are so rich in historical interest as Natchez, situated on the eastern bank of the river, two hundred and eighty miles north of New Orleans. The city is divided into two sections, known as Natchez-on-the hill and Natchez-under-the-hill. The latter is built on a narrow strip of land between the bluff and the river, and includes the landings and principal business houses. It possesses neither architectural nor scenic beauty. It was formerly the resort of gamblers, river thieves and other desperate characters.

Broad and well-shaded roads connect it with Natchez-on-the-hill, which is beautifully located on a cliff nearly two hundred feet high overlooking the river. The latter has abundance of shade trees, and many handsome residences and other buildings. The houses are principally of brick, and surrounded by ample and attractive gardens.

Along the whole front of the city, on the brow of the cliff, is a park from which fine views can be obtained up and down the river. Adjoining this park is a National Cemetery, laid out and decorated in a tasteful manner. The Court House is in a public square, shaded with trees, and the Masonic Temple is a handsome building. The Catholic Cathedral has a spire one hundred and twenty-eight feet high, and there are other churches architecturally worthy of notice.

Natchez is the shipping-port of a large and fertile cotton region, and holds commercial intercourse with the whole Mississippi Valley. Its population in 1860 was 13,553. But the blockade of the Mississippi and the general prostration of business in the South during the Rebellion affected the city disastrously, so that even at the conclusion of the war it did not at once recover, and in 1870 its population had decreased to about 10,000. Since that time it has been gradually regaining lost ground, and is now on the road to prosperity.
(Willard Glazier, *Down the Great River . . . ,* 395–96)

Natchez on the Hill, From the Marine Hospital. Drawn by A[lfred] R. Waud. From *Harper's Weekly* 10 (July 14, 1866): 441. Wood engraving, 4 7/16 x 20 11/16 in. (11.3 x 52.5 cm).

John W. Reps

Natchez Under The Hill. Drawn by A[lfred] R. Waud. From *Harper's Weekly* 10 (July 14, 1866): 441. Wood engraving, 4 5/16 x 8 1/4 in. (11 x 20.9 cm).

John W. Reps

Natchez-Under-The-Hill. Drawn by A[lfred] R. W[aud]. From *Every Saturday* n.s. 3 (August 19, 1871): 185. Wood engraving, 6 x 9 in. (15.2 x 22.8 cm).

John W. Reps

Folio 15.   Beginning as a Frontier Military Post, Vicksburg Becomes an Important Mississippi River Port

Francis Baily describes the site of Vicksburg on his trip down the Mississippi in 1797

About five o'clock we came to the Walnut Hills. . . . Here there is a strong fort kept up by the Spaniards. It is an irregular fortification, occupying a great part of the hill on which it stands, which is very high and steep. . . .

Walnut Hills is a beautiful situation for a town, and an advantageous one for a fort. There are two forts at this place, one of them commands the other, being situated upon an eminence behind it. The few houses which are scattered around it, and the green bank on which they stand, surround[ed] with flowering, verdant, and lofty trees, presented at once a picturesque and romantic appearance to our eyes, fatigued with the uniformity of the prospect to which we had for so many miles been witness.

(Baily, *Journal of a Tour in Unsettled Parts of North America in 1796 & 1797*, 146–47)

A Yankee visitor in 1835 records the extensive cotton trade conducted through the port of Vicksburg

Vicksburg is about two miles below the Walnut hills, one of the bluffs of the Mississippi, and five hundred from the Balize. It contains nearly two thousand inhabitants. Thirty thousand bales of cotton, about one eighth of the whole quantity shipped by the state at large, are annually shipped from this place. In this respect it is inferior only to Natchez and Grand Gulf, the first of which ships fifty thousand. There is a weekly paper published here, of a very respectable character, and well edited, and another is in contemplation. There are also a bank, with two or three churches, and a handsome brick court-house, erected on an eminence from which there is an extensive view of the Mississippi. . . .

There is no town in the south-west more flourishing than Vicksburg. It is surrounded by rich plantations, and contains many public-spirited individuals; whose co-operation in public enterprises is opening new avenues of wealth for the citizens, and laying a broad and secure foundation for the future importance of the town. It is already a powerful rival of Natchez: but the two places are so distant from each other, that their interests will always revolve in different circles. The situation of this town, on the shelving declivity of a cluster of precipitous hills, which rise abruptly from the river, is highly romantic. The houses are scattered in picturesque groups on natural terraces along the river, the balcony or portico of one often overhanging the roof of another. . . . Cotton is often conveyed to Vicksburg . . . from a distance of one hundred miles in the interior.

([Ingraham], *The South-West. By a Yankee*, 2:169–70)

A guide to the Mississippi describes the city as it existed in 1848

Vicksburgh [*sic*] . . . is the county-seat of Warren county, Mississippi. It is situated on a hill, the highest part of which is two hundred feet above high water mark. The principal business part of the city is situated on the bottom, along the river. It was incorporated as a town in 1825, and as a city, in 1836. The country surrounding it is a black loamy soil, well adapted to the cultivation of all kinds of grain, tobacco, cotton, &c. The principal product is cotton, of which seventy-five thousand bales are annually shipped from here. Within the few past years, Vicksburgh has been improving very rapidly, and the fine section of country, with which it is surrounded, as well as the beautiful site of the city, and the fine harbor of the river (which is here from ninety to three hundred feet deep), all give it superior advantages, for a rapid and healthy growth. There is a railroad extending from it to Jackson, the seat of government, a distance of fifty miles. The city contains a court house, five churches, three academies, a hospital, a theater, twelve schools, and two foundries, doing a good business. The population is about five thousand.

(*Conclins' New River Guide*, 100)

A popular illustrated journal tells its readers about Vicksburg in the mid–1850s

Situated . . . on a high bluff, elevated 200 feet above the level of the river, [Vicksburg's] location leaves nothing to be desired. The scenery in the neighborhood is exceedingly beautiful. . . . Vicksburg . . . has several churches, some of which are noble specimens of architecture. Its large public school is an admirable institution, and receives about five hundred pupils annually. A large business is done here in the preparation and the making of bricks for building, and some 90,000 bales of cotton are sent hence to New Orleans annually. The town contains every element of progress and prosperity. The future of these western cities, though susceptible of prediction from data that admit of no dispute, presents so grand and dazzling a prospect as, if delineated would awaken incredulity in those who have not made their progress a special study. If their moral and intellectual progress had not kept pace with their physical advancement, we should fear to look ahead. But from the elevated views of their citizens, we look with confidence for their prosperity.

("View of Vicksburg, Miss.")

VICKSBURG.

Vicksburg, Mississippi. Drawn by H[enry] Lewis. [Printed by C. H. Muller, Aachen.] Published by Arnz & Co., Düsseldorf, [1854–1857]. Lithograph, 6 3/8 x 8 5/16 in. (16.2 x 21.9 cm).

Minnesota Historical Society

Vicksburgh, Miss. [Drawn by Otto Onken?] Lithographed by A[dolphus F.] Forbriger. Printed by Onken's Lith, Cin[cinnati] O[hio], [1851]. From William Wells, *Western Scenery; or, Land and River, Hill and Dale, in the Mississippi Valley.* Lithograph, 5 3/4 x 7 15/16 in. (14.7 x 20.2 cm).

Public Library of Cincinnati and Hamilton County

View of Vicksburg, Mississippi. Unsigned. From *Ballou's Pictorial Drawing-Room Companion* 9 (August 25, 1855): 121. Wood engraving, 5 5/8 x 9 1/2 in. (14.3 x 24.1 cm).

John W. Reps

Vicksburg, from the Old Spanish Fort. Drawn by A[lfred] R. Waud. From *Harper's Weekly* 10 (July 14, 1866): 441. Wood engraving, 4 3/4 x 20 11/16 in. (12 x 52.5 cm).
John W. Reps

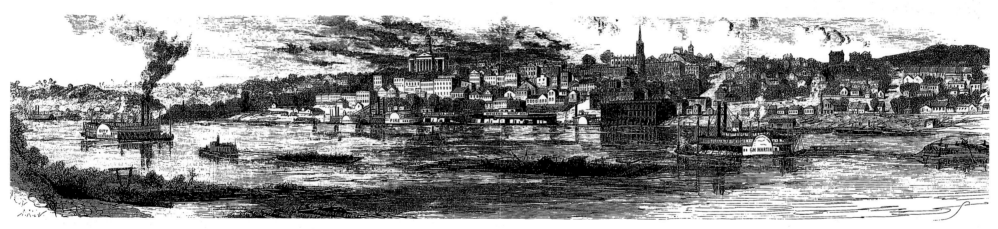

A General View of Vicksburg. Drawn by A[lfred] R. W[aud]. From *Every Saturday* n.s. 3 (August 19, 1871): 188–89. Wood engraving, 3 3/4 x 18 7/8 in. (9.5 x 48 cm).
John W. Reps

Folio 16.   A Prolonged Siege during the Civil War Devastates Vicksburg, and It Fails to Recover Its Former Prominence

The artist of the Harper's Weekly *sketch just seen provides a vivid description of Vicksburg to accompany it*

Vicksburg is called the "City of Hills," but it would be equally appropriate to name it the City of Ravines. Built on one of the bluff formations of the Mississippi Valley, it presents a picturesque sight from the river and neighboring heights. The sketch is made from a hill once the site of a Spanish fort, and during the siege of Vicksburg, a portion of the Confederate line of defenses. Prominent is the Court-house, still showing the marks of the peppering it got from the Yankees. Below the left façade is the house, formerly a bank, now headquarters of the Freedmen's Bureau. To the right is a flag-staff and a fort, the highest in the line, and where "Whistling Dick"—a gun well known to the Union army—had its eyrie. Another flag-staff, away to the left of the picture, shows the headquarters of the commander of the Department, that fine old warrior, General Wood. Negro-huts dot the middle distance, while to the right the river stretches off into the distance, showing a little of the opposite shore, where Grant camped a large portion of his army and tried to make a canal.

The trees and gardens of Vicksburg give it a delightful appearance. Choice flowers and shrubs flourish almost spontaneously, blossoming even through the winter. As it rained all the time I was there I can testify to the superior capabilities of the soil in the matter of mud. At other times the inhabitants say the dust is unbearable, which, indeed, is the case in all the Mississippi towns and cities. Capacious culverts are there to carry off the water, but for all that it cuts ravines through the roads, and occasionally renders the streets impassable. One block from the Washington Hotel there was a gully cut through the street by the rain, ten or twelve feet deep. The Post-office and a number of stores and houses were flooded by leaky roofs, without, however, disturbing the equanimity of the owners to any degree.
(A[lfred] R. W[aud], "Pictures of the South: Vicksburg")

A traveler tells of the city's condition in 1873

Vicksburg, the tried and troubled hill-city, her crumbling bluffs still filled with historic memorials of one of the most desperate sieges and defences of modern times, rises in quite imposing fashion from the Mississippi's banks in a loop in the river, made by a long delta, which at high water is nearly submerged. The bluffs run back some distance to an elevated plateau. In the upper streets are many handsome residences. The Court-House has climbed to the summit of a fine series of terraces; here and there a pretty church serves as a land-mark; and the remains of the old fort . . . are still visible on a lofty eminence. From the grass-grown ramparts one can . . . overlook the principal avenue—Washington street, well-lined with spacious shops and stores, and . . . see the broad current sweeping round the tongue of land on which the towns of De Soto and Delta stand, and the ferries plying to the landings of the railroad which cuts across North Louisiana to Shreveport; can see the almost perpendicular streets scaling the bluff from the waterside, and, down by the river, masses of elevators and warehouses, whence the white, stately packets come and go. There is evidence of growth; neat houses are scattered on hill and in valley in every direction; yet the visitor will find that money is scarce, credit is poor, and that every tradesman is badly discouraged.
(King, *The Great South*, 1:287–88)

An Australian visitor in 1876 is unimpressed by what he sees

From the natural strength and importance of its position Vicksburg has often been called the "Quebec of the Mississippi," but the town itself is miserable, the streets for the most part being unpaved, and the buildings irregular, and generally constructed of wood or brick. From the terrace of the Court House, the view of the river, and of the vast tracts of forest, extending as far as the eye can reach, is, however, very fine.
(Falk, *Trans-Pacific Sketches*, 255–56)

By 1881 when Willard Glazier stopped in Vicksburg it had finally regained some of its lost commercial vitality

Vicksburg is situated on the eastern bank of the Mississippi, at the lower end of the immense Yazoo basin, created by the union of the river of that name with the Mississippi some twelve miles above. It is in the midst of some of the best scenery on the Lower Mississippi, being located on bluffs known as Walnut Hills, which extend for two miles along the river and rise gradually to a height of five hundred feet. It is about midway between Memphis and New Orleans, and is the largest city between them. As seen from the river it presents a highly picturesque appearance, and loses none of its attractiveness on a nearer approach. . . .

Its existence dates only from 1836, when a planter by the name of Vick settled there and founded the town. Members of his family still reside there. . . .

Vicksburg is now a city of about fourteen thousand inhabitants, and is the chief commercial mart of that section of the Mississippi. It has rallied from the vicissitudes which it suffered during the war, and is now a prosperous, as well as a beautiful city.
(Glazier, *Down the Great River*, 367–68, 374)

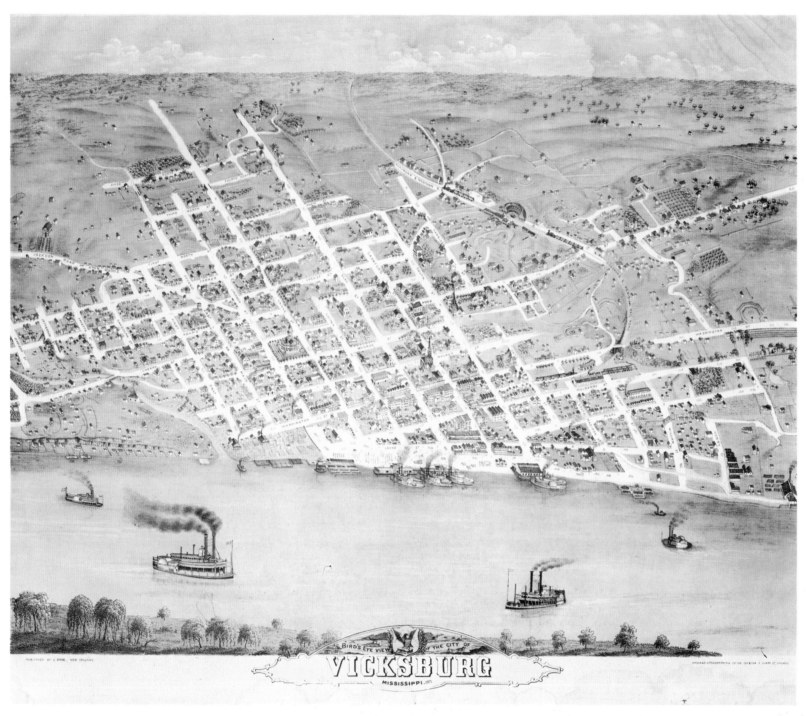

Bird's Eye View of the City of Vicksburg Mississippi 1871. [Drawn by Camille N. Drie?] Printed by Chicago Lithography Co., 150, 152 & 154 S. Clark St., Chicago. Published by C. Drie, New Orleans. Lithograph, 23 7/8 x 29 in. (60.8 x 73.8 cm).

Old Court House Museum, Vicksburg

Vicksburg, Miss. 1891. Drawn and published by C[lemens] J. Pauli, 726 Central Avenue, Milwaukee. Lithograph, 21 1/8 x 33 1/16 in. (53.8 x 84.2 cm).
Old Court House Museum, Vicksburg

Vicksburg, Mississippi from the air, October 14, 1988.

Alex MacLean

Folio 17.   The Two Most Important Nineteenth-Century Mississippi River Towns in Arkansas Have Different Experiences

Helena gains an entry in 1850 in an important guide to places on the river

Helena . . . is the county seat of Phillips county, Arkansas. It contains one church, thirteen stores, one newspaper printing office, three saw mills, and a population of about four hundred. . . . Considerable cotton, brought down the St. Francis river, and from the interior country, is shipped from this place.
(*Conclins' New River Guide*, 94)

An artist and an author in 1871 call Helena a prosperous place

Helena . . . presents, as will be seen by our picture, a thriving appearance. Remains of fortifications used in the late war, are still visible on the high ground back of the town, but the town itself shows no scars, at least to one passing on the river.
(Ralph Keeler and A[lfred] R. Waud, "From Vicksburg to Memphis, with Some Account of an Explosion")

Willard Glazier in 1881 thinks Helena has an excellent future

Helena . . . has become, since the Civil War, a very progressive town, and is growing rapidly in importance. It offers many advantages for navigation and commerce, and the only drawback to its still greater advancement is the destructive agency of the Mississippi, which occasionally threatens it with inundation. If it can protect itself against the overflows, Helena, from its peculiarly favorable position, is destined to become one of the first cities on the Lower Mississippi. Located in a fertile cotton section, the facilities for shipment of that staple to other ports is apparent. It is eighty miles below Memphis, and is the terminus of the Arkansas Midland, and the Iron Mountain and Helena railroads. . . .

The present population of Helena is about four thousand, and it supports two banks and five newspapers.
(Glazier, *Down the Great River*, 359–60)

Mark Twain in 1882 notes Helena's flood-prone site

Helena occupies one of the prettiest situations on the Mississippi. Her perch is the last, the southernmost group of hills which one sees on that side of the river. In its normal condition it is a pretty town; but the flood (or possibly the seepage) had lately been ravaging it; whole streets of houses had been invaded by the muddy water, and the outsides of the buildings were still belted with a broad stain extending upwards from the foundations. Stranded and discarded scows lay all about; plank sidewalks on stilts four feet high were still standing; the board sidewalks on the ground level were loose and ruinous,—a couple of men trotting along them could make a blind man think a cavalry charge was coming; everywhere the mud was black and

deep, and in many places malarious pools of stagnant water were standing. A Mississippi inundation is the next most wasting and desolating infliction to a fire.
(Twain, *Life on the Mississippi*, 336)

In 1871 Every Saturday's *correspondent and artist note that Napoleon is being eroded by the river's action*

You have a faithful representation of what is left of Napoleon, Arkansas. It used to have the reputation of being the wickedest town on the Mississippi, but the streets once vocal with the "sharp note of the pistol and the pleasing squeak of the victim" have all caved into the river. Napoleon may be said to be wrecked on a sand-bar a few miles below, on the opposite side of the river, for there the caving earth is depositing.
(Keeler and Waud, "From Vicksburg to Memphis," 284)

Willard Glazier visits a nearly extinct Napoleon in 1881

Below the mouth of the Arkansas is, or rather was, the town of Napoleon, at one time a place of enterprise and importance on the lower Mississippi, but now represented by only a few scattered houses, the most demoralized-looking hamlet we had seen since leaving . . . the other end of the river. The banks were tumbling into the stream day by day. Houses had fallen into the current which was rapidly undermining the town. Here and there chimneys were observed standing in solitude, the buildings having been torn down and removed to other localities in order to save them.
(Glazier, *Down the Great River*, 362–63)

In his Life on the Mississippi, *Mark Twain includes this passage of dialogue about Napoleon*

"I have come to say good-bye, captain. I wish to go ashore at Napoleon. . . ."
The captain laughed . . . and said,—. . . .
"Why, hang it, don't you know? There *isn't* any Napoleon any more. Hasn't been for years and years. The Arkansas River burst through it, tore it all to rags, and emptied it into the Mississippi!"
"Carried the whole town away?—banks, churches, jails, newspaper-offices, court-house, theatre, fire department, livery stable,—everything?"
"Everything. Just a fifteen-minute job, or such a matter, Didn't leave hide nor hair, shred nor shingle of it, except the fag-end of a shanty and one brick chimney. This boat is paddling along right now, where the dead-centre of that town used to be; yonder is the brick chimney,—and all that's left of Napoleon."
(Twain, *Life on the Mississippi*, 361–62)

Helena, Arkansas. [Drawn by Alfred R. Waud.] From *Every Saturday* n.s. 3 (September 16, 1871): 284. Wood engraving, 4 x 8 7/8 in. (10.1 x 22.6 cm).

John W. Reps

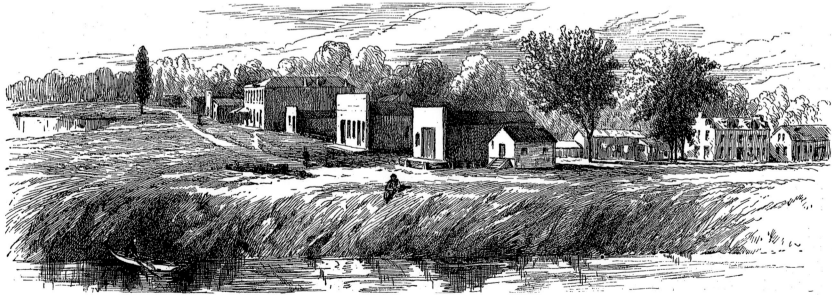

Napoleon, Arkansas. [Drawn by Alfred R. Waud.] From *Every Saturday* n.s. 3 (September 16, 1871): 284. Wood engraving, 3 1/4 x 9 in. (8.2 x 22.8 cm).

John W. Reps

Folio 18.   Early Visitors Note the Favorable Location for a City at Chickasaw Bluffs

Francis Baily describes the spot in 1797

At Chickasaw Bluffs there are about five or six families settled, who may be called half-Indians; that is, they are persons who, in habit and manners, are nearly allied to them, and have generally married into the Indian families. It is situated at the mouth of Wolfe river, of which it forms the southern bank. The Spaniards had lately a fort here, which they preserved merely to keep their chain on this river. . . .
(Baily, *Journal of a Tour in Unsettled Parts of North America in 1796 & 1797*, 142)

Another visitor in 1806 provides more information about conditions at the site

The Chickasaw Bluff is a very high red bank on the eastern side of the river. On it are erected a fort, barracks for a company of soldiers and a few artillery men, and houses and stores for two State commissioners. . . . The high plain on which the buildings are erected, is very beautiful; but, like the other settlements on the Mississippi . . . is limited, and subsides into ponds and swamps. It maintains about a dozen families, who raise corn, breed poultry and pigs, and supply boats descending the river with what common provisions they may want. . . . The view of the fort, on approaching it from the opposite side, has a very fine and picturesque effect. In consequence of the bend in the river, it is hurried on the view from a very favourable point. In the distance, the principal bluff forms a noble object. . . . On its summit, stands a lonely watch-tower; on its brow, the garrison and fort mounted with guns. The gardens and improvements are elevated and extensive; and the offices and commissioners' buildings add greatly to the general effect.
(Ashe, *Travels in America, Performed in 1806*, 297–98)

One of the owners of land at Chickasaw Bluffs tells his partner they must be first to lay out a town on the site

You will see an official account from Gen. Jackson published in the *Whig* that he has made a treaty with the Chickasaws. . . . We must proceed to lay off a town [on our land] by this time 12 months [hence]. I suspect [if] the country settles as fast as I think it will . . . we must not let the owners of property on the Bluffs of the Mississippi above us be beforehand in laying off towns, as it might damp the sale of ours.
(John Overton, Letter to James Winchester, October 25, 1818, p. 197)

John Overton promotes the new town with an advertisement in a Philadelphia newspaper

The plan and local situation of Memphis is such as to authorize the expectation that it is destined to become a populous city . . . being from twenty to thirty feet above the highest flood, it is always dry. . . . This is the only site for a town of any magnitude on the Mississippi, between the mouth of the Ohio and Natchez. The western bank is uniformly too low and subject to inundation, and the eastern affords no other situation sufficiently high, dry, level, and extensive, together with a rich surrounding country competent to support it.
(Philadelphia *Portfolio*, as quoted in Edward F. Williams III, "Memphis' Early Triumph over Its River Rivals")

An early surveyor in West Tennessee recalls the slow sales of lots in Memphis after its founding in 1819

Judge John Overton, of Nashville, Tennessee, one of the proprietors of the new town of Memphis, was here with his plan of the upper part of Memphis . . . and on several days had offered some of his lots for sale; very few were sold and they for small prices, I rather think from thirty and forty dollars to one hundred dollars would cover the range of prices. . . .

Judge Overton did not seem to be discouraged at the low prices and short sales, and only offered the lots for sale to afford all who might be disposed to invest, an opportunity to do so. He said that he knew it took many people to make a large town and the country contiguous must be settled before it could grow much.

Judge Overton donates lots to old settlers to avoid suits over land ownership

He was quite liberal in donating lots to nearly all of the old settlers. To T. D. Carr he gave two lots whereon to build a tavern for the accommodation of the persons attending the land office. It consisted of six or eight one-story round-pole cabins, very low, and floored with old boat plank, the cracks daubed with clay, after the manner of Indian huts. To A. B. Carr he gave one lot for the location of a horse-mill and one lot out on Bayou Gayoso for a ten-yard site.
(Col. James Brown, "Early Reminiscences of Memphis and West Tennessee," 403)

Timothy Flint sees Memphis in 1820, two years after its founding, but mentions the place only in passing

Below New Madrid . . . there are two villages commenced, the one on the high bluff, formerly called Fort Pickering, and now Memphis . . . , and another at the St. Francis bluffs, in the territory of Arkansas. They are both inconsiderable.
(Flint, *Recollections of the Last Ten Years in the Valley of the Mississippi*, 212)

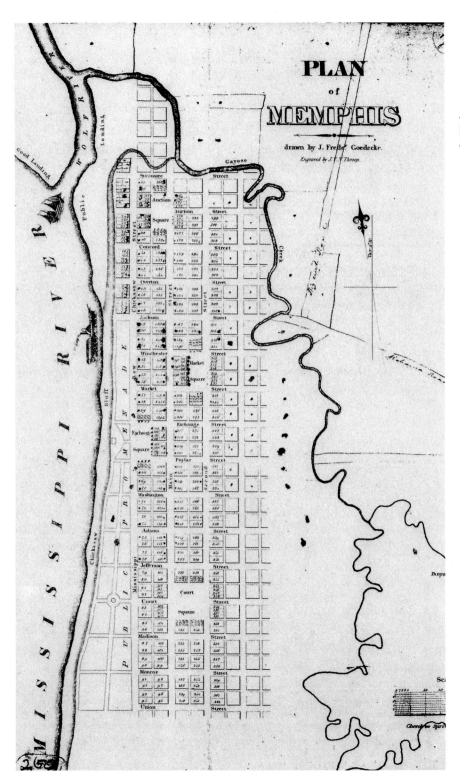

Plan of Memphis. Drawn by J. Fredek Goedecke. Engraved by J. V. N. Throop. [Published, 1819.] Engraving, 19 x 23 1/2 in. (48.2 x 59.7 cm).

Tennessee State Archives

Memphis. [Drawn by Charles-Alexandre Lesueur, ca. 1828. Printed in France before 1846.] Lithograph, 5 5/16 x 7 13/16 in. (13.5 x 19.8 cm).

Edward Caldwell Collection, Knox College Library, Galesburg, Ill.

Folio 19.   Memphis Begins to Grow, but Its Development Proves Painfully Slow

A Methodist minister in 1827 found Memphis to consist of a few cabins, two or three houses, and four or five stores

This place is seven miles north of the line which separates Tennessee from Mississippi. It is not yet so rich, or so populous, as the ancient capital of Egypt. There are four or five stores, and perhaps ten log-houses, with two or three poor frame houses. A large framed house is to be erected here this season for a tavern. The land of the back country is rich, but very sparsely settled, and the people are poor.

(J. Orin Oliphant, ed., *Through the South and West with Jeremiah Evarts in 1826*, 120)

A young doctor comes to Memphis in 1828 intending to settle but leaves after seeing its primitive state

I went to Memphis, Tennessee, hoping to find a good opening for future work in that new place. . . . It was then a small town, ugly, dirty, and sickly. While supper was being got for me at the tavern, I walked through the miserable streets, and out upon the banks of the river. I shall never forget the dreariness of that night, nor the despondency into which I fell when I tried to bring myself to consider this as my future home. I passed much of the night in reflection, and became convinced that I could not maintain myself there. Everything pointed to the certainty that in a short time this squalid village must grow to be a great and wealthy city, but I had no confidence in my destiny as one of the builders of it. For many years the population would be rough and lawless, and the locality and sanitary condition of the town promised that disease and death would hold high carnival there. . . .

My courage failed, and, after an early breakfast, I turned my face homewards.

(Reuben Davis, *Recollections of Mississippi and Mississippians*, 25–26)

Mrs. Trollope wades through the mud to see Memphis in 1828

Memphis stands on a high bluff, and at the time of our arrival was nearly inaccessible. The heavy rain which had been falling for many hours would have made any steep ascent difficult, but unfortunately a new road had been recently marked out, which beguiled us into its almost bottomless mud, from the firmer footing of the unbroken cliff. Shoes and gloves were lost in the mire, for we were glad to avail ourselves of all our limbs, and we reached the grand hotel in a most deplorable state. . . .

The town stretches in a rambling, irregular manner along the cliff, from the Wolf River, one of the innumerable tributaries to the Mississippi, to about a mile below it. Half a mile more of the cliff beyond the town is cleared of

trees, and produces good pasture for horses, cows, and pigs; sheep they had none. At either end of this space the forest again rears its dark wall, and seems to say to man, "so far shalt thou come, and no farther!" Courage and industry, however, have braved the warning. Behind this long street the town straggles back into the forest, and the rude path that leads to the more distant log dwellings becomes wilder at every step.

(Mrs. [Frances] Trollope, *Domestic Manners of the Americans*, 42)

A British military officer visits Memphis in 1831 and likes what he sees

I was much pleased with the site and appearance of Memphis in Tennessee; it is pleasantly situated on a high bluff . . . and commands an extensive view up and down the river, and across the Arkansas territory, an unbroken forest to the base of the rocky mountains. The town now contains a thousand inhabitants. The framehouses [*sic*] had a clean look about them; and the hotel where I put up was a respectable extablishment [*sic*], kept by a colonel of militia, with the effigy of the great Washington swinging before the door.

(J. E. Alexander, *Transatlantic Sketches*, 254–55)

A minister and frequent visitor to Memphis compares the city of 1831 with what he sees in 1845

In 1831 Memphis contained about three hundred inhabitants. At that time there was no organized church in the place, except the Presbyterian, which contained eight or ten members. There are now nearly two hundred and fifty members in that church. . . . The City now contains a population of between five to six thousand souls, between thirty and forty lawyers, more than forty physicians, three female schools, four male schools, seven ministers, five houses of worship and three others under contract.

(E. C. Tracy, *Memoir of the Life of Jeremiah Evarts*, 239)

In 1846 Sir Charles Lyell looks at the site of Memphis with a geologist's eye

The town on which this ancient and venerable name is conferred, appears the newest of the large places we have yet seen on the Mississippi. It is growing with great rapidity, standing on a bluff now fifty two feet above the level of the water when the river is high. . . .

Such a site for a town, in spite of the slow undermining of the cliffs, is permanent by comparison with the ordinary banks of the river for hundreds of miles continuously.

(Charles Lyell, *A Second Visit to the United States of America*, 2:171)

H. Lewis pinx.

Lith. Jnst. Arnz & Cᵒ Düsseldorf

MEMPHIS . TENESSEE.

DIE STADT MEMPHIS. TENESSEE.

Memphis, Tennessee. Drawn by H[enry] Lewis. [Printed by C. H. Muller, Aachen.] Published by Arnz & Co., Düsseldorf. Lithograph, 5 13/16 x 7 3/4 in. (14.8 x 19.6 cm).

Minnesota Historical Society

Memphis, Ten. [Drawn by Otto Onken?] Lithographed by A[dolphus F.] Forbriger. Printed by Onken's Lith, Cin[cinnati] O[hio], [1851]. From William Wells, *Western Scenery; or, Land and River, Hill and Dale, in the Mississippi Valley.* Lithograph, 5 3/4 x 7 7/8 in. (14.7 x 20 cm).
Public Library of Cincinnati and Hamilton County

Memphis, Tennessee. Unsigned. From *Ballou's Pictorial Drawing-Room Companion* 8 (February 17, 1855): 108. Wood engraving, 6 x 9 1/4 in. (15.2 x 23.5 cm).
Olin Library, Cornell University

Memphis. Drawn by F[rederick] Piercy. Engraved by C[harles] Fenn. From Piercy, *Route from Liverpool to Great Salt Lake Valley* (1855). Steel engraving, 7 1/2 x 10 1/8 in. (19 x 25.7 cm).

John W. Reps

Folio 20.   Memphis Begins to Prosper in the 1850s but Suffers from the Effects of the Civil War a Decade Later

A guide to Mississippi River ports published in 1850 describes Memphis as a major center of trade

Memphis . . . is beautifully situated on the fourth Chickasaw bluff, just below the mouth of Wolf river. . . . The bluff . . . is thirty feet above the highest floods, and its base is washed by the river, for a distance of three miles, while a bed of sand-stone, the only known stratum of rocks below the Ohio, juts into the stream, and forms a convenient landing. From the Ohio to Vicksburgh, a distance of six hundred and fifty miles, it is the only site for a commercial mart, on either side of the Mississippi.

The appearance of Memphis from the river, is very beautiful and imposing. Some distance from the brow of the bluff, a handsome range of fine buildings extends for several squares, and gives an air of business to it, which is manifested by few places of its size. This point has been selected by the United States government, for the erection of a new Navy Yard, and the necessary buildings for that purpose are now in course of erection, on a large scale. The beautiful situation of Memphis, and its connection with a fine country, together with the great distance from any other point on the river, where a large city could be built, give it superior advantages in becoming a place of great importance. Immense quantities of cotton are grown in the interior country, and this is the principal mart and shipping point for it. One hundred and twenty thousand bales of cotton are annually shipped from this place. It contains, at present, six churches, an academy, two medical colleges, a number of private schools, a large number of stores, some of them doing an extensive business, an office of the Magnetic Telegraph, and a population of ten thousand.

(*Conclins' New River Guide*, 92–94)

A visitor in 1855 criticizes the city's muddy, unpaved streets

On a high, bold bluff we descry two miles of handsome buildings and our boat rounds to, so as to bring her head up stream, and in a few moments we land at Memphis. The shore is thronged with carriages and porters. The hotels are not half a mile away, and the fare demanded is the . . . sum of ten shillings. . . .

It was late at night, and in a rather heavy shower: in fact, the rain amounted to an inundation, and the water in the streets was two feet deep. The excuse for high fares at Memphis was, that it was muddy. There was no mistake about that. The streets are broad, the side walks well laid, the buildings fine, but the streets had never been paved, and the stumps of the forest trees were in some of the public squares.

(Thomas L. Nichols, *Forty Years of American Life*, 167)

An English visitor in 1859 predicts a great future for Memphis

Everything new is built on a superior scale equal to anything of the kind in one large town in England. The time will come when it will be a very large place, when the railways are more fully developed, as it is surrounded by a fertile cotton country on each side of the river, which is *the* great communication to New Orleans. Even now as at Atlanta you see a magnificent store rising by the side of a wooden shanty which probably ten or fifteen years ago was not considered a bad sort of house when the Red Indians were more common than they are now in these parts. . . .

The levee (what would be called a wharf in England) on the river is covered with bales of cotton, all exposed. A stranger would either think it never rained or that cotton was not of much value. The increased annual export of cotton from this place is very great. I have no doubt of its some day being a large city. There is a great trade on the river. Steamers constantly up and down. . . .

I consider Memphis to be particularly well laid out in a sanitary point of view. The main streets are crossed at right angles, cutting it into blocks, through the center of which is a narrow passage sufficient to clear away the refuse from every house without coming into the main street. I don't mean to say that this plan obviates dirt in the main streets in Memphis—for what American town is clean?—but in any new town in England it would be a very first-rate plan of building houses.

The great peculiarity in these mushroom cities is that notwithstanding these good houses and stores, if they have made a foot pavement at all it is of wood. The main street is as nature left it, mud axletree deep if the weather be wet, or sand, as the case may be. It is very characteristic of the people— the Americans get a city built leaving the roads and such minor details to another generation.

(John Henry Vessey, *Mr. Vessey of England* . . . , 101–3)

In 1867 Memphis seems a depressing place to a visiting actor

What Memphis may have been when it flourished in Egyptian soil one has little opportunity of judging, but since its transplantation to the banks of the Mississippi, it has enjoyed the unenviable distinction of being considered the worst place in that by no means respectable neighbourhood. . . .

The dust blew in perfect torrents through the streets. There was nothing to be seen but the Levee, or wharf, a shabby town, and a few miserable grey squirrels in the public garden, so I returned to the hotel, and sat outside the door surrounded by a group of wild-looking expectorators.

(George Rose, *The Great Country; or, Impressions of America*, 208–9)

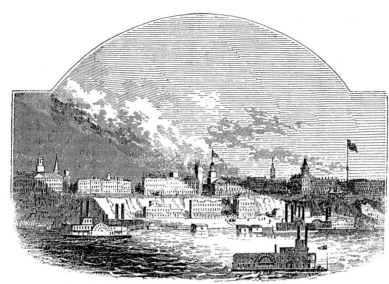

View of Memphis from the West bank of the Mississippi. [Drawn by John Warner Barber or Henry Howe.] From Barber and Howe, *Our Whole Country* (1863), 2:829. Wood engraving, 3 x 3 7/8 in. (7.6 x 9.8 cm).

Olin Library, Cornell University

The Levee at Memphis, Tenn.—Hauling Sugar and Cotton from their Hiding-Places for Shipment North. Drawn by Alex. Simplot. From *Harper's Weekly* 6 (July 5, 1862): 417. Wood Engraving, 5 x 9 1/4 in. (12.7 x 23.5 cm).

Olin Library, Cornell University

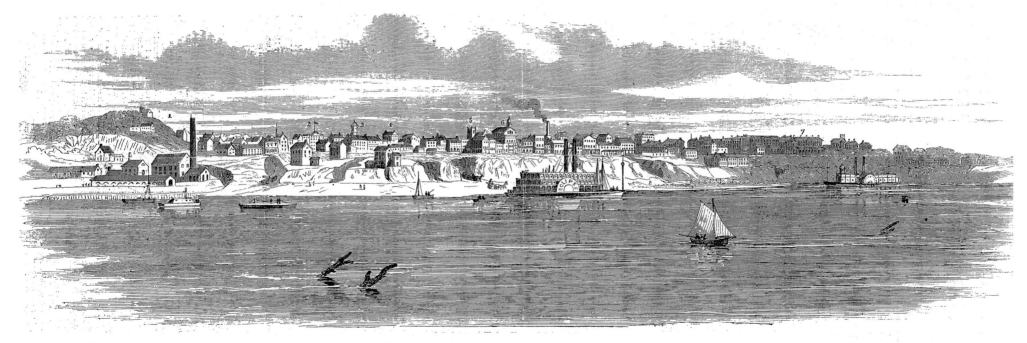

General View of the City of Memphis, Tennessee, from Hopefield, on the Arkansas Side. Unsigned. From *Harper's Weekly* 6 (May 31, 1862): 348. Wood engraving, 5 1/8 x 14 in. (13 x 35.5 cm).

Olin Library, Cornell University

City of Memphis, Tennessee, After the War. Drawn by A[lfred] R. W[aud]. From *Harper's Weekly* 10 (May 5, 1866): 281. Wood engraving, 6 1/16 x 13 3/4 in. (15.4 x 35 cm).
Olin Library, Cornell University

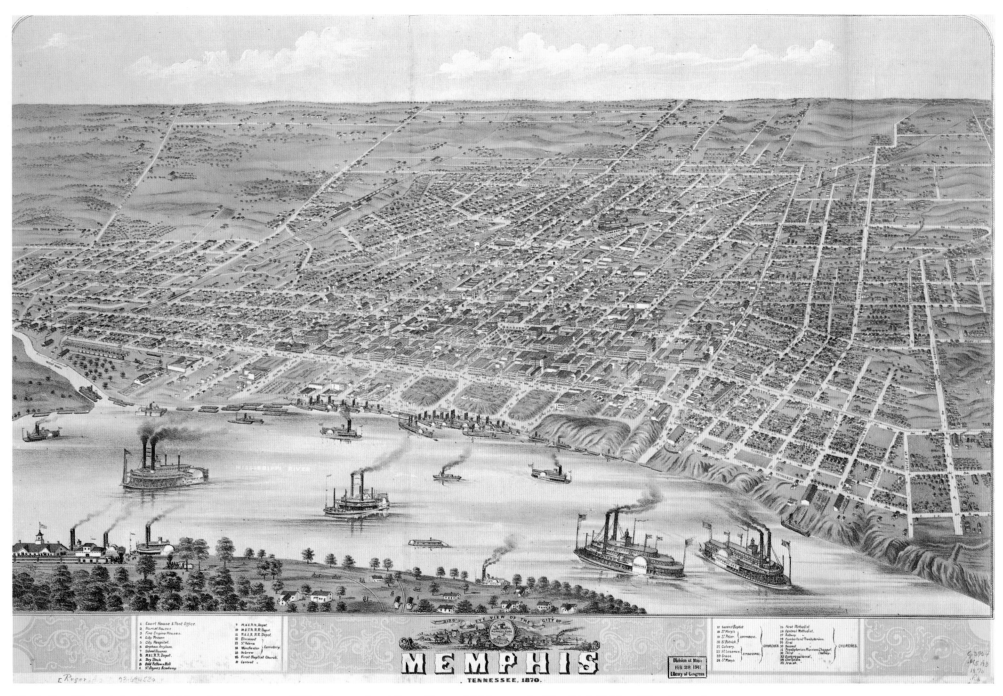

Bird's Eye View of the City of Memphis, Tennessee 1870. [Drawn by Albert Ruger.] Lithograph, 22 x 34 3/16 in. (56 x 87 cm).

Geography and Map Division, Library of Congress

Folio 21.   Postwar Memphis Regains Its Former Prosperity Despite a Major Epidemic

By 1873 Memphis seems to have recovered from the disruptions the Civil War brought

From the river Memphis presents quite an imposing appearance, stately piles of buildings running along the bluff, at whose foot stretches a levée, similar to those of all the other river towns. . . . The streets of Memphis are broad, regular, and lined with handsome buildings; there is but one drawback to their perfection, and that is a wooden pavement, so badly put down, and so poorly cared for, that a ride over it in an omnibus is almost unendurable. In the centre of the town is an exquisite little park, filled with delicate foliage, where a bust of Andrew Jackson frowns upon the tame squirrels frisking around it. . . . Since the terrible visitation of yellow fever in 1873, the City Government has made most extraordinary efforts to secure perfect drainage and cleanliness in the streets; and Memphis certainly compares favorably in this respect with any of its riparian sisters, Northern or Southern. On the avenues leading from the river toward the open country there are many lovely residences surrounded by cool and inviting lawns; the churches and school buildings are handsome and numerous, and there is an air of activity and thrift which I was not prepared to find manifested after the severe experiences through which the city has passed.
(King, *The Great South*, 264–65)

An Australian author records his impressions of Memphis in 1876

The lofty stores and warehouses, the rows of shops on the broad street along the river, and the number and size of the public and private edifices, attest the results of the development of commerce created in a great measure by the Mississippi. Memphis is the outlet of a large cotton district, and exports 400,000 bales annually. It has fine public buildings and hotels, a theatre, eighteen churches, two medical colleges, five daily and three weekly newspapers, besides numerous banks and insurance offices. It is connected by railway with New Orleans, Charleston, Louisville, and Little Rock; and possesses foundries and manufactories of boilers and machinery. Its population is estimated at something over 30,000. . . . Memphis is a wonderful place, and impressed me with the idea of progress more than any other place in the States.
(Falk, *Trans-Pacific Sketches*, 253–54)

Mark Twain revisits Memphis in 1882 and finds a different and improved city

This is a very different Memphis from the one which the vanished and unremembered procession of foreign tourists used to put into their books a long time ago. In the days of the now forgotten but once renowned and vigorously hated Mrs. Trollope, Memphis seems to have consisted mainly of one long street of log-houses, with some outlying cabins sprinkled around rearward toward the woods; and now and then a pig, and no end of mud. That was fifty-five years ago.
(Twain, *Life on the Mississippi*, 321–23)

An American travel writer traces the city's development to 1884

Twenty years after its foundation the population had increased to three thousand three hundred and sixty; in 1884, it had reached nearly fifty thousand. Memphis has attained the dignity of being the most important point on the river between Saint Louis and New Orleans. The city is very tastefully and conveniently planned, and is adorned with many elegant and substantial private residences and public structures. The Esplanade, between Front street and the river, forms a fine addition to the city, and here we find the Custom House, a splendid specimen of architecture, built of the best quality of marble from the Tennessee quarries. The business streets are wide and regular and lined with handsome stores. Many of the private residences are surrounded with beautiful lawns, ornamented with classic statuary and flowers in profuse variety. The city occupies an area of over three square miles, a handsome park, filled with trees, adorning its centre. . . . Intersecting the city is the Bayou Gayoso, with several branches, which, up to the year 1860, was the receptacle of most of the city drainage. Since that date over forty miles of sewers have been constructed and the city is now provided with a very superior and effective system of drainage. The facilities for transportation by railway are abundant in every direction, and to these are added an excellent and well-appointed street railway.
(Glazier, *Down the Great River*, 354–55)

Charles Dudley Warner admires Memphis in 1885 but dislikes its streets

The traveller . . . does not need figures to convince him of the business activity of the town; the piles of cotton beyond the capacity of storage, the street traffic, the extension of streets and residences far beyond the city limits, all speak of growth. There is in process of construction a union station to accommodate the six railways now meeting there and others projected.

As to its external appearance, it must be said that the city has grown so fast that city improvements do not keep pace with its assessable value. . . . The city offices are shabby, the city police quarters and court would disgrace an indigent country village, and most of the streets are in bad condition for want of pavement.
(Warner, *Studies in the South and West*, 297–98)

A View of Memphis, Tenn. Drawn by A[lfred] R. W[aud]. From *Every Saturday* n.s. 3 (September 23, 1871): 305. Wood engraving, 9 1/4 x 12 in. (23.4 x 30.4 cm).

John W. Reps

Perspective Map of the City of Memphis, Tenn. 1887. Published by Henry Wellge & Co., Milwaukee. Lithograph, 24 3/4 x 40 3/4 in. (63 x 105 cm).

Geography and Map Division, Library of Congress

Memphis, Tennessee, from the air, October 13, 1988.

Alex MacLean

Folio 22.   Early Observers of Cairo Note the Difficulties Encountered in Creating a City on an Unfavorable Site

Timothy Flint records the failure of the first attempt in 1818

A speculation was got up, to form a great city at the delta, and in fact they raised a few houses upon piles of wood. The houses were inundated, and when we were there, "they kept the town," as the boatmen phrased it, in a vast flat boat, a hundred feet in length, in which there were families, liquor-shops, drunken men and women, and all the miserable appendages to such a place. To render the solitude of the pathless forest on the opposite shore more dismal, there is one gloomy-looking house there.
(Flint, *Recollections of the Last Ten Years in the Valley of the Mississippi*, 64)

In 1839 the Cairo Company promises extensive improvements

The company . . . will proceed to make levees, embankments, canals, dry docks, and erect warehouses, stores and shops, for the convenience of every branch of commercial business; also buildings adapted for every useful mechanical and manufacturing purpose; likewise dwelling houses, of such description and cost, as will suit the taste and convenience of every citizen. The buildings will be principally of stone and brick, and the plan, system, style and location such, as will best accommodate the business of the place.
("Prospectus," quoted in J. C. Wild, *The Valley of the Mississippi Illustrated in a Series of Views*, 89)

An English traveler in 1841 finds no evidence of the promised improvements

Nothing is seen but a few small dwellings of the humblest class of workmen, not exceeding 20 in number, and the whole population of the spot did not appear to exceed 100. So injudiciously conducted were the first operations on the spot, that the infant settlement had already been completely submerged; and but a few weeks since, all its inhabitants were obliged to abandon it, to avoid being drowned! Instead of raising the site of the proposed city to a sufficient height to secure it from the annual overflow of the river, which ought to have been the very first operation, the few dwellings erected here, are not 10 feet above the level of the present surface of the streams, both of which are much below their maximum height; and every year, therefore, the same submersion of them may be expected. That the site is an eligible one, as far as mere position is concerned, there cannot be a doubt . . . ; but then it wants elevation to secure it from overflow. . . . If these desiderata should be supplied, no doubt a great city might be made to grow up here; but under the present aspect of things, there seems to be no well-founded hope of the Cairo of the Mississippi ever resembling the Cairo of the Nile, in any thing but its name.
(J[ames] S[ilk] Buckingham, *The Eastern and Western States of America*, 3:81–82)

Charles Dickens, possibly an unhappy investor in Cairo city bonds, cannot find a kind word to write about the place in 1842

At length . . . we arrived at a spot so much more desolate than any we had yet beheld, that the forlornest places we had passed, were, in comparison with it, full of interest. At the junction of the two rivers, on ground so flat and low and marshy, that at certain seasons of the year it is inundated to the house-tops, lies a breeding-place of fever, ague, and death; vaunted in England as a mine of Golden Hope, and speculated in, on the faith of monstrous representations, to many people's ruin. A dismal swamp on which the half-built houses rot away; cleared here and there for the space of a few yards; and teeming, then, with rank unwholesome vegetation, in whose baleful shade the wretched wanderers who are tempted hither, droop, and die, and lay their bones; the hateful Mississippi circling and eddying before it . . . ; a hotbed of disease, an ugly sepulchre, a grave uncheered by any gleam of promise; a place without one single quality, in earth or air or water, to commend it: such is this dismal Cairo.

On his return from St. Louis, Dickens fires another verbal salvo at the place

We came again in sight of the detestable morass called Cairo; and . . . lay alongside a barge, whose starting timbers scarcely held together. It was moored to the bank, and on its side was painted "Coffee House;" that being, I suppose, the floating paradise to which the people fly for shelter when they lose their houses for a month or two beneath the hideous waters of the Mississippi.
(Charles Dickens, *American Notes*, 143, 155)

Another foreign visitor tells his readers about the unfortunate history and location of Cairo

It was, at one time, intended to build a city at the confluence of the [Ohio and Mississippi rivers], which, had it started into being, would have been a formidable rival to St. Louis. The Chief obstacle in the way of the project was, that the site on which the town was to rest was very frequently under water. Cairo was to have been its name, but it by no means follows that because one Cairo can stand ankle deep in the sands of the desert, another could so up to the knees in the marshes of the Ohio. For the present, therefore, the Cairo of the West is a mere phantasy.
(Mackay, *The Western World; or, Travels in the United States in 1846–47*, 141–42)

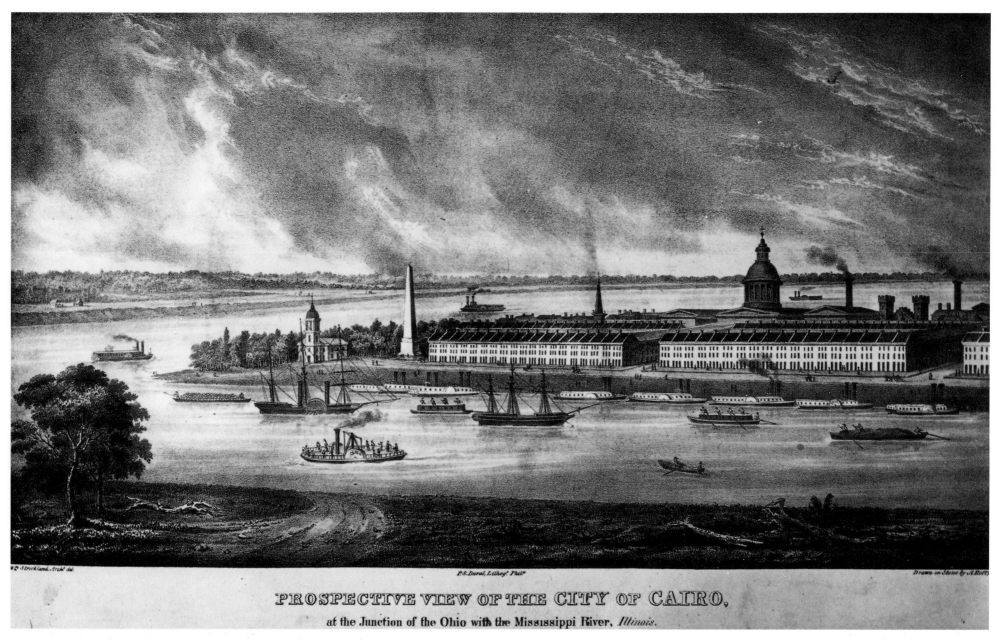

PROSPECTIVE VIEW OF THE CITY OF CAIRO,
at the Junction of the Ohio with the Mississippi River, *Illinois.*

Prospective View of the City of Cairo, at the Junction of the Ohio with the Mississippi River, Illinois. Drawn by Wm. Strickland. Lithographed by A[lfred] Hoffy. Printed by P. S. Duval, Lithogr. Phil[adelphia], 1838. Lithograph, 10 9/16 x 19 7/16 in. (25.8 x 49.3 cm).

Preston Player Collection, Knox College Library, Galesburg, Ill.

The thriving City of Eden, as it appeared on paper.
Drawn by Phiz [pseud. for Hablot Knight
Browne]. From Charles Dickens, *The Life and
Adventures of Martin Chuzzlewit* (London, 1843).
Etching, 3 3/4 x 5 3/4 in. (9.5 x 14.6 cm).

Rare Books, Olin Library, Cornell University

The thriving City of Eden as it appeared in fact. Drawn
by Phiz. From Dickens, *The Life and Adventures of
Martin Chuzzlewit*. Etching, 4 1/2 x 6 in.
(11.4 x 15.2 cm).

Rare Books, Olin Library, Cornell University

Cairo. Illinois. [Drawn by John Caspar Wild.] From Wild, *The Valley of the
Mississippi Illustrated in a Series of Views* (1841). Lithograph,
5 3/4 x 9 1/8 in. (14.6 x 23.2 cm).

St. Louis Mercantile Library Association

View of Cairo, Junction of the Ohio and Mississippi Rivers. Drawn by Kilburn. From *Ballou's Pictorial Drawing-Room Companion* 11 (August 30, 1856): 140. Wood engraving, 5 1/8 x 9 1/2 in. (13 x 24.1 cm).

John W. Reps

Folio 23.   Visitors to Cairo Continue to Criticize the City and Note the Drawbacks of the Flood-prone Site

Edward Dicey, an English correspondent during the Civil War, can find nothing complimentary to say about the Cairo he saw in 1862

There are some places in the world which, when you get to, your first thought is—how shall I get away again; and of these Cairo is one. . . .

The whole town is below the level of the river, and would be habitually under water, were it not for the high dykes which bar out the floods. As it is, Cairo is more or less flooded every year, and when I was there the whole town was under water, with the exception of the high jetty which fronts the Ohio. On this jetty, the one great street of the town, the railroad runs, and opposite the railroad are the hotels and stores, and steam-boat offices. On the land side of the jetty there stretches a town of low wooden houses standing, when I saw them, in a lake of sluggish water. Anything more dismal . . . can hardly be conceived. . . .

The smoke of the great steamboat chimneys hung like a pall over the town, and . . . the inhabitants were obviously too dispirited to do what little they could have done to remedy the unhealthiness of their town. Masses of putrid offal, decaying bones, and dead dogs, lay within eye-sight (not to allude to their proximity to the nasal organ) of the best dwellings in the city. . . .

The truth is, that the town is a mere depot for transhipping goods and passengers at the junction of the Ohio and Mississippi rivers, and the great Illinois Central railroad. There is money to be made there, and therefore people are always found to come and settle at Cairo for a time. But the time, either by choice or stern necessity, is always a very short one.
(Edward Dicey, *Six Months in the Federal States*, 2:116–19)

An Australian observer reaches the same conclusions in 1875

Cairo is built on a bank of slimy mud. As the steamer approached the desolate embankment, which seemed the only barrier between the low land on which the town is built and the waters of the great river rising about it, it certainly was difficult to imagine that sane men, even though they be speculators, could have fixed upon such a spot, on which to place the site of a city—an emporium of trade and commerce. The town itself is a collection of brick houses and wooden shanties, and the streets are rendered almost impassable by mud. A more desolate-looking place cannot be conceived.
(Falk, *Trans-Pacific Sketches*, 251–52)

An American explorer, author, and lecturer summarizes Cairo's situation and offers a cautious vision of the future

Cairo is said to be the geographical centre of the trade and population of our country. At the junction of two of its greatest rivers it would naturally seem to invite commerce, and also seem to occupy the very position for the metropolis of the Mississippi Valley. So reasoned the early settlers, and Cairo sprang into existence. But beyond its geographical position at the mouth of the Ohio . . . it possessed no natural advantages. The ground was low and annually overflowed during the spring freshets. . . .

Since that time large sums of money have been expended in improvements, chiefly in the construction of levees to protect it from inundation; but trade and commerce have in a great measure passed it by. . . . Steamers upon the Mississippi and the Ohio make Cairo one of their regular stopping-places, and a number of railroads centre here. . . . If railroads and river facilities could make a town, then surely Cairo ought to be one of the most prosperous in the West.

Cairo is now a city of eleven thousand still hopeful inhabitants. It has several good hotels, and a fine Custom House of cut stone. . . . The country buildings are also large and handsome. The levee keeps within bounds the two rivers which, not a generation ago, almost yearly united and spread out in a broad expanse of water several miles in extent at that point. But it does not give consistency to the Illinois mud, which, stickier and deeper even than that of the Chicago of early days, still turns the streets into semi-fluid canals at certain seasons of the year. Neither can it keep back the malaria which infests the lower portion of the State of Illinois. . . .

It is not a handsome city, though there are some fine buildings, and its general architecture has improved of late years. The flat unpicturesque country and the yellow flood of the Mississippi possess, neither of them, elements of beauty. Its future may possibly be brighter than its past, though it will probably never reach the goal of its early ambition.
(Glazier, *Down the Great River*, 339–42)

Mark Twain visits Cairo in 1882 and confidently predicts future prosperity

Cairo is a brisk town now; and is substantially built, and has a city look about it which is in noticeable contrast to its former estate, as per Mr. Dickens's portrait of it. However, it was already building with bricks when I had seen it last—which was when Colonel (now General) Grant was drilling his first command there. . . . Cairo has a heavy railroad and river trade, and her situation at the junction of the two great rivers is so advantageous that she cannot well help prospering.
(Twain, *Life on the Mississippi*, 280)

1. COURT HOUSE.
2. SCHOOL HOUSES.
3. MARKET HOUSE.
4. I.C.R.R. DEPOT.
5. GAS WORKS.
6. EPISCOPAL CHURCH.
7. CATHOLIC.
8. METHODIST.
9. PRESBYTERIAN.
10. LORETTO CONVENT.
11. CUSTOM HOUSE.
12. U.S. COMMISSARY.
13. ST CHARLES HOTEL.

CHURCHES.

CAIRO.
ILLINOIS 1867.

Cairo. Illinois 1867. Drawn by A[lbert] Ruger. Printed by Chicago Lithographing Co. Lithograph, 19 3/4 x 28 1/4 in. (50.2 x 71.8 cm).
Geography and Map Division, Library of Congress

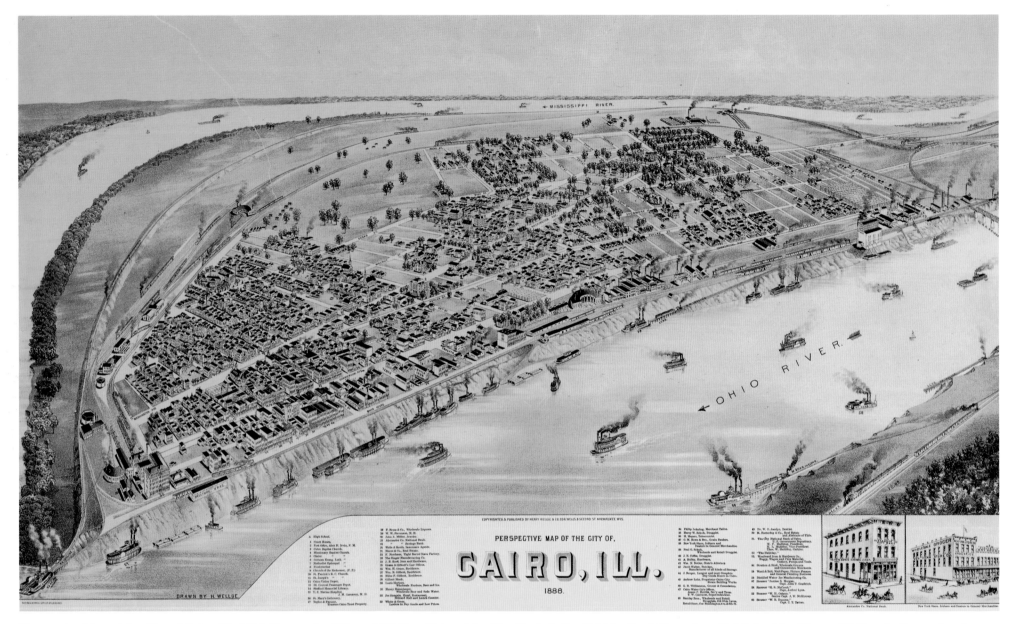

Perspective Map of the City of Cairo, Ill. 1888. Drawn by H[enry] Wellge. Printed by The Beck & Pauli Lith. Co. Milwaukee. Published by Henry Wellge & Co. cor[ner] Wells & Second St. Milwaukee, Wis. Lithograph, 18 7/8 x 33 3/8 in. (48 x 85 cm).

Geography and Map Division, Library of Congress

Cairo, Illinois, from the air, October 13, 1988.

Alex MacLean

Folio 24.   Cape Girardeau in Missouri and Kaskaskia and Cahokia in Illinois Remind Travelers of Their French Origins

In 1834 Cape Girardeau seems of small importance

In ascending the Mississippi River from the mouth of the Ohio, several towns are seen in succession, on each side of the river, after having passed 50 miles.

Cape Girardeau is the first town on the Missouri side. It is a small place, but will eventually be one of much importance. It is situated on a bluff of considerable elevation, and a rich country spreads out from it. It is 50 miles from the junction of the Ohio and Mississippi.
([Baird], *View of the Valley of the Mississippi*, 243)

The compiler of a Missouri gazetteer in 1867 describes a substantially larger community

Cape Girardeau, the commercial city, and the most important place in [Cape Girardeau] County, is located upon a commanding site, overlooking the Mississippi River. . . . The best private residences are in the outskirts of the town, and the few old French buildings, valued by some for their antiquity and past history, add nothing to the beauty of the place. . . . This place, in 1850, had a population of only about 800, which has within ten years increased to 3000.
(Nathan H. Parker, *Missouri as It Is in 1867* . . . , 210–11)

Edmund Flagg tells of his visit to Kaskaskia in 1836

A low sandy beach stretched itself more than a mile along the river, destitute of trees, and rounding itself gently away into a broad green plain. Upon this plain . . . at the distance of a few hundred yards from the water, is situated all that now remains of "old Kaskaskia." From the centre rises a tall Gothic spire, hoary with time, surmounted by an iron cross; and around this nucleus are clustered irregularly, at various intervals, the heavy-roofed, time-stained cottages of the French inhabitants. These houses are usually like those of the West India planters—but a single story in height—and the surface which they occupy is, of course, in the larger class, proportionably increased. They are constructed, some of rough limestone, some of timber, framed in every variety of position—horizontal, perpendicular, oblique, or all united—thus retaining their shape till they rot to the ground, with the interstices stuffed with the fragments of stone, and the external surface stuccoed with mortar; others—a few only—are framed, boarded, etc., in modern style. Nearly all have galleries in front, some of them spacious, running around the whole building, and all have garden-plats enclosed by stone walls or stoccades [*sic*]. . . .

The view [from the church belfry] was extremely beautiful: the settlement scattered for miles around, with the quaint little cottages and farms all smiling in the merry sunlight, could hardly fail of the lovely and picturesque. . . . The Nunnery at Kaskaskia is a large wooden structure, black with age, and formerly a public house. With this institution is connected a female seminary, in high repute throughout this region, and under superintendence of ten of the sisters. A new nunnery of stone is about being erected.

Flagg also sees Cahokia on the same trip

Cahokia . . . is supposed to have been settled by the followers of La Salle during his second expedition to the West in 1683, on his return from the mouth of the Mississippi. More than a century and a half has since elapsed; and the river, which then washed the foot of the village, is now more than a mile distant. . . .

For many years Cahokia, like old Kaskaskia, was the gathering-spot of a nomadic race of trappers, hunters, miners, voyageurs, engagés, *couriers du bois*, and adventurers, carrying on an extensive and valuable fur-trade with the Indian tribes of the Upper Mississippi. This traffic has long since been transferred to St. Louis, and the village seems now remarkable for nothing but the venerableness of age and decay. All the peculiarities of these old settlements, however, are here to be seen in perfection. The broad-roofed, whitewashed, and galleried cottage; the picketed enclosure; the kitchen garden. . . . Here, too, is the gray old Catholic church, in which service is still regularly performed by the officiating priest. Connected with it is now a nunnery and a seminary of education for young ladies.
(Edmund Flagg, *The Far West: or, a Tour Beyond the Mountains* . . . , 2:28–30, 63–64, 117–18)

John Caspar Wild also sees the two villages and draws their images in 1841

The accompanying view [of Kaskaskia] was taken from the east bank of the Kaskaskia river. . . . Under the territorial government its prosperity was at the highest; it then numbered about seven thousand inhabitants, and many fine public buildings, among them, a spacious capitol, a Jesuit college and a cathedral, not a vestige of either of which is now remaining. . . .

The following is about the present state of [Cahokia]: A convent, court house, post office, catholic chapel, three taverns, five or six groceries, one general store and between sixty and seventy houses. Since [1837] the population has advanced about twenty-five or thirty per cent. The houses of the town are straggling, hence its actual extent is not obvious.
(Wild, *The Valley of the Mississippi Illustrated*, 61–62, 106)

Capital View of Cape Girardeau. Drawn and lithographed by A. Bottger. Printed by Chas. Robyn & Co. 51 Chestnut St. cor of 3d. St. Louis, Mo. 1858.
Lithograph, 10 5/16 x 27 1/8 in. (51.8 x 69.1 cm).

Missouri Historical Society

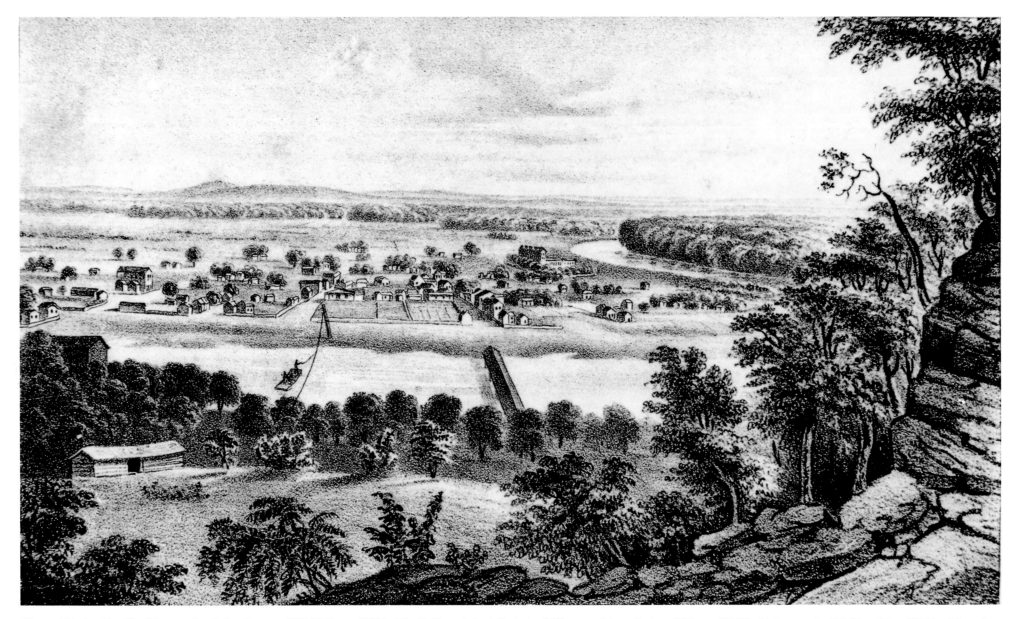

View of Kaskaskia, Ills. [Drawn by John Caspar Wild.] From Wild, *The Valley of the Mississippi Illustrated in a Series of Views* (1841). Lithograph, 5 3/8 x 8 in. (13.7 x 23 cm).
St. Louis Mercantile Library Association

Cahokia, Illinois. [Drawn by John Caspar Wild.] From Wild, *The Valley of the Mississippi Illustrated.* Lithograph, 6 1/8 x 8 7/8 in. (16 x 22.6 cm).

St. Louis Mercantile Library Association

Folio 25.   St. Louis Grows from a Crude and Tiny Frontier Settlement in the Early Years of the Nineteenth Century

The American officer assuming control of St. Louis at the time of the Louisiana Purchase describes the place in 1804

St. Louis, the capital of Upper Louisiana, is situated on the west bank of the Mississippi, eighteen miles below the mouth of the Missouri, and fourteen miles above that of the Merimak [*sic*]. . . . It was founded in 1764 . . . for the purposes of trade . . . , and since that period, St. Louis has been the emporium of trade in Upper Louisiana. In 1766 this village received a large accession of inhabitants from the opposite side of the river, who preferred the government of Spain to that of England. The situation of the town is elevated; the shore is rocky, which effectually prevents the encroachments of the river. It has two long streets running parallel with the Mississippi, with a variety of others intersecting them at right angles. It contains about one hundred and eighty houses, and the best of them are built of stone. Some of them, including the large gardens, and even squares, attached to them, are enclosed with high stone walls; and these, together with the rock scattered along the shore and about the streets, render the air uncomfortably warm in summer. A small sloping hill extends along in the rear of the town, on the summit of which is a garrison, and behind it an extensive prairie, which affords plenty of hay, as also pasture for the cattle and horses of the inhabitants.

He mentions efforts to fortify St. Louis

After the attack made on St. Louis in 1780 by the governor of Michillimakinak, the Spanish government found it necessary to fortify the town. It was immediately stockaded, and the stone bastion and the demilune at the upper end of it were constructed. In 1794 the garrison on the hill in the rear of the town and government house, was completed. In 1797, when an unfriendly visit was expected from Canada, four stone towers were erected at nearly equal distances in a circular direction round the town, as also a wooden blockhouse near the lower end of it. It was contemplated to enclose the town by a regular chain of works, and the towers were intended to answer the purposes of bastions. But as the times grew more auspicious, the design was abandoned, and the works left in an unfinished state.
(Stoddard, *Sketches, Historical and Descriptive, of Louisiana*, 18–19)

A longtime observer of the development of the Mississippi valley tells his readers about the town's appearance

St. Louis, as you approach it, shows, like all the other French towns in this region, to much the greatest advantage at a distance. The French mode of building, and the white coat of lime applied to the mud or rough stone walls, give them a beauty at a distance, which gives place to their native meanness, when you inspect them from a nearer point of view. The town shows to very great advantage, when seen from the opposite shore. . . . The site is naturally a most beautiful one, rising gradually from the shore to the summit of the bluff, like an amphitheatre. It contains many handsome, and a few splendid buildings. The country about it is an open, pleasant, and undulating kind of half prairie, half shrubbery. A little beyond the town, there is considerable smooth grass prairie. . . . Just beyond the skirts of the town, are some old, white stone forts, built in Spanish times, as defences against the Indians, which have a romantic and beautiful appearance. A little northeast of the town, you see a mound of a conical form and considerable elevation, an interesting relic of the olden time.
(Flint, *Recollections of the Last Ten Years in the Valley of the Mississippi*, 81–82)

An emigrant's guide published in Philadelphia in 1834 notes how St. Louis has grown and prospered

This city is growing rapidly in importance. Situated on an elevated bank, it is above the overflow of the river, and must prove a healthy place, especially as the small ponds in its vicinity are becoming drained. Two streets parallel with the river are on the first bank: the rest of the city stands upon the second bank, which spreads out into a vast plain to the west. The streets in the old part of the city are rather too narrow for convenience. But it is altogether a place of great business. It is the centre of trade for the states of Missouri and Illinois, and indeed for the Valleys of the upper Mississippi and Missouri, and it is nearly in the centre of the entire Valley of the Mississippi. The houses which have been built by the American part of the population, which greatly predominates over the French, and is now more than two-thirds of the whole, are principally of brick. The present population is about seven thousand. . . .

The amount of business done here is very great. . . . Besides the flat and keel boats, which are very numerous, I have seen twenty steam-boats lying along the wharves of this city at once. Steam-boats from every part of the Valley of the Mississippi visit this place, besides those boats which may be called regular traders or packets, between this place and various others. . . .

Last summer there were 6 steam-boats regularly employed between St. Louis and New-Orleans, besides many others which occasionally ran between these places.
([Baird], *View of the Valley of the Mississippi*, 244–46)

Partial View of St. Louis. Unsigned. Engraved by [William L.] Leney and [William] Rollison in New York City. Published by the Bank of St. Louis in 1817. Line engraving on $10.00 banknote, 2 11/16 x 6 11/16 in. (6.9 x 17 cm). View only, 1 3/8 x 2 5/8 in. (3.4 x 6.6 cm).

Eric and Evelyn Newman Collection

Unsigned and undated advertising card view for Steamboat *Peoria.* [St. Louis (?), 1832–1834.] Lithograph, view only, 5 3/8 x 19 5/8 in. (13.2 x 49.8 cm).

Missouri Historical Society

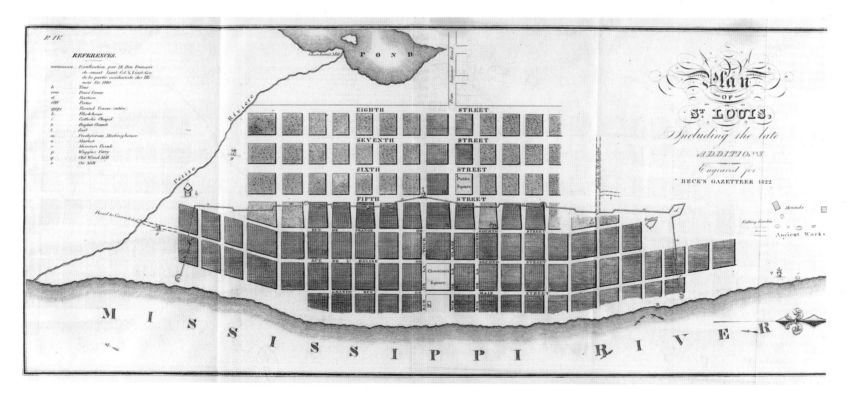

Plan of St. Louis, Including the late Additions. From Lewis C[aleb] Beck, *A Gazetteer of the States of Illinois and Missouri* (1823). Engraving, 6 1/4 x 15 3/8 in. (15.9 x 39 cm).

Eric and Evelyn Newman Collection

Folio 26.   Several Authors Record Their Impressions of St. Louis in the 1830s

A visitor in 1834 uses a nautical image to emphasize the curious appearance of St. Louis caused by ethnic differences

The aspect of the town partakes of the characteristics of all of its original possessors: In one section you find it built up entirely with the broad, steep-roofed stone edifices of the French, and the Spaniard's tall stuccoed dwelling raising its tiers of open corridors above them, like a once showy but half-defaced galleon in a fleet of battered frigates; while another will present you only with the clipper-built brick houses of the American residents,—light as a Baltimore Schooner, and pert-looking as a Connecticut smack.

He praises the site of the city and the plan of newer neighborhoods

That part of the town immediately upon the river is built, in great measure, on a rock that lies a few feet below the surface of the soil; the stone excavated in digging the cellars affording a fine material for the erection of some substantial warehouses that line the wharf. The site, for a great city, apart from its admirable geographical position, is one of the finest that could be found; and having been laid out of late years with broad rectangular streets, St. Louis, will, however it may increase in size, always be an airy, cheerful-looking place.

([Charles Hoffman], *A Winter in the West*, 2:72–74)

Edmund Flagg analyzes the St. Louis of 1836 for his readers

The city of San' Louis, now hoary with a century's years, was one of those early settlements planted by the Canadian French up and down the great valley. . . . There is an antiquated, venerable air about its narrow streets and the ungainly edifices of one portion of it; the steep-roofed stone cottage of the Frenchman, and the tall stuccoed-dwelling of the Don, not often beheld. A mellowing touch of time, which few American cities can boast, has passed over it, rendering it a spot of peculiar interest to one with the slightest spirit of the antiquary, in a country where all else is new. The modern section of the city, with its regular streets and lofty edifices, which, within the past fifteen years, has arisen under the active hand of the northern emigrant, presents a striking contrast to the old.

The site of St. Louis is elevated and salubrious, lying for some miles along the Mississippi upon two broad plateaux or steppes swelling up gently from the water's edge. Along the first of these . . . are situated the lower and central portions of the city, while that above sweeps away in an extensive prairie. . . . The latter section is already laid out into streets and building-lots; elegant structures are rapidly going up, and, at no distant day, this is destined to become the most courtly and beautiful portion of the city. It is at a pleasant remove from the dust and bustle of the landing, while its elevation affords a fine view of the harbour and opposite shore. . . .

Flagg lists the major public buildings

St. Louis, like most Western cities, can boast but few public edifices of any note. Among those which are to be seen, however, are the large and commodious places of worship of the different religious denominations; an elegant courthouse, occupying with its enclosed grounds one of the finest squares in the city; two market-houses, one of which, standing upon the river-bank, contains on its second floor the City Hall; a large and splendid theatre, in most particulars inferior to no other edifice of the kind in the United States; and an extensive hotel, which is now going up, to be called the "St. Louis House," contracted for one hundred and twenty thousand dollars. The Cathedral of St. Luke, the University, Hospital, Orphan Asylum, and the "Convent of the Sacred Heart," are Catholic Institutions, and well worthy of remark.

(Flagg, *The Far West*, 1:143–44, 164)

Mrs. Eliza Steele records her impressions of St. Louis as the decade closes

The appearance of St. Louis, from the water, is very much like Albany, as it is built upon rising ground, consisting of two plateaus of land, the last elevated several feet above the other, but its water craft gave it quite a different character. We are used in our cities to behold the water in front, bristling with masts, but here we saw steamboats alone, there being about seventy moored at the wharves, which gave a novel and western appearance, to the scene. . . . The city of St. Louis stretches a mile along the elevated shore, and nearly the same distance back. We almost fancied ourselves in New York again, so great was the stir upon the wharf. The ware-houses, of brick or limestone, made of the rock upon which they stand, appeared filled with goods and customers, boxes and bales, carts and barrows were floating about, and every one seemed active. . . . We missed our good wharves at home, and even the paved bank of Alton, for a shower had rendered the shore muddy. Surely some Yankee might contrive a more commodious landing; something that might rise and fall with the river, or a long pier.

([Eliza R.] Steele, *A Summer Journey in the West*, 183–84)

St. Louis in 1832. From an original Painting by Geo Catlin in Possession of the Mercantile Library Association. Drawn on stone and published, [St. Louis (?), 1865–1869]. Lithograph, 12 1/2 x 19 1/4 in. (31.8 x 48.9 cm).

Collection of A. G. Edwards & Sons, Inc.

Saint Louis, 1832. From a Painting by L. D. Pomarade [i.e. Pomarede]. From Camille N. Dry and Rich[ard] J. Compton, *Pictorial St. Louis: The Great Metropolis of the Mississippi Valley* (1875). Lithograph, 12 3/4 x 18 7/8 in. (32.3 x 48.1 cm).

Collection of A. G. Edwards & Sons, Inc.

Folio 27.   St. Louis Becomes the Most Imposing Settlement in the Upper Mississippi Valley

A young resident of St. Louis describes his impressions of the city as he sees it in 1838

There are a great number of buildings going up at this time [July 15]; some are very fine and built of permanent materials such as hammer dressed limestone, cut stone, & brick; some of the buildings display considerable taste and order, and would be considered an ornament to any city east of the mountains; some very elegant and spacious storehouses have been & are erecting. . . .

The public buildings are a court house & jail, two market houses, 4 hotels, one Theatre, a Convent of Nuns, one College, the St. Louis Hospital . . . , 8 churches: 2 for Presbyterians, one for Methodists, one for Epsicopalians [*sic*], one for Baptists, one for Unitarians, the Roman Catholic Cathedral & an African meeting house. There are two Orphan Asylums . . . & two Public School houses. The Court house . . . is a neat Brick building with a respectable Portico in front of an Elliptical form supported by 3 brick columns of the Ionic order plastered & marbled. . . .

The principal or lower Market is situated on Market street between front & Main streets. . . . It is so constructed that the lower part fronting on Front street is made into store rooms; these rent to tolerable good advantage . . . ; above these is the Market, or rather the Butchers stands or stalls . . . ; in the centre is the public buildings for the use of the City, such as the Mayors office, town Counsils [*sic*] room, the Calaboso or watch house, with some other rooms. This building shows to a tolerable good advantage when comeing [*sic*] up the river. . . .

The National Hotel situate on the southwest corner of Market & Third street is at this time, I think, the best house in the City. . . . The City Hotel at the corner of Third & Vine streets is in a very pleasant part of the city and is very much thronged at this time. . . . The others are the Missouri Hotel & Union Hotel, both on Main street; the Union is on the corner of Oak street & the Missouri is on the next street above. These are old houses and are not so much resorted by strangers. . . . They no doubt once were the principal houses in the city, but like ancient Babylon, their Glory has departed.

The writer describes Chouteau's Pond at the southern edge of the built-up area

Cho[u]teaus Pond . . . is a beautiful sheet of clear & mostly spring water, immediately back of the City. There are a number of lots laid out beyond it and ere long some part of the Pond will be in the City limits. It is about 3 miles long (when full of water) and about 1/4 of a mile wide. The water is clear & beautiful but not so wholesome as the river water. . . . The outlet or lower end of the Pond is at the city & about half a mile from the river. There has been an artificial enbankment [*sic*] raised here for the purpose of erecting a mill; the embankment is about 100 yards long. There is a midling large and commodious mill now rebuilding here by one of the Mr. Chouteaus, but the greatest misfortune is, there will not be a sufficiency of water the year round, & sometimes the greater part of the year too.
(Miller, "The Journal of Henry B. Miller," 248, 251–53, 271–72)

An English travel writer records his impressions of St. Louis in 1841

The plan of the town has more of regularity than might have been expected, considering its origin and recent transfer to the Americans. What is still called the French quarter, which forms the southern portion of the town, was badly built, with narrow streets, and small and mean houses; though these are all fast disappearing, to make way for better edifices. But the American portion of the city is as regularly laid out, and as well executed, as any town of similar size in the Union. Like New Orleans, Cincinnati, and Pittsburgh, it has a fine slope from the front street, which faces the river, down to the water, which now extends for about two miles along the river's bank, and at which about 100 steamboats were lying at the time of our visit, each having its bow close into the beach, with a few planks for separate communication with the shore, and their hulls hanging diagonally to the stream, all being kept in their relative positions by the force of the current pressing downward on their quarters or sterns.

From Front Street, which has only one side to it—the levee or walk in front of it being open to the river—there are several other parallel streets receding back from the stream, and ascending gradually up to the level plain. . . . Those nearest the river are almost exclusively occupied by stores and places of business; while the private residences are in the streets more remote from the river and on the hill. . . .

Of the public buildings in St. Louis, the principal is the Court House, which is nearly in the centre of the town. Though at present a large and beautiful building, it is now undergoing enlargement and decoration. . . . A very spacious Hotel is also building, in the immediate vicinity of the Court House, which has a longer frontage, and covers more ground, than the Astor House at New York. . . . There is also an immense Theatre, the exterior of which appeared to me to be as large as the Opera House in London, and which, when finished, will be an imposing structure. All these are so advantageously placed, that they will be highly ornamental to the city.
(Buckingham, *The Eastern and Western States of America*, 3:117–18)

North East View of St. Louis. From the Illinois Shore. Drawn, lithographed, [and published in 1840] by J[ohn] C[aspar] Wild. Printed at the *Missouri Republican* Office, St. Louis. Lithograph, 11 1/16 x 15 5/16 in. (28.1 x 39 cm).

Missouri Historical Society

South East View of St. Louis from the Illinois Shore. Drawn, [lithographed, printed, and published in 1840] by J[ohn] C[aspar] Wild in St. Louis. Lithograph, 11 15/16 x 15 3/16 in. (30.4 x 38.7 cm).

Missouri Historical Society

View of St. Louis from South of Chouteaus Lake. [Drawn, lithographed], printed, and published [in 1840] by J[ohn] C[aspar] Wild in St. Louis. Lithograph, 10 7/8 x 15 3/16 in. (27.7 x 38.7 cm).

Missouri Historical Society

View of Front St. Looking North from Walnut. Drawn, [lithographed], printed, and published [in 1840] by J[ohn] C[aspar] Wild in St. Louis. Lithograph, 9 3/4 x 15 in. (24.8 x 38.1 cm).

Missouri Historical Society

Folio 28.   Visitors to St. Louis in the Middle of the Nineteenth Century Witness the Results of Prosperity and Fire

An observer from Scotland in the late 1840s provides information about the city for his readers

St. Louis is a most striking town as seen from the river. The ground on which it is built slopes gently up from the water, its flatter portion being occupied by the business part of the town which adjoins the quays. For some distance the river is lined with piles of lofty and massive store warehouses, indicating the existence of an extensive "heavy business." The wharves are thronged with craft of different kinds, but from the inland position of the town the steamers greatly predominate. The city is handsomely built, chiefly of brick; and for comfort, elegance, and general accommodation, few establishments in the United States can compare with the Planters' Hotel, in which we took up our quarters. The principal streets run parallel with the river, being rectangularly intersected by others which run back from it. . . . Within its precincts, particularly about the quays, and in Front and First streets, it presents a picture of bustle, enterprise, and activity; whilst on every hand the indications of rapid progress are as numerous as they are striking. (Mackay, *The Western World; or, Travels in the United States in 1846–47*, 2:129)

John Hogan writes of St. Louis in a series of newspaper articles published as a book in 1854

Some of our principal streets have been built up so elegantly, as to have entirely changed their appearance within a year or two, and a person who left here in 1852, even, if he were now to return, would scarcely recognize the thronged thoroughfares. Some beautiful edifices have been recently erected here; I especially refer to that beautiful block of stores on the east side of Fourth Street, extending from Locust to Vine Streets . . . to be known hereafter as the "Ten Buildings". . . . The buildings are all four stories high, the front embellished by a massive finish, and together they present a beautifully imposing appearance, not exceeded probably by any block of buildings in the West, and few, indeed, in the East. The architect, Mr. William Rumbold (who also designed that magnificent building on Olive Street, not yet quite finished, the High School of the St. Louis Board of Public Schools), has introduced into these buildings many beautiful features, greatly adding to their finish and appearance.

Doubtless, the day is not distant when Fourth Street will be as well supplied with all the various articles in the fancy and fashionable line, and be as prominent a promenade as is to be found anywhere in the West. All the new stores recently erected are being occupied . . . and when fashionable stores begin to occupy that upper part of the street, it will not be very long, until all the smaller shops and dwelling houses . . . will be driven back, and made to give way before the march of improvement.

Hogan recalls the devastating fire of 1849, which caused terrible damage but led to the construction of many new buildings

What a diversity there was in the houses on Main and Second Streets, as well as on the Levee or Water Street, prior to that terrible night in May, 1849, when the devouring element swept over this devoted region like a sea of fire, scarcely leaving a house to tell the story! . . . But what a change was produced by that apparently disastrous fire! The narrow streets were widened, and the houses that have arisen on those ashes are now business palaces, built in continuous blocks of stone, brick and iron, capable of resisting and preventing such another conflagration. If a person long a resident of St. Louis, but who had left here before that great fire, were to return now, he would be lost; none of the old "land marks" being left to guide him. The narrow streets, the inconvenient houses, have given place to rows of four and five story brick stores, equal to the business purposes of those of any city in the land. . . .

The "Old Market House" had even to "give way" before the march of improvement, and now a beautiful block of thirteen stores, five stories high, fills its place on the levee, between Market and Walnut Streets. That fire gave an immense impetus to building in St. Louis. . . .

Fourth Street, a beautiful, wide, American street, which began to be built up for residences some twenty-five years ago, is now being turned entirely to business, and some of the most beautiful houses in the city are being erected up and are now occupied there.
([John Hogan], *Thoughts about the City of St. Louis, Her Commerce and Manufactures, Railroads, &c.*, 152–53, 163–64)

Another foreign visitor, Charles Mackay, summarizes the industrial accomplishments of St. Louis

The manufactures of St. Louis are numerous and important, and comprise twenty flour-mills, about the same number of saw-mills, twenty-five founderies, engine and boiler manufactories and machine-shops, eight or ten establishments engaged in the manufacture of railroad cars and locomotives, besides several chemical, soap, and candle works, and a celebrated type foundery, which supplies the whole of the Far West with the types that are absolutely necessary to the creation of all new cities in the wilderness. (Charles Mackay, *Life and Liberty in America; or, Sketches of a Tour in the United States and Canada in 1857–8*, 145)

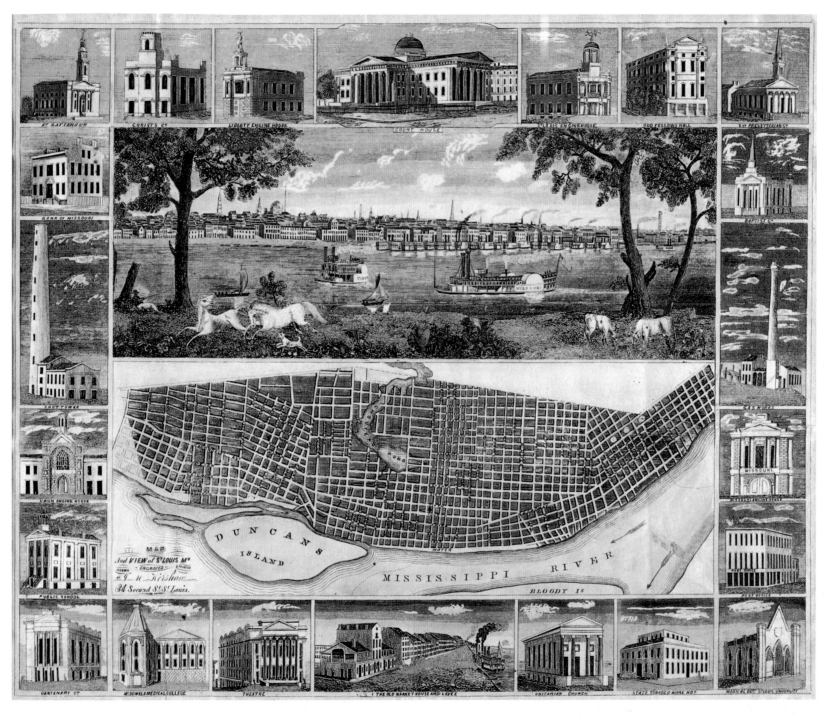

Map and View of St. Louis Mo. Drawn and printed by J[ames] M. Kershaw, 34 Second St., St. Louis. From J. H. Sloss, *The St. Louis Directory for 1848 . . .* (St. Louis: Charles and Hammond, 1848). Lithograph, 8 1/2 x 10 1/2 in. (21.6 x 26.7 cm).

Eric and Evelyn Newman Collection

Saint Louis, Mo. in 1855. Printed and published by Leopold Gast & Brother [St. Louis], 1855. From [John Hogan], *Thoughts about the City of St. Louis, Her Commerce and Manufactures, Railroads, &c* (1854). Engraving on stone, 7 3/4 x 51 3/8 in. (19.7 x 130.5 cm).
Collection of A. G. Edwards & Sons, Inc.

St. Louis. Drawn by H[enry] Lewis. [Printed by C. H. Müller, Aachen.] Published by Arnz & Co., Düsseldorf, [1854–1857]. Lithograph, 5 7/8 x 7 13/16 in. (15 x 19.9 cm).
Research Collections, Lovejoy Library, Southern Illinois University, Edwardsville

View of St. Louis, Missouri. Drawn by G[eorge] Hofmann, based in part on a daguerreotype by [Thomas M.] Aesterly [i.e. Easterly]. Engraved by E[mil] B. Krausse. Printed in New York by W. Pate. Published by C[harles] A. Cuno, Krausse & Hofmann, 31 South Main St. St. Louis, Mo, [1854]. Line engraving, 25 x 36 in. (63.5 x 91.4 cm).

Collection of A. G. Edwards & Sons, Inc.

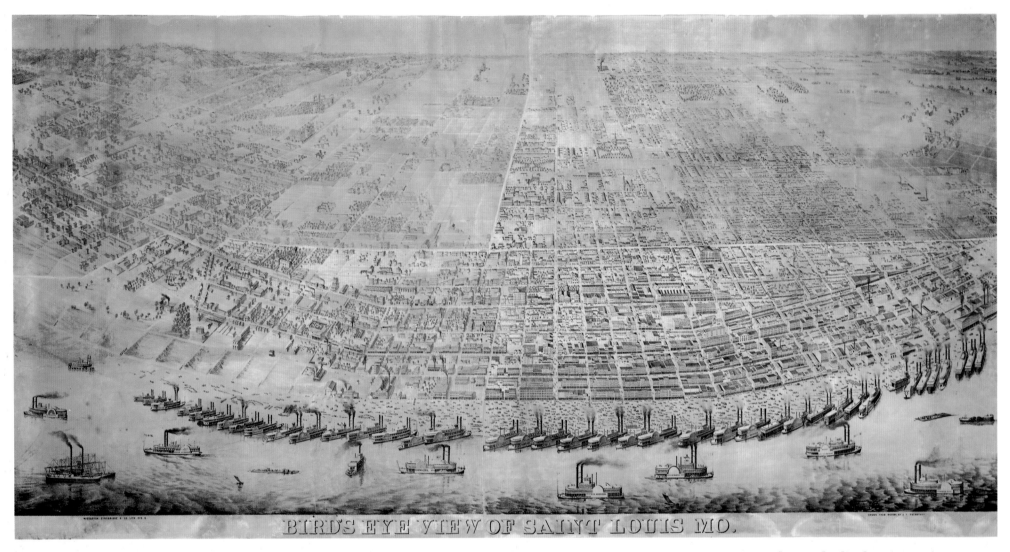

BIRD'S EYE VIEW OF SAINT LOUIS MO.

Bird's Eye view of St. Louis Mo. Drawn [and published?] by J[ames] T. Palmatary in 1858. Printed by Middleton Strobridge & Co., Cin[cinnati] O[hio]. Lithograph, 54 x 93 in. (137.5 x 236.7 cm).

Missouri Historical Society

Detail from *Bird's Eye view of St. Louis Mo.* Drawn [and published?] by J[ames] T. Palmatary in 1858. Printed by Middleton Strobridge & Co., Cin[cinnati] O[hio]. Lithograph, 54 x 93 in. (137.5 x 236.7 cm).

Missouri Historical Society

Folio 29.   St. Louis Becomes a Major Metropolis

One observer describes the city as seen from an insurance company's office building

Looking down upon the St. Louis of to-day . . . one can hardly believe the vast metropolis spread out before him represents the growth of only three-quarters of a century. The town seems as old as London. The smoke from the Illinois coal has tinged the walls a venerable brown, and the grouping of buildings is as picturesque and varied as that of a continental city.

From the water-side, on ridge after ridge, rises acres of solidly-built houses, vast manufactories, magazines of commerce, long avenues bordered with splendid residences. A labyrinth of railways bewilders the eye; and the clang of machinery and the whirl of a myriad wagon-wheels rise to the ear. The levée is thronged with busy and uncouth laborers; dozens of white steamers are shrieking their notes of arrival and departure; the ferries are choked with traffic; a gigantic and grotesque scramble for the almost limitless West beyond is spread out before one's vision.

He tells his readers about the several concentrations of business activities and the development of fashionable residential districts

As the ridges rise from the river, so rise the grades of social status. Mingled with the wholesale establishments, and the offices of mining and railway companies in Main and Second streets, parallel with the river, are hundreds of dirty and unhealthy tenement houses; on Fourth, and Fifth, and Sixth streets, and on those running at right angles with them, are the principal hotels, the more elegant of the shops and stores, the fashionable restaurants, and the few places of amusement which the city boasts; beyond, on the upper ridges, stretching back to Grand avenue, which extends along the summit of the hill, are the homes of the wealthy.

The passion for suburban residences is fast taking possession of the citizens of St. Louis, and several beautiful towns have sprung up within a few miles of the city, all of which are crowded with charming country houses.
(King, *The Great South*, 1:217–19, 222–23)

An Australian traveler of the time mentions some of the notable buildings of St. Louis

St. Louis possesses some fine public buildings. The Court House is built of limestone in form of a Greek cross, with fine Doric porticoes, and surmounted by a large cupola, from the top of which a grand view of the city, river, and surrounding country is obtained. The Four Courts buildings, in which . . . the different Courts are held, is a beautiful freestone edifice, very ornate, having in its rear a jail, constructed of iron, semi-circular in form, so arranged, that all the cells can be overlooked at the same time by a single

warder. A new building is in course of erection, to be occupied as a Post-Office and Custom House, and will when completed be very fine, and a great improvement on the present inconvenient building; as will also the new Exchange now being built. Other fine edifices are the Masonic Temple, the City Hall, the St. Louis Life Insurance building, and the Republican Newspaper building.
(Falk, *Trans-Pacific Sketches*, 243–44)

Harper's Weekly describes St. Louis in 1888

St. Louis is fast losing its identity as a semi-southern city. It is taking on the manners and customs and vigor and breeziness that characterize the wide-awake Western towns. New life has been infused into it within the past five or six years. The St. Louis of to-day has the elements of a great city, with prospects of a near future that will make it . . . the great metropolis of the Southwest. On every hand is seen the steady march of improvement in architecture, in streets, in parks, and in modes of transportation. In the business part of the city the two and three story buildings that so long lined its thoroughfares are passing away, and in their places are springing up magnificent structures of stone and iron, towering skyward, with all the advantages of the modern metropolitan style of architecture. Solid blocks of granite ring beneath the iron-shod hoof of the commercial steed, and no more do clouds of limestone dust arise to blind the pedestrian.
("St. Louis of To-Day," 421)

The author of a book on western cities describes St. Louis at the turn of the century

St. Louis . . . acquired Forest Park, the greatest natural public city park in the country, after Fairmount in Philadelphia, also O'Fallon Park, but little less magnificent. Through the philanthropic generosity of Henry Shaw she acquired Tower Grove Park, which is perhaps the finest specimen of the park artificial to be found anywhere. Later, Mr. Shaw left to the city by will his botanical garden, an institution famous the world over for its collection of plants of almost every species. . . .

The city lost its river trade but has made up for it in utilization of the railroads. . . . It is one of the wealthiest cities in the country, a city of homes, and a city of perhaps more beautiful homes widely distributed in different sections than are to be found elsewhere. . . . The city has to-day a population of 575,000. In the suburban territory there are over 700,000 more people in close relationship daily and almost hourly with the business and social life of the city.
(Lyman P. Powell, *Historic Towns of the Western States*, 367, 370–72)

THE CITY OF ST. LOUIS.

The City of St. Louis. Drawn by [Charles R.] Parsons and [Lyman] Atwater. Published by [Nathaniel] Currier & [James] Ives, New York, 1874. Lithograph, 21 1/4 x 32 5/8 in. (55.3 x 83 cm).

Collection of A. G. Edwards & Sons, Inc.

Specimen Page, From Manufacturing Portion of the City. Undated and unsigned view of a portion of St. Louis [drawn by Camille N. Dry]. Published by Compton & Company, No. 3, St. Louis Life Insurance Building, Cor. Sixth and Locust, St. Louis, [1874?]. Lithograph, 13 x 18 1/2 in. (33 x 47 cm).
Missouri Historical Society

Untitled portion of view of St. Louis [drawn by Camille N. Dry]. From Camille N. Dry and Rich[ard] J. Compton, *Pictorial St. Louis: The Great Metropolis of the Mississippi Valley* (1875). Lithographic facsimile, 13 x 18 1/2 in. (33 x 47 cm).
John W. Reps

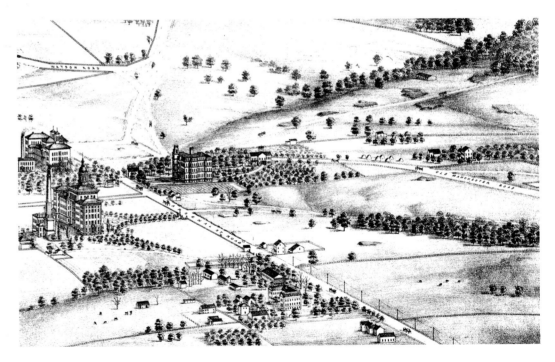

Plates 1, 2, 21, and 22 [drawn by Camille N. Dry]. From Compton and Dry, *Pictorial St. Louis.* Each lithograph, 13 x 18 1/2 in. (33 x 47 cm).

Collection of A. G. Edwards & Sons, Inc.

St. Louis in 1896. Drawn, printed, and published in St. Louis by Charles Juehne. Lithograph, 23 1/2 x 40 in. (59.7 x 101.7 cm).

Geography and Map Division, Library of Congress

St. Louis, Missouri, from the air, September 30, 1987.

Alex MacLean

Folio 30.   Despite Its Early Start, St. Charles Remains a Place of Only Modest Size and Importance

A visitor in 1820 finds St. Charles entering a period of modest prosperity at the end of its first forty years of existence

When Lewis and Clark ascended the Missouri, the town of St. Charles was said to contain one hundred houses, the inhabitants deriving their support principally from the Indian trade. This source having in a great measure failed, on account of the disappearance of the aborigines, before the rapid advances of the white population, the town remained in a somewhat declining condition for several years; but as the surrounding country was soon occupied by an agricultural population, a more permanent though less lucrative exchange is taking the place of the Indian trade. Accordingly within two or three years, many substantial brick buildings had been added, and several were now in progress: we could enumerate, however, only about one hundred houses. There are two brick kilns, a tanyard, and several stores. (Edwin James, comp., *Account of an Expedition from Pittsburgh to the Rocky Mountains Performed in the Years 1819, 1820,* 1:126–27)

A state gazetteer provides a description and historical summary of St. Charles in 1823

St. Charles . . . is built on a narrow space between the river and a considerable bluff, which admits of but one street. The site is elevated beyond the inundations of the river, but the bank is continually wearing away.

The town . . . was first founded by the French in 1780, by whom it was also called *Pette Cote,* and they continued in possession if it for a long time. Its advantageous and healthy situation, however, soon attracted the attention of the Americans; and after the cession of Louisiana, it increased rapidly. Within the last few years its increase has been very considerable. The houses which have recently been built, are of brick, and generally of a uniform style. At present it contains about 1200 inhabitants; and it may safely be affirmed, that they are not surpassed in industry and enterprise. Being the present seat of government, it is the residence of the state officers. (Lewis C. Beck, *A Gazetteer of the States of Illinois and Missouri,* 316–17)

A traveler in 1836 finds St. Charles attractive

A long line of neat edifices, chiefly of brick, with a few ruinous old structures of logs and plastering, relics of French or Spanish taste and domination, extend along the shore; beyond these, a range of bluffs rear themselves proudly above the village, crowned with their academic hall and a neat stone church, its spire surmounted by the cross.

Ten years ago . . . the pleasant little village of St. Charles was regarded as quite the frontier-post of civilized life; now it is a flourishing town, and an early stage in the traveller's route to the Far West. . . . The site of the town is high and healthy, upon a bed of limestone extending along the stream, and upon a narrow *plateau* one or two miles in extent beneath the overhanging bluffs. Upon this interval are laid off five streets parallel with the river, only the first of which is lined with buildings. (Flagg, *The Far West,* 1:268, 276–77)

John Caspar Wild tells his readers about St. Charles in a book published in 1841

St. Charles . . . was the temporary seat of government of the State until the first of October, 1826. . . . While the town enjoyed the perogatives [*sic*] of a State capitol, it flourished and promised to be a place of very great importance, but it since declined considerably, until recently a new impetus has been given it, and it has renewed its promise of future consequence. It numbers at present upwards of fifteen hundred inhabitants, and is the third town in population in the State. . . . The "main street" is about a mile and a half long, and is straight, level and McAdamized, with well-paved sidewalks. A large proportion of the buildings are substantially built of brick. There are in the town, ten stores and a number of mechanic's shops, a large steam flouring mill, a saw mill, etc. The Presbyterian and Methodist congregations have each a brick church, and the Roman Catholics a stone church in the town, and the German Lutherans have a stone church a short distance from the town. . . . The public buildings, connected with the government of the town and county, consist of a court house, jail, county and town clerks' office etc.; there is also a fine brick market house. (Wild, *The Valley of the Mississippi Illustrated,* 41)

John Warner Barber and Henry Howe describe St. Charles in their guide to the western states published in 1863

St. Charles . . . for a long time was regarded as the rival of St. Louis. The opening of the North Missouri Railroad has added much to its prosperity. It is handsomely situated on the first elevation on the river from its mouth. The rocky bluffs in the vicinity present beautiful views of both the Mississippi and Missouri Rivers. Quarries of limestone, sandstone, and stone coal have been opened near the town. The village is upward of a mile long, and has several streets parallel with the river. It contains the usual county buildings, several steam mills, etc., a Catholic convent, a female academy, and St. Charles College, founded in 1837, under the patronage of the Methodists. Population about 3,000. (Barber and Howe, *Our Whole Country,* 2:1294–95)

View of St. Charles. Missouri. Drawn by J[ohn] C[aspar] Wild. From Wild, *The Valley of the Mississippi Illustrated in a Series of Views* (1841). Lithograph, 6 1/8 x 8 3/8 in. (15.6 x 21.3 cm).

St. Louis Mercantile Library Association

VIEW OF THE CITY OF ST. CHARLES MO.

View of the City of St. Charles, Mo. Unsigned. Lithographed by H. G. Haerting. Printed by A. Janicke & Co. Lith. 41 Chestnut St. [St. Louis]. Published by Ortloff, 1850. Lithograph, 14 1/8 x 24 1/2 in. (36 x 62.4 cm).

Missouri Historical Society

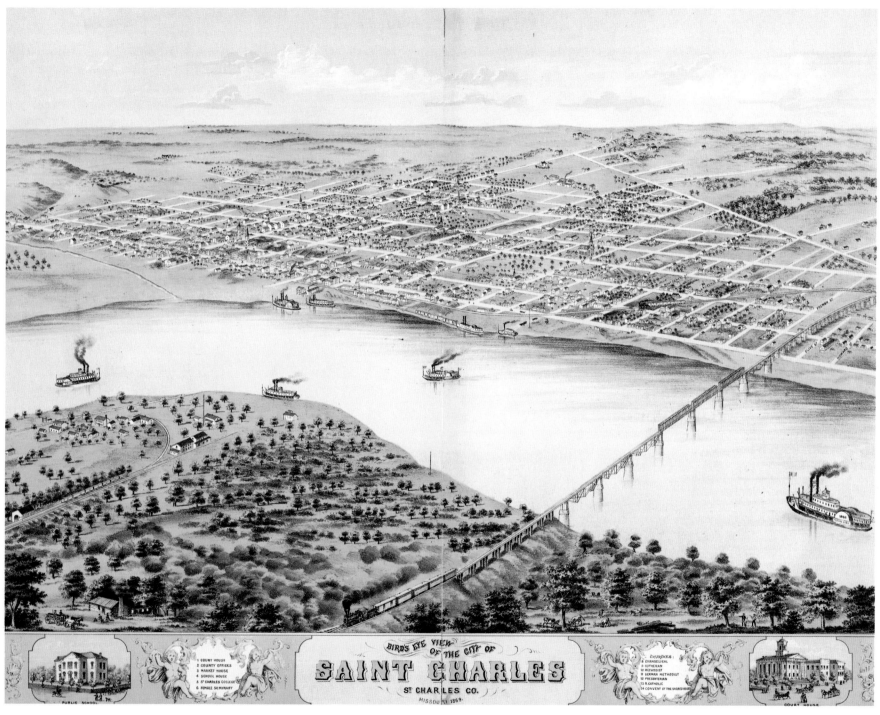

Bird's Eye View of the City of Saint Charles, St. Charles Co., Missouri 1869. Drawn by A[lbert] Ruger. Lithograph, 20 1/2 x 26 in. (52.1 x 66.1 cm).
Geography and Map Division, Library of Congress

Folio 31.   Alton, Illinois, Begins Its Existence and Experiences Modest Growth on a Site near the Mouth of the Missouri River

An emigrant's guide to the Mississippi published in 1834 provides few details about the place

Alton stands on the Mississippi, one mile above the mouth of the Missouri, sixteen miles below the entrance of the Illinois, twenty-two above St. Louis, and sixty west of Vandalia. There are two neighbouring villages, called Upper and Lower Alton. The prospect is, that Alton will become a place of great business. The population is between 500 and 1000. This will be an important station for building steam and other boats. Vast numbers of hogs and cattle, are here slaughtered for the New Orleans market.
([Baird], *View of the Valley of the Mississippi*, 228)

Edmund Flagg's description of Alton in 1836 mentions the state penitentiary

The far-famed village of Alton, situated upon the Illinois shore a few miles above the confluence, soon rose before us in the distance. When its multiform declivities shall have been smoothed away by the hand of enterprise and covered with handsome edifices, it will doubtless present a fine appearance from the water; as it now remains, its aspect is rugged enough. The Penitentiary, a huge structure of stone, is rather too prominent a feature in the scene. Indeed, it is the first object which strikes the attention, and reminds one of a gray old baronial castle of feudal days more than of anything else. The churches, of which there are several, and the extensive warehouses along the shore, have an imposing aspect, and offer more agreeable associations. . . .

The place has been laid off by its proprietors in liberal style; five squares have been reserved for public purposes, with a promenade and landing, and the corporate bounds extend two miles along the river, and half a mile into the interior. Yet Alton, with . . . its situation, on one section abrupt and precipitous, while in another depressed and confined, and the extensive alluvion lying between the two great rivers opposite, it is believed, will always render it more or less unhealthy; and its unenviable proximity to St. Louis will never cease to retard its commercial advancement.

The *city* of Alton, as it is now styled by its charter, was founded in the year 1818 by a gentleman who gave the place his name, but, until within the six years past, it could boast but few houses and little business. Its population now amounts to several thousands, and its edifices for business, private residence, or public convenience are large and elegant structures. . . . The streets are from forty to eighty feet in width, and extensive operations are in progress to render the place as uniform as its site will admit.
(Flagg, *The Far West*, 1:117–20)

A tourist in 1840 gives her impressions of Alton's appearance

Turning a sharp angle . . . we found ourselves before a large imposing looking town, built upon the bank of the river, which came sloping down from the bluffs behind. This we learned was Alton. While our crew were mooring our boat upon the steep bank, we gazed with great curiosity and interest upon this place, larger than any we had seen since leaving Detroit fourteen hundred miles behind. To the left the rocks were crowned by a large solid looking building which we were told was the penitentiary. In front was a row of high ware-houses made of limestone, filled with goods and men; while a mass of houses and steeples at our right were brightly reflecting the rays of the sinking sun. The shore presented a busy scene; men and carts and horses were transporting goods or luggage, or busily employed Macadamizing the bank—a great improvement upon the wharves we had passed.
(Steele, *A Summer Journey in the West*, 172)

John Warner Barber and Henry Howe describe Alton as they see it about 1862

The site of the city is quite uneven and broken, with high and stony bluffs, and in front of it the Mississippi runs almost a due course from east to west. The city contains a splendid city hall, 10 churches, and a cathedral in its interior superior to anything of the kind in the western states. Five newspapers are published here. As a manufacturing point, Alton has hardly an equal on the Mississippi River, and the city is now in a flourishing condition, having at hand limestone for building purposes, mines of bituminous coal, beds of the finest clay for brick and earthen ware, with railroad and steamboat communication to every point. . . . Population about 10,000.
(Barber and Howe, *Our Whole Country*, 2:1087–88)

When Willard Glazier sees Alton in 1881 the town has become industrialized and the penitentiary has been removed

Manufactories of various kinds are abundant. Among these are iron-foundries, woolen-mills, flour-mills, glass-works, a castor-oil-mill, planing-mills, several lumber-yards and steam saw-mills, and agricultural implement factories. Lime and building stone of a very superior quality are largely exported from Alton. . . . The State Penitentiary, established here in 1827, was removed some years since to Joliet. The buildings are still in existence and were utilized during the Rebellion as a government prison of war.
(Glazier, *Down the Great River*, 310–11)

View of Alton, Illinois. [Drawn by John Caspar Wild.] From Wild, *The Valley of the Mississippi Illustrated in a Series of Views* (1841). Lithograph, 5 5/8 x 7 13/16 in. (14.3 x 19.8 cm).

St. Louis Mercantile Library Association

Alton am Mississippi (in Illinois). [Drawn by Th. Anders?] Printed and published by the Kunstanst. d. Bibliogr. Instit. in Hildbh. From Charles A. Dana, ed., *The United States Illustrated: In Views of City and Country, with Descriptive and Historical Texts*, vol. 2, *The West: or the States of the Mississippi Valley and the Pacific* (New York: Hermann J. Meyer, [1853–1854]). Steel engraving, 5 x 6 1/4 in. (12.7 x 15.8 cm).

John W. Reps

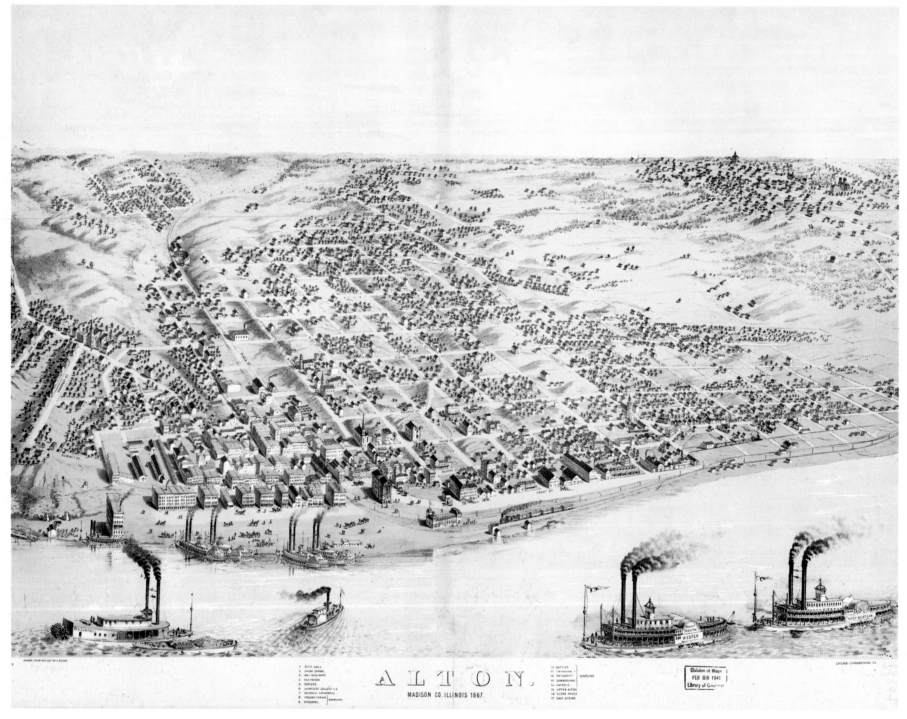

Alton. Madison Co. Illinois 1867. Drawn by A[lbert] Ruger. Printed by the Chicago Lithographing Co. Lithograph, 20 1/8 x 28 1/2 in. (51.2 x 72.5 cm).
Geography and Map Division, Library of Congress

Alton, Illinois, from the air, September 29, 1987.

Alex MacLean

Folio 32.   Henry Lewis Sketches and Describes Several Small Towns He Visited in 1848

An artist draws and tells about the curious craft from which he sketched towns of the Mississippi

In the foreground . . . is one of our overnight camps as well as the unusual little boat which we used to ply the river, making sketches at leisure for the present work. A vessel like it had probably never before been seen on the Mississippi, and every place we stopped on our journey, it aroused no small sensation.

When we arrived at Fort Snelling, we secured two Indian canoes. These we fastened firmly together, leaving an open space of four feet between them. We then boarded over the middle section of the boats, thus making a platform eight feet wide and ten feet long. Over this we built a roof, and on the sides we hung temporary walls of canvas for protection against sun and rain. Inside, various compartments were built to hold books, weapons, a tent, provisions, etc. . . . We . . . had to take a considerable supply of food on board, for the crew consisted of three men. . . .

The "Minnehaha" (for so we christened the boat, in memory of the waterfall at St. Anthony, which the Indians knew by this name) served its purpose perfectly. She sailed along quietly and safely, never rocking, so that there was no difficulty in making sketches on board. . . .
In order to sketch, we always had to cast anchor. That is speaking figuratively, for instead of an anchor we used a heavy stone tied to a rope to bring our boat to a standstill. So passed day after day until we had traversed the entire distance from the Falls of St. Anthony and had drawn all interesting points on both shores.

Lewis records in pen and ink and words his impressions of Grafton, Illinois

The city of Grafton stands on a plateau under the bluffs on the east side of the river, at the confluence of the Illinois and the Mississippi, forty miles above St. Louis. Grafton has a good landing and also possesses wide and fertile environs, besides inexhaustible quarries which provide material suitable for building, so that, generally speaking, the place has favorable prospects for becoming a center of extensive trade.

Louisiana, Missouri, catches the attention of the artist, who writes about the place in the mid–1850s

Louisiana, a busy little town in Missouri, 105 English miles above St. Louis, is famous for its flour mills. In 1851 it had a population of about 300. The aspect of the town, which we sketched for our illustration at sunrise, was one of the most charming of our entire journey.

Lewis also captures the image of Warsaw, Illinois, and includes a few words about its location and appearance

Warsaw, Illinois . . . is located on the east bank of the Mississippi, in Hancock County, Illinois, 175 miles above St. Louis. It is a small, vigorous, rapidly growing city, surrounded by numerous settlements and a farming population which together exert a favorable influence on the development of the community. Fort Edwards, a well-known frontier post . . . formerly stood on the hill on the other side of the city. . . . During the Mormon war this place was the scene of many disturbances.

At Bellevue, Iowa, the Lewis party attracts the attention of curious but friendly residents

It was a beautiful August evening when we dropped anchor opposite Bellevue and at once began sketching. It wasn't long till a brisk activity was noticeable on the shore. First two or three people showed up, who viewed the strange boat with obvious curiosity. Their intent staring out over the river soon drew a crowd of curious people who, without knowing what was actually going on, also turned their noses to the opposite bank. Finally a boat, manned by four or five armed persons, took off from the shore and approached us cautiously. When they had come within hailing distance, we called to them to come on board, and in a few minutes they drew alongside. The conversation opened with the customary greeting, *"How goes it, stranger?"* "I reckon you're prospecting," said one of the Bellevuers, doubtless the chosen speaker for the group. "No," was the answer. "Government surveyors, perhaps," he continued, and got a negative answer for the second time. "Well then," he called out, "What in the world are you doing?" *"I take the Mississippi."* "Take the Mississippi?" he cried out in astonishment. "Well, why not? Where in the d—l do you want to take it?" We finally explained that this was a matter of "taking a picture and not the actual Father of Waters." But who can describe his astonishment when we showed him the sketchbook which contained Bellevue. He looked alternately at the book and then at the town and cried out repeatedly. "Yes, that's it. Yes, indeed; d—d natural!" Next he turned several pages and found neighboring scenes and landscapes which he also recognized. Then we told him that in this way the entire Mississippi was to be taken, and finally it was to be painted on a great canvas several hundred yards long. *"Well I swan, stranger,"* he exclaimed, *"You are one!"* He meant that to be a great compliment.
(Lewis, *The Valley of the Mississippi Illustrated*, 208–10, 215–16, 260, 277–79)

The Artist's Encampment. Drawn by H[enry] Lewis. [Printed by C. H. Muller, Aachen.] Published by Arnz & Co., Düsseldorf, [1854–1857]. Lithograph, ca. 6 1/2 x 8 1/4 in. (16.5 x 21 cm).

Research Collections, Lovejoy Library, Southern Illinois University, Edwardsville

View on the Fever River. Drawn by H[enry] Lewis. [Printed by C. H. Muller, Aachen.] Published by Arnz & Co., Düsseldorf, [1854–1857]. Lithograph, ca. 6 1/2 x 8 1/4 in. (16.5 x 21 cm).

Research Collections, Lovejoy Library, Southern Illinois University, Edwardsville

The Town of Louisiana, Missouri. Drawn by H[enry] Lewis. [Printed by C. H. Muller, Aachen.] Published by Arnz & Co., Düsseldorf, [1854–1857]. Lithograph, ca. 6 x 7 1/2 in (15.3 x 19.1 cm).

Historic New Orleans Collection

Warsaw, Illinois. Drawn by H[enry] Lewis. [Printed by C. H. Muller, Aachen.] Published by Arnz & Co., Düsseldorf, [1854–1857]. Lithograph, 6 3/8 x 8 5/16 in. (16.2 x 21.9 cm).

Minnesota Historical Society

Port Byron, Illinois, and Berlin, Iowa. Drawn by H[enry] Lewis. [Printed by C. H. Muller, Aachen.] Published by Arnz & Co., Düsseldorf, [1854–1857]. Lithograph, ca. 6 3/8 x 8 5/16 in. (16.2 x 21.9 cm).

Research Collections, Lovejoy Library, Southern Illinois University, Edwardsville

Bellevue, Iowa. Drawn by H[enry] Lewis. [Printed by C. H. Muller, Aachen.] Published by Arnz & Co., Düsseldorf, [1854–1857]. Lithograph, ca. 7 1/8 x 9 3/4 in (18.1 x 24.8 cm).

Research Collections, Lovejoy Library, Southern Illinois University, Edwardsville

Folio 33. The Boyhood Home of Mark Twain Serves Its Role as a Small River Port

John Warner Barber and Henry Howe describe Hannibal as they saw it at the beginning of the 1860s

Hannibal . . . on the western bank of the Mississippi is 15 miles below Quincy, Ill., and 153 above St. Louis. It is a flourishing town and the shipping port of a large quantity of hemp, tobacco, pork, etc. raised in the vicinity. Stone, coal, and excellent limestone for building purposes, are abundant. Its importance, however, is principally derived from its being the eastern terminus of the Hannibal and St. Joseph Railroad, a line extending directly across the northern part of the state, and which, at this point, connects this great western railroad with the system of railroads eastward of the Mississippi. Hannibal was laid out in 1819, and incorporated in 1839. It is one of the most thriving towns on the Mississippi, has numerous manufacturing establishments, an increasing commerce, and about 8,000 people.
(Barber and Howe, *Our Whole Country*, 2:1291)

On his voyage down the Mississippi in 1881, Willard Glazier finds Hannibal a busy industrial community

Hannibal is a busy commercial city in Marion County, Missouri, on the west side of the river. . . . Its favorable position and extensive railroad connections have contributed largely to its rapid growth and prosperity, the latter being clearly indicated by the large number of fine residences on the surrounding slopes. The Mississippi is crossed here by a splendid iron bridge adapted for railroad, wagon and passenger travel. The city is rapidly increasing in extent and importance, and is the supply-point for large quantities of tobacco, pork, flour and other produce. The leading trade is in lumber with other parts of the State, as well as with Kansas and Texas, and it claims to be one of the most extensive lumber markets on the western bank of the Mississippi. The manufactories include iron foundries, car-shops, machine-shops, several large tobacco works, beef-curing establishments, saw-mills, flour-mills, and the lumber yards are fifteen in number. Coal and limestone abound in the vicinity, and the manufacture of lime is a prominent industry. It possesses a city hall, a Catholic seminary, several good public schools, including a high school, and daily and weekly newspapers. Hannibal College was established in 1868, under the auspices of the Methodist Episcopal Church, South, and is in a flourishing condition. The present population is about fifteen thousand and everything about the city wears the aspect of industrial prosperity.
(Glazier, *Down the Great River*, 302–3)

Mark Twain pays a nostalgic visit to Hannibal on his tour of the Mississippi River in 1882

At seven in the morning we reached Hannibal, Missouri, where my boyhood was spent. I had had a glimpse of it fifteen years ago, and another glimpse six years earlier, but both were so brief that they hardly counted. The only notion of the town that remained in my mind was the memory of it as I had known it when I first quitted it twenty-nine years ago. That picture of it was still as clear and vivid to me as a photograph. I stepped ashore with the feeling of one who returns out of a dead-and-gone generation. I had a sort of realizing sense of what the Bastille prisoners must have felt when they used to come out and look upon Paris after years of captivity, and noted how curiously the familiar and the strange were mixed together before them. I saw the new houses—saw them plainly enough—but they did not affect the older picture in my mind, for through their solid bricks and mortar I saw the vanished houses, which had formerly stood there, with perfect distinctness.

It was Sunday morning, and everybody was abed yet. So I passed through the vacant streets still seeing the town as it was, and not as it is, and recognizing and metaphorically shaking hands with a hundred familiar objects which no longer exist; and finally climbed Holiday's Hill to get a comprehensive view. The whole town lay spread out below me then, and I could mark and fix every locality, every detail.

Twain realizes that the small village of his boyhood has become a city

Hannibal . . . is no longer a village; it is a city, with a mayor, and a council, and water-works, and probably a debt. It has fifteen thousand people, is a thriving and energetic place, and is paved like the rest of the west and south—where a well-paved street and a good sidewalk are things so seldom seen that one doubts them when he does see them. The customary half-dozen railways centre in Hannibal now, and there is a new depot which cost a hundred thousand dollars. In my time the town had no specialty, and no commercial grandeur; the daily packet usually landed a passenger and bought a catfish, and took away another passenger and a hatful of freight; but now a huge commerce in lumber has grown up and a large miscellaneous commerce is one of the results. A deal of money changes hands there now.

Bear Creek—so called, perhaps, because it was always so particularly bare of bears—is hidden out of sight now, under islands and continents of piled lumber, and nobody but an expert can find it.
(Twain, *Life on the Mississippi*, 524, 545–46)

Hanibal, Missouri. Hannibal in Missouri. Drawn by H[enry] Lewis. [Printed by C. H. Muller, Aachen.] Published by Arnz & Co., Düsseldorf. Lithograph, 5 7/8 x 7 5/8 in. (15 x 19.4 cm).

Minnesota Historical Society

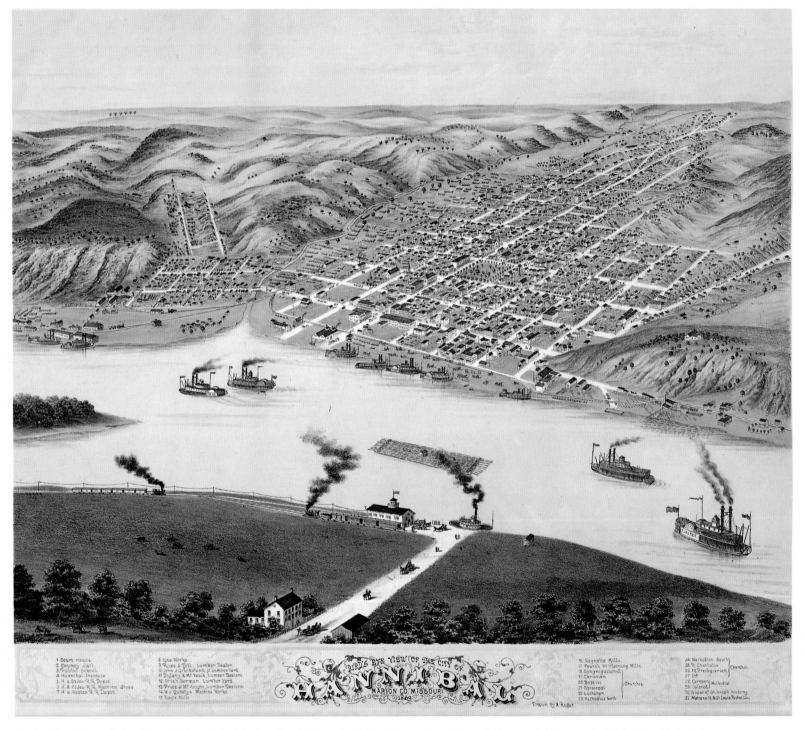

Bird's-Eye View of the City of Hannibal, Marion Co. Missouri. 1869. Drawn by A[lbert] Ruger. Lithograph, 20 1/8 x 25 3/4 in. (51.2 x 65.4 cm).

Amon Carter Museum

Hannibal, Missouri, from the air, October 12, 1988.

Alex MacLean

Folio 34.   Founded on Public Land as a New Illinois County Seat, Quincy Begins Its Existence in 1825

An early resident tells how county commissioners surveyed the town plat and put lots up for auction

Quincy was established as the county seat in July, 1825. . . . Judge [Henry H.] Snow, greatly assisted by Willard Keyes, surveyed and drew up the first plat of the town. In after years he called it the "Model City." . . . The County being named Adams, the Town Quincy, to complete the full name of the then President of the United States, the public square, now called Washington Park, was called "John's Square." . . .

On Wednesday, November 9, 1825, the Commissioners made an order employing Henry H. Snow to survey the Town of Quincy, and to draw plats thereof. . . .

The original town contained two hundred and thirty lots, the general size of which is 99 x 198 feet. . . . Agreeably to public notice previously given, the County offered for sale on the 13th of December, 1825, a number of these town lots . . . at public auction to the highest bidder. Fifty-one lots were sold to different individuals for the aggregate amount of $714.

The same author recalls Quincy in 1834 when he arrived

Quincy then contained about five hundred inhabitants. The old Land Office Hotel, sometimes called the bed-bug hotel, was the largest tavern. There were some half a dozen very respectable frame houses, a good many log houses, including a log Court House and jail, and several smaller frame houses and two small brick houses in the town. The inhabitants of the county outside of Quincy numbered from ten to twelve hundred souls.
(Henry Asbury, *Reminiscences of Quincy, Illinois . . .* , 29–31, 51)

A local newspaper in 1836 boasts of Quincy's growth and prosperity

We do not believe that there is a town in the state of Illinois, saving perhaps Chicago, which has increased at any time with the rapidity of Quincy for the past summer and fall. Besides the Court House (the old brick on the east side of the public square), the Methodist Church, (on Vermont street) one store and two dwellings of brick, there has been erected between sixty and ninety frame buildings for stores, machine shops, &c. There has been upwards of two hundred mechanics and laborers, who were not residents of the town in constant employ, and work for a hundred more, if they could have been procured. The business of the town has increased in proportion to its growth. The increase of our population has been so great, that it is impossible for them all to procure houses for love or money. The situation of Quincy—the fine country in the vicinity, and the landing of steamboats

equalled by few and surpassed by none on the Mississippi, offer sufficient inducements to merchants and mechanics who wish to make a permanent location. If in the course of ten years, and perhaps sooner, Quincy is not the largest town on the Mississippi above the mouth of the Ohio, except St. Louis, then we will confess that we are destitute of the gift of prophecy.
(*Quincy Argus and Illinois Bounty Land Register*, November 8, 1836)

An English travel writer visits Quincy in 1841 and predicts a great future when rail service becomes available

[At Quincy] we ascended the hill from the landing, and were agreeably surprised to find a large and pretty town occupying the level plain above. In the centre is a square as large as Russell or Grosvenor Squares in London, with a hotel, occupying more ground than the Clarendon, presenting four points of about 200 feet each. . . . What led to the rapid rise and extensive scale designed for this place, was the fixing on the spot on which it stands, as the terminus of a railroad from the Illinois to the Mississippi river; but the general stagnation with respect to funds has caused this to be suspended for the present, though when it shall be completed, Quincy can hardly fail to become a town of considerable size and importance.
(Buckingham, *The Eastern and Western States of America*, 3:163)

The newspaper announces the railroad's arrival—but not until 1856

The especial event of the time was the completion of the railroad to Galesburg on the last day of January . . . making the connection with Chicago complete. It was a jubilee time, and the satisfaction and anticipations of the people was [*sic*] told by the press as follows . . .

"The event is an important one and inaugurates a new era. . . . For years our citizens have been looking with an intense interest to the consummation of this enterprise which was to open, and which has opened, to Quincy, a future radiant with every promise of prosperity. A new vitality and a new strength has been given to our city, apparent in the immense increase of business in all departments, transacted during the past season. . . ."

No event ever occurred . . . that was hailed with more of universal satisfaction than the final construction of this road. It was felt to be the one needed resource to free traffic and travel from its winter thraldom when the river was closed by ice and to establish the place on conditions of equality with the surrounding rival cities, and in it the citizens had freely embarked their means and their hopes.
(John Tillson, *History of the City of Quincy, Illinois*, 163)

QUINCY, ILL:

Quincy, Ills. Unsigned. Printed by P. S. Duval & Son, Philad[elphia], ca. 1859. Lithograph, 33 1/2 x 48 1/2 in. (85.2 x 123.4 cm).

Historical Society of Quincy and Adams County

Publ. by Haerting and Ortloff.   Lith & print. in Colors by L. Gast. Bro. & Co St. Louis Mo.

View of the City of Quincy, Ill.

View of the City of Quincy, Ill. Drawn by H. G [L?] Haerting. Printed by L[eopold] Gast Bro[thers] & Co., St. Louis, Mo. Published by Haerting and Ortloff, ca. 1860. Lithograph, 23 1/2 x 29 1/2 in. (59.9 x 75 cm).

Historical Society of Quincy and Adams County

Quincy, Illinois, from the air, October 11, 1988.

Alex MacLean

Folio 35.   Quincy Prospers and Develops into an Attractive Community

John Warner Barber and Henry Howe in 1862 describe the city in their history and guide to the West

Quincy . . . is situated on a beautiful elevation, about 125 feet above the Mississippi, and commands a fine view for five or six miles in each direction. It is 109 miles from Springfield, 268 miles from Chicago, by railroad, and 160 above St. Louis. It contains a large public square, a court house, many beautiful public and private edifices, several banks, a number of extensive flouring and other mills, and manufactories of various kinds, with iron founderies, machine shops, etc. Flour is exported to a great extent, and large quantities of provisions are packed. The bluffs in front of the city may be considered as one vast limestone quarry, from which building stone of a hard and durable quality can be taken and transported to any section of the country, by steamboat and railroad facilities immediately at hand. Five newspapers are printed here, three daily and two in the German language, one of which is daily. Population about 16,000.
(Barber and Howe, *Our Whole Country*, 2:1086)

A visitor in 1877 tells his readers of the busy scene that greeted his eye upon reaching Quincy

Animated and bustling enough is the scene now before us and before the beautiful city of Quincy, from its elevation on the grand old bluffs that rise more than a hundred feet above the majestic river, affording delightful views of the surroundings to the tourist and the forty or fifty thousand people who are proud, as who would not be to call this charming city home.

Below us, as we stand upon the summit of the bluffs, are the river landings with steamers receiving and discharging their wealth of boxes, bales, barrels, and crates of freight. Yonder is a beautiful bridge extending across the river; there the Court House, of fine architectural proportions, and very many imposing edifices for business, and scores of elegant residences; there we see incoming and outgoing railway trains on roads that radiate from the city in all directions; we count a couple-of-dozen church spires, and many school-houses, and to whatever point we turn our eyes—stretching beyond the range of sight, are grounds of great fertility with their golden plush of grain, thrifty orchards laden with ripening fruit, and gardens of rare beauty. The air is balmy and refreshing; the city surely is healthful as well as busy.
(I. Winslow Ayer, *Life in the Wilds of America*, 118)

The special report on cities in the census of 1880 provides information about the city's past and present

In January, 1825, the legislature provided for the organization of Adams county, fixing its boundaries as they now exist, and appointed commissioners to locate the county-seat. . . . In November of the same year, the town was surveyed and laid off, and on the 13th of December the first sale of lots took place. For ten years the growth of Quincy was not rapid, owing, in a great measure, to her distance from other settlements. In 1830 the first regular church was organized. . . . In 1834 the town was incorporated and trustees were elected. In 1837 the first hotel was built, and in 1840 a city charter was granted. . . . The opening of railroads and the developing of coal-mines in the vicinity insured her subsequent growth and prosperity. . . .

There are 88 miles of streets in the city, 7 miles being paved with broken stones (macadam) and 8 with gravel. . . . The gutters are laid with limestone rock, and are from 5 to 10 feet wide. With the exception of the business portion of the city, trees are planted, as a rule, on all improved blocks. . . .

The horse-railroads in the city have a length of 4 1/4 miles. They use 15 cars and 65 mules, and give employment to 14 men. The rate of fare is 5 cents. Three omnibuses, with 8 horses and 6 men, carry annually 25,000 passengers to all parts of the city at the uniform rate of fare of 25 cents. . . .

The total area of the public parks in Quincy is 30 acres. They are 5 in number, and except one of 15 acres, which is projected but not yet improved, are too small for driving purposes. They are scattered over the city, 2 being suburban and 3 centrally located.
(U.S. Census Office, *Report on the Social Statistics of Cities*, 2:530–33)

Mark Twain stops at Quincy in 1882 during his visit to the land of his youth

Quincy is a . . . brisk, handsome, well-ordered city; and now, as formerly, interested in art, letters, and other high things. . . .

In the beginning Quincy had the aspect and ways of a model New England town: and these she has yet: broad, clean streets, trim, neat dwellings and lawns, fine mansions, stately blocks of commercial buildings. And there are ample fair-grounds, a well kept park, and many attractive drives; library, reading-rooms, a couple of colleges, some handsome and costly churches, and a grand court-house, with grounds which occupy a square. The population of the city is thirty thousand. There are some large factories here, and manufacturing, of many sorts, is done on a great scale.
(Twain, *Life on the Mississippi*, 555–56)

Quincy, Ill. 1878. [Drawn by Clemens J. Pauli?] Printed and published by Beck & Pauli, Milwaukee, Wis. Lithograph, 20 1/2 x 26 3/4 in. (52 x 67.9 cm).
Historical Society of Quincy and Adams County

Folio 36.   Alexandria, Missouri, and Keokuk, Iowa, Occupy Sites at the Mouth of the Des Moines River

A county historian in 1887 recalls the origins of Alexandria

The survey and plat . . . was made . . . in September, 1833. This plat contained four public squares, and seventy-three blocks. It was nicely laid out on a large scale. . . .

The original proprietors of Alexandria anticipated a large future commercial city, and in many ways the site chosen for it was very favorable toward the fulfillment of their anticipations. . . . But the failure to make the Des Moines [River] navigable, and the still more serious failure to prevent the occasional inundation of the site . . . has defeated the greatest anticipations of those who once thought it would become a large city. . . .

From about the year 1858 to 1872 Alexandria was famous for the large amount of pork packed and shipped annually, and at one time it ranked as the greatest pork-packing and shipping point on the river above St. Louis. . . . In the season of 1869–70 . . . the price of pork then went down, and caused a failure of nearly all of the pork packers. Pritchett, Gartrell & Co. . . . owned a large five-story brick block facing the river. . . . About the year 1875, . . . this firm . . . and about six other business houses were consumed by fire. The pork-packing business was abandoned in 1872, . . . and this loss was a serious drawback to the commercial prosperity of the town, and the great fire which followed added very much to its commercial depression.
(*History of Lewis, Clark, Knox and Scotland Counties, Missouri,* 336–38)

An Iowa gazetteer describes Keokuk, a dozen miles north of Alexandria

Keokuk is situated upon a bluff 150 feet above high-water mark in the Mississippi, is laid out one mile square, and contains a population of nearly 7000. Its streets are wide and regular, and are being graded and McAdamized with rapidity. Main Street, 100 feet in width, is McAdamized through the city for a distance of one mile. The city contains six brick-yards, two lumber-yards, one flouring and grist-mill, two foundries, one machine shop, five hotels, &c. . . . This city also contains the Iowa Medical College, a State institution, and a Female Seminary, besides two other female institutes, and a number of private schools.
(N. Howe Parker, *Iowa as It Is in 1855* . . . , 152–53)

The compilers of a history and guide to the United States mention the waterpower resources of Keokuk and summarize its history

The site of Keokuk is remarkably fine. It covers the top and slopes of a large bluff, partially around which the Mississippi bends with a graceful curve, commanding a fine prospect to the south and north. . . . A portion of the great water power at this point is used in various manufactories, flouring mills, founderies, etc. The Mississippi, upward from this place, flows over a rocky bed of limestone, called the *Rapids,* 12 miles in extent, falling, in that distance 24 1/2 feet, making it difficult for the larger class of steamboats to pass. The city contains several splendid public buildings, the medical department of the State University, hospital, some eight or nine churches, and about 13,000 inhabitants.

The plat of the village of Keokuk was laid out in the spring of 1837, and in the ensuing June a public sale of town lots was held, and attended by a very large crowd. One boat was chartered in St. Louis, and numbers came up on other boats. Only two or three lots, the south-west corner of Main-street and the levee, and one or two others lying contiguous, were sold. . . .

In 1840, the main portion of Keokuk was a dense forest. . . . About a dozen cabins comprised all the improvements. In the spring of 1847, a census of the place gave a population of 620. Owing to the unsettled state of the titles, but little progress was made till 1849. From that time until the autumn of 1857 it had a rapid growth.
(Barber and Howe, *Our Whole Country,* 2:1255–56)

The author of a book on the American West visits Keokuk in 1877

Passing Fort Madison . . . we reach the city of Keokuk—"the Gate City of Iowa,"—so called from its position, it being at the head of navigation for large vessels on the Mississippi, and two miles from the mouth of the Des Moines River, at the foot of the lower rapids of the Mississippi, which are twelve miles in extent, with a fall in that distance of about twenty-five feet, over ledges of rock. A canal would greatly conduce to the general prosperity, and will no doubt in early time be constructed. The city . . . now has a population of nearly 25,000. It is one of the most flourishing and enterprising of our western cities. Its foundries, flour-mills, and many other industries give to it deserved distinction. . . . A bridge nearly 2,300 feet in length extends from the city across the river.
(Ayer, *Life in the Wilds of America,* 116)

Willard Glazier sees the new canal around the rapids in 1881

The Government Canal is a grand work, by means of which the dangers arising from rocks and shoals in the rapids, that formerly interfered with navigation, are entirely obviated, and large vessels pass through in perfect safety on their way up and down the river. The cost of the canal to the Government was nearly four million dollars. The largest steamboats find ample room at Keokuk for loading and discharging freight and passengers.
(Glazier, *Down the Great River,* 295–96)

Drawn from Nature by J.B.Miller.

Wm Schuchman, lith Pittsburgh, Pa

CITY OF ALEXANDRIA, MO.

City of Alexandria, Mo. Drawn by J. B. Miller. Printed by Wm. Schuchman, Pittsburgh, Pa., after 1849. Lithograph, 6 3/8 x 8 5/16 in. (16.2 x 21.9 cm).
Amon Carter Museum

KEOKUCK , JOWA .

Keokuk, Iowa. Drawn by H[enry] Lewis. [Printed by C. H. Muller, Aachen.] Published by Arnz & Co., Düsseldorf, [1854–1857]. Lithograph, 5 15/16 x 7 11/16 in. (15 x 19.5 cm).

Preston Player Collection, Knox College Library, Galesburg, Ill.

East view of Keokuk. [Drawn by John Warner Barber or Henry Howe.] From Barber and Howe, *Our Whole Country* (1863), 2:1255. Wood engraving, 3 3/16 x 4 in. (8 x 10.1 cm).

Olin Library, Cornell University

Folio 37.   The Mormons under Joseph Smith Transform a Nearly Vacant Site into a Large City before Leaving for the West

Mormon leader Joseph Smith tells of his decision to build a city on the site of the paper town of Commerce

When I made the purchase of [land for Nauvoo], there was one stone house and three log houses . . . in this vicinity, and the place was literally a wilderness. The land was mostly covered with trees and bushes, and much of it so wet that it was with the utmost difficulty a footman could get through, and totally impossible for teams. Commerce was so unhealthful, very few could live there; but believing that it might become a healthful place by the blessing of heaven to the Saints, and no more eligible place presenting itself, I considered it wisdom to make an attempt to build up a city.
(Joseph Smith, *History of the Church of Jesus Christ of Latter-Day Saints . . .* , 3:175)

A visitor in 1845 sees Nauvoo on the eve of its evacuation

We passed the famous city of Nauvoo, said to contain from 15 to 20,000 inhabitants (doubtless exaggerated), and presents a fine appearance from the river on account of the peculiar prominence given to the temple, now in process of erection. This edifice is built of a grey stone, two stories in height with a tier of portholes between the two ranges of windows. From the distance at which I saw it, merely the general outlines of the building could be seen. The main body of the building appeared to be externally complete except the roof, and there seemed to be the tower or steeple only to be carried up to a further height.
(William W. Greenough, "Tour to the Western Country," 346)

An observer visiting the town in July 1846 records his impressions of the now-ruined city

The Mormon City occupies an elevated position, and, as approached from the south, appears capable of containing a hundred thousand souls. But its gloomy streets bring a most melancholy disappointment. Where lately resided no less than twenty-five thousand people, there are not to be seen more than about five hundred; and these, in mind, body and purse, seem to be perfectly wretched. In a walk of about ten minutes, I counted several hundred chimneys, which were all at least that number of families had left behind them, as memorials of their folly, and the wickedness of their persecutors. When this city was in its glory, every dwelling was surrounded with a garden, so that the corporation limits were uncommonly extensive; but now all the fences are in ruin, and the lately crowded streets actually rank with vegetation. Of the houses left standing, not more than one out of every ten is occupied, excepting by the spider and the toad. Hardly a window

retained a whole pane of glass, and the doors were broken, and open, and hingeless. . . .

Yet, in the centre of this scene of ruins, stands the Temple of Nauvoo, which is unquestionably one of the finest buildings in this country. It is built of limestone . . . and . . . is one hundred and twenty-eight feet in length, eighty feet wide, and from the ground to the extreme summit it measures two hundred and ninety-two feet.

[From] the belfry of the Temple . . . I had an opportunity to muse upon the superb panorama which met my gaze upon every side. I was in a truly splendid temple,—that temple in the centre of a desolate city,—and that city in the centre of an apparently boundless wilderness. To the east lay in perfect beauty the grand Prairie of Illinois . . . and on the west, far as the eye could reach, was spread out a perfect sea of forest land, entering which, I could just distinguish a caravan of exiled Mormons, on their line of March to Oregon and California.
(Charles Lanman, *A Summer in the Wilderness . . .* , 30–31, 33)

A river guide published in 1850 recalls Nauvoo's history

Nauvoo . . . is the site of the celebrated Mormon city, which was laid out about 1840, by Joseph Smith and his followers. It is situated on a handsome plain, on an elevated bank, extending for some distance from the river. The city was laid out on a very extensive plan, and intended to be the great city, to which all should look, as the Jews do toward Jerusalem. A great many houses were erected, some of them on a very magnificent scale, and the city was fast being filled with the adherents of that sect, from all parts of the country. A temple was also in course of erection, which, for vastness of dimensions and splendor of design, was intended to be without a rival in the Union. But, difficulties having arisen among the members of the community, and between them and the citizens of the surrounding country, Joseph Smith . . . and Hiram, his brother, were arrested, and thrown into prison, in Carthage the county-seat, where they were, on the 27th of June, 1844, murdered, by an armed mob, in disguise, who overpowered the guard, stationed at the jail. New troubles subsequently arising, the Mormons were expelled from the state. Many of them returned to their former homes . . . ; but a large body banded together, and started toward Oregon, with the intention of there raising up a city, which should fill the place of that one, which had proved so disastrous to them. Nauvoo has since declined rapidly. A religious denomination were about making a contract for the purchase of the Temple, for a college, but it was destroyed in October, 1848, by an incendiary, who fired it in the cupola, and it is now a heap of ruins.
(*Conclins' New River Guide*, 73–74)

NAUVOE, Jllinois.

Nauvoe, Illinois. Drawn by H[enry] Lewis. [Printed by C. H. Muller, Aachen.] Published by Arnz & Co., Düsseldorf, [1854–1857]. Lithograph, 5 7/8 x 7 3/4 in. (14.7 x 19.3 cm).

Minnesota Historical Society

Nauvoo (Mississippi). [Drawn by Th. Anders?] Printed and published by Kunstanst. d. Bibliogr. Instit. in Hildbh. From Charles A. Dana, ed., *The United States Illustrated: In Views of City and Country, with Descriptive and Historical Texts,* vol. 2, *The West: or the States of the Mississippi Valley and the Pacific* (New York: Hermann J. Meyer, [1853–1854]). Steel engraving, 4 7/8 x 6 1/4 in. (12.4 x 15.8 cm).

John W. Reps

Nauvoo, from the Mississippi, Looking Down the River. Unsigned. From *Gleason's Pictorial Drawing-Room Companion* 7 (July 22, 1854): 36. Wood engraving, 7 x 9 1/8 in. (17.8 x 23.2 cm).

John W. Reps

Nauvoo. Drawn by F[rederick] Piercy. Engraved by C[harles] Fenn. From Piercy, *Route from Liverpool to Great Salt Lake Valley* (1855). Steel engraving, 7 1/4 x 10 5/16 in. (18.4 x 26.1 cm).

John W. Reps

Folio 38.   Fort Madison, Iowa, Achieves Urban Status at the Site of an Early Military Establishment

In 1836, a year after the town was laid out, Albert Lea praises its site and predicts a prosperous future

This is the site of old Fort Madison which was abandoned by its garrison and burnt during the last war with Britain. Nature seems to have designed this place for the trade of an extensive back country. It has an excellent landing, the only good one from Fort Des Moines to Burlington; and the locality is well adapted to an extensive city. By casting the eye upon the map it will be perceived that all the fine country between Des Moines River and Chauqua . . . River must do its import and export business at this point. (Albert M. Lea, *Notes on Wisconsin Territory, with a Map*, 35–36)

A county history of 1879 recounts how the town plat was surveyed twice

Gen John H. Knapp and Nathaniel Knapp arrived . . . in 1833 . . . and . . . in the fall of 1835 the Knapps staked out a town, the eastern limit being what is now Oriental street and the western limit a point about half-way between Cedar and Pine streets. . . .

At that time, there was some open ground about the ruins of the old fort, but all the lower portion of the present town was heavily timbered with oak, black walnut, elm, sycamore and ash, and game abundant within what is now the city limits. There were but four cabins on the present town site. . . . Settlers began to arrive soon after, and the Knapps began selling lots. In 1836, there was quite an influx of new-comers, and quite a number of cabins were erected. . . .

At that time, the whole of the town of Fort Madison was above the offset in Front street, with the exception of a few whisky-shanties along the bank of the river below. As the town plat was originally laid out, there were fractional lots between Front street and the river for three blocks opposite and below the old fort. . . .

On the 2d of July, 1836, Congress passed an act, designating certain tracts of land [in Iowa] to be laid off into town lots, one of which was the present site of Fort Madison. This act was supplemented by another act, passed March 3, 1837, by which William W. Coriell, George Cubbage and M. M. McCarver were appointed commissioners to make the survey. Their plat extended from Oriental street on the east to Occidental street on the west, and back from the river to Ninth street; and those claimants by pre-emption to the land included in the town plat were not allowed to exceed one acre in town lots, nor more than one outlot. Certificates were issued to such claimants by the Commissioners. The first sale of lots in the new town was made at the Land Office, in Burlington, in the fall of 1838. It was conducted in the same manner as the general land sales. Those persons who had acquired

rights, either by pre-emption or by purchase of lots in the old plat made by the Knapps, were protected by provisions in the law. (*History of Lee County, Iowa* . . . , 592–96)

The author of a state history published in 1876 provides further information about early settlement at this location

Fort Madison was once a military post of great importance, but since 1853, it has never been used for such purposes, and the Indians who had long felt its presence as a standing menace, removed every vestige of the old block houses by fire as soon as they found it would be safe. This is now the county seat of Lee county. . . . The first settlement that is recorded, after the soldiers had been withdrawn, was made in 1832, and the town was incorporated by act of congress four years afterwards. . . .

Before Iowa had been admitted to the honors and responsibilities of a sovereign state, the general government ordered the erection of a penitentiary here, and that work was completed in 1842. . . . The state is now the director of operations in that establishment, and so great are its attractions for a certain class, that the place is never empty.

Educational facilities attract his attention

The public schools maintained in this place are very efficient, the buildings plain and substantial, but sufficient for all purposes, and the corps of educators equal to any in the state. There is, in addition, . . . a special opportunity in Fort Madison for those who aspire to collegiate honors, as the academy which prospers here gives a classical course in addition to its primary and academic training.

He identifies the industries most important in the local economy

Manufacturing timber is somewhat of a specialty with the people of Fort Madison. Pine lumber is shipped from here by millions of feet annually, and it would be perilous to attempt to enumerate how many millions of laths and shingles are here made ready for transportation. Planing mills are in full blast, and manufactories of various kinds abound more and more every year. The facilities for shipment from Fort Madison are not so numerous as the like privileges enjoyed by Keokuk, but they are such as to command a good local and general trade, which will not be allowed to retrograde as long as the citizens and men of business on the spot continue to be wise and energetic. (Charles R. Tuttle, *An Illustrated History of the State of Iowa* . . . , 563)

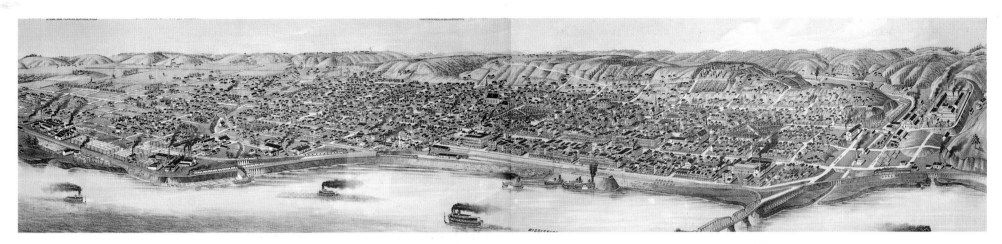

Perspective Map of Fort Madison, Ia. 1889. Drawn by H[enry] Wellge. Published by the American Publishing Co. 205 Second St. Milwaukee, Wis. Lithograph, 13 3/8 x 37 in. (38 x 96 cm).

Geography and Map Division, Library of Congress

Fort Madison, Iowa, from the air, October 12, 1988.

Alex MacLean

Folio 39.   Burlington Joins the Ranks of Other Successful Towns in Iowa on the Mississippi River

A young visitor from St. Louis likes what he sees when he travels to Burlington in 1838

This town makes a beautiful appearance; from the river comeing [*sic*] down it shows to good advantage. The town plat is beautiful—quite a treat after leaving Galena. The town is built on what are here called the Flint Hills, there being some small hills in the back part of the town and some larger above and below which come to the river. The ground lays about 10 feet above high water mark with a beautiful landing and a handsome situation for a levee or wharf. The soil here is rather sandy and the streets tolerable dry. The streets are wide and intersect each other at right angles.
(Miller, "The Journal of Henry B. Miller," 239)

The compiler of an emigrant's guide to Iowa gives his impressions of Burlington in 1846

The view of the city, as presented from the opposite shore, or in ascending or descending the Mississippi, is extremely picturesque. The main part of the city is situated within an amphitheatre, formed by the surrounding hills, but the buildings are rapidly extending over these eminences and sloping declivities, and the neat white residences, frequently interspersed with spacious structures of brick, rising above each other in each succeeding street, form a striking contrast with the forest crowned hills with which the whole is encompassed.
(J[ohn] B. Newhall, *A Glimpse of Iowa in 1846, or the Emigrant's Guide and Territorial Directory*, 67–68, 71)

A writer in an eastern pictorial journal provides his readers with a brief description of the city

This flourishing place . . . was laid out in 1834. It is . . . situated on the west bank of the Mississippi, 88 miles southwest from Iowa City, to which the seat of government was removed from Burlington in 1839. . . . It is finely situated, and surrounded by hills of gentle ascent and moderate elevation, affording many fine building sites. The streets are regular, its private residences neat and elegant, and its churches and other public buildings large and handsome. Its manufactures and workshops attest the activity and enterprise of the people, and its commercial facilities, while accounting for its rapid growth, give assurance that it will, before many years, become a vast and wealthy city.
("Burlington, Iowa," 252)

John Warner Barber and Henry Howe include a description of Burlington in their history and travel guide published in 1863

The city was organized under a charter from the Territory of Wisconsin, in 1838. It is regularly laid out and beautifully situated. Part of the city is built on the high grounds or bluffs, rising in some places about 200 feet above the river, affording a beautiful and commanding view of the surrounding country: with the river, and its woody islands, stretching far away to the north and south. It has a variety of mechanical and manufacturing establishments. The pork packing business is carried on extensively. It is the seat of Burlington University, and contains 12 churches, and about 14,000 inhabitants.
(Barber and Howe, *Our Whole Country*, 2:1252–53)

Willard Glazier catalogs the achievements of Burlington in the early 1880s

Burlington [has] a well-organized police force, fire department, water-works, gas, street-cars, a fine public library, churches, public schools, two colleges, one of the best opera-houses in the West, a splendid boat-club house, and commerce, trade and manufactures of a character to warrant the belief of her citizens that in a few more years she will rank among the first of western cities. The private residences are exceedingly attractive in appearance, and nothing could be more beautiful than the view from those on the summit of Prospect Hill. . . . The little park on North Hill is a delightful resort in the summer, with its fountain and walks and seats under the shade of the maples and elms. North of the Catholic Cemetery is Black Hawk Amphitheatre. . . .

The levee is a very fine one, embracing a quarter of a mile of solid paved roadway, with a gradual slope, making the landing easy of access. . . . Large rafts of lumber from up-river are received and landed at Burlington to be stored in the yards to dry, after which it is shipped by railway to various points in Iowa, Illinois, Missouri, Kansas, and Nebraska. The amount of lumber shipped from Burlington is a large item in her general trade. The smokestacks of the manufactories are seen in all parts of the city. The Murray Iron Works are large and substantial buildings. The Burlington Plow Company, Wolfe's Furniture Factory, and Buffington Wheel Works, and many others, are fully up to the times in the character and amount of their products. . . .

A splendid iron bridge crosses the river at this point, built by the Chicago, Burlington and Quincy Railroad Company. It consists of nine spans and is about two thousand two hundred feet in length.
(Glazier, *Down the Great River*, 279–81)

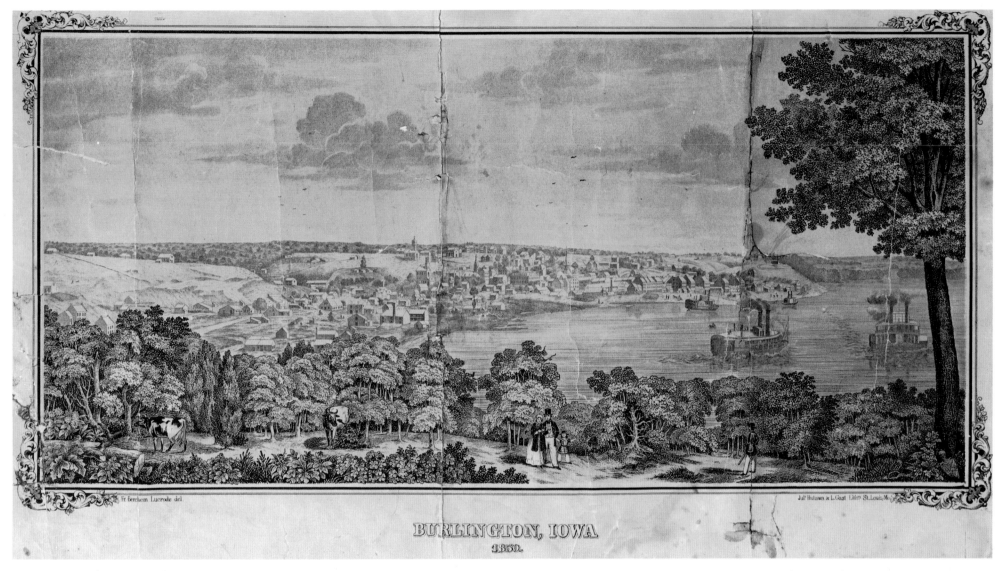

Burlington, Iowa. Drawn by Fr. Berchem Lucrode. Printed by Jul[iu]s Hutawa & L[eopold] Gast, Lith., St. Louis, 1850. Lithograph, 11 3/8 x 22 3/4 in. (29 x 58 cm).

State Historical Society of Iowa, Iowa City

Onken's Lith. Cin. O.   Copy Right secured.   A. Forbriger, Lith.

BURLINGTON, IOWA.

Burlington, Iowa. Unsigned. Lithographed by A[dolphus F.] Forbriger. Printed by Onken's Lith. Cin[cinnati] O[hio], [1851]. From William Wells, *Western Scenery; or, Land and River, Hill and Dale, in the Mississippi Valley.* Lithograph, 5 13/16 x 7 7/8 in. (14.8 x 20 cm).
Public Library of Cincinnati and Hamilton County

View of Burlington, Iowa. Unsigned. From *Ballou's Pictorial Drawing-Room Companion* 8 (April 21, 1855): 252. Wood engraving, 5 5/8 x 9 1/4 in. (14.3 x 23.5 cm).
Olin Library, Cornell University

VIEW OF BURLINGTON, IOWA.

City of Burlington, Iowa. Drawn and copyrighted by William Bourne, 1858. Printed by Endicott & Co. Lithograph, 17 1/2 x 25 3/8 in. (44.4 x 64.4 cm).
Muscatine Art Center

1889 Perspective Map of the City of Burlington, Ia. Drawn by H[enry] Wellge. Published by the American Publishing Co. 205 Second Str. Milwaukee, Wis. Lithograph, 17 1/4 x 32 1/4 in. (44 x 82 cm).

Geography and Map Division, Library of Congress

Burlington, Iowa, from the air, October 12, 1988.

Alex MacLean

Folio 40.   Muscatine Develops at a Strategic Location on a Westward Bend of the Mississippi

A county history published in 1879 recalls the town's origins

In May, 1836, the proprietors [John Vanater and Benjamin Clark] employed Maj. William Gordon, then a resident of Rock Island, to survey a town on their claim. When the first plat was made, the name of "Newburg" was given the town; but before the work had progressed very far that title was discarded, and the name of Bloomington was bestowed . . . which designation was retained for about twelve years. Owing to the proximity of Bloomington, Ill., mail-matter was frequently sent astray, and to avoid that difficulty the name was changed to . . . Muscatine. . . .

The town of Bloomington was incorporated by act of the Territorial Legislature, approved January 23, 1839. . . .

At the time of its incorporation, the town contained a population of seventy-one souls, and boasted of thirty-three buildings.
(*History of Muscatine County, Iowa* . . . , 501, 507)

A new resident describes Muscatine in 1853 in a letter to his father

Iowa as yet is quite new, she has a few smart towns on the river, (among which this is one of the smartest) which derive their business directly and indirectly from the agricultural resources of the surrounding country, which are at present quite extensive and daily increasing. . . .

Land in this town is worth from $100 to $125 per front foot in the business portion of the town. One mile out, good locations for farms are worth from $15. to $25. per acre. . . .

The site of this town is very rough, a succession of hills and valleys, requiring a great deal of grading and filling up to make it as it should be. The reason why it was chosen is that the river here makes a large elbow, and this town is built on the outer point of the elbow, thus securing a larger extent of country, the trade of which can reach this point and can't be turned off from it. The town getting the best location of course gets the most trade. The great rival of this place is Davenport, thirty miles above. It is the most beautiful western town I have seen and about the size of this (about 5000 inhabitants) but they don't at present do half the business that they do here. . . .

To give you an idea of the emigration here; there are more emigrant wagons than the ferry boat can take across the river in the day time; sometimes there are fifteen or twenty wagons waiting on the eastern shore to come across, and when I rode out yesterday, I met fifteen wagons going a distance of five miles, on the main road, that came into the state in another direction. This is what you see at our point.
(Isaac Lane Usher, "Letters of a Railroad Builder," 16–20)

A Boston magazine in 1855 explains the benefits of Muscatine's location and mentions some of the results

The city of Muscatine derives its importance, in a commercial point, mainly from its peculiar location. It is situated on the extreme western bend of the Mississippi River, and is thus thrown into the interior, as it were, of the State. It is the landing point on the river for a large tract of country, and in this respect has the advantage over every other city in Iowa. . . . The number of inhabitants is about 6000, and is increasing rapidly. The trade at this point is immense; far beyond any calculations that would be made by any one not cognizant of the fact. New branches of business are being constantly introduced, and all classes of labor are in demand. A contract has been entered into by the city council to have the city lighted by gas during the present year. There was a very large emigration last year to this portion of Iowa, and from present indications it will be much larger during this year.
("City of Muscatine, Iowa," 73)

An Iowa historian tells his readers about Muscatine in 1876

The city is not young and new, but although many of the blocks are old and touched by the tooth of time, there are some very fine buildings, quite new, and very substantial, and as the progress of decay or accident may increase the area of dilapidation, the city like the fabled bird will rise from its ashes, more glorious than ever before. This site was first named Bloomington, and the appellation was changed upon due deliberation some years afterward. . . .

Within the current decade, the growth of the place has been more remarkable than at any former period in its development. Lands have gone up in value, building lots have been in demand at fair prices, and great enterprise has been displayed in the erection of stores for the rapidly increasing demands of traffic. . . .

There are several manufactories in Muscatine city and suburbs, many of them identified with the lumber trade, going on to make up into doors and sashes the material which the sawing mills employ some five hundred men in preparing for the market, and in selling in the several yards. Besides there are factories in which furniture of all kinds is made; carriage and wagon shops, extensive flouring mills, agricultural implement manufactories, and an endless range of industries which will go on increasing their importance as long [as] the country back of the city, and the union at large, can find a market for goods of genuine merit.
(Tuttle, *An Illustrated History of the State of Iowa*, 608–9)

PAINTED AND LITHO; BY J.C.WILD.

BLOOMINGTON; IOWA.

Bloomington, Iowa [i.e. Muscatine, Iowa]. Drawn and lithographed by J[ohn] C[aspar] Wild, ca. 1844. Lithograph, 18 3/8 x 24 in. (46.7 x 61 cm).
Muscatine Art Center

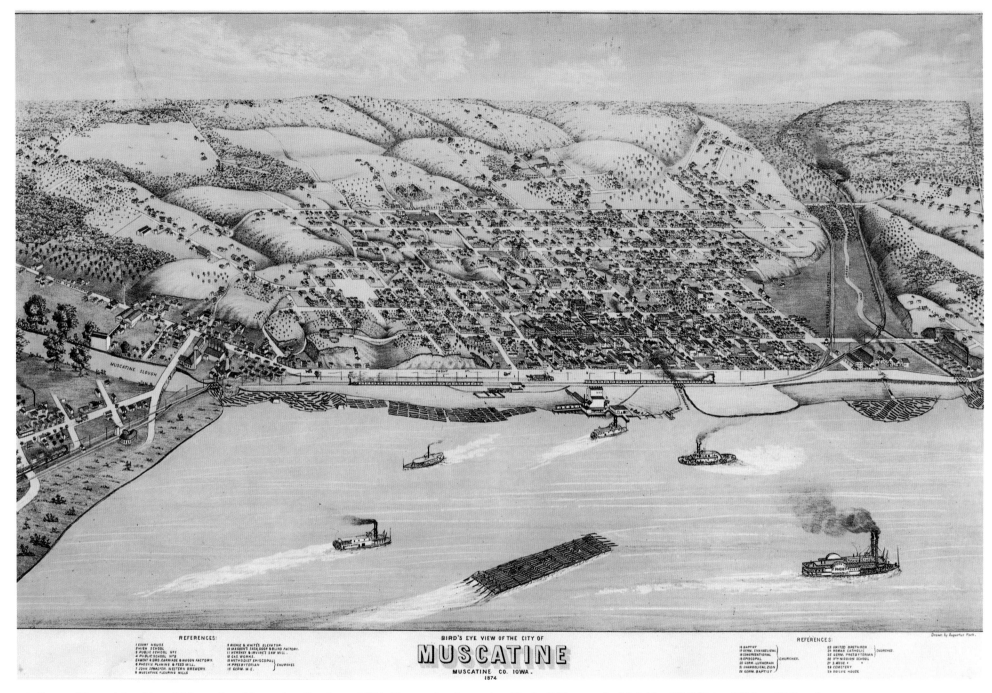

BIRD'S EYE VIEW OF THE CITY OF

MUSCATINE

MUSCATINE CO. IOWA.
1874

Bird's Eye View of the City of Muscatine, Muscatine Co., Iowa, 1874. Drawn by Augustus Koch. Lithograph, 15 3/4 x 25 3/4 in. (40.1 x 65.5 cm).
Muscatine Art Center

1. COMMERCIAL HOTEL.   4 MUSCATINE MILLS.   7. NEVADA MILLS.   10. SCHOOL HOUSE.   13. CHURCH   16. SCHOOL HOUSE.
2. SCHAEFERS BREWERY.   5. ELEVATOR.   8. M.E. CHURCH.   11. CATHOLIC CHURCH.   14. EPISCOPAL CHURCH   17. FLOUR MILLS
3. CHURCH.   6. OPERA HOUSE.   9. PRES. CHURCH.   12. NATIONAL HOTEL   15. COURT HOUSE   18. STEAM SAW MILLS.

BIRD'S EYE VIEW OF MUSCATINE CITY MUSCATINE COUNTY IOWA.

STATE OF IOWA

Bird's Eye View of Muscatine City Muscatine County Iowa. Unsigned. Printed by Chas. Shober & Co. Props. Chicago Lith. Co.
From A. T. Andreas, *Atlas of the State of Iowa* (1874). Lithograph, 9 x 12 in. (22.8 x 30.5 cm).
Muscatine Art Center

Folio 41.   Rock Island, Illinois, Develops on a Strategic Site at the Upper Falls of the Mississippi

A British traveler in 1855 describes Rock Island during the construction of a railroad bridge across the Mississippi

Rock-island city, 181 miles from Chicago, is the present terminus of the railway; but a bridge is being built across the Mississippi at this point, and it is intended to carry on the railway . . . through the State of Iowa to the Missouri river. The city is on the east bank of the river, not on the island, which belongs to the government of the United States. There are the ruins of a dismantled fort—Fort Armstrong—upon it. On the opposite side of the Mississippi is Davenport, an older city than Rock-island. Both are increasing very rapidly. As an instance of this, a gentleman in the train told me he lately bought a lot of land in Rock-island city for $480, for which he could now get $1000, cash down, and $1200, half cash now, and half in twelve months; and that he lately bought a piece of land in Iowa for $100, and re-sold it immediately for $300. . . .

The south end of the island terminates in an abrupt cliff, of thirty to forty feet height. The empty wooden buildings of the deserted fort look desolate enough. The island is not settled, being reserved for military purposes. The railway will cross it. The bridge over the narrowest channel is nearly completed. The one over the main channel will be a noble structure. It will open with a swivel bridge for the passage of boats. There are rapids above this, terminating with the island; but I did not go far enough to see them, although I would have liked to have seen some activity in this great mass of water, for otherwise it is impossible to estimate its magnitude. Any way it was curious to think of the "father of waters" driving saw-mills!
(William Ferguson, *America by River and Rail . . .* , 423–24)

John Warner Barber and Henry Howe inform their readers about the site of Rock Island as they found it in 1862

Rock Island City, and county seat of Rock Island Co., is situated on the Mississippi River, opposite the city of Davenport, 2 miles above the mouth of Rock River, 178 W. by S., from Chicago, and 131 N.N.W. of Springfield. It is at the foot of the Upper Rapids of the Mississippi, which extend nearly 5 miles, and in low stages of water obstruct the passage of loaded vessels. It is a flourishing manufacturing place, at the western terminus of the Chicago and Rock Island Railroad.

It derives its name from an island three miles in length, the southern extremity of which is nearly opposite the town. The principal channel of the river is on the west side of the island, while that on its eastern side has been so dammed as to produce a vast water power above and a good harbor below. The island forms one of the capacious buttresses of the immense railroad bridge across the Mississippi connecting the place with Davenport, and

creates a junction between the railroad from Chicago and the Mississippi, and the Missouri Railroad through Iowa.
(Barber and Howe, *Our Whole Country*, 2:1096–97)

The special report on cities for the U.S. Census of 1880 includes information about the history of Rock Island

The first house within the present city limits of Rock Island was erected in 1826 by George Davenport and Russell Farnham, Indian traders, the location being known as Farnhamburg. The vicinity was gradually settled by the early pioneers, who came there in order to be within the protection of fort Armstrong. In 1835 the commissioners of Rock Island county . . . entered at the Galena land-office a fractional quarter-section of land in what is now the central part of the city, and laid out a town called Stephenson, which was made the county-seat. . . . The state legislature . . . in March, 1841, changed the name to Rock Island, and incorporated it as a town, under a board of 9 trustees. . . .

The first railroad, the Chicago and Rock Island, came into the city in 1856; up to that time the city had made slow progress as to wealth and population, but since then it has had a steady and rapid growth.
(U.S. Census Office, *Report on the Social Statistics of Cities*, 2:542)

Willard Glazier tells his readers about the island from which the city takes its name and about the railroads serving the vicinity

Rock Island . . . has been appropriated by the United States Government since 1804. . . . A fort was erected here in 1816, and named Fort Armstrong, in honor of the then Secretary of War. It was garrisoned by United States troops until May, 1836. . . . In 1862, an Act of Congress converted the Island into an arsenal for the National Government, and such it remains to this day. . . . [Here are] substantial quarters for the commander and his subordinate officers, soldiers' barracks, a complete system of sewerage, a bridge, connecting the Island with the city of Moline; roads, streets and avenues across the Island; a water-power wall, powder-magazine, pump-house, and . . . the manufacture of stores for the army and machinery for the various shops in which the material of war is extensively fabricated. . . .

It is on the line of the great transcontinental highway. The Chicago, Rock Island and Pacific Railroad, passing through Rock Island, connects the eastern trunk lines with the Union Pacific at Omaha; and here also are depots of the Chicago, Milwaukee and Saint Paul; the Chicago and Northwestern; the Chicago, Burlington and Quincy; the Rock Island and Peoria, and the Rock Island and Mercer County railways.
(Glazier, *Down the Great River*, 258–59, 267)

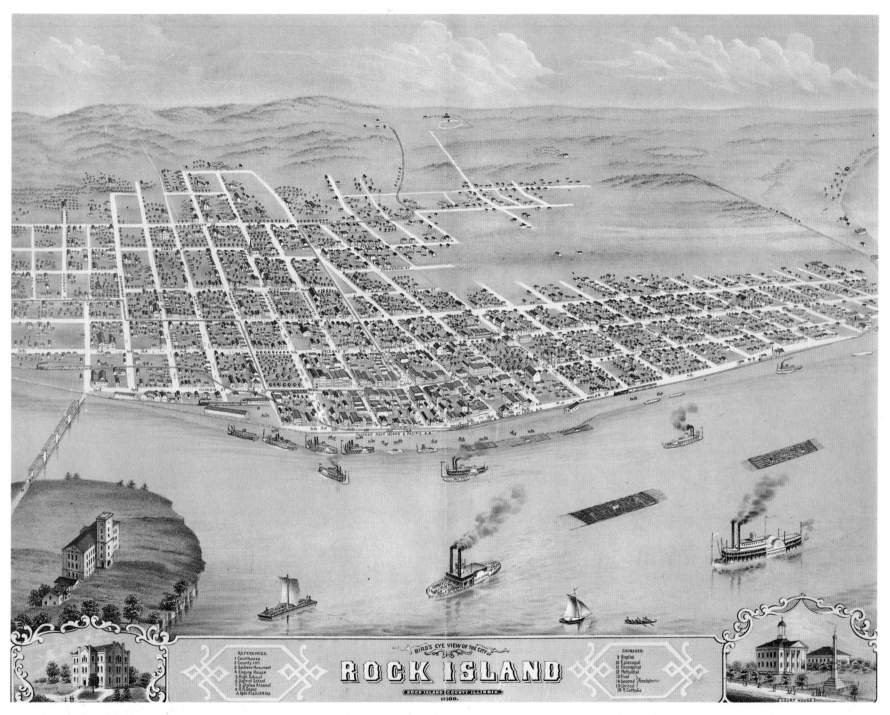

Bird's Eye View of the City of Rock Island Rock Island County Illinois 1869. [Drawn by Albert Ruger.] Printed by the Chicago Lithographing Co., Chicago. Published by Ruger & Stoner, Madison, Wis.

Geography and Map Division, Library of Congress

Rock Island. [Drawn by Alfred R. Waud.] From William Cullen Bryant, ed., *Picturesque America, or The Land We Live In,* vol. 2 (1874). Wood engraving, 2 7/8 x 9 3/16 in. (7.3 x 23.3 cm).

John W. Reps

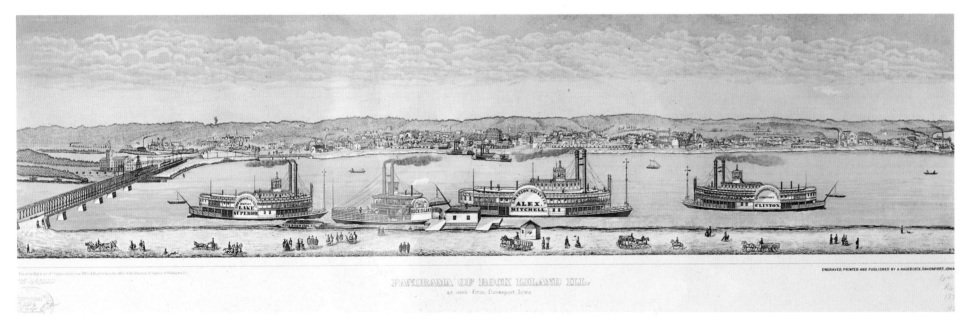

Panorama of Rock Island, Ill. as Seen from Davenport, Iowa. Drawn, printed, and published by A[ugustus] Hageboeck, Davenport, Iowa, ca. 1874. Lithograph, 6 11/16 x 24 3/8 in. (17 x 62 cm).

Geography and Map Division, Library of Congress

Rock Island, Ill. Drawn by H[enry] Wellge. Published by the American Publishing Co., 205 Second Str. Milwaukee, Wis., [1889]. Halftone lithographic facsimile of original lithograph, 29 x 28 in. (48.4 x 71.2 cm).

Muscatine Art Center

Rock Island, Illinois, from the air, October 12, 1988.

Alex MacLean

Folio 42.   Moline, Illinois, Gains Recognition as a Rising Midwestern Manufacturing Center

A local history recalls the founding and early growth of Moline

In 1843, Charles Atkinson, D. B. Sears and others . . . laid out the town of Moline. . . . The plat thus laid out constituted the original town of Moline. Subsequently Charles Atkinson laid out his first addition, which was followed by his second addition in 1856; since which, various additions have been made from time to time, till the place has reached its present corporate dimensions. It extends on the east to the city limits of Rock Island.
(*The Past and Present of Rock Island County, Ill.*, 185)

The Postmaster writes about Moline for an Illinois gazetteer and business directory of 1859

Moline . . . has already gained the title of the "Lowell of the West." . . . A dam has been built across from the Illinois shore to the head of the island, thus affording one of the very best water powers in the whole western country. A stock company has been formed with a view to turn this power to account. Prominent among other manufacturing establishments is Deare's [*sic*] Plow manufactory. A large number of other manufactories and mills are in successful operation, and extensive improvements are continually going forward. Only a few miles distant are large coal fields, which will eventually become a source of revenue. . . . The future of Moline is destined to be one of unprecedented importance as a manufacturing town, the enterprise of its inhabitants being a sure guarantee. Population, 3,000.
(Absalom B. Williams, "Moline," 144)

A county history describes Moline's largest industry in 1877

The Deere & Co. Plow Works have the reputation of being the largest establishment of the kind in the world. They employ over 600 hands, and the works have a capacity of 500 steel plows, cultivators, sulky and gang plows every working day in the year, making a grand aggregate of 150,000 implements. . . . The new foundry erected last season is a substantial building 100 by 60 feet in size, the old foundry building now being used for pattern shops and core room. The main building, four stories high, contains the blacksmith shop, stocked with the latest improved machinery, the grinding and polishing room, etc. The wood-work shops occupy a building of similar design, three stories in height. . . . For convenience and expedition in shipping, a railroad track runs through the front end of the main building, beside which is the elevator, communicating with each floor of the building.
(*The Past and Present of Rock Island County, Ill.*, 185)

Capt. Willard Glazier explores Moline in 1881

Passing along its main street, parallel to the river, we see little else than factories, some of considerable size, and the busy hum of machinery salutes our ears for more than a mile, as we walk, and look with wonder on these signs of the march of western industry and progress. The motive power produced by a fall in the Mississippi at this point, and utilized for the driving of machinery, is the source of all this energy, and has made Moline one of the busiest and most flourishing places in the western country. The National Government has of late years greatly improved this motive power for the benefit, mainly, of the United States Arsenal works on the island, but no less has it contributed to the solid advantage of the enterprising settlers on the adjacent mainland, and hence Moline, the "City of Mills," has attained its present importance. . . . The great plow-factory of Messrs. Deere & Company is known far and wide, while many other establishments of scarcely less celebrity flourish side by side on the river's bank, giving employment to large numbers of people.

Glazier mentions some of the town's buildings

Educational and religious matters are not forgotten by this busy people. Besides several excellent schools, including a handsome and commodious High School, the site of which overlooks the city, and is in every respect a credit to the citizens, Moline has a flourishing Public Library, containing many thousand volumes of theological, historical, biographical and scientific works, together with a good assortment of fiction. Here are also several churches of the various religious denominations.

He makes some additional observations

In population Moline is smaller than either Davenport or Rock Island City, but in manufacturing importance it far excels them both. The source of its growth and prosperity—the water-power—will doubtless continue to operate as such for generations untold, and Moline will eventually fill the entire space between the Mississippi and Rock River at this point. Sylvan Water, the poetic designation given to a portion of the Great River lying between the city and Rock-Island Arsenal, has been the scene of the annual regatta of the Mississippi Valley Amateur Rowing Association, for which it is found to be eminently adapted. A substantial bridge uniting Moline with the arsenal crosses it, and from this a view is obtained of the extensive government works now in progress for the permanent improvement of the water-power.
(Glazier, *Down the Great River*, 249–51)

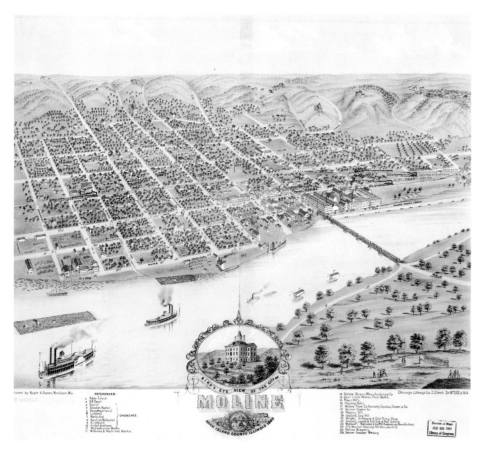

Bird's Eye View of the City of Moline Rock Island County Illinois 1869. [Drawn by Albert Ruger.] Printed by the Chicago Lithogr. Co. S. Clark St. No. 152 & 154. Published by Ruger & Stoner, Madison, Wis. Lithograph, 17 x 21 3/4 in. (43.3 x 55.3 cm).

Geography and Map Division, Library of Congress

Moline, Ill. 1889. Drawn by H[enry] Wellge. Published by the American Publishing Co., 205 Second Str. Milwaukee. Lithograph, 17 1/2 x 26 5/8 in. (29.2 x 67.6 cm).

Muscatine Art Center

Folio 43.   Early Accounts Describe What Davenport Was Like during Its First Decades

The first priest in the region tells of the beginnings of Davenport in the 1830s

In 1836 Mr. [Antoine] LeClaire began to convert his cultivated land into a city named Davenport, which was first designed on a map with straight streets of noble breadth, leaving at regular intervals spaces for squares and courthouses, with a broad open road on the river front for commercial purposes. His faith did not let him forget the needs of religion, for, in the city he was planning, he selected a square in an advantageous position for the erection of the Catholic church. In 1836 many speculators and other persons wishing to enjoy the opportunities offered to the first settlers in new areas bought a large tract of land near the beginning city of Davenport. A number of frame houses were raised there before the spring of the next year. . . .

In 1837 Davenport had about one hundred inhabitants . . . ; in 1843 there were more than twelve hundred . . . , five churches of various denominations, a magnificent hotel, a court house (for the city is now the county seat), several schools, people engaged in ordinary and luxury trades, professions of every kind, a flourishing commerce with other small towns in the interior. . . . One who in 1835 had seen the lodges of the poor Indian on the grassy plain and sees it now covered with new brick houses, presenting to the traveler a lively and symmetrical city where many stately steamboats land, is tempted to wonder if what he sees is an illusion rather than a reality. (Samuel Mazzuchelli, *The Memoirs of Father Samuel Mazzuchelli, O.P.*, 170–73)

A local historian writes of Davenport in 1854

The year 1854 was distinguished as a busy one. . . . The growth of the town has always been concomitant with the settling of the back country, the establishment of manufacturing interests, and the development of other resources. There has been at no time a retrogression, or a stand-still, indicating a fictitious progress, or an over-growth. Thus, in 1854, the population increased nearly or quite three thousand. The base of this growth was the railroad connection, *six* saw mills, turning out from twenty to thirty thousand feet of lumber each per day; two foundries and machine shops; some twenty-four runs of burrs, dozens of smith and wagon shops, one wholesale plow factory, turning out one hundred plows per week, one Pork packing establishment, and a County population of about thirteen thousand. (Franc B. Wilkie, *Davenport Past and Present*, 120)

An Iowa gazetteer published in 1855 provides a detailed description of Davenport

The Mississippi Bridge, now being built at Davenport, connects the Chicago and Rock Island, and the Mississippi railroads; making one continuous line . . . from Chicago to the Missouri River. . . . The bridge will span the Mississippi on the Rapids, where the current is compressed to a narrow space, so that boats, to strike the piers on either side, would first have to surmount rocks which Nature has had fixed as impediments to navigation for centuries. . . . Simply a skeleton railroad bridge, the draw will always be up, save when the cars are actually crossing; which never can occur when a steamboat is passing, except by the grossest negligence. . . .

One beholds Davenport spread out upon a gently sloping plain nearly two miles long, and one-half to three-fourths of a mile wide, fronting on the river, which runs, at this point, nearly west; and the streets range parallel to the four cardinal points of the compass. . . .

The city of Davenport, since the completion of the Chicago and Rock Island Railroad, has moved forward with rapid strides. The present population of the city is about 8000.

The gazetteer quotes a dispatch from the St. Louis Republican

"We have two flouring-mills, six saw-mills, two planing-mills, one plow factory, two sash and blind factories, and two foundries, all operated by steam-engines, and doing a thriving business.

The stores, numbering over one hundred, have passed through the transition state, from general country groceries to distinct and well appointed establishments, representing separately each prominent branch of commercial enterprise. . . . Our hotels, six in number, are insufficient for the accommodation of strangers. Our banking-houses, of which there are three, are sound and healthy. Our real estate offices, which are too numerous to enumerate, are converting money into property, and property into money, daily, at prices which, although comparatively high, make both buyer and seller rich. All kinds of business, and classes of business men, thrive and prosper. Two abutments, and three piers of the great Mississippi bridge are completed. . . .

Davenport is becoming an important lumber depot. Besides the six saw-mills in operation here, cutting some fifteen or twenty millions of feet per annum, it is supplied by rafts from the pineries, which, on account of the spacious eddy at East Davenport, are induced to touch here before seeking another market. . . ."

Five large new churches, dedicated last fall, rear their turrets towards heaven; a new collegiate building, an extensive building for a female school, two market houses, and several stores, of architectural proportions, are among the edifices of last year's growth. (Parker, *Iowa as It Is in 1855*, 91, 167, 171–72)

[Davenport, Iowa, Fort Armstrong, Rock Island and Moline, Illinois.] Untitled gouache painting by John Caspar Wild, 1844.

Putnam Museum of History & Natural Science, Davenport, Iowa

East View of Davenport. Iowa T. Fort Armstrong on Rock-Island. Ill. Town of Rock-Island. Ill. Moline. Drawn and Lithographed by J[ohn] C[aspar] Wild, [1844]. Lithograph, 22 1/8 x 30 3/4 in. (56.3 x 78.3 cm).

Putnam Museum of History & Natural Science, Davenport, Iowa

Davenport, Iowa. Drawn by E. P. Gillett. Printed by J. H. Buffords, 260 Washington St., Boston, [1855?]. Lithograph, 16 15/16 x 25 5/16 (43.1 x 64.4 cm).

Putnam Museum of History & Natural Science, Davenport, Iowa

City of Davenport, Iowa. From the Original Picture in the Possession of Geo. L. Davenport. Drawn [and published] by Rufus Wright. Printed by Sarony, Major & Knapp, 449 Broadway, N.Y., [1858]. Lithograph, 18 5/8 x 27 3/4 in. (47.4 x 70.6 cm).

Putnam Museum of History & Natural Science, Davenport, Iowa

Folio 44.   Rufus Wright Depicts Davenport in 1858 and for His Efforts Is Supported by the Local Press

The newspaper announces that Wright's drawing can now be seen

City of Davenport.—Mr. Wright's picture of our city may be seen in the show window of Geo. W. Ells & Co, Le Claire Row. It will soon be lithographed and fully colored in the best possible style, at the famous establishment of Messrs. Sarony & Major, of New York City. In view of this enterprise, which is a true display of talent and skill, we would urge upon the public the importance of subscribing liberally to this production, as it is the best ever painted.

(Davenport *Daily Iowa State Democrat,* February 9, 1858, 1)

A rival picture is also described—one that apparently was never published

Mrs. Codding's picture of the City of Davenport is now executed, and is on exhibition at the office of J. Dial & Co. Main street, where Mr. Monger, agent for Mrs. C. will take pleasure in receiving subscriptions for the lithographic copies to be made therefrom. Mrs. C. has spent a large amount of time, and has spared no pains to make this work acceptable to all, and in this respect we think she is not disappointed. The numerous visitors who examine this painting, are unanimous in its praise, and we trust this generous and appreciative public will extend the enterprise a liberal patronage, and furnish her, ample remuneration for the large amount of time patience and skil [*sic*] bestowed upon it. Those who have not seen the painting should call at the place above named, while yet it remains on exhibition.

(Davenport *Daily Iowa State Democrat,* February 13, 1858, 1)

A newspaper reporter sees and praises a proof copy of Wright's lithograph

Wright's Picture of Davenport.

Mr. Wright introduced us into his studio yesterday, and showed us the proof sheet of his new picture of our city, just received from Messrs. Sarony, Major & Co., Lithogr[a]phers, of New York City. The picture as it will be when completed, is by far the best representation of our city ever produced, and goes far ahead of what we had expected. The entire plan is taken with a truthful pencil—nothing superfluous, nothing wanting—and reflects great credit upon Mr. Wright's artistic taste and skill. It is to be seen by all. Mr. Wright informs us that, he will canvas for subscriptions in a few days.

Readers learn that purchase is only by advance subscription

Those wishing to obtain one of those beautiful pictures must subscribe *now—positively now,* as there will be no extra numbers struck off for subsequent sale. Let every citizen who wishes to preserve the landmarks of the onward progress of our city, as appears from time to time, subscribe for this work of art, have it put in a frame and suspended upon the walls of your parlors and offices as a memento of the past. We would advise all to do so who have the means.

(Davenport *Daily Iowa State Democrat,* May 19, 1858, 1)

Wright appeals to citizens of Davenport to support his project by subscribing to copies of his lithograph

To the Citizens of Davenport:—At an expense of much time and trouble, I have at last succeeded in producing a truthful and beautiful lithographic view of your city.—Owing to the fact of there having been *three previous failures* in this same enterprise, I resolved to get this up without previous assurances in the shape of subscriptions—which I did with a few generous exceptions.

I visited New York, and there, at a very large additional expense, engaged the first lithographing firm in this country to do the work. The result is that I have received the proof sheet of by far the best lithographic view that was ever made of this city, and one which I am not ashamed to offer to you, and one which is well worthy of your patronage.

Now, it remains with you to say whether I shall be compensated for my trouble and expenditures, or lose the whole. I will trust to your verdict.

Owing to ill health, I am unable to call upon you myself, and have, therefore, authorized Mr. H. Eastman to solicit subscriptions for me.

The proof sheet is a sample of the picture as it will be, with the exception of a few errors which I have ordered corrected, and the census table, since 1830 to the present time, to go upon the lower margin.

Respectfully, RUFUS WRIGHT.

The newspaper earnestly recommends that residents of Davenport heed Wright's call for support

Remarks.—The foregoing is submitted to the public in all confidence that the labors of this artist, who has labored assiduously, and expended no small amount of means to give a truthful portrait of our city, will be amply or at least suitably rewarded by the liberal patronage of the public. When it is considered that the work presented by Mr. Wright is a very valuable acquisition to any citizen, that it is truthful in delineation, and exactly what every citizen of Davenport should have, we trust it will be generally subscribed to. Encourage and upbuild home talent by extending patronage to home artisans who have shown themselves worthy. We trust our readers when called upon by Mr. Eastman, agent for soliciting subscriptions, will "come down" with the ready, and secure the only correct painting of the City of Davenport ever produced.

(Davenport *Daily Iowa State Democrat,* May 29, 1858, 1)

City of Davenport, Iowa. Unsigned. Lithographed and published by Ch[arle]s Vogt & Co., 1865. Printed by J. Mc Kittrick & Co., St. Louis, Mo.
Lithograph, 21 5/8 x 28 5/8 in. (55 x 72.9 cm).

Putnam Museum of History & Natural Science, Davenport, Iowa

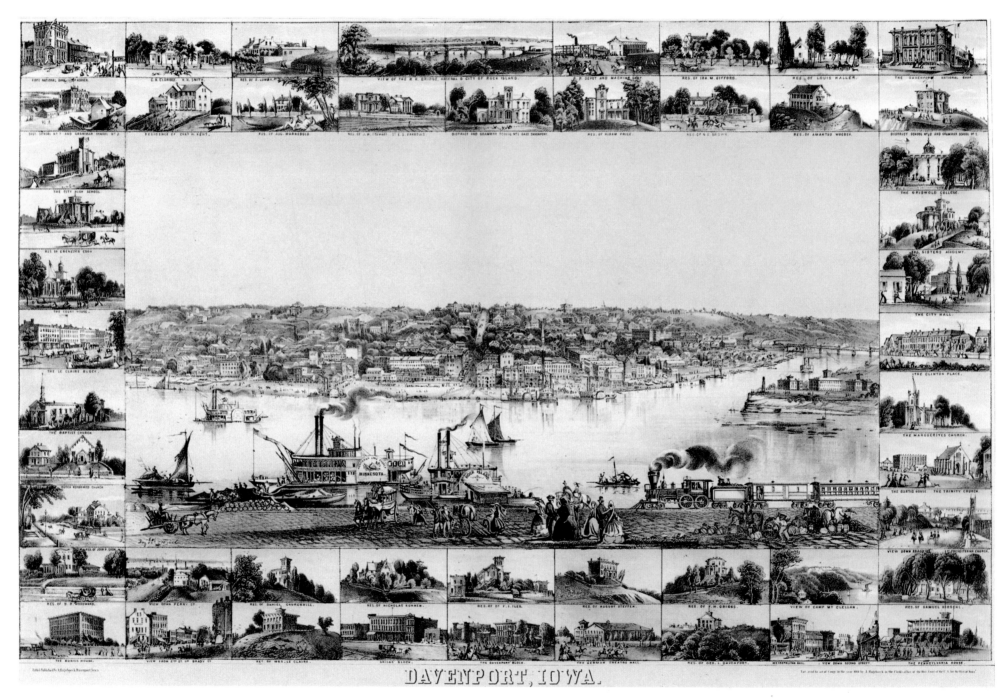

Davenport, Iowa. Drawn and published by A[gustus] Hageboeck, 1866. Lithograph, 18 1/2 x 29 1/4 in (47 x 74.4 cm).

Putnam Museum of History & Natural Science, Davenport, Iowa

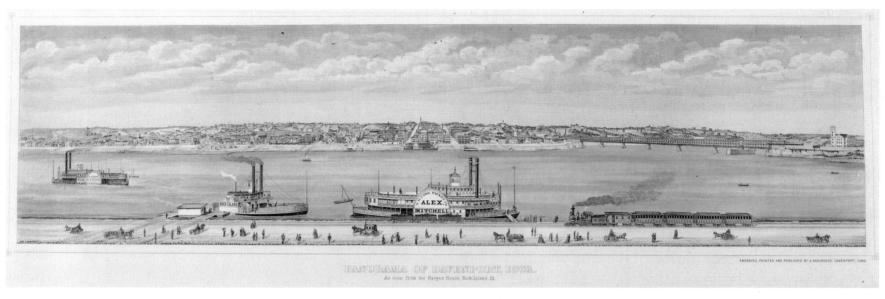

Panorama of Davenport, Iowa. As Seen from the Harper-House, Rock-Island, Ill. Drawn by Aug. Lambrecht. Engraved [*sic*], printed, and published by A[ugustus] Hageboeck, Davenport, Iowa, [1872–1874?]. Lithograph, 7 3/8 x 24 15/16 in. (18.7 x 63.5 cm).

Putnam Museum of History & Natural Science, Davenport, Iowa

Davenport, Iowa. River Front. The most beautiful City on the Mississippi, 1875. Population 25,000. From the Arsenal Tower. Die schönsteStadt am Mississippi, 1875. Einwohner Zahl 25,000. Vom Thurme des Arsenals. Drawn by Frank Jervis. Printed by National Lith. Institute, Chicago. Published by Jervis & Wolfe, Davenport, Iowa, Aug. 1875. Lithograph, 19 x 32 in. (48.2 x 81.3 cm).

Putnam Museum of History & Natural Science, Davenport, Iowa

Folio 45.   Davenport Prospers, Grows, and Changes in the Decades of the 1860s and 1870s

In their history and geography published in 1863, John Warner Barber and Henry Howe include an entry on Davenport

Davenport, a flourishing city, the county seat of Scott, is beautifully situated on the right bank of the Mississippi, at the foot of the upper rapids, opposite the town of Rock Island, with which it is connected by a most magnificent railroad bridge, the first ever built over the Mississippi. The great railroad running through the heart of the state, and designed to connect the Mississippi and Missouri Rivers, has its eastern terminus at Davenport. . . . The rapids extend 20 miles above this place, and the navigation of the river is somewhat obstructed by them during the time of low water. The city is built on ground which rises gradually from the water, with a chain of rounded hills in the back ground. Davenport contains about 12,000 inhabitants.

The city derived its name from Col. George Davenport, who was born in England, in 1783. He came to this country when a young man, entered the U.S. army as sergeant, and saw considerable service, on the frontier, in the war of 1812. After the war, he settled on Rock Island, opposite this town, and engaged in trading with the Indians. That vicinity was densely settled by them. The village of Black Hawk was there in the forks of Rock River and the Mississippi.

(Barber and Howe, *Our Whole Country*, 2:1244)

A historian of Iowa tells his readers about Davenport in a volume published in 1876

Davenport is favored in situation, and it is still more fortunate in the type of its inhabitants, who are a pushing and intellectual combination of all that is most valable [*sic*] in American city life. The population, which in 1839 was less than five hundred, had grown to two thousand in less than twelve years, and within ten years from that time, was twelve thousand. In the year 1870, when the people were numbered, Davenport had a population of more than twenty thousand, and it is safe to say that, by the time the union has completed its centennial, there will be thirty thousand persons in and around that city.

He finds Davenport's appearance impressive and notes that the city enjoys the latest improvements

The appearance of the city is decidedly imposing, all the aspects of a commercial and manufacturing town strikes the visitor at the first glance. Vast business blocks, tall chimneys, thronged streets and a populace full of the affairs of the moment, without time or inclination for the idle curiosity of the villager. The improvements of the age are here represented in their latest form—streets lighted with gas, traversed by street railroads, and reticulated

with water pipes which will not allow the streams to escape from man's control, until the very topmost rooms in the greatest buildings have been visited to serve his needs.

He emphasizes the importance of the railroads to Davenport and mentions the construction of a replacement bridge

The railroads continue to favor their own interests and those of the city by making this place one of their main depots. The Chicago, Rock Island and Pacific Railroad does a large business here, and the same may be said of the Davenport and St. Paul. The general government, uniting with the first named of these companies, has recently . . . constructed a new bridge of wrought iron to replace the bridge first constructed to unite Davenport with Rock Island. The present structure rests upon massive piers and abutments of stone, and has been built to accommodate carriages and pedestrians as well as for the use of the railroad, hence the share in construction borne by the general treasury. The city is one of the largest grain depots in the west, and the great water power available here, added to the many other causes which unite to make this an immense storehouse for the industrial forces throughout Iowa, must force the growth of this metropolis to immense proportions.

(Tuttle, *An Illustrated History of the State of Iowa*, 635)

The author of a book of travels in the American West informs his audience about Davenport in 1877

Davenport . . . is one of the chief cities of Iowa. It may be regarded as the principal city, in view of its importance in a commercial point of view. . . .

The view of the city of Davenport, as we approached it [from upriver] was strikingly beautiful. The city is built upon an inclined plain a mile or two in width, and extending from the river point back to a range of very high bluffs, the slopes of which are dotted here and there with elegant residences, while gardens, orchards, shade trees and lawns present a scene of beauty. At a little distance from the city, perhaps three or four miles, the bluffs open into Pleasant Valley, as the prairie is called, and the name is most appropriate. . . .

The city has a population of about thirty thousand, and is notable for its extensive manufactures of various kinds, among which are superior cotton fabrics, etc. Everything in and about the city denotes thrift, prosperity and remarkable enterprise. Its history, from its incorporation in 1838, to the present time, has been most gratifying, and reflects the highest credit upon its people.

(Ayer, *Life in the Wilds of America*, 114–15)

DRAWN BY C. J. PAULI, MILWAUKEE, WIS.

AMERICAN OLEOGRAPH CO. MILW—

DAVENPORT, IOWA IN 1876
FROM THE EAST.

Davenport, Iowa in 1876, From the East. Drawn by C[lemens] J. Pauli. Printed by the American Oleograph Co., Milwaukee. Lithograph, 17 13/16 x 24 in. (45.3 x 61 cm).

Putnam Museum of History & Natural Science, Davenport, Iowa

Folio 46.   The United States Census and Other Sources Provide Information about Davenport in the 1880s

A special report of the Census of 1880 summarizes the changes during the past thirty years

The year 1850 began a new era, and the prospect of soon being connected with the eastern cities by rail gave an impetus to Davenport. In 1851, a city charter was obtained. In 1854 the first train came to Rock Island from Chicago, and the same year saw the corner-stone laid for a bridge over the Mississippi, connecting Davenport with Rock Island, Illinois. Immigration, which had begun a few years previously, increased, new industries sprang up, and business rapidly increased. From this time forward the progress of the city has been steady, with . . . the exception of the financial crises of 1857 and 1873.

The report tells about the city's streets and parks

The total length of streets is about 135 miles, of which 35 miles are paved with broken stone. . . . The sidewalks are chiefly of wood, a few being of stone or brick. Gutters are laid with flat stones. An ordinance lately passed fixes the width of streets north of Fifth street at 40 feet and the width of sidewalks at 20 feet, with 14 feet of the latter reserved for grass-plots and trees; but "so far this is only on paper. . . ." There are 12 1/2 miles of horse-railroads in the city, using 35 cars, with 96 horses and mules, and giving employment to 30 men. . . . There are no regular omnibus lines, but the hotels have omnibuses running to and from the railroad stations. . . .

There are 3 parks, aggregating 7 1/2 acres: *Court House Square*, 2 1/4 acres: *Washington Park*, 3 acres; with another of 2 1/4 acres. In addition to these, there is *Shooting Park*, area 25 acres. The former are owned by the city and the latter by a private company; it is, however, open to the public at all times, and, being situated on a high point overlooking the river, with many shade trees, is much resorted to. Washington park cost $5,000. The annual cost of maintenance for the 3 parks belonging to the city is $700, and they are controlled by a committee of the city council.
(U.S. Census Office, *Report on the Social Statistics of Cities*, 2:720–21)

On his visit in 1881, Willard Glazier extols the beauty of the site but criticizes the upkeep of Davenport's sidewalks

Davenport, in the beauty of its location, excels all the other cities in the State. Handsome homes dot the bluffs. River views, for residences, have been extensively occupied by the well-to-do citizens, and the scope of country brought within the range of the eye from some of these hill-top dwellings is scarcely to be excelled for beauty by anything I have seen on the river.

The drainage is of nature's own making—the city being built on a declivity. There is much room for improvement in the sidewalks here. Possibly the citizens are too busy to give thought to a subject that concerns them only externally. Strangers, however, notice their defective, and in many cases dilapidated, condition, and make uncharitable remarks. The same applies to the County Court House, which is, without exception, the meanest I have seen in any city east of the Rockies and north of "Dixie." . . .

The educational advantages are proportioned to the size of the city. Here are twelve school-buildings, including that of the High School, erected in 1874, at a cost of sixty-five thousand dollars. . . . Griswold College, belonging to the Protestant Episcopal diocese of Iowa, occupies a very picturesque site overlooking the river. The Roman Catholic Academy of the Immaculate Conception is . . . surrounded by beautiful grounds and appears as quiet and retired as if miles away from the hum of the restless city. . . . Four Baptist, four catholic, one Christian, two Congregational, four Episcopal, one Hebrew, three Lutheran, four Methodist, one Unitarian and four Presbyterian churches afford strong evidence of progress in the cause of religion.

Mercy Hospital is under the management of the Sisters of Mercy, and was opened in 1868. It has grown to large proportions and receives and cares for patients without reference to their religious denomination.
(Glazier, *Down the Great River*, 256–58)

A survey of American economic progress lauds Davenport as a railroad and manufacturing center

Davenport . . . is on the Great Western route from Chicago, and is the centre of numerous railroads. A large iron bridge . . . spans the river at this point and connects the city with Rock Island; it has railroad, carriage, and pedestrian accommodation. The scenery in this vicinity is unsurpassed on the North Mississippi, and the city, which is on a commanding bluff, affords a fine view of the river.

The manufactures consist of cotton and woolen goods, agricultural implements, flour, carriages, furniture, lumber, etc. It is situated in the midst of a fine agricultural district, and has a large trade with the surrounding country. It has a fine court-house, City Hall, gas-works, water-works, over 30 churches, schools, banks, Opera-house, a Catholic Academy, Seminary, Hospital, and an Episcopal College. . . . Population, 1870, 20,038; 1880, 25,000; 1886, 32,000.
(J. H. Beale, *Picturesque Sketches of American Progress. Comprising Official Descriptions of Great American Cities* . . . , 132)

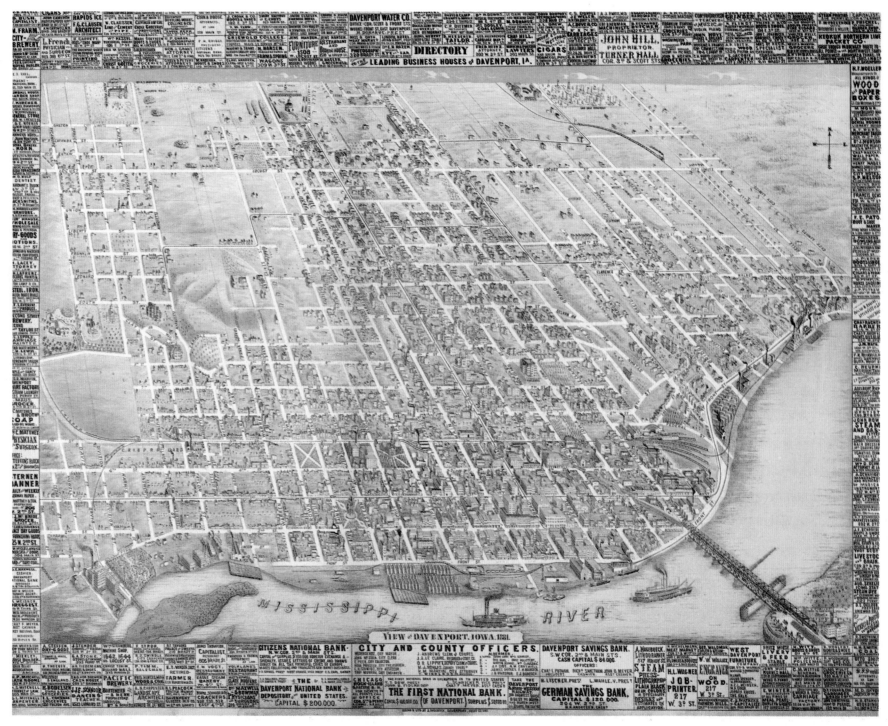

View of Davenport, Iowa, 1881. Drawn, lithographed, [and printed] by A[ugustus] Hageboeck. Lithograph, 22 7/8 x 28 1/16 in. (58.2 x 71.4 cm).

Putnam Museum of History & Natural Science, Davenport, Iowa

Davenport, Ia. 1888. Drawn by H[enry] Wellge. Published by the American Publishing Co., Milwaukee. Lithograph, 20 1/2 x 39 3/4 in. (52.2 x 101.1 cm).

Geography and Map Division, Library of Congress

Davenport, Iowa, from the air, October 12, 1988.

Alex MacLean

Folio 47.   Galena, Illinois, Is a Mississippi River Town Although Located a Short Distance up the Fever River

The second son of an English earl finds himself in this lead-mining town in 1835

This town, which has risen to some importance, and to a population of several thousands during the last few years, is situated on Fever River, about five miles from the point where it falls into the Mississippi. The Galenians, anxious for the healthy reputation of their river, have circulated a story that "Fever River" is an awkward corruption of the old French name of "Riviére des Fêves," or *Bean* River; but I see little reason to credit this version. . . . However, it is of little consequence: the place is as healthy as any other on the Mississippi banks; but its site is singularly inconvenient and circumscribed, being surrounded on the north and west by high bluffs, so as to render its increase to any extent almost impossible; while the ground on which it is built is so abrupt, that you have to climb a bank steep as the side of a house, in order to get from one street to another, and, in rainy weather, nothing short of stilts or Greenland boots can save a pedestrian from the mud and filth.

The inhabitants have hitherto cared little about paving, improving, or lighting the streets, as the land has not been as yet in the market; consequently the property still belongs to Congress, and the only existing title is a right of pre-emption.

(Murray, *Travels in North America during the Years 1834, 1835, & 1836,* 2:77–78)

A resident of St. Louis visits Galena and provides some details about its plan and appearance

The town of Galena is situated on the north side of Fever river . . . six miles from the Mississippi; nature seems to have been very sparing in her advantages, as far as regards the cite [*sic*] of a city here; the appearance that the town now makes is rather uninviting to strangers and lovers of regular built roomy cities. The town is built in a ravine along the river and bluffs; the streets are very narrow and miry, being the mudiest I ever saw; there are two principal streets running lengthwise, and in some places three; the streets appear to be no more then [*sic*] 30 feet wide and the space between the streets in some places are no more than 50 or 60 feet; in some places they may [be] upwards of 100. The buildings are intended to extend from one street to another clear through the block and so percipitate [*sic*] is the rise in many places between 1st and 2nd streets in most of places that the 2d story on first street will be the 1st on second street. Back of 2d street the bluffs rise about twice as high as the houses in most places, and are very steep . . . ; the inhabitants talk of grading the bluffs down and filling up some of the low ground about the middle of the town that adjoins the river. . . . If this project succeeds, it will make more room to build and give the town the appearance

of an amphtheatre [*sic*]. This is not yet done and will perhaps not soon be accomplished.

(Miller, "The Journal of Henry B. Miller," 237–38)

Harper's New Monthly Magazine tells its readers about this little western mining metropolis in 1853

Galena['s] growth has been rapid, and its future is bright, while the mineral wealth around remains inexhaustible; but so unfavorable is its location between the two high shores of Fever River, for other business than that which gave it birth, that should the buoyancy of lead fail to keep it up, it must sink. The business street is at the foot of the bluff, and the dwellings are scattered over its summit a full hundred feet above, to which the people ascend by flights of steps. Art and business have given the town almost every attraction which it possesses. The narrow Fever River is filled with steamboats and other craft, and the mart is full of rough miners, and the implements of labor and trade incident to their business. One seems to be pent up in a chasm; but ascend the bluff to the dwellings, and there is beauty, neatness, and taste. The houses are pleasant, and around them are gardens and shade trees, and delightful walks. But all adjacent to this pretty creation of taste, is the forbidding and desolate hill country of the lead region. All is poverty on the surface, but riches below.

("Sketches on the Upper Mississippi," 180–81)

Harper's Magazine reports about Galena again in 1858, illustrating its article with a small wood engraving

Our view of Galena is as it once was, but these towns come up in a night, and grow, like the prophet's gourd, so fast that one can hardly keep pace with them. It is the metropolis of the great lead region, and ships away annually 42,000,000 pounds of the metal, which is valued at $1,780,000, and gives direct employment to about two thousand people. In the region round about the ground is penetrated with pits and diggings, many of which extend deep below the surface. Thousands of tons of zinc and copper ores are dug out and lie on the surface, unused for want of coal to smelt them. The town contains about ten thousand people, and is charmingly built on the rising banks of a branch of the Mississippi; it has churches of many kinds—Baptist, Presbyterian, Episcopal, Methodist, and Roman Catholic—and is well supplied with schools, newspapers, and mills and shops in abundance. Galena will not go backward. Railroad trains rush in daily, bearing their loads of freight and passengers, and her levee is busy in receiving and discharging cargoes from steamboats that ply up and down the Mississippi.

("The Upper Mississippi," 447)

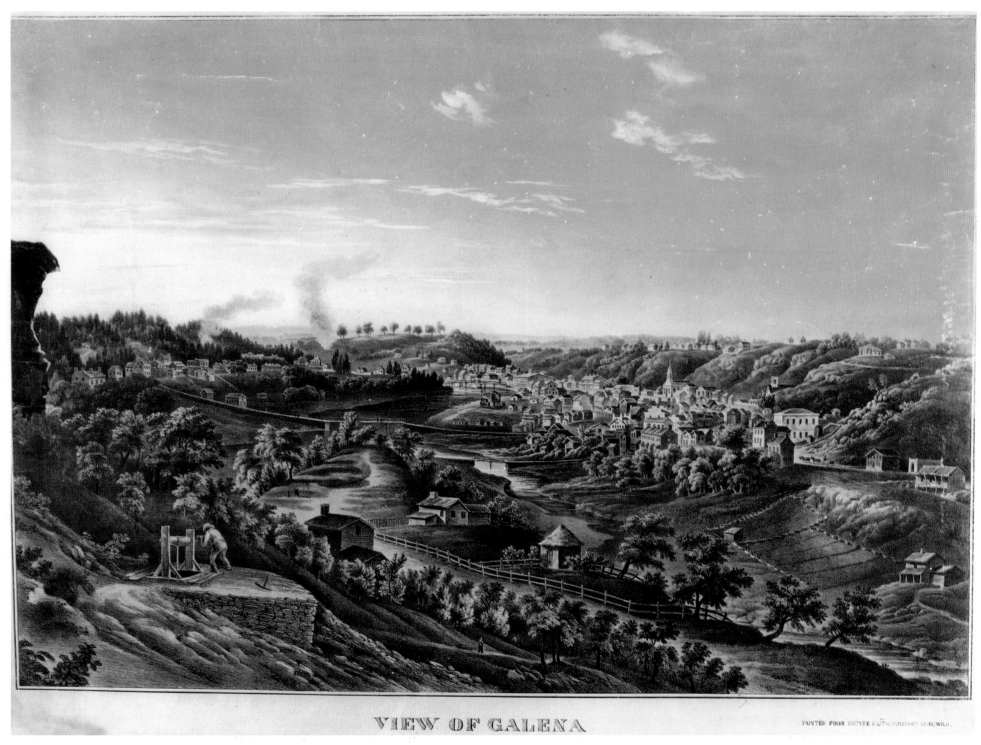

VIEW OF GALENA

View of Galena, Illinois. Drawn and lithographed by J[ohn] C[aspar] Wild, ca. 1844. Lithograph, 20 5/8 x 30 in. (52.5 x 76.3 cm).

Galena/Jo Daviess County Historical Society and Museum

Galena, Ill. Unsigned. Lithographed by A[dolphus F.] Forbriger. Printed by Onken's Lith. Cin[cinnati] O[hio], [1851]. From William Wells, *Western Scenery; or, Land and River, Hill and Dale, in the Mississippi Valley.* Lithograph, 5 13/16 x 7 7/8 in. (14.8 x 20)

Public Library of Cincinnati and Hamilton County

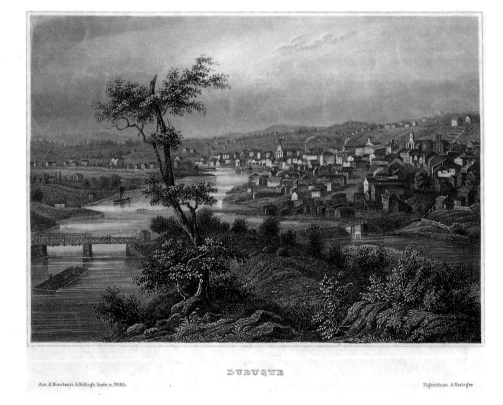

Dubuque [i.e. Galena]. [Drawn by Th. Anders?] Printed and published by the Kunstanst. d. Bibliogr. Instit. in Hildbh. From Charles A. Dana, ed., *The United States Illustrated: In Views of City and Country, with Descriptive and Historical Texts*, vol. 2, *The West: or the States of the Mississippi Valley and the Pacific* (New York: Hermann J. Meyer, [1853–1854]). Steel engraving, 5 x 6 1/4 in. (12.7 x 15.8 cm).

John W. Reps

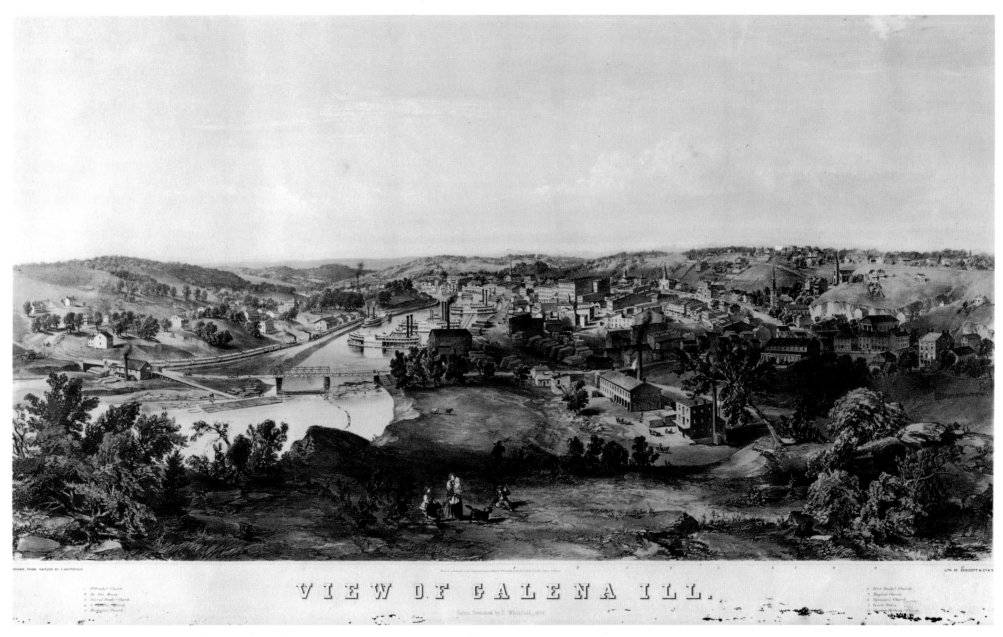

View of Galena, Ill. Drawn and published by E[dwin] Whitefield, 1856. Printed by Endicott & Co., N. Y. Lithograph, 19 1/2 x 36 in. (49.5 x 91.5 cm).

Galena/Jo Daviess County Historical Society and Museum

Folio 48.   Several Writers Provide Information about the Early Years of Dubuque

A pioneer clergyman in the region recalls Dubuque's beginnings

The little episcopal city of Dubuque dates its origin from 1833; before then, the whole western shore of the Mississippi, which forms the great Territory of Iowa, was still inhabited by different Indian tribes. The government having bought from these tribes the land adjoining the river, by various treaties, or, to speak more correctly, by large sums of money, many thousand citizens of the Republic settled there in a few months, but particularly in the neighborhood of Dubuque on account of the lead mines. The traffic in this valuable metal created the city of Dubuque, named for the last French trader who . . . died in 1811. . . .

In July, 1835, the rising city of Dubuque numbered about two hundred and fifty persons—perhaps a thousand including those in the vicinity where they were excavating in search of lead veins.
(Mazzuchelli, *The Memoirs of Father Samuel Mazzuchelli*, 147)

A military officer, Albert Lea, provides a list of business activities in 1835

This is the center of the mining region of the Iowa District. The operations in these mines were commenced in the year 1832, when the country was still in the possession of the Indians; and in 1833, after the acquisition of the District by the United States, the town was laid out and permanently settled. It contained in the autumn of 1835, about twenty-five dry goods stores, numerous groceries, four taverns, a court house, a jail, and three churches. One of these, the Catholic, is a beautiful little building. Ten steamboats, which run between this and Saint Louis, are partly owned here; and there is also here a steam ferryboat. . . .

In the autumn of 1835 the population was about 1200 and was rapidly increasing. The people of this town are exceedingly active and enterprising, carrying on an extensive trade in the products of their mines, and in supplying the miners with the necessities and comforts of life. Every thing here is in a flourishing condition, for all labor is well paid.
(Lea, *Notes on Wisconsin Territory*, 40–41)

Henry Miller visits Dubuque a few years later in 1838 and records his impressions

The town makes rather a hard & ragged appearance, many of the buildings very temporary and but few elegant or even neat; there are but 3 brick houses in the town which are very common; there are a number of stores and groceries with 2 tolerable decent Hotels. . . . The river in front of the town is full of Islands, and but a narrow channel to come up, which gives it rather an unpromising appearance to strangers at first sight. Immediately back of the town the ground rises into bluffs which are upwards of 100 feet high. The Bottom on which the town is laid out on is about 1/2 to 3/4 of a mile wide at the upper end, and runs to a point; it is about 2 miles long. The principal part of the town is built at the lower end of the plain or point.
(Miller, "The Journal of Henry B. Miller," 235)

John Plumbe, Jr., describes Dubuque in 1839

Du Buque . . . now contains its elegant cathedral, stone and wooden churches, its brick banking house, its theatre, court house, jail, land office, surveyor-general's office, towering warehouses, splendid stores, hotels, billiard rooms, spacious brick mansions, a large double steam sawmill, a printing establishment employing some ten or twelve individuals, a lyceum, a temperance society, reading rooms, a museum, a postoffice with tri-weekly mail from the east, a tri-weekly mail for the southeast, a semi-weekly mail from St. Louis, and a weekly mail respectively from the north and the west; besides a daily river mail when steamboats run.

A classical school and a ladies' academy are here also to be found, in addition to a seminary incorporated by the legislature at its last session.

A splendid new court house, too, is to be built here this season, of brick; the materials for manufacturing which are found close to the town.

Numerous stores and dwellings, of brick and frame, are also now being put up, giving to Du Buque, in addition to the many fine buildings hitherto erected, the appearance of an old settled place. Her business is very considerable in exporting the production of the various lead furnaces in the surrounding neighborhood.
(John Plumbe, Jr., *Sketches of Iowa and Wisconsin*, 75–76)

By the mid–1840s Dubuque sheds its frontier image and emerges as a modern city

Dubuque . . . is the seat of justice of Dubuque county; contains the Surveyor-General's office for Wisconsin and Iowa; U.S. Land office for the northern district of Iowa; a tasteful and spacious Catholic cathedral; a brick Court house; several neat and commodious churches; a bank; several good hotels; two printing offices; numerous tasteful residences, and between twenty and thirty extensive mercantile establishments; likewise, most of the trades and mechanical occupations usually found in the Eastern cities. . . .

From the high cliffs, which bound the western side of the town, the prospect is surpassingly beautiful. The eye of the traveller traces the city, almost beneath his feet, stretched out on the broad plateau of green, the compact portion presenting its parallel streets, with the uniform ranges of houses and lofty stores, together with numerous neat and tasteful residences that are sprinkled over the suburbs of the town, the whole presenting a panorama of rare and attractive beauty.
(Newhall, *A Glimpse of Iowa in 1846*, 72–73)

DUBUQUE; IOWA.

Dubuque, Iowa. Drawn and Litho by J[ohn] C[aspar] Wild, ca. 1844. Lithograph, 21 5/8 x 30 11/16 in. (55 x 78 cm).

Putnam Museum of History & Natural Science, Davenport, Iowa

Folio 49.   Dubuque Newspapers Boast about the City during the Boom Years of the 1850s

The newspaper calls attention to the shortage of housing despite much construction

A Town Full—The city of Dubuque is literally filled. There has been a greater call for houses within the last two months than ever before known. Houses are being finished every day, but are all engaged long before they are complete. More are building, however; don't be discouraged.
(Dubuque *Daily Miners' Express,* October 23, 1850)

The editors of the paper see unlimited prosperity ahead

Never did a spring open in Dubuque with more flattering prospects of a healthy and lucrative trade. Our hotels are crowded beyond their capacity to accommodate; our merchants, buildings and mechanics are active; our smelting mills and foundries, etc., are enjoying a season of the highest prosperity; our streets are crowded with immigrant wagons; the demand for dwellings and business houses is beyond the capacity of our property holders to meet; the best and fastest steam ferry boat on the Mississippi is actively engaged; the harbor improvement is progressing rapidly; and everywhere is seen growth and prosperity. . . .

Within a few months there has been established in this city a large foundry, rope works, soap and candle factory and steam saw mill, and there is now being erected an additional steam saw mill.
(Dubuque *Daily Miners' Express,* April 9, August 12, 1852)

The boom continues into 1853, and the local newspaper boasts of the city's glorious future

New houses are going up in all parts of the city on ground hitherto unoccupied and old buildings (and often good ones) are tearing down to make room for more substantial and magnificent edifices. Our hotels are thronged with strangers and the tide of immigration, though the season is far advanced, is still unchecked. Business of all kinds is stirred with astonishing activity. These things are apparent to every eye. The natural advantages of Dubuque are rapidly developing under the thoroughgoing enterprise of her people. These things let us know that a brilliant future for Dubuque is no longer hypothetical. . . .

No period within the history of Dubuque has presented a greater amount and variety of improvements than the present. Buildings are going up or being torn down in all directions. One year ago we predicted 20,000 population in the space of five years. We were then laughed at. One thing is settled, Dubuque is to be the great central business focus of the northwest.
(Dubuque *Daily Miners' Express,* June 29, August 3, 1853)

A reader points out the need for harbor improvements

All know our city has suffered greatly for the last fifteen years in her business and reputation, at home and abroad, in consequence of the extreme difficulty of getting to and from the river in low water. Strangers destined for Dubuque (ladies not infrequently) have been landed from steamboats at night upon the outer island and were compelled to grope their way by land and slough to the city, benumbed and saturated with rain. Our own merchants, business men and hotel keepers can attest the hardships they have been subjected to, in getting to and from the river a great portion of the year.
(John King, in the Dubuque *Daily Miners' Express,* March 14, 1854)

The newspaper predicts the future population and reports on recent developments

In.whatever part of the city you visit you will discover the preparations for extensive building this spring and summer. We understand that contracts for the erection of some twenty new business houses on Main street are already let. There never has been a spring within the history of Dubuque when such an activity prevailed in the building line. . . .

From present unmistakable indications Dubuque in 1855 will be a city of ten if not twelve thousand inhabitants. Scarcely a day goes by that it does not bring new acquisitions to the city. The streets are crowded with strangers, new signs are going up in every direction and strangers daily inquire in vain for dwellings and business houses. Business men predict that three times the number of buildings will go up this season than have ever gone up in any one season before.
(Dubuque *Daily Miners' Express,* March 11, 14, 1854)

The newspaper notes the arrival of the railroad at Dunleith across the Mississippi and a bridge to the steamboat landing

Yesterday morning about half past seven o'clock the construction train of the Illinois Central railroad came through to the terminus of the road opposite this city. Passenger trains will commence running regularly to and from Dubuque and Dunleith on Monday next. This event should be commemorated by our citizens. . . .

There is now a bridge across the slough and connecting the main island with the business part of the city. Boats are now landing on the outer island and hacks and carts are running to and from Main street to the deep water of the Mississippi. This is an important fact for Dubuque. Seventh street also will soon be completed to the deep water of the main river.
(Dubuque *Express and Herald,* June 2, 13, 1855)

General View of the City of Dubuque, Iowa. [Drawn by J. C. Wolfe.] Engraved by Kilburn. From *Ballou's Pictorial Drawing-Room Companion* 13 (October 31, 1857): 281. Wood engraving, 9 11/16 x 13 7/16 in. (24.6 x 34.1 cm).

John W. Reps

View of Dubuque, Iowa. Drawn by Miss Lucinda Farnham. Printed by J. Cameron, 208 Broadway, New York, [1852–1855]. Lithograph, 21 5/8 x 29 7/8 in. (55 x 76 cm).

Dubuque County Historical Society

Dubuque. Drawn by [Henry W. Petit]. [Printed by Endicott & Co., 59 Beekman St., N.Y.] [Published by W. J. Gilbert, 100 Main St. Dubuque, Iowa, 1860.] Lithograph, 16 1/8 x 26 3/8 in. (41 x 67.1 cm).

State Historical Society of Iowa, Iowa City

Folio 50.   Dubuque's Boom Days Continue into the 1850s, but the City Suffers in the Depression of 1857

An Iowa gazetteer describes the city in 1855

The city of Dubuque, one of the largest and most densely populated in the state, is handsomely situated upon a natural terrace. The streets run parallel to each other, and owing to the peculiar soil at this location, are never muddy. This city is more compactly built, and contains a greater proportion of fine buildings than any other place in the State. Among these the Catholic Cathedral, court-house, and hotels stand prominent. The city is bounded on the west by a range of high cliffs, from which the prospect of the city and county is entrancingly beautiful. . . .

The population of Dubuque County, according to the census of 1854, is 16,513; and of the city, according to West's Statistics, 10,000. The number of buildings erected in the city last year was 332.

(Parker, *Iowa as It Is in 1855*, 127)

A visitor in 1855 arrives from the railroad terminus at Dunleith on the opposite shore

We arrived about seven and the scene was enchanting. The bold eastern bluff overlooked a broad reach of the "father of waters," stretching both upwards and downwards, smooth and clear; opposite, lay the town of Dubuque, nestled in a receding hollow, embraced by hills, and almost lost in their shade. To crown all, the sun was going down behind the distant hills of Iowa . . . and imparting a sort of fairy light to the whole scene. Such was the picture we gazed on from the deck of the small steamer which carried us across the mighty Mississippi. . . .

We strolled about the town, already of considerable size, and a bustling place. There are furniture manufactories, a foundry, and all the appearance of a rapidly-rising town. What may be called the business-town, is built on a gentle slope a little above the level, to which the river rises in the season of high-water, while the eminences behind afford very fine sites for private residences.

(Ferguson, *America by River and Rail*, 403, 406)

Early in 1857 the local newspaper notes and applauds the rise in real estate values

It is almost incredible to what a degree real estate has appreciated in this city within a twelve-month past. Take the Miller farm near town. A year or two ago it sold for $130 an acre. Now it is rated at $1000 an acre. A short time ago Mr. Sanford bought two lots corner of Seventh and Iowa streets for $30,000. The same lots were offered a year ago for $6,000 and could not find a purchaser at that price. It is within bounds to say that all the real estate within the city limits of Dubuque has doubled in value within a year.

(Dubuque *Express and Herald*, January 28, 1857)

On the eve of a national depression the Dubuque newspaper recalls the town's history and looks to a rosy future

Twelve years ago (1844) Dubuque was what we may call a small village, remarkable for nothing more than its being in the lead mining region. It had then, if our recollection be correct, about 700 inhabitants all told. There was not a single street of what is now the city of Dubuque graded. There were but two brick houses, most of the rest of the buildings being frame shanties. A few stores were sufficient to supply Dubuque and all the country for six miles around in Iowa with all the commodities of household, mechanical and agricultural use. . . . The hotels then were the Jefferson, the Washington and the Western, three frame buildings, not a vestige of which remains we believe to awaken in the minds of the old settlers reminiscences of the early days of Dubuque. . . . Look at Dubuque now and judge whether she does not give warrant for future greatness which we anticipate she will ere long attain.

(Dubuque *Express and Herald*, February 4, 1857)

In 1858 a new mayor describes the results of the speculative boom of the early 1850s

The outward signs of prosperity are awfully deceptive. They indicate the disease and corruption at work upon the citadel of life. Notwithstanding the apparent prosperity our city has become profligate, spendthrift, has wasted her substance and ruined her credit and good name by fast living, by projecting and carrying on costly improvements and going into expense thus incurred. She is forced to make short loans and pay exorbitant interest until the regular interest upon the funded debt, together with heavy shares upon short loans, are swallowing up almost her entire revenue.

(H. S. Hetherington, "Inaugural Address as Mayor of Dubuque," 124)

In 1863 John Warner Barber and Henry Howe describe Dubuque

Dubuque, the largest city, and the first settled place in the state . . . extends two miles on a table area, or terrace, immediately back of which rise a succession of precipitous bluffs, about 200 feet high. A small marshy island is in front of the city, which is being improved for business purposes. The beautiful plateau on which the city was originally laid out, being too limited for its growth, streets have been extended up and over the bluffs, on which many houses have been erected of a superior order, among which are numerous elegant residences. The Dubuque Female College is designed to accommodate 500 scholars. The Alexander College, chartered in 1853, is located here, under the patronage of the Synod of Iowa. Several important railroads terminate at this place, which is the head-quarters and principal starting place for steamboats on the northern Mississippi.

(Barber and Howe, *Our Whole Country*, 2:1234–35)

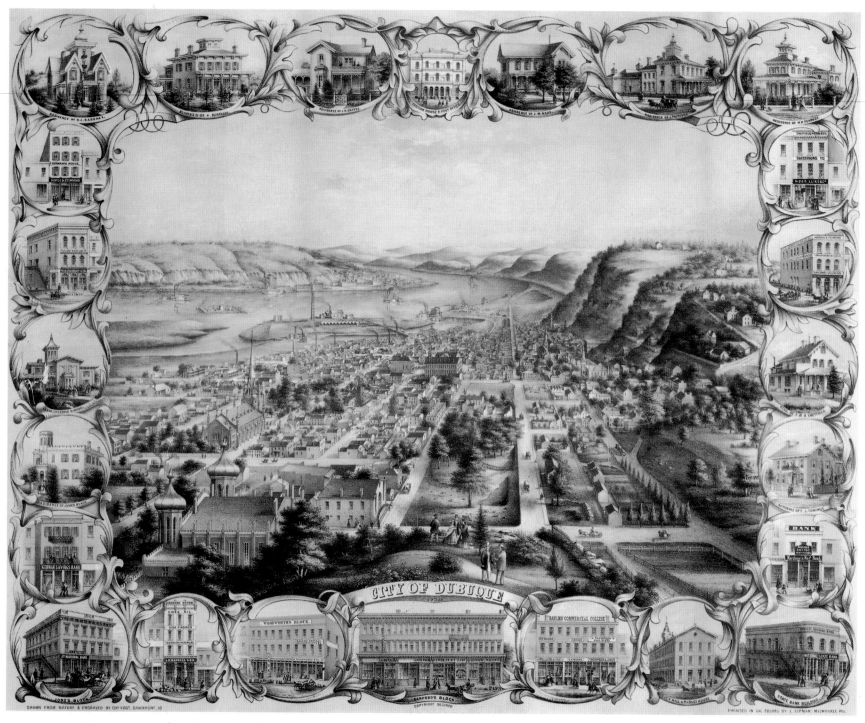

City of Dubuque Iowa. Drawn from nature & engraved [i.e. lithographed] by Chas. Vogt, Davenport, Io[wa]. Printed by L. Lipman, Milwaukee, Wis., ca. 1866. Lithograph, 20 1/2 x 25 7/8 in. (52 x 65.7 cm).

Research Center for Dubuque Area History

Drawn & Pub'd by Alex. Simplot, Nº 8 Main Street.   Chicago Lithographing Co. Nº 150, 152 & 154, S. Clark St. Chicago.

DUBUQUE , IOWA. 1870.

Dubuque, Iowa 1870. Drawn and pub'd by Alex. Simplot, No. 8 Main Street. Printed by Chicago Lithographing Co. No. 150, 152 & 154 S. Clark St. Chicago. Lithograph, 12 1/4 x 21 3/4 in. (31.1 x 55.3 cm).

Research Center for Dubuque Area History

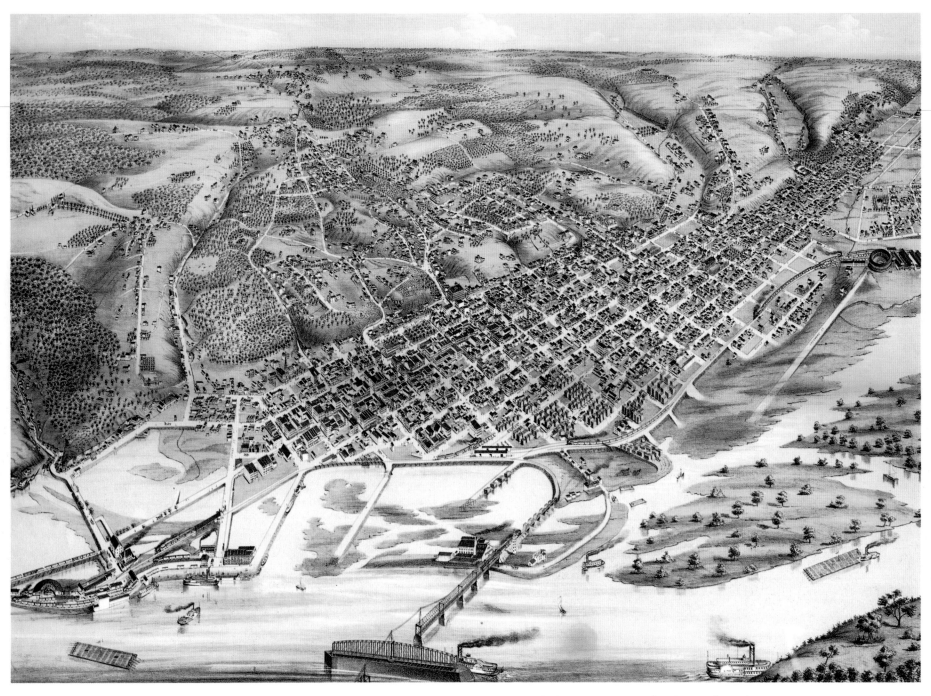

Birds Eye View of the City of Dubuque Iowa 1872. Drawn by Augustus Koch. Lithograph, 25 3/4 (matted) x 34 11/16 (matted) in. (65.4 x 88.1 cm).
Research Center for Dubuque Area History

Folio 51.   Visitors to Dubuque and One of Its Residents Record Their Impressions of the City after the Civil War

The readers of a famous American work on the scenic wonders of the country learn about how the city looked

At Dubuque the bluffs are nearly three hundred feet high, . . . but at the base there is a broad level, about sixteen feet above the Mississippi. On this plateau are all the business houses, the hotels and the factories. Above, connected with paths that have been cut through the solid limestone, are the streets of the dwelling houses.

The approaches to these upper houses are mostly by stairs that might easily be called ladders, without exposing one to a charge of being sarcastic; but it is worth the trouble of mounting these ladders a few times every day to have such a landscape unrolled before the eye. There is a stretch of bare, sandy island in the center of the river, across which comes the railway bridge of the Illinois Central railroad. There is, at the farther end of the island, a large shot factory, and close to it the shot tower, which darts up into the blue sky like a light flame. Beyond rise the bluffs of the eastern shore, which here are very hilly, and present beautiful contrasts of green verdure with glaring white. . . . This is the outward look.

The author finds a picturesque jumble of walls, stairs, and houses in these hilly residential quarters of Dubuque

There is an absolute confusion of lines. Here is a wall, there a stairway. Above that wall is a house, with more stairways. Then comes another wall, and perhaps another house, or a castellated mass of limestone, overlooking the architectural muddle. It is as quaint as any of the scenes in the old cities of Lombardy upon the slopes of any mountains, among the terraces cultivated with the grape, the olive and the fig.
(R. E. Garczynski, "The Upper Mississippi, from St. Louis to St. Anthony's Falls," 333)

A resident crosses the frozen river in 1876 to look back on the city from Dunleith

We took a walk in the afternoon across the ice on the Mississippi to Dunleith, a small town opposite to Dubuque. . . . We went to the top of the Dunleith bluffs in order to get a good view of Dubuque, &c. Dubuque looks very fine from this point. It occupies a sort of semicircle by the side of the river worn out by the water at some former period, and the cliffs behind are more than half covered with buildings, &c. At the south end of the town lies the Irish quarter, and there are some poor little shanties in it and nothing fine in its best parts. The business part of the town lies in the middle. The stores are mostly 3 stories high with a cellar underneath; the usual frontage of each store 22 1/2 feet and 113 through to the alley behind. A block of buildings

is about 270 ft. front by 113. The western portion of the town is nearly all German. There houses are better by far than those of the Irish, but not so good as those of the Americans and English which are principally situated on the cliffs and slopes behind.
(James L. Broderick, *The Character of the Country: The Iowa Diaries of James L. Broderick, 1876–1877*, 48–49)

The author of a book of travels in the American West visits Dubuque in 1877

Crossing the bridge which spans the river connecting Iowa with Illinois . . . we found ourselves in the beautiful and busy city of Dubuque, claiming, and justly so I should say, a population of 40,000. No locality upon the river could present more natural advantages for a city, none could be more picturesque, interesting and grandly beautiful than that upon which the city is situated. Rising gradually from the river bank and extending back for perhaps half-a-mile, is a plateau or table land, upon which the business portion of the city stands. Upon wide and cleanly [*sic*] streets are imposing buildings—stores, warehouses, factories and shops of all kinds, elegant public buildings and many fine residences. A semi-circular range of bluffs rises to an altitude of nearly 250 feet above the river, the highlands being adorned with delightful residences and their ornamental surroundings.
(Ayer, *Life in the Wilds of America*, 108, 110)

Willard Glazier in 1888 provides a word picture of the city

In 1870 the population of Dubuque had increased to over eighteen thousand. A street railway was added to the facilities for passenger transit; and steady progress made it all that pertains to a healthy municipal growth. Among the manufactures of this thriving city are those of steam-engines, boilers, threshing-machines, casting and work of iron-foundries and machine-shops, coppersmith work, tobacco, window-shades, churns, fanning-mills, trunks, soap, flour, wagons and carriages, furniture, planing-mill work, cooperage, brick, vinegar and many others.

Glazier mentions the lumber trade that many towns along the Mississippi depended on

The trade in lumber affords a striking contrast. In 1834 a small raft of pine boards, the first that ever descended the Upper Mississippi, furnished the material for a frame building used as a boarding-house in Dubuque. In 1870 fifty million feet of pine lumber were sold from fifteen Dubuque lumberyards, and the trade has very considerably increased since that date.
(Glazier, *Down the Great River*, 242)

Bridges on the Mississippi, at Dubuque. [Drawn by Alfred R. Waud.] Engraved by Filmer. From William Cullen Bryant, ed., *Picturesque America, or The Land We Live In*, vol. 2 (1874). Wood engraving, 6 3/8 x 9 1/8 in. (16.2 x 23.1 cm).

John W. Reps

Dubuque, From Kelly's Bluff. Drawn by A[lfred] R. W[aud]. Engraved by Richardson. From Bryant, ed., *Picturesque America*, vol. 2. Wood engraving, 6 5/16 x 8 13/16 in. (16 x 22.4 cm).

John W. Reps

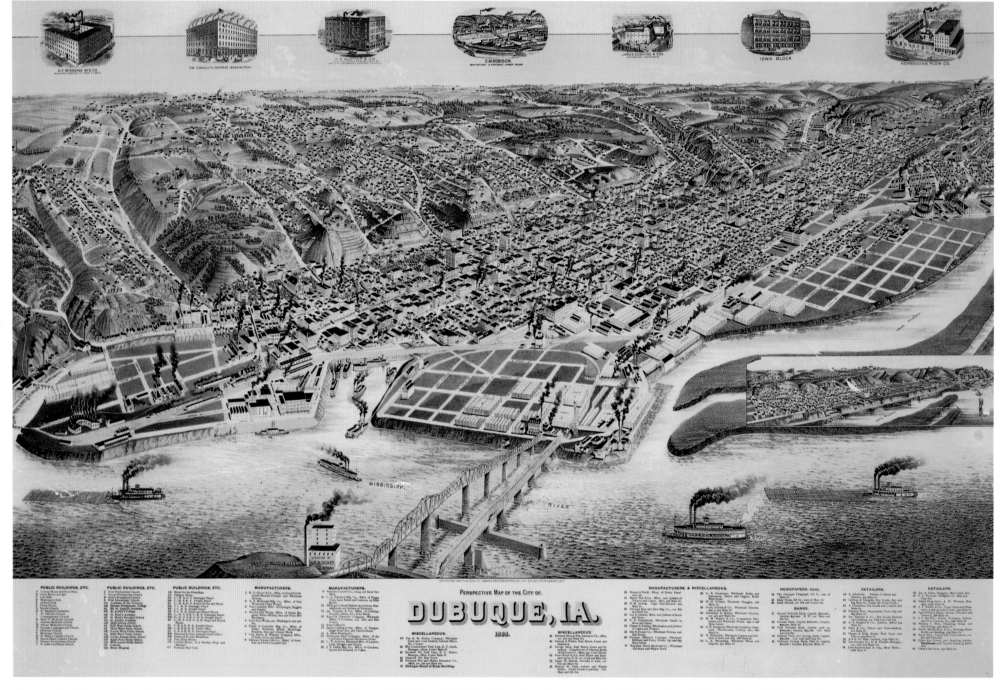

Perspective Map of the City of Dubuque, Ia. 1889. Drawn by H[enry] Wellge. Published by the American Publishing Co., Milwaukee. Lithograph, 21 1/4 x 39 1/2 in. (54 x 102 cm).

Dubuque County Historical Society

Dubuque, Iowa, from the air, October 12, 1988.
Alex MacLean

Folio 52.   McGregor and Guttenberg Develop as Linear Settlements in Northeastern Iowa

An Iowa history published in 1876 provides a description and history of McGregor

McGregor is situated on the bank of the Mississippi, opposite Prairie du Chien, one hundred and ninety-nine miles from Milwaukee, by the Milwaukee and St. Paul Railroad, which crosses the river at this point, and gives the town access to a valuable line of travel through the northwest. The Chicago, Dubuque and Minnesota Railroad, running from Chicago to Dubuque, passes through McGregor to Winona, Minnesota, where it connects with other valuable lines. In the year 1857, McGregor was a village of less than three hundred souls, and now its population exceeds four thousand, and there is before this lively and wide awake town a very prosperous future. Northern Iowa and southern Minnesota find in this town their best outlet, and the success of the younger town is a killing commentary on the lifelessness of the town on the further bank. During the season when the river can be navigated there are boats of the best description to be availed of for travel to St. Paul, on the one hand, or to Dubuque and St. Louis on the other. Crossing the river to Prairie du Chien another range of travel and traffic opens up, and the commercial advantages of this center of business can hardly be overstated.

The early French traders named the ravine in which McGregor is built, "Coolie de Sioux." The bluffs rise on either hand to a height of four hundred feet, and the position has beauty as well as convenience to recommend it. A ferry from Prairie du Chien was established in 1836, by the man from whom the town took its name, and the place was at once known for miles around as McGregor's landing. From that date the town slowly rose and in spite of diversions which were made at one time to diminish its importance. The cabin built by McGregor, the ferryman, marked the beginning of the now great commercial center. The village was incorporated in 1857, and its improvements would alone serve to testify the growth of which it is capable. There is a considerable share of manufacturing effected in the town, and the records, which have been obtained to show the amount of business transacted within twelve months, show a total of nearly sixteen million dollars. (Tuttle, *An Illustrated History of the State of Iowa*, 468–69)

An Iowa gazetteer issued in 1865 traces the origins and growth of the German community of Guttenberg

The first municipal election was held in 1851. Since that time the growth of the town has been both upward and rapid. Every year has witnessed new and substantial buildings, and a large increase of trade and business.

Since the incorporation of the town large sums have been annually expended in public improvements. Good roads have been made leading to every part of the surrounding country. The town has an excellent steam ferry boat, which during the season of navigation plies regularly between this place and Glen Haven, three miles up the river on the Wisconsin side.

The buildings are mostly of stone, of which material of an excellent quality is obtained from the bluff back of town.

There are now in the place seven general stores; two groceries; two clothing stores; two hardware, stove and tin shops; two drug stores; three millinery and fancy stores; four blacksmith and saddler shops; two wagon and carriage shops; one gun shop; three furniture shops; four hotels; five breweries; several warehouses; two flouring mills; and one saw mill, together with the usual number of mechanical shops. The Lutheran and Catholic are the leading church denominations.

The commercial advantages of Guttenberg are not surpassed by any town of the same size on the river. It annually ships and receives large quantities of produce and merchandise. The principal articles of export are wheat, flour, barley, oats, corn, potatoes, pork, lard, beef and pig lead.

The country in the vicinity of Guttenberg is beautiful, healthy and remarkably fertile and is settled with an intelligent and enterprising class of farmers.

The resources of the surrounding country are unsurpassed. Independent of the unrivalled fertility of the soil, it possesses abundant sources of wealth in its vast forests of timber and the rich mines of lead ore. North of the town are large tracts of timber for building, fencing and other purposes; while to the south and west the forests extend for many miles and abound in choice varieties of oak, walnut, hard maple, ash and basswood.

The bluffs immediately back of town abound in lead ore, and on Miner's Creek, within two or three miles of town, several rich veins of mineral have been discovered and profitably worked.

The advantages for manufacturers are good. Miner's Creek in the rear of town affords good water power, which has already been rendered available to some extent. The "Big Spring" at the upper end of town can be made profitable in the propulsion of light machinery. Steam power can be used to good advantage, and at small cost, owing to the abundance of timber. With these facilities manufacturers could be established, and carried on profitably at this point.

From the bluffs immediately back of town issue numerous springs of excellent water; sufficient in quantity to supply the inhabitants of a large city. (*Iowa Gazetteer*, as quoted in W. W. Jacobs, "A History of Guttenberg," 8–9)

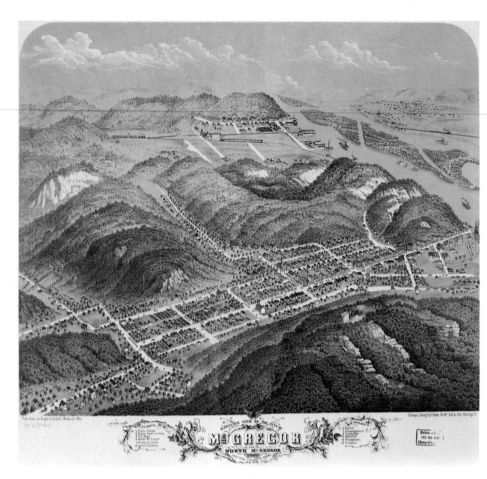

Bird's Eye View of the City of McGregor and North McGregor Clayton County, Iowa 1869. [Drawn by Albert Ruger.] Printed by the Chicago Lithog. Co. S. Clark St. No. 152 & 154, Chicago, Ill. Published by Ruger & Stoner, Madison, Wis. Lithograph, 18 1/16 x 22 in. (45.8 x 55.8 cm).

Geography and Map Division, Library of Congress

McGregor, Iowa, from the air, October 11, 1988.

Alex MacLean

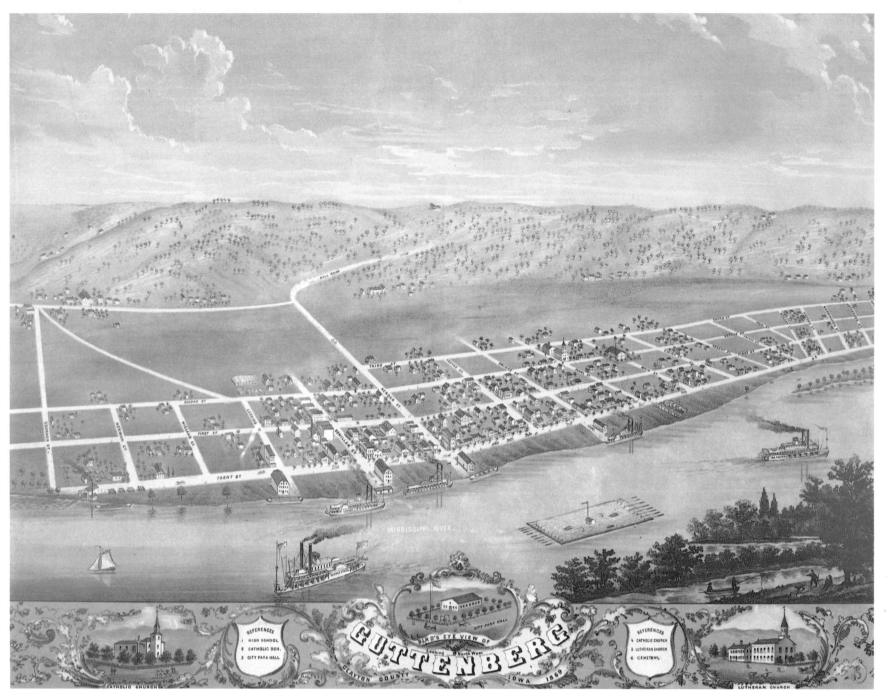

Bird's Eye View of Guttenberg Clayton County Iowa 1869 Looking North West. [Drawn by Albert Ruger.] Printed by Merchants Lithographing Co. Chicago. Published by Ruger & Stoner, Madison, Wis. Lithograph, 16 1/8 x 21 3/8 in. (40.9 x 54.3 cm).

Geography and Map Division, Library of Congress

Guttenberg, Iowa, from the air, October 11, 1988.

Alex MacLean

Folio 53.   Once One of the Most Important Indian Trading Posts, Prairie du Chien, Wisconsin, Falters with Age

A visitor in 1846 tells something of the history of the place

Prairie Du Chien is undoubtedly one of the most interesting and beautiful places on the Mississippi. It takes its name from the fact that it was once the camping place of a Fox Indian Chief, whose name was—*The Dog.* The prairie extends along the river for about ten miles; on the one hand it slopes gently down to the river, and on the other is bounded by a range of bluffs, which are some five hundred feet high, and exceedingly picturesque. The houses that shelter the inhabitants of this place are planted without any order, but as it is one of our most ancient trading posts, there is a rude and romantic appearance about them which is quite refreshing. Here, in the form of an isolated square, lie the barracks of Fort Crawford, where the discordant sounds of the drum and shrill whistle of the fife are often heard; while in another part of the plain are the ruins of an old fortress almost level with the ground. Now a lonely Catholic church is seen holding forth its gilded cross; and now, the store of the Indian trader is surrounded with a herd of Winnebagoe Indians, who resort here for the purposes of trade. (Lanman, *A Summer in the Wilderness,* 35)

In 1846 the young town lies in the shadow of the fort used for Indian trading

Prairie du Chien, the seat of justice of the county, and the only village of much size and importance in it, is situated on the Mississippi, about four or five miles above the mouth of the Wisconsin, on a level plain or prairie, about six miles long and two miles wide. This prairie is bordered on one side by the Mississippi, and on the other by high rocky bluffs, with scattered trees. . . . It is one of the oldest of the French settlements, or trading posts; but the first permanent settlement was commenced in 1783. Fort Crawford is located here, near the south part of the "new town" of St. Friole, as it is sometimes called to distinguish it from the more ancient or "old town," which lies a mile and a half above, and is separated from it by an arm of the Mississippi called the "Grand Maris de St. Friole." Below the fort, the "City of Prairie du Chien" has been laid out, but the *city* is much smaller than the town. Prairie du Chien is about five hundred and forty miles above St. Louis. (I. A. Lapham, *Wisconsin: Its Geography and Topography, History, Geology, and Mineralogy,* 194)

John Warner Barber and Henry Howe describe Prairie du Chien in their guide and history of 1862

Prairie Du Chien, the county seat of Crawford county, stands upon the left bank of the Mississippi, at the terminus of the Milwaukie and Mississippi Railroad, about three miles above the mouth of Wisconsin River. . . . It is beautifully situated on a dry alluvial prairie, about six miles in length along the river, by two miles wide. The southern and widest portion of the prairie is gently undulating, and so high above the river as never to be subject to inundation, and it is one of the best sites for a town on the river. The water is deep, affording natural and spacious harbors. On the opposite side of the river the bluffs rise directly from the water, are covered with a thick growth of forest trees, and are only broken by ravines, which afford roadways into the country west from the river. There is no room for any considerable town to be built on the river elsewhere, nearer than Dubuque, seventy miles south of this place, and for a distance of nearly one hundred miles north, on account of the high bluffs which rise, like the highlands of the Hudson, from the water's edge. Prairie du Chien can never have a competitor for the western trade between those limits.

There are two landings here, one at the terminus of the Milwaukie and Mississippi Railroad, on the slough around the eastern side of an island in the Mississippi, the other, McGregor's landing, about 1 1/2 miles northward of the railroad depot. (Barber and Howe, *Our Whole Country,* 2:1190–91)

Willard Glazier visits Prairie du Chien in 1881 and records his impressions

Prairie du Chien, the county-seat of Crawford County, is situated on the eastern bank of the Mississippi, on a level plain or prairie about nine miles long and between one and two miles wide. . . . It was one of the oldest of the French trading-posts, but the first permanent settlement was located there in 1783. . . .

Like many of its neighbors up and down the river, Prairie du Chien had great expectations in its youth. It was confident of becoming the chief town of the Mississippi. It is situated five hundred and forty miles north of Saint Louis, in the midst of a productive agricultural and mineral region. But though one or more railroads touch it, the great through-lines of the continent passed it by; and for that, and other reasons, more or less difficult of explanation, but which act as a sort of Providence in shaping the ends of rough-hewn cities, it remains scarcely more than a town, having but about three thousand inhabitants. It is, however, an important local shipping-post, and has a number of manufactories. Saint John's College and Saint Mary's Female Institute are located here, under control of the Catholic Church. (Glazier, *Down the Great River,* 231–32)

PRAIRIE DU CHIEN, WISCONSIN
in 1830

Prairie Du Chien, Wisconsin, in 1830. Drawn by H[enry] Lewis. [Printed by C. H. Muller, Aachen.] Published by Arnz & Co., Düsseldorf, [1854–1857]. Lithograph, 6 1/8 x 7 11/16 in. (15.5 x 19.5 cm).

Minnesota Historical Society

Prairie du Chien Crawford County Wisconsin 1870. [Drawn by Albert Ruger.] Printed by the Chicago Lithog. Co. No. 150, 152 & 154, S. Clark St. Chicago. Published by Ruger & Stoner, Madison, Wis. Lithograph, 22 x 28 in. (56 x 71.3 cm).

State Historical Society of Wisconsin

Prairie du Chien, Wisconsin, from the air, October 11, 1988.

Alex MacLean

Folio 54.   La Crosse, Wisconsin, Grows from a Small Settlement to Become an Important Lumber Town and Trading Center

A state gazetteer published in 1853 summarizes the early history of La Crosse and records the status of development

La Crosse . . . is situated on a prairie 5 miles long and 3 wide, on the Mississippi river, immediately below the mouth of the Black and La Crosse rivers, and about equidistant between Galena and St. Paul. The prairie is high enough from the river to be free from all danger of innundation [*sic*], and as a site for a village or city, is unsurpassed by beauty and natural advantages by any spot on the river. The first claim was made by H. J. B. Miller and Nathan Myrick, who took up their residence in 1842. The Government survey was not made until 1847; John M. Levy opened a store in 1846, and the next year erected the first hotel. Nothing was done towards laying out the town until after the advent of Timothy Burns, now Lieutenant Governor of the State, to whom it is largely indebted for its present progress. A post office was established in 1844. The plat was surveyed in May 1851. In the second year of its organization, the town paid into the State treasury over $900. The population in March, 1853, in the village, was 543. It contains 4 stores of general assortment, 1 drug, 1 hardware, 1 furniture, 1 stove and tin, 3 groceries, 1 bakery, 1 livery stable, 1 harness, 4 tailor, 3 shoemaker shops, and mechanics of every description; 6 physicians, 6 lawyers, 4 clergymen, 3 religious societies, a division of the Sons of Temperance, a Free Masons' lodge, 1 church edifice, court house, steam saw mill and grist mill, and 5 hotels. La Crosse, from the advantages of its position, cannot fail to become one of the largest and most important places in the Northwest. . . . It has been selected as the terminus of a rail road from Milwaukee, and the route selected is the most feasible one from Lake Michigan to the Mississippi, north of Dubuque.
(John Warren Hunt, *Wisconsin Gazetteer . . .* , 122–23)

A local history written a quarter of a century later tells of the early economic boom in the mid–1850s

The spring of 1853 was early in its arrival. . . . The streets of La Crosse were filled with strangers attracted hither—some to engage in legitimate business, some to embark in speculations, and others to continue their explorations into the lumber regions of the Black River country. New stores and warehouses had been contracted for, or were in progress of building; the saw-mill was in active operations, and others were promised.
(*History of La Crosse County, Wisconsin*, 401)

The authors of a guide and history of the West report on conditions in La Crosse when they saw it in the early 1860s

La Crosse, the capital of La Crosse county, is beautifully situated on the Mississippi, at the mouth of La Crosse River, 200 miles N.W. of Milwaukie by railroad, and 303 miles below St. Paul, by the river. It contains a large number of saw mills, and considerable quantities of pine lumber are manufactured. It is a place of rapid increase and prosperity, and its merchants transact a heavy business with the adjacent country, which is rapidly filling up. Population, in 1853, 300; and in 1860, about 4,000.
(Barber and Howe, *Our Whole Country*, 2:1199–1200)

In 1880 the U.S. Census summarizes its information about public transportation in La Crosse

The horse-railroads have a total length of 2 miles. There are 5 cars and 13 horses in use, while employment is given to 7 men. There were 100,000 passengers carried during the year, the rate of fare being 5 cents. There are no regular omnibus lines, but 3 vehicles with 12 horses, and employing 7 men, carry passengers to all parts of the city at rates of fare of from 25 to 50 cents.
(U.S. Census Office, *Report on the Social Statistics of Cities*, 2:651)

Willard Glazier visits La Crosse in 1881 and describes what he saw and learned

The growth and development of La Crosse, in a very few years, are in truth no less amazing than creditable to its enterprising pioneers and citizens. The first settler . . . landed here in November, 1841. . . . In . . . 1856, the town had attained sufficient size and importance to be made a city. To-day it has a population of over twenty thousand of as live, go-ahead citizens as are to be found in the valley of the Great River. . . .

It will afford some idea of the dimensions of the city to say that it has about thirty miles of graded streets, and forty-five miles of sidewalks. The fire department and the police force rank at a high standard of efficiency. Electric light for the streets and stores is furnished by . . . four towers, each one hundred and fifty feet high, and nine masts, and the streets at night are consequently well illuminated. The public schools are eleven in number in addition to the High School. . . . Twenty-five churches administer to the religious requirements of the various denominations and nationalities, some of them handsome specimens of church architecture. The Public Library contains about eight thousand volumes adapted to the mixed population.
(Glazier, *Down the Great River*, 222, 225)

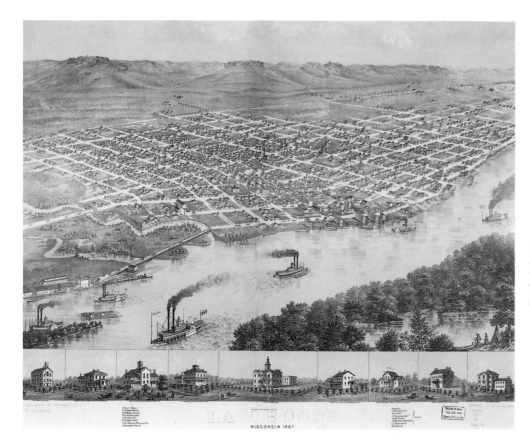

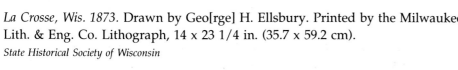

Bird's Eye View of the City of La Crosse Wisconsin 1867. Drawn by A[lbert] Ruger. Printed by the Chicago Lithographing Co. 152 & 154 Clark St. Chicago. Lithograph, 20 13/16 x 28 1/4 in. (53 x 72 cm).

Geography and Map Division, Library of Congress

La Crosse, Wis. 1873. Drawn by Geo[rge] H. Ellsbury. Printed by the Milwaukee Lith. & Eng. Co. Lithograph, 14 x 23 1/4 in. (35.7 x 59.2 cm).

State Historical Society of Wisconsin

LA CROSSE, WIS.

1. Court House. Jail.	12. White & Co., Flour Mill.	22. Methodist Episcopal Church.	32. Green Bay R. R. Depot.
2. City Hall.	13. Thornsby & James, Foundry.	23. St. Rosa de Viterbo Convent, Motherhouse of the	33. Gund's Brewery.
3. First Ward School House.	14. M Funk's Boiler Shops.	Francois Sisters.	34. Eagle Brewery, I. Hofer.
4. St. Joseph's Cathedral.	15. J. Paul's Saw Mill.	24. Orphan Asylum.	35. Zeisler's Brewery.
5. Congregational Church.	16. C. L. Colman's Saw Mill.	25. St. Wenceslaus Church, (Bohemian.)	36. C. M. and St. Paul R. R. Depot.
6. Episcopal Church.	17. Segelke, Kohlhaus & Co., Sash and Blind Factory.	26. Michel Bros. Brewery.	37.
7. First Baptist Church.	18. M. E. Church.	27. Turner Hall.	38. Dean, Smith & Co., Machine Shops.
8. First Presbyterian Church.	19. St. Mary's Catholic Church.	28. Reformed Church.	39. A. Hirsheimer & Co., Plow Works.
9. Post Office Building.	20. Universalist Church.	29. Armory Building.	40. A. Hirsheimer, City Mills.
10. German Lutheran Church.	21. Third Ward School House.	30. Engine House.	41. Hutt & Horton's Factory.
11. Second Ward School House.		31. Heilman's Brewery.	42. Southern Minnesota Depot.

La Crosse, Wis. 1876. Drawn by C[lemens] J. Pauli. Printed by the American Oleograph Co. Lith. Milwaukee. Lithograph, 17 1/4 x 23 15/16 in. (43.8 x 60.8 cm).

State Historical Society of Wisconsin

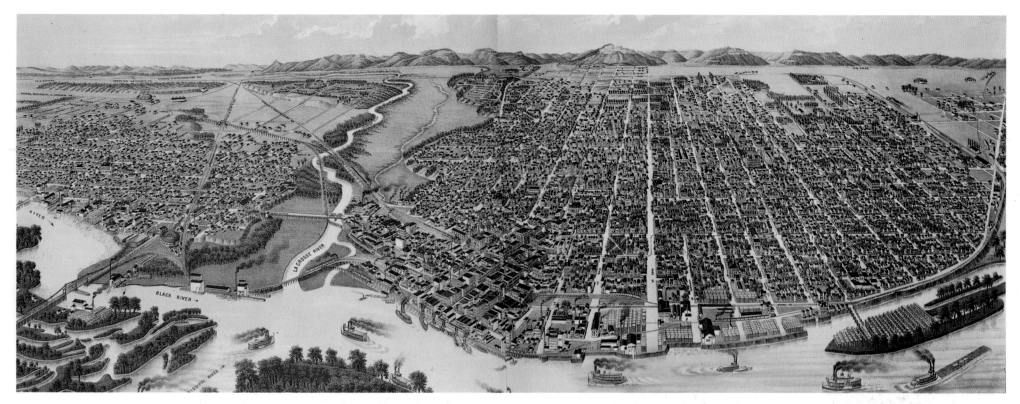

La Crosse, Wis. County Seat of La Crosse County. 1887. Unsigned. Printed by The Beck & Pauli Lith Co. Milwaukee. Published by H[enry] Wellge 205 Second St. Milwaukee, Wis.

Geography and Map Division, Library of Congress

La Crosse, Wisconsin, from the air, October 3, 1989.

Alex MacLean

Folio 55.   Winona, Minnesota, Takes Its Place among the Many Towns Founded along the Upper Mississippi in the 1850s

In 1848 Henry Lewis climbs to the top of the bluff overlooking the site of Winona and foresees a city at that location

The view from the top of the mountain well repays the exertion of the climb. Four hundred feet below the astonished spectator . . . a beautiful plain stretches from the water to the hills which form the background on both shores. . . .

But how will it look in a hundred years? Then the wanderer may well stand on that mountain top, but he will look down on the church spires of "Winona City," and in the distance he will see a hundred villages instead of one little house. Hundreds of ships and boats of all kinds will rock on the bosom of the mighty river and the canoe of the savage will be known only in legend.
(Lewis, *The Valley of the Mississippi Illustrated*, 123)

A local historian at the end of the nineteenth century recalls the city's origins

The original plat of Winona, surveyed, June 19th 1852, . . . was bounded on the north by the Mississippi river, on the east by Market street, on the south by Wabasha street and on the west by Washington street. It comprised a square, each side of which was six full blocks. This plat was enlarged from time to time by "additions," until at the close of 1856, the platted area on Wabasha prairie covered a tract of ground fully two miles in extent from east to west, and nearly half that distance from north to south. The principal of these additions was . . . known as Huff's survey of . . . 1854, and extended from the original town plat . . . a total length of seven blocks and a fraction, and covering an area considerable [*sic*] larger than the original plat itself.

This addition does not now appear on the maps as such, and for years has been included and its blocks numbered as a part of the original town plan.

The Winona of 1897, with its population of 23,000, can scarcely be recognized as the barren, sandy, Wabasha prairie of 1851.

He lists the trades and occupations in 1856 as evidence of the diverse character of the growing city at an early date

There were fourteen attorneys-at-law and nine physicians waging war against crime and death, (when not retained on the other side,) and about 150 business housed [*sic*], stores, shops, etc., distributed as follows: dry goods, 14; groceries and provisions, 16; clothing, 7; hardware and tin, 6; drugs, 5; boots and shoes, 4; furniture, 4; books, 2; wholesale liquor, 2; hotels and taverns, 13; eating houses and saloons, 10; lumber yards, 5; blacksmith shops, 3; warehouses, 4; brick yards, 2; livery stables, 2; sign painters, 3; watchmakers, 3; butchers, 2; wagon and carriage shops, 2; fanning-mill maker, 1; gunsmith

shops, 2; bakeries, 2; dentists, 3; daguerrean artist, 1; banking offices, 6; real estate and insurance, 10; printing offices, 2; harness shops, 2; barber shops, 3. To these may be added five churches and two schools, and you have a fair summary of Winona's business at the close of 1856.
(Lafayette Houghton Bunnell, *Winona (We-No-Nah) and Its Environs on the Mississippi in Ancient and Modern Days*, 406–7)

By 1869 the population reached nine thousand according to one traveler

Winona [is] a pleasant town, delightfully situated on a low prairie, elevated but a few feet above the river. The bluffs at this point recede, giving ample room for a town site with a ravine behind it. . . .

This city of Winona fifteen years ago had about one hundred inhabitants. It was a place where steamers stopped to take wood and discharge a few packages of freight, but to-day it has a population of nine thousand. Looking out upon it from the promenade deck of the steamer, we see new buildings going up, and can hear the hammers and saws of the carpenters. It already contains thirteen churches and a Normal School with three hundred scholars, who are preparing to teach the children of the State.
(Charles Carleton Coffin, *The Seat of Empire*, 10–11)

Willard Glazier in 1881 likes what he sees during his visit to Winona

In its location and surroundings, Winona is extremely picturesque, standing as it does on a plateau nine miles long by three broad on the west bank of the river, and environed by lofty bluffs. . . .

The city is laid out with the utmost regularity, the streets wide and chiefly at right angles; the business blocks compactly built of wood and stone are generally of a very substantial character. Many of the private residences are elegantly designed and are suggestive of wealth and refinement. The whole appearance of the place betokens business activity and prosperity. In population, Winona is the fourth city in the State and claims to be third in commercial importance. . . .

Besides water communication north and south, Winona has within her limits the stations of the Chicago, Milwaukee and Saint Paul; the Green Bay, Winona and Saint Paul, and several branch lines of railway.

As a lumber distributing point, this city is one of the most important of the Upper Mississippi, while its saw-mills, flour-mills, wagon factories and other manufacturing establishments give a very good idea of the extent to which its capital and industries have been developed in the course of a few years by its enterprising inhabitants.
(Willard Glazier, *Headwaters of the Mississippi . . .*, 245)

Winona, Minn. 1866. Drawn by Geo H. Ellsbury. Printed by Chas Shober, Chicago. Lithograph, 5 7/8 x 20 9/16 in. (15 x 52.3 cm).
Amon Carter Museum

Winona, Minn. [Drawn by George H. Ellsbury?] Printed by Chas. Shober & Co. props. Chicago Lith. Co. Copyright by Geo H. Ellsbury and Vernon Green, 1874. Lithograph, 17 1/8 x 28 1/4 in. (43.5 x 72 cm).
Amon Carter Museum

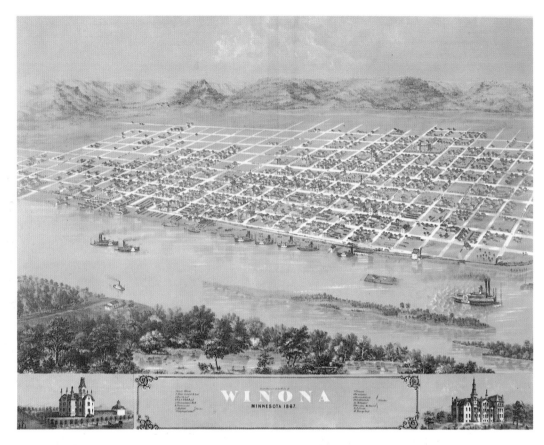

Birds Eye View of the City of Winona Minnesota 1867. Drawn by A[lbert] Ruger. Printed by Chicago Lithographing Co., 152 & 154 Clark St. Chicago. Lithograph, 22 1/2 x 28 1/2 in. (57.2 x 72.4 cm).

Geography and Map Division, Library of Congress

Winona, Minn. 1889. Drawn by C[lemens] J. Pauli. Published by C. J. Pauli & Co. Lithograph, 18 x 40 in. (45.8 x 101.7 cm).

Geography and Map Division, Library of Congress

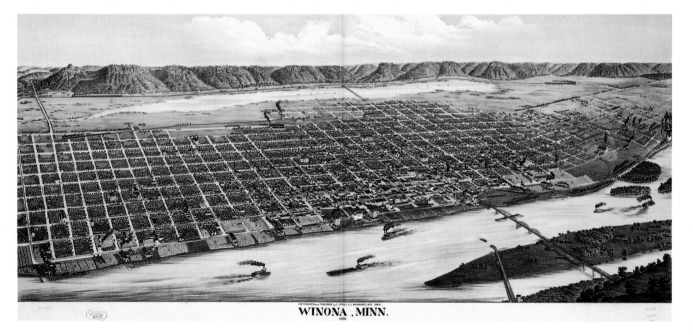

Winona, Minnesota, from the air, July 15, 1989.

Alex MacLean

Folio 56.   Alma, Wisconsin, and Red Wing, Minnesota, Occupy Strategic Sites below and above Lake Pepin on the Mississippi

A county history of 1888 tells its readers about Alma and its early days

The city of Alma . . . has a length of five miles in a straight line north and south, but considerably more along the Mississippi. . . . For about five miles[,] high and steep bluffs extend, there being no level land between them and the river and sloughs, except the bottoms or islands. The city proper, is situated on the slope of the bluffs, and has but two streets running in the direction of the river, though quite a number crossing them, of which, however, but few are practicable, though some of them have been put into such a condition between Main and Second Streets as to afford communication. Second Street is from 50 to 60 feet above the level of Main Street. The railroad, running close to, or in fact upon part of Main Street in the Lower Addition, it was found necessary to build a graded road from the junction of Main Street with North Street, to the junction of Hill Street with Second Street in order to prevent accidents to teams becoming frightened by the approach of trains. . . . What was the Village, and is now the City, of Alma, was part of the Town of Alma. . . . In 1868 it was found desirable to dissolve this connection and the place was incorporated as a village. Owing to some defects in the charter, which could not readily be amended, the citizens applied for a city charter, which was granted by the legislature of 1885.
(L. Kessinger, *History of Buffalo County, Wisconsin*, 611–12)

W. H. Mitchell in 1869 recalls the origins of settlement at Red Wing in Minnesota

Nestled among the high hills that rise in such majestic grandeur on the western bank of the Mississippi, and that seem standing sentinel over the wealth and beauty of the lovely valley they are guarding, lies the young city of Red Wing. . . .

Not a score of years since it was called Red Wing's Village. . . . Where then were only the tepees of the natives of the soil, now stand the halls of learning, and the steeples from a dozen church towers point the way to the throne of Him who gave these valleys to the sons of men. . . .

The beauty of the location of Red Wing has ever been the theme of comment by the visitor, or even the passing tourist. The plateau upon which the city is mostly built, is about forty feet above the river, and is entirely surrounded by high hills or bluffs, except on the side next the river. . . .

On the 13th of June, 1849, Rev. J. W. Hancock, with his family, entered upon the duties of a missionary at this station. The [Indian] village at that time comprised about three hundred inhabitants. . . .

In the autumn of 1850, a Mr. Snow having procured an Indian traders license, built a trading house near the present Steamboat landing and kept Indian goods for sale. In 1851 he took into partnership with him Mr. Calvin Potter. Soon after this Mr. Snow died of cholera, in St. Paul. Potter continued the business till the Indians were removed. The building used by Potter as a trading house, was afterwards converted into a hotel and called the Eastern house. A portion of it is still standing, and serves as the back wing of the Metropolitan Hotel.

The honor of selecting Red Wing as the site of a future town, and the place for business, belongs to Hon. Wm. Freeborn, then a resident of St. Paul. . . .

We cannot perhaps do better than to introduce an extract from Rev. Mr. Hancock's reminiscences [*sic*]. He says:

> Mr. Freeborn was soon on the ground, and having bought out Messrs. Potter & Bush announced his purpose of having a town surveyed and platted. Troops of claim hunters visited the spot during that season and many and amusing were the strifes about who should hold this or that favored claim in the surrounding country. As yet there had been no United States survey, and each man was permitted to mark off his own 160 acres. . . .
>
> Very few of the first claim hunters remained as permanent residents. They had come too soon. It was dull business to wait until the land could be surveyed and brought into market, boarding one's self in a log cabin eight or ten feet square, without any floor or window. Nobody thought of raising wheat at that time. Our flour, pork and butter, all came from down the river.

(W. H. Mitchell, *Geographical and Statistical Sketch of the Past and Present of Goodhue County*, 160–65)

By 1888 Red Wing has become a thriving marketing and manufacturing center

Red Wing has the reputation of being one of the largest primary wheat markets in the country, having handled grain to the amount of nearly three million bushels. Some of its manufactures also are acquiring a wide reputation. . . . Lumber and all its products are in a flourishing condition; laths, shingles, sashes, doors and blinds, hubs, spokes, felloes and every variety of bent-work being manufactured extensively. Boots and shoes, furniture, stoneware, boilers and wagons, have also found a solid footing. The lime and stone business has developed during the past few years into an important industry. Common and pressed brick are also extensively made here, and have acquired an excellent reputation throughout the Northwest. Steam-engines and heavy and light castings are manufactured.
(Glazier, *Down the Great River*, 202)

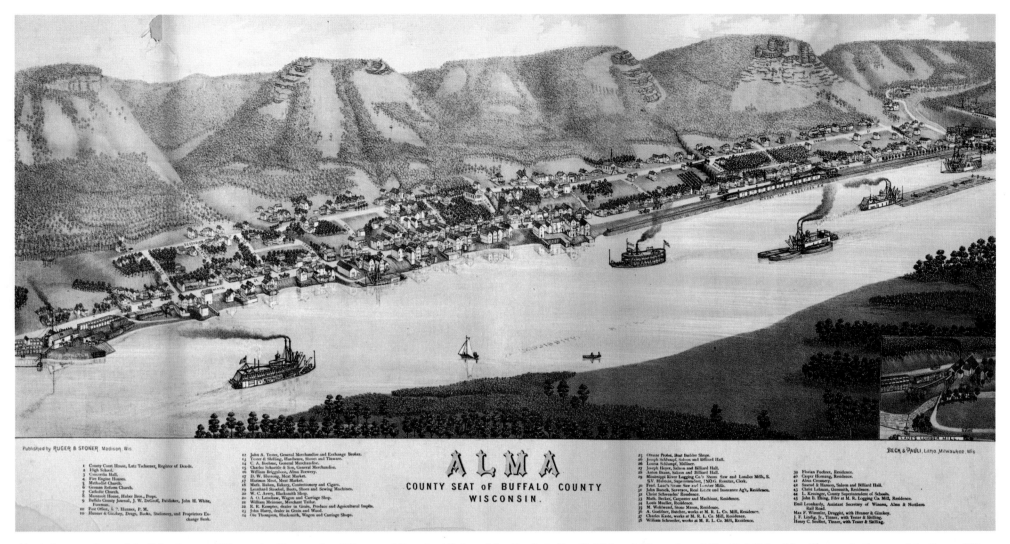

Alma County Seat of Buffalo County Wisconsin. Drawn by H[erman] Brosius. Printed by Beck & Pauli, Litho. Milwaukee, Wis. Published by Ruger & Stoner, Madison, Wis., [1880]. Lithograph, 11 x 26 5/16 in. (28 x 67 cm).

State Historical Society of Wisconsin

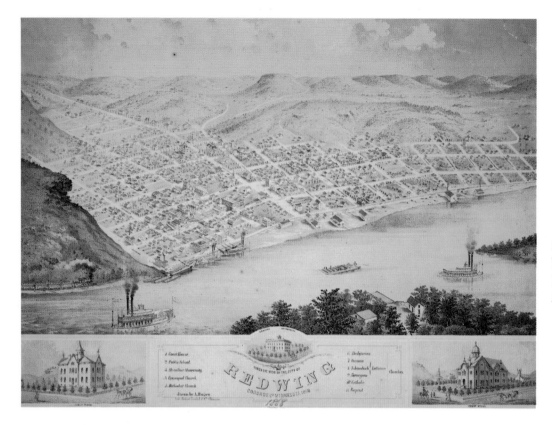

Bird's Eye View of the City of Red Wing Goodhue Co. Minnesota 1868. Drawn by A[lbert] Ruger. Printed by Robert Teufel & Co. Chicago. Lithograph, 18 1/2 x 24 1/2 in. (47.1 x 62.3 cm).
Minnesota Historical Society

Red Wing, Minn. Drawn by Geo[rge] L. Richards. Printed by the Milwaukee Lith & Eng. Co. Published by Josehp [*sic*] M. Wolfe, 1874. Lithograph, 16 5/8 x 27 7/8 in. (42.3 x 70.9 cm).
Minnesota Historical Society

Red Wing, Minnesota, from the air, August 15, 1989.
Alex MacLean

Folio 57.   South of St. Paul on the West Bank of the Mississippi, Hastings Begins Its Existence in the 1850s

A book on Minnesota published in 1857 describes the beginnings of settlement

Hastings, three miles above the mouth of the St. Croix, on the opposite side of the Mississippi, had no existence as a town until 1853. The rush of immigration to this point has known no parallel out of our young territory. Property has gone up here with a rapidity that astonishes men of the greatest sagacity, and the inhabitants are numbered by hundreds; churches and schools have been organized, and every department of business has its representatives. In short, Hastings is one of the "smart" "fast" towns, where no money is lost by investment.

Since writing the above, I have made a visit to this precocious young town, for the avowed purpose of obtaining a sketch of it, to embellish the pages of this book, but failed, with the jocose assurance, that "the business activity and bustle have been such that they have not kept still a sufficient time to obtain a daguerreotype impression. . . ."

We looked over the surprising town—only three years old—with its neat and tasteful residences, its substantial business blocks, and fifty-six stores, all doing above a *living* business! The world affords no finer farming country than stretches back from Hastings, for fifty or sixty miles, supporting it greatly by its products. . . .

Hastings numbers four Protestant churches, and the Roman Catholics have one. With their usual foresight, they have laid the foundation for immense wealth, having early secured a large amount of real estate in the heart of the town. What a blessing to the world would Protestants manifest the same commendable zeal!
(Harriet E. Bishop, *Floral Home or, First Years of Minnesota* . . . , 228–30)

A local newspaper reports some events in 1857

Lots in Barker's Addition now ready for sale. Large size, handsomely located, with splendid view of the steamers on the river.

New residences are springing up in all directions. Down in Barker's Addition, up in the west, and out on the prairie, all over the city new houses greet the eye and carry the conviction that Hastings is rapidly advancing in population.

Mr. Edison's large new building is being pushed forward in the right spirit. In a week or two the visitors' attention will be attracted to this noble edifice. We are proud of the enterprise Mr. Edison has manifested in rearing this structure.
(Newspaper accounts found in cornerstone of the Irving School building in 1899, as quoted in the Hastings *Gazette*, July 15, 1899)

A county history published in 1863 provides additional information about the origin and growth of Hastings

In June, 1857, Mr. Wheelock, editor of the St. Paul *Press*, in speaking of the city of Hastings, says: "We recollect when Hastings was considered one of the 'paper towns' they tell us of in the eastern papers and elsewhere. It was a 'paper town' apparently, in 1854. In 1855 this paper began to be written in legible characters, and before the fall of that year was already marked with the impress of a bold hand. *God has made some towns.* We have positive faith in the indications of nature. Now Hastings we consider a foregone 'conclusion' from its very situation. It has one of the best landings on the upper Mississippi. Its site is merely the terminal slope of the prairie country which stretches illimitably in its rear till it reaches the Minnesota river on one side and the magnificent valleys of the Cannon and Straight rivers on the other. . . ."

On the first of January, 1856, there were about 700 inhabitants. During the year 1856 the number of inhabitants nearly trebled, as will appear from the following extract from the Hastings *Journal* of that date: "According to the census, recently taken, there are four hundred and twenty-five scholars between the ages of four and twenty-one years. There are seven hundred and ten minors. There are twelve hundred and eight persons of full age. There are seven hundred and eighty females, and eleven hundred and thirty-eight males. The whole number of inhabitants is 1918. More than two-thirds of these, 1280, came since the opening of navigation, April 18, 1856." More than three-fourths of all the buildings in town were erected that year. The following year the county seat was removed by a vote of the people, from Mendota to this city, on the 17th day of March (St. Patrick's Day), 1857, and the county records were removed to Hastings on the 2d day of June following.
(W. H. Mitchell, *Dakota County. Its Past and Present* . . . , 122–23)

Willard Glazier visits the little city in 1891 and tells his readers what he sees

Hastings is a pretty little city of modest pretensions, claiming a population of only about five thousand. In pioneer days it aspired to first place among the leading cities of Minnesota, and I am told was at one time considered the rival of Saint Paul and Minneapolis. While it has not been able to reach the goal of its ambition, it has made considerable progress, and will doubtless in the course of another decade show a creditable increase in population and commercial importance.
(Glazier, *Headwaters of the Mississippi*, 255–56)

Bird's Eye View of the City of Hastings Dakota Co. Minnesota 1867. Drawn by A[lbert] Ruger. Printed by the Chicago Lithographing Co. 152 & 154, Clark St., Chicago. Lithograph, 20 x 24 in. (50.8 x 61 cm).

Geography and Map Division, Library of Congress

Hastings, Minnesota, from the air, July 15, 1989.

Alex MacLean

Folio 58.   St. Paul Grows Rapidly from Its Origins as a Tiny Frontier Post

Henry Lewis recalls the pioneer settlement he sketched in 1848 and notes its development to 1855

A small Indian trading post, called St. Paul's, . . . contained only some forty or fifty families. . . . The view of St. Paul as given in the illustration is as it appeared [then]. . . . Since that time great changes have taken place. . . . Such was the great rush to this new paradise, that, at one time, there were more than 1,300 persons living in tents who could not get houses to shelter themselves.

A statehouse, court house, churches, schoolhouses, library, and Athenaeum have all been built, and St. Paul now begins to assume the appearance of a large and flourishing town.
(Lewis, *The Valley of the Mississippi Illustrated*, 57, 85, 88)

A visitor to the upper Mississippi valley in 1849 describes the new town of St. Paul

About three miles above Kaposia we obtained an indistinct view of St. Paul, across a point of woodland, around which the river makes a very·short bend. On turning this point at a distance of a mile from St. Paul, a fine view of the town suddenly opened before us. My first impression of the place, as seen from this point, was a very favorable one. Its elevated situation gives it a commanding appearance. Its new frame buildings, glistening with the reflection of the rising sun, imparted to it an air of neatness and prosperity. . . .

Every thing here appeared to be on the high-pressure principle. A dwelling-house for a family could not be rented. The only hotel was small, and full to overflowing. Several boarding-houses were very much thronged. Many families were living in shanties made of rough boards fastened to posts driven in the ground, such as two men could construct in one day. It was said that about eighty men lodged in a barn belonging to Rice's new hotel, which was not yet completed. Two families occupied tents while I was there. . . .

The central portion of the town is a beautiful level plateau, terminating, on the river, in a precipitous bluff, about eighty feet high. This bluff recedes from the river at the upper and lower end of the town, forming two landings —the upper and lower. Considerable rivalry prevails between the upper and lower town. . . . Part of the lower town is situated on a bench, about twenty feet lower than the plateau above mentioned, which, extending around it in a semicircular form, gives the land below the appearance of a large basin. Most of the buildings in the lower town are situated on the lower bench. The ascent from the landing into this lower town is more precipitous than in the upper, which is reached by a low and easy grade. In the rear of the town, the ground rises gradually into a very high bluff. The town-site is

a pretty one, affording ample room for stores or dwellings to any extent desirable. I could not but regret, however, that, where land is so cheap and abundant, some of the streets are narrow, and that the land on the edge of the high bluff, in the center of the town, was not left open to the public, instead of being cut up into small lots. It would have made a pleasant place for promenading, affording a fine view of the river, which is now liable to be intercepted by buildings erected on those lots.

He provides a census of major buildings

On the 13th of June [1849] I counted all the buildings in the place, the number of which, including shanties and those in every state of progress, from the foundation wall to completion, was one hundred and forty-two. Of the above, all, except about a dozen, were probably less than six months old. They included three hotels, one of which is very large, and is now open for the accommodation of travelers; a state house, four warehouses, ten stores, several groceries, three boarding-houses, two printing-offices, two drug stores, one fruit and tobacco store, one or two blacksmith's shops, one wagon shop, one tinshop, one or two baker's shops, one furniture-room, a billiard and bowling saloon, one school-house, in which a school of about forty children is kept by a young lady, and where divine services are performed every Sabbath. . . . There is also a Catholic church, where meetings are held every alternate Sabbath.
(E. S. Seymour, *Sketches of Minnesota, the New England of the West . . .* , 95, 97–100)

By the end of 1850 the embryonic city could boast of several new churches

Improvements are going on in Saint Paul with an astonishing rapidity. A great change is noticeable every month: but the greatest change that has taken place of late is with regard to churches. Three months ago, all the houses of public worship to be seen here were the Methodist house, a very commodious brick building, besides an old Catholic church built of logs. Now we have in addition to these, a Presbyterian house which would not compare unfavorably with those of Chicago; the Baptist and Episcopalian, all of which are ready for public services. They occupy the most prominent points in the embryo city and can be seen from a great distance in approaching the town from the South East. We consider the building of so many churches, in so short a time, a good enterprise, indeed, for a place two years old, and containing only twelve or fifteen hundred inhabitants.
(St. Paul *Minnesota Pioneer*, February 6, 1851)

St. PAUL'S.

St. Paul, Minnesota. Drawn by H[enry] Lewis. [Printed by C. H. Muller, Aachen.] Published by Arnz & Co., Düsseldorf, [1854–1857]. Lithograph, 6 3/8 x 8 5/16 in. (16.2 x 21.9 cm).

Minnesota Historical Society

Folio 59.   St. Paul Continues to Grow at a Rapid Pace

A writer in the local newspaper at the beginning of 1853 comments on the town's swift pace of development

We are never more sensibly impressed with the fact of the wonderful growth of our town than while passing from the upper end of the town to the lower, in the evening, when the lights gleam from the dwellings, in multitudinous twinkling, like fire flies in a meadow. Then along Third street for an eighth of a mile, the shops are so illuminated as to give the scene a city aspect. Three years ago, last spring, there was scarcely a store on that street. Indeed, if we rightly remember, the bluff above the Post Office was not graded and made passable until the summer of '51. Previous to that the only carriage way from the lower end of town to the upper, was in front of the Central House. Next season, Fourth street will begin to show out.
(St. Paul *Minnesota Pioneer,* January 20, 1853, 2)

An eastern reporter also finds the city's rate of growth impressive

St. Paul is one of the hundred wonders of America. Here, five years ago, were only a few log huts; now there is a large and rapidly growing village of almost four thousand white people, with handsome public buildings, good hotels, stores, mills, mechanics' shops, and every other element of prosperity. St. Paul is upon the north (or left) bank of the Mississippi, which here flows in an easterly direction from the mouth of the St. Peter. The central portion of the village is upon a beautiful plateau, almost a hundred feet above the river; the remainder is chiefly near the water, and already there is a strife for supremacy between the "upper" and "lower" towns. The first sale of government lands there took place in 1848, and the ground upon which St. Paul is built was purchased in 1849 for the government price—one dollar and a quarter an acre.
("Sketches on the Upper Mississippi")

An English traveler in 1854 likes what he sees at St. Paul

St. Paul is perhaps the best specimen to be found in the States, of a town still in its infancy with a great destiny before it. Its progress hitherto has been equalled only by Chicago. In 1847 a few trading huts, rejoicing under the sobriquet of Pig's Eye—a name still retained by some rapids just below the town—marked the site of the present city; and it occurred to some of the French traders and Yankee squatters . . . to mark out what is called in the States a town plat, without apparently any anticipation of the important results which were ultimately to attend their speculation; indeed, they were somewhat old-fashioned in their notions, and laid out their plat in what one of the present citizens . . . calls "little skewdangular lots, about as large as a

stingy card of gingerbread broke in two diagonally." The consequence was, that for the first two years there was very little temptation to put anything upon the said lots; but in 1849 some celebrated go-ahead speculators took up the thing. . . . At this time there were half-a-dozen log-huts, a hotel, a couple of stores, a log Catholic chapel, and about 150 inhabitants. . . . Colonel James M. Goodhue arrived in the same year to start a paper, which he intended to call "The Epistle of St. Paul." The good people there, however, had discrimination enough to object to the name, and so he called it the *Minnesota Pioneer. . . .*

There are now four daily, four weekly, and two tri-weekly papers, which is pretty well for a Far West town only five years old. . . . There are four or five hotels, and at least half-a-dozen handsome churches, with tall spires pointing heavenward, and sundry meeting-houses, and a population of seven or eight thousand to go to them, and good streets with side-walks, and lofty brick warehouses, and stores, and shops, as well supplied as any in the Union; and "an academy of the highest grade for young ladies;" and wharves at which upwards of three hundred steamers arrive annually, bringing new settlers to this favoured land, and carrying away its produce to the south and east. . . .

The view of St. Paul and the banks of the river just below it is very beautiful, and I was thankful for a stoppage upon the Pig's Eye, as the delay enabled me to take a sketch of the town.
(Laurence Oliphant, *Minnesota and the Far West,* 252, 254, 284)

An observer comments that St. Paul's future is no longer in doubt

[St. Paul] has passed its doubtful era. It has passed from its wooden to its brick age. Before men are certain of the success of a town, they erect one story pine shops; but when its success appears certain, they build high blocks of brick or granite stores. So now it is common to see four and five story brick or stone buildings going up in St. Paul. . . .

I have had an agreeable stroll down upon the bluff, south-east from the city, and near the elegant mansion of Mr. Dayton. . . . As I stood looking at the city, I recalled the picture in Mr. Bond's work, and contrasted its present with the appearance it had three or four years ago. What a change! Three or four steamers were lying at the levee; steam and smoke were shooting forth from the chimneys of numerous manufactories; a ferry was plying the Mississippi, transporting teams and people; church steeples and domes and great warehouses stood in places which were vacant as if but yesterday; busy streets had been built and peopled; rows of splendid dwellings and villas, adorned with delightful terraces and gardens, had been erected.
(Christopher Columbus Andrews, *Minnesota and Dacotah . . . ,* 36–37)

Stanley. Del.

Sarony, Major & Knapp, Lith.ᵉ 449 Broadway N.Y.

SAINT PAUL.

Saint Paul. Drawn by [John Mix] Stanley in 1853. Printed by Sarony, Major & Knapp, Liths 449 Broadway N.Y. From *Reports of Explorations and Surveys . . . for a Railroad from the Mississippi River to the Pacific Ocean*, General Report, book 1, 1860, plate I. Lithograph, 6 1/2 x 9 5/16 in. (16.5 x 23.6 cm).

John W. Reps

UPPER LANDING.   P. S. Duval & Co. steam lith press, Phila.   LOWER LANDING.   On stone by J. Queen.

CITY OF ST. PAUL,
Capital of Minesota.

Published by **THOMPSON RITCHIE**.

City of St. Paul, Capital of Minnesota. Drawn by [Max] Strobel. Lithographed by J[ames Fuller] Queen. Printed by P. S. Duval & Co. steam lith press, Phila[delphia]. Published by Thompson Ritchie, 1853. Lithograph, 13 1/8 x 19 3/4 in. (33.4 x 50.3 cm).

Minnesota Historical Society

Saint Paul, Capitol of Minnesota, May, 1856. Drawn by S. H[olmes] Andrews. Printed by Endicott & Co. N.Y. Published by C. Hamilton & Co. Lithograph, 14 5/8 x 22 3/4 in. (37.2 x 57.9 cm).

Minnesota Historical Society

Folio 60.   St. Paul Continues to Receive Attention from Writers Who Tell about the City's Major Features

A visitor in 1856 mentions some of the city's shortcomings as well as attractions

Like all new and growing places in the west, St. Paul has its whiskey shops, its dusty and dirty streets, its up and down sidewalks, and its never-ceasing whirl of business. Yet it has its churches, well filled; its spacious school-houses; its daily newspapers; and well-adorned mansions. There are many cottages and gardens situated on the most elevated part of the city, north and west, which would not suffer by a comparison with those cheerful and elegant residences so numerous for six to ten miles around Boston.
(Andrews, *Minnesota and Dacotah*, 37)

The report on cities in the Census of 1880 summarizes the booms and busts of St. Paul development from 1854 to 1873

The rapid growth of Saint Paul and of the territory produced one of the most remarkable periods of speculation and inflation, especially in real estate, ever known in American history. It began to be marked in 1854 or 1855; grew intense in 1856, and in 1857 the wild speculative frenzy had grown to be a perfect madness, which appeared to affect all classes. In August of that year it met with a sudden check by the financial panic which began in New York city. The revolution affected Saint Paul with extreme severity, and a trying period of depression set in. . . . During this period there were scarcely any new buildings erected, and the tax duplicate shows a remarkable falling off in the assessed valuation. Real estate was utterly unsalable.

Some improvement began to be noticed in 1860, but was of transient duration, as the secession movement soon produced another period of depression, and the years 1861 and 1862 were years of extreme distress. . . .

From 1865 to the fall of 1873 was one of the busy and prosperous periods of the city. Numerous fine and costly public buildings, business blocks, dwellings, schools, churches, etc. and works of improvement were constructed. Real estate became almost as inflated as during the "kiting" days of 1857. But the financial revulsion in the fall of 1873 again utterly prostrated everything.
(U.S. Census Office, *Report on the Social Statistics of Cities*, 2:697)

Anthony Trollope, the English novelist, records his observations about St. Paul in 1862 for his large reading public

St. Paul contains about fourteen thousand inhabitants, and, like all other American towns, is spread over a surface of ground adapted to the accommodation of a very extended population. As it is belted on one side by the river, and on the other by the bluffs, which accompany the course of the river, the site is pretty, and almost romantic. Here also we found a great

hotel,—a huge square building, such as we in England might perhaps place near to a railway terminus, in such a city as Glasgow or Manchester; but on which no living Englishman would expend his money in a town even five times as big again as St. Paul. . . . Look at the map, and see where St. Paul is. Its distance from all known civilization . . . is very great. Even American travellers do not go up there in great numbers.
(Anthony Trollope, *North America*, 147)

A writer describes the city in 1869

We approach St. Paul from the south. . . . We ride over a long wooden bridge, one end of which rests on the low land by the railroad station, and the other on the high northern bluff, so that the structure is inclined at an angle of about twenty degrees, like the driveway to a New England barn where the floor is nearly up to the high beams. We are in a city which in 1849, twenty years ago, had a population of eight hundred and forty, but which now has an estimated population of twenty-five thousand. . . . To ride through the streets of St. Paul; to behold its spacious warehouses, its elegant edifices, stores piled with the goods of all lands, the products of all climes . . . ; to behold the streets alive with people, crowded with farmers' wagons laded with wheat and flour; to read the signs, "Young Men's Christian Association," "St. Paul Library Association"; to see elegant school-edifices and churches, beautiful private residences surrounded by lawns and adorned with works of art,—to see this . . . and to think that this is the development of American civilization, going on now as never before, and destined to continue till all this wide region is to be thus dotted over with centres of influence and power, sends an indescribable thrill through our veins.
(Coffin, *The Seat of Empire*, 16–18)

A St. Paul newspaper in 1874 remarks on the number and character of new dwellings

We doubt if during any previous year so many dwelling houses have been got under way so early in the season. Some of the structures are costly, of tasty architecture, and provided with all modern convenience, others are built in blocks, with three, four or more complete houses under one roof, for tenement purposes, while still others are for those of smaller means, built, in the majority of cases, for a home by some hard working, saving mechanic and day laborer—small, but in most cases, tasty and comfortable structures, but all going to make up a large and prosperous city.
(St. Paul *Daily Pioneer*, April 29, 1874, 4)

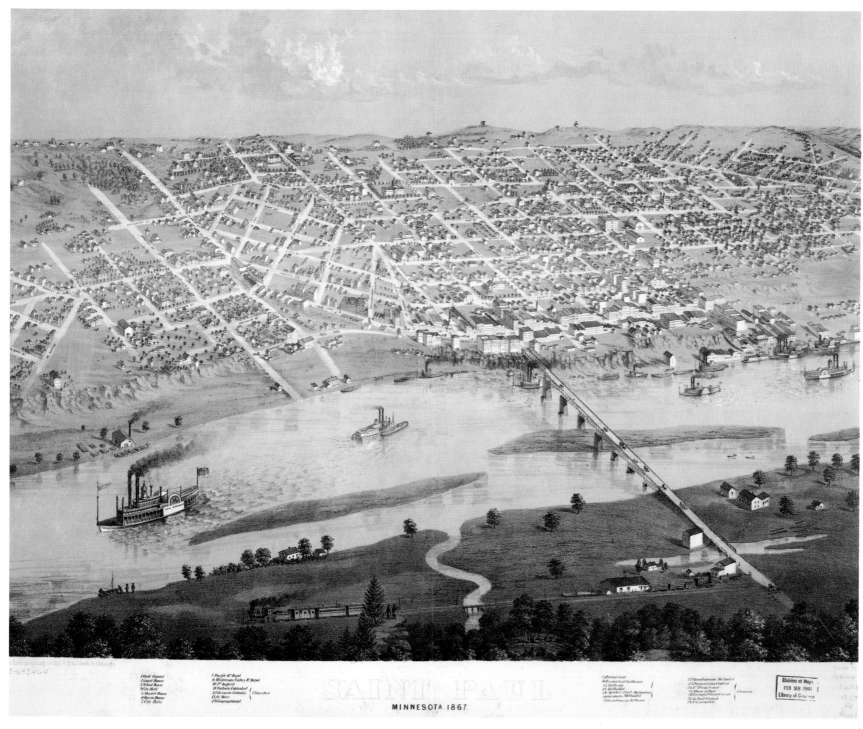

Saint Paul, Minnesota, 1867. Drawn by A[lbert] Ruger. Printed by Chicago Lithographing Co. 152 & 154, Clark St. Chicago. Lithograph, 22 1/2 x 28 in. (57.2 x 71.1 cm).

Geography and Map Division, Library of Congress

ST. PAUL, FROM DAYTON'S BLUFF.

St. Paul, From Dayton's Bluff. Drawn or engraved by N Orr & Co. From William Cullen Bryant, ed., *Picturesque America, or The Land We Live In*, vol. 2 (1874). Wood engraving, 6 5/16 x 9 1/16 in. (16 x 23 cm).

John W. Reps

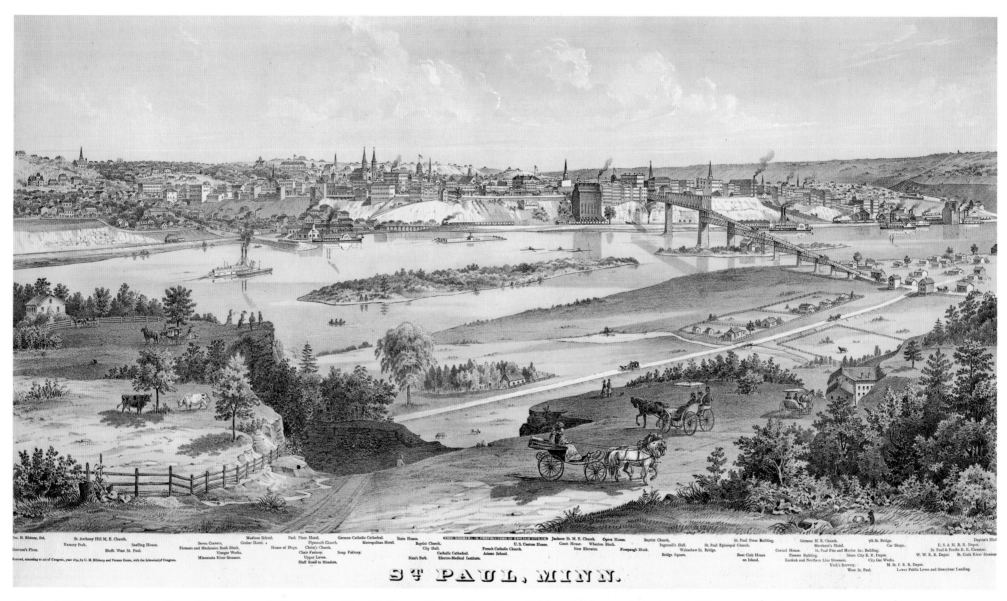

ST PAUL, MINN.

St. Paul, Minn. Drawn by Geo. H. Ellsbury. Lithographed by Hoffman. Printed by Chas. Shober & Co., proprietors of Chicago Lith. Co. Copyright 1874 by G. H. Ellsbury and Vernon Green. Lithograph, 16 1/2 x 29 7/16 in. (42 x 74.9 cm).

John W. Reps

Folio 61.   In Only Four Decades St. Paul Becomes a Major City

A writer views the city from a vantage point on Summit Avenue

I ascended the Observatory on Summit Avenue to see the bird's-eye view of the "saintly city" which lies in the broad valley of the Mississippi. . . . In the river valley is the modern city, its streets gradually stretching up their long arms towards the surrounding cliffs. The towers and steeples of stately churches break the uniformity of the buildings below; huge warehouses, crowded with furs from the icy regions which lie to the north, or with the tropical fruits borne thither on the river's broad bosom from the fair southern lands which line its banks, flank the quays. Fairy-like iron bridges, which look in the distance like the delicate tracery of lacework, span the river in several directions. Here too converge from all parts of the mainland a dozen lines of iron road. On the river huge rafts of logs are floating, the harvest of the great pine-forests which fringe its head-waters, waiting for the flood-tide to carry them to their destinations in the south. Steamers convey the traveller from this point over the long two-thousand-mile course of the Mississippi. . . .

Upon the cliffs, which rise in lofty terraces, tier upon tier, above the river valley, are the princely houses of the men who have grown rich side by side with the marvellously exotic growth of this new country. Nestling in parks, where the primeval oaks and beeches still stand in their old grandeur, are country mansions, which might have been designed by a Scott or a Pugin, some built of the dazzling white limestone of the surrounding cliffs, others of a delicate pink stone found in a neighbouring quarry, with roofs of variegated slate, and picturesque dormers, and lordly stabling, and model dairies, like nothing I have ever seen but such places as Strawberry Hill, or some of the villas whose velvet lawns stretch down near Richmond or Twickenham to the banks of Father Thames.

(Maurice Farrar, *Five Years in Minnesota. Sketches of Life in a Western State*, 53–57)

A famous nineteenth-century travel writer gives his impressions of the city

The original town was regularly laid out, but the additions are irregular. The streets are well graded and generally paved. The third terrace is underlaid by a stratum of limestone from twelve to twenty feet thick, and of this material many of the buildings are constructed. The city has several excellent hotels, and many churches belonging to the various denominations of Christians. Five bridges cross the river; lines of horse-cars connect all parts of the city, and a system of sewerage drains it of all impurities. The State Capitol—in process of erection when I saw it—occupies one entire square, on an elevation overlooking the city and river. The Opera House, on Wabasha Street,

seating about twelve hundred persons, is a large and handsome building. The Academy of Sciences contains about one hundred and thirty thousand specimens in natural history. The Historical Society and Library Association have each fine public libraries. The public and private schools of Saint Paul are all of the first order of excellence, and there are several female seminaries of a high grade. A Protestant and a Catholic Orphan Asylum and three hospitals represent the public charitable institutions. . . .

It is a thorough business city, its chief thoroughfares being lined with large and well-built stores and warehouses; the movement of the people on the streets indicating the hurry and preoccupation of pressing business pursuits. . . . The retail trade of Saint Paul is very large, and it is also in great part the wholesale centre of a large circle of smaller towns.

Its double line of river banks affords ample wharfage. It is surrounded by a network of railways, connecting it with the large and growing city of Minneapolis, and with every town of importance in Minnesota and adjoining states. These secure permanence to its prosperity, since railroads, even more than rivers, make flourishing cities in the present day.

(Glazier, *Down the Great River*, 190–91)

Mark Twain provides a humorously perceptive impression of the city

St. Paul is a wonderful town. It is put together in solid blocks of honest brick and stone, and has the air of intending to stay. . . . Population of the present year (1882): 71,000; . . . number of houses built during three-quarters of the year, 989. . . . St. Paul's strength lies in her commerce—I mean his commerce. He is a manufacturing city, of course,—all the cities of that region are—but he is peculiarly strong in the matter of commerce. . . .

He has a custom-house, and is building a costly capitol to replace the one recently burned—for he is the capital of the State. He has churches without end. . . .

There is an unusually fine railway station; so large is it in fact, that it seemed somewhat overdone, in the matter of size, at first; but at the end of a few months it was perceived that the mistake was distinctly the other way. The error is to be corrected. . . .

It is a very wonderful town, indeed, and is not finished yet. All the streets are obstructed with building material, and this is being compacted into houses as fast as possible, to make room for more—for other people are anxious to build, as soon as they can get the use of the streets to pile up their bricks and stuff in.

(Twain, *Life on the Mississippi*, 427–28)

St. Paul, Minnesota, 1883 State Capital and County Seat of Ramsey Co. Drawn by H[enry] Wellge. Vignettes by H[erman] Brosius. Printed by Beck & Pauli, Lithographers, Milwaukee, Wis. Published by J. J. Stoner, Madison, Wis. Lithograph, 25 1/2 x 40 1/16 in. (65 x 102 cm).

Minnesota Historical Society

St. Paul, Minn, January, 1888. Unsigned. Printed by Orcutt Litho. Co., Chicago. Published by J. H. Mahler Co., St. Paul, Minn. Lithograph, 20 13/16 x 39 11/16 in. (53 x 101 cm).

Minnesota Historical Society

St. Paul, Minnesota, from the air, July 16, 1989.

Alex MacLean

Folio 62.   The Town of St. Anthony across the Mississippi from Early Minneapolis Attracts Comment

The report on American cities in the 1880 census summarizes the history of St. Anthony and Minneapolis

The establishment of a military post at Fort Snelling . . . in 1819 attracted . . . attention to the spot. In 1822 the water-power was first utilized by a small saw-mill built by the quartermaster of the fort in order to get lumber with which to finish the buildings at the fort; a grist-mill was subsequently added. . . . In 1847, Mr. W. A. Cheever purchased . . . a large share in the water-power, and steps were at once taken to improve it and to erect mills. . . . The Saint Anthony town site was surveyed in the spring of 1849. Minnesota territory was organized during the winter of 1848-'49, and this gave a further impetus to the place. . . .

At this time the . . . military reservation of Fort Snelling extended over most of the present site of Minneapolis. In 1849 Hon. Robert Smith . . . and John H. Stevens secured permits from the government to occupy 160 acres each on the reservation. . . . In 1854 John H. Stevens had his claim surveyed and laid out into a town plot. The Smith claim also was soon surveyed into blocks and lots. At the close of 1854 it was estimated that the town contained 100 buildings and about 1,000 inhabitants. In that year the first flouring-mill (not a permanent one), and also the first bridge, were built. . . . In 1854 the "Minneapolis Bridge Company" was organized, and a fine wire suspension bridge was erected, the first bridge ever thrown across the Father of Waters. It was dedicated in January, 1855, with a great celebration. In March it was almost destroyed and had to be chiefly rebuilt. After that it did good service till 1877, when the present magnificent structure was erected in its place. (U.S. Census Office, *Report on the Social Statistics of Cities*, 2:687–88)

An English visitor in 1849 predicts a glorious future

Saint Anthony, which is laid out on the east side of the Mississippi, directly opposite the cataract, is a beautiful town-site. A handsome, elevated prairie, with a gentle inclination toward the river bank, and of sufficient width for several parallel streets, extends indefinitely up and down the river. In the rear of this another bench of table-land swells up some thirty feet high, forming a beautiful and elevated plateau. A year ago there was only one house here; now there are about a dozen new framed buildings, including a store and hotel, nearly completed. During the summer, it is expected that a large number of houses will be erected. Lots are sold by the proprietor, with a clause in the deed prohibiting the retail of ardent spirits on the premises. . . .

That it will eventually become a great manufacturing town there is no doubt. Water power in Minnesota is abundant, but this at St. Anthony is so extensive, and so favorably situated, that it will invite a concentration of mechanical talent, and of population, whereby the necessary facilities for profitable manufacturing will be abundantly afforded. It is not, indeed, expected that a Lowell, of mushroom growth, will spring up here in a day. Such a state of things, if practicable, is not desirable. But let the town only keep pace with the country, a city will spring up in these polar regions (as some people choose to call this country) sooner than is generally anticipated. (Seymour, *Sketches of Minnesota*, 125–26)

By 1854 St. Anthony appears to be well on the way to prosperity

There was only one house there in 1849; now it contains a population of about two thousand. It promises to be an extensive manufacturing town, and depot of all the future productions of the extreme Upper Mississippi. Steamboats ascend from New Orleans to Fort Snelling, and small steamers are now navigating the Mississippi above the Falls of St. Anthony, a distance of about one hundred and eighty miles. The city of St. Anthony has good hotels, and will hereafter be a place of great resort for summer tourists. Now that railways are about to connect the Atlantic with the Mississippi for land travel, and fine steamers are daily traversing the whole length of the great lakes, the tide of fashionable Summer travel which has been heretofore at flood at Niagara, will flow on to the Falls of St. Anthony; and those who have been accustomed to angle in Lake George or the clear lakes and streams of Northern New England, will cast their lines ere long in the green depths of the remote Itaska. ("Sketches on the Upper Mississippi," 189–90)

Another visitor in 1854 confirms the dual role of early St. Anthony

St. Anthony is already a curious mixture of a manufacturing town and a watering-place. The extreme beauty of the scenery in the neighbourhood, the attractions of the Falls themselves, and the comfortable and civilised aspect of the town, are beginning to render it a fashionable summer resort, and picturesque villas are springing up on all available sites; but upon the bank of the river saw-mills, foundries, shingle-machines, lath-factories, &c., keep up an incessant hubbub—delightful music to the white man, who recognises in the plashing [sic] of water, and the roar of steam, and the ring of a thousand hammers, the potent agency which is to regenerate a magnificent country, and to enrich himself.

The first dwelling-house was only erected in this city in the autumn of 1847. . . . There are now numerous manufactories, shops, newspaper offices, and young ladies; four organised churches . . . ; while the importance of the place has been much increased by its having been selected as the location for the university of Minnesota . . . opened in 1851. (Oliphant, *Minnesota and the Far West*, 244–45)

WHITEFIELD'S ORIGINAL VIEWS OF NORTH AMERICAN CITIES, Nº 38

VIEW OF ST ANTHONY, MINNEAPOLIS AND ST ANTHONY'S FALLS.

(FROM CHEEVER'S TOWER.)

View of St. Anthony, Minneapolis and St. Anthony's Falls (From Cheever's Tower). Drawn [and published] by E[dwin] Whitefield. Printed by Endicott & Co., New York, [1857]. Lithograph, 24 x 36 in. (61 x 91.5 cm).

Minnesota Historical Society

Minneapolis and Saint Anthony Minnesota 1867. Drawn by A[lbert] Ruger. Printed by the Chicago Lithographing Company, 152 & 154 Clark St. Lithograph, 22 x 27 1/4 in. (55.9 x 70.5 cm).

Geography and Map Division, Library of Congress

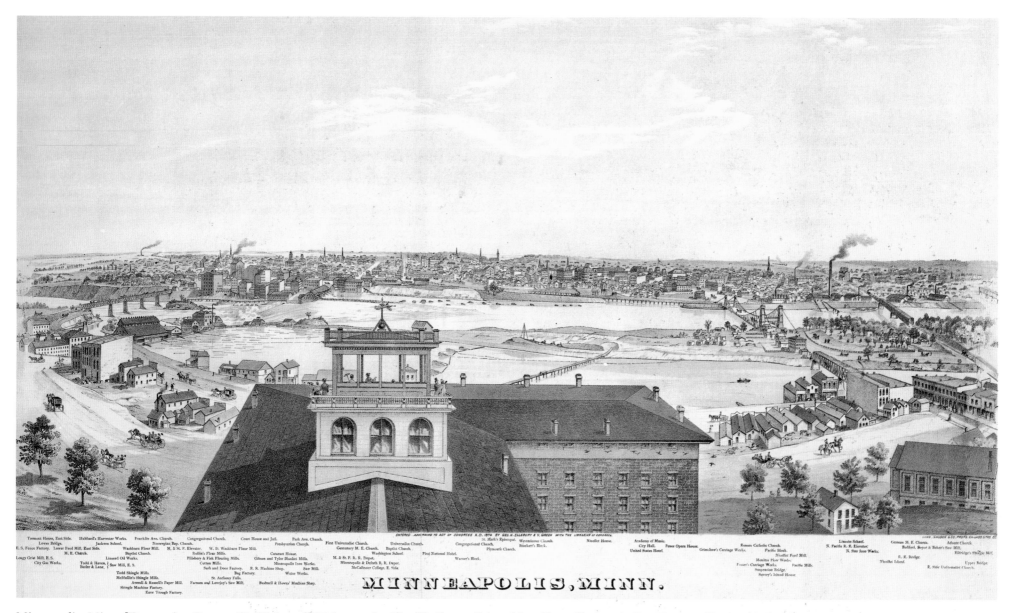

Tremont House, East Side.   Hubbard's Harvester Works.   Franklin Ave. Church.   Congregational Church.   Court House and Jail.   Park Ave. Church.   First Universalist Church.   St. Mark's Episcopal.   Westminster Church.   Nicollet House.   Academy of Music.   Lincoln School.   German M. E. Church.
Lower Bridge.   Jackson School.   Norwegian Bap. Church.   Presbyterian Church.   Blanket's Block.   City Hall.   Pence Opera House.   N. Pacific R. R. Elevator.   Radford, Boyce & Todd's Saw Mill.
E. S. Fence Factory.   Lower Feed Mill, East Side.   Washburn Flour Mill.   M. & S. F. Elevator.   W. D. Washburn Flour Mill.   Centenary M. E. Church.   Baptist Church.   Universalist Church.   Congregational Church.   Pacific Block.   N. State Iron Works.   Advent Church.
M. E. Church.   Baptist Church.   Radlin's Flour Mills.   Cataract House.   Washington School.   Plymouth Church.   Nicollet Fuel Mill.   Eldridge's Shingle Mill.
Leavy Grist Mill, E. S.   Linseed Oil Works.   Pillsbury & Fisk Flouring Mills.   Gibson and Tyler Blanket Mills.   First National Hotel.   Warner's Block.   Monitor Plow Works.   R. R. Bridge.
City Gas Works.   Todd & Haven,   Saw Mill, E. S.   Cotton Mills.   Minneapolis Iron Works.   M. & St. P. R. R. Depot.   Fraser's Carriage Works.   Pacific Mills.   Nicollet Island.   Upper Bridge.
Butler & Lane,   Sash and Door Factory.   E. R. Machine Shop.   Saw Mill.   Minneapolis & Duluth R. R. Depot.   E. Side Universalist Church.
Todd Shingle Mills.   Bug Factory.   Water Works.   McCalester College, E. Side.
McMullin's Shingle Mills.   St. Anthony Falls.
Averell & Russell's Paper Mill.   Farnum and Lovejoy's Saw Mill.   Bushnell & Howe's' Machine Shop.
Shingle Machine Factory.
Eave Trough Factory.

ENTERED ACCORDING TO ACT OF CONGRESS A.D. 1874 BY GEO. H. ELLSBURY & V. GREEN WITH THE LIBRARIAN OF CONGRESS.

MINNEAPOLIS, MINN.

Minneapolis, Minn. [Drawn by George H. Ellsbury?] Lithographed by Hoffman. Printed by Chas. Shober & Co., Prop's. Chicago Litho Co. Copyright by Geo. H. Ellsbury & V[ernon] Green, 1874. Lithograph, 16 5/8 x 29 3/8 in. (42.3 x 74.8 cm).

John W. Reps

Folio 63.   Minneapolis Continues Its Growth and Also Continues to Attract Visitors

Anthony Trollope makes fun of the city's name and seems unimpressed by the community

Till I got there I could hardly believe that in these days there should be a living village called Minneapolis by living men. I presume I should describe it as a town, for it has a municipality, and a post-office, and, of course, a large hotel. The interest of the place however is in the saw-mills.
(Trollope, *North America*, 149)

A newspaper from its nearby rival, St. Paul, praises Minneapolis almost as it might its own city

In the spring of 1853 . . . there was only one house in all this broad expanse. . . .

Now . . . two miles of roofs stretch away till they join the sky; Dean's great steam-mill and the fine Catholic Church in the foreground, emblems of devotion and of industry; in the background, Gale's second addition, a hundred new houses, scattered like foam upon an emerald sea; at the right, the river, shining in the morning sun, and slipping downward under its four bridges: a mile above, the new one, opened last fall to the public; lower down, the spans of the Pacific railroad; near this, the suspension bridge that has done noble service . . . ; and away below the misty ghost that constantly haunts the place where the river breaks its neck in its fall, hangs high, like a quiver of telegraph wires, the lower bridge, just finished—a broad, solid, picturesque structure, commanding a superb water panorama. . . .

Minneapolis is one of the handsomest new cities in the Union. With the disadvantage of looking unfinished and disheveled, it enjoys the advantage of having been definitely planned and laid out by men of prescience, who foresaw its great destiny. Its streets are all as straight as an arrow, and range from 80 to 120 feet in width. Very few cities in the world have so many householders to the population—most of the mechanics owning the houses they occupy. Considerable architectural taste is shown on its school houses, churches, business blocks and private residences; though here there is much that is raw, vulgar and outre, that experience and age will correct. When its present population of 31,000 grows to 50,000, for which three or four years will suffice, its streets will be well shaded with fine trees, and Minneapolis will be one of the handsomest cities in the world.
(St. Paul *Daily Pioneer*, June 21, 1874, supplement, 1)

The 1880 census report on U.S. cities points out some deficiencies in this vigorously growing place

The city engineer, in his report to the city council for the year ending April 1, 1880, said: "I would here call attention to the necessity of adopting some more durable material for the construction of our roadways, sidewalks, and crossings than the ordinary dirt or mud roadway and wooden side- and cross-walks, especially for the business portion of our city."

Nearly all the sidewalks of the city are made of pine lumber. A few blocks have cobble-stone gutters, the rest being of earth. As fast as improvements are made shade-trees are set out. . . .

The total length of horse-railroad track in the city is 9 miles; total number of cars, 21; of horses, 90; of men employed, 35; of passengers carried during the year, 987,267. The rate of fare is 5 cents. . . .

There are no artificial parks, but in the suburbs there are small lakes, groves, etc., which supply their place. Within 3.5 miles of the city there are 4 lakes, each about 1.5 miles in length and the same in breadth; in them the water is clear and cool, and there are plenty of fish. The celebrated falls of Minnehaha are but 3 miles distant. . . .
(U.S. Census Office, *Report on the Social Statistics of Cities*, 2:690–91)

A New England newspaper tells its readers about this new town

Though a young city, Minneapolis, unlike most others of the western sisterhood, is surprisingly orderly and respectable. The stranger entering at its gates, or rather alighting at its railroad station, is impressed with the cleanliness and decency of its general appearance. The main business thoroughfare into which you pass directly from the station, though it may be evening and the sidewalks may be full of people, is as quiet and the crowd is as well-behaved, as would be the case in a New England city. . . .

Minneapolis did not grow; it was built and mainly in the last decade, during which its population has increased by 269 per cent, now exceeding 48,000. Its streets were laid out straight and regular as the lines on a checker-board. The business part of the town is by the river, the great flour mills and other factories of course close beside it. Back from the river and running out on to the plain are the dwellings of the town's prosperous people. And here again is the New England influence apparent. Each man seems to vie with his neighbor in making his home pretty and attractive. The places are not so showy as they are neat, comfortable and tasteful. Blocks of houses are rare; the prevailing style is the wooden cottage, of infinite variety in pattern, each surrounded by its own plot of green turf. . . . There are also not a few handsome brick mansions, belonging to the more wealthy manufacturers. Illustrating the rapidity with which Minneapolis is still growing in wealth and population, is the fact stated to me by one of her prominent citizens, that there are fully 1000 new buildings of all sorts in process of construction here this summer.
(*Springfield* [Massachusetts] *Weekly Republican*, September 23, 1880)

Panorama of Minneapolis, Minn. Drawn, printed, and published by A[gustus] Hageboeck, Davenport, Iowa, 1873. Lithograph, 7 1/4 x 24 1/4 in. (18.4 x 61.6 cm).
Geography and Map Division, Library of Congress

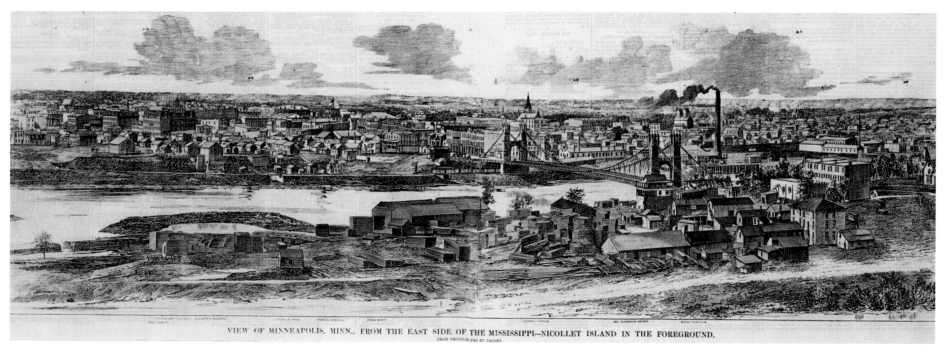

View of Minneapolis, Minn., From the East Side of the Mississippi—Nicollet Island in the Foreground. From photographs by Jacoby. From *New York Daily Graphic,* August 17, 1878. Wood engraving, 9 x 26 7/8 in. (22.8 x 68.3 cm).
Minnesota Historical Society

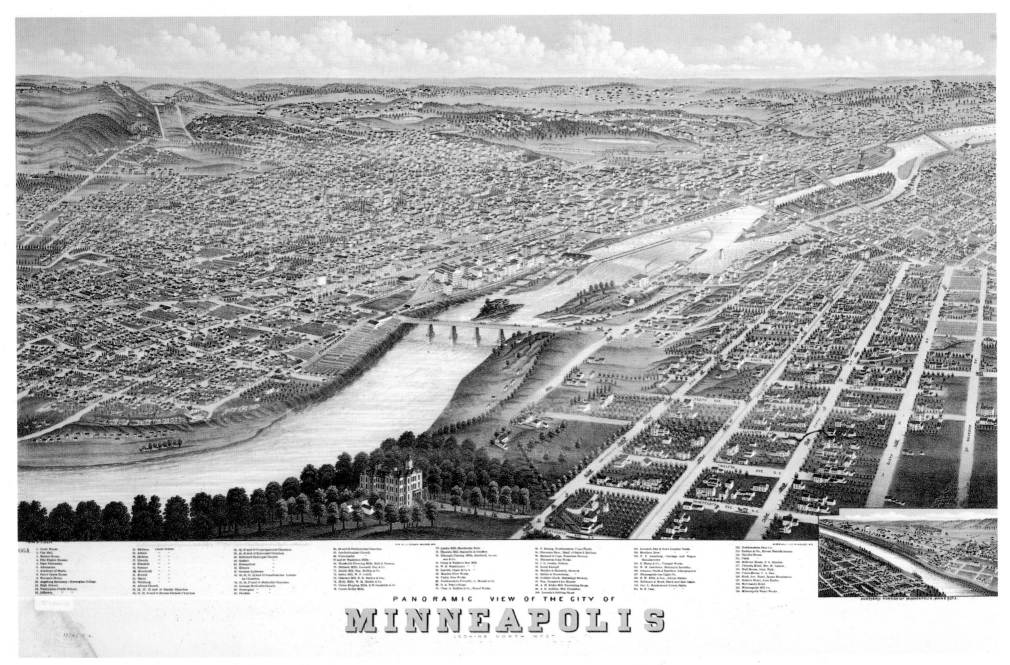

Panoramic View of the City of Minneapolis, Minnesota, 1879 Looking North West. Drawn by A[lbert] Ruger. Printed by [Adam] Beck & [Clemens J.] Pauli, Lith., Milwaukee.
Published by J[oseph] J[ohn] Stoner, Madison, Wisconsin. Lithograph, 20 1/2 x 32 1/2 in. (52.1 x 82.6 cm).

Geography and Map Division, Library of Congress

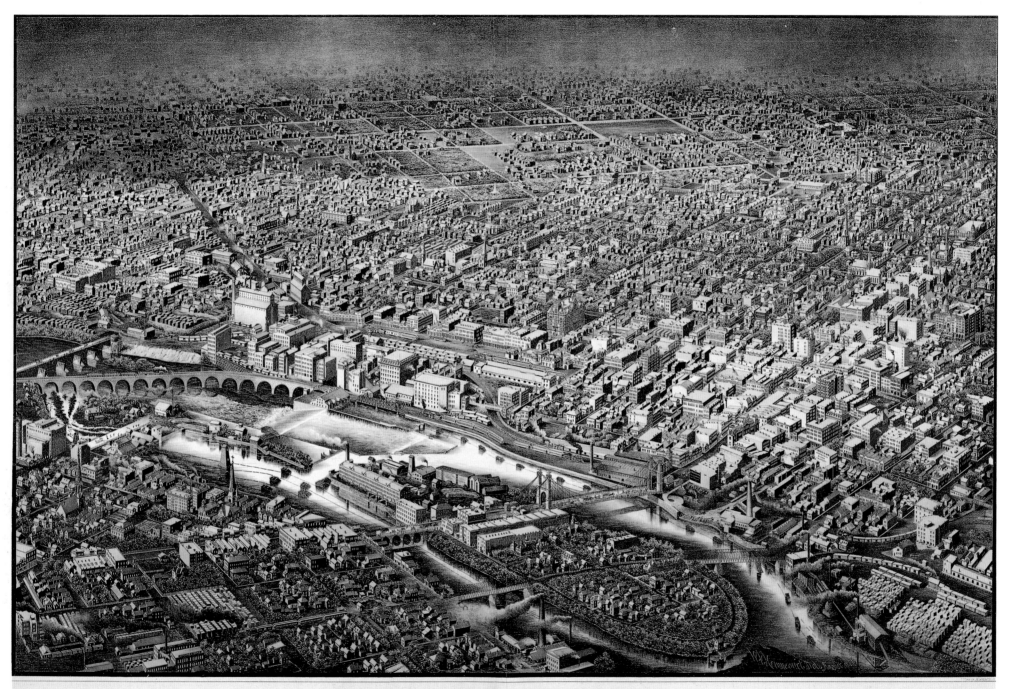

MINNEAPOLIS, MINNESOTA.

Minneapolis, Minnesota. Drawn and copyright by W. V. Herancourt. Lithographed by I[sador] Monasch, 1885. Lithograph, 27 1/2 x 40 1/2 in. (69.9 x 103 cm).
Minnesota Historical Society

Folio 64.   By the Mid–1880s Minneapolis—Now United with St. Anthony—Grows to Rival St. Paul in Importance

In 1881 Willard Glazier captures the character of Minneapolis in his book on the Mississippi

Minneapolis proper is situated on the west side of the river, while Saint Anthony, which by mutual agreement has become united to the first-named city, is on the east side—the two forming one city under the name of Minneapolis. It is ten miles from Saint Paul. The city proper is built on broad esplanades overlooking the river and its falls, rapids, and picturesque bluffs. It is the first place of magnitude reached in descending the river. The streets are laid out at right angles, eighty feet in width, bordered by sidewalks twenty feet wide, with double rows of trees on each side. The founders of western cities have gained wisdom from the mistakes of those of the eastern coast. Notwithstanding the broad expanse of country, which to the early colonists seemed limitless, the cities and towns built on and near the Atlantic seaboard were modeled upon European plans, even to the narrow streets and compact rows of buildings. Not so in the West. The original plans of our western towns are so wisely designed that no future increase of population, with its attendant demands for dwelling and business houses can ever transform them into an aggregation of dense, stifling streets and lanes, such as are too often found in our first-class eastern cities. Health and beauty are two objects which have been steadily kept in view in their foundation. Though their rude beginnings have not always been attractive, the possibilities of beauty are always there and time is sure to develop them.

He lists the educational and religious institutions in Minneapolis

The University of Minnesota is located here, and there are several other important educational institutions. The public schools are in every respect excellent; the Athenaeum Library contains about ten thousand volumes, while the University possesses one of several thousand. There are more than sixty churches of all denominations, and some of the sacred edifices are very handsome.

Glazier points out the importance of the lumbering and milling enterprises in Minneapolis

The logs which fill the Mississippi above the Falls, sometimes even to the point of obstructing navigation, all have their destination at Minneapolis. Here they are converted into lumber and laths and sent to distant sections of the country, perhaps in the form of huge rafts again set afloat upon the river. The lumber business of this city is immense, probably exceeding that of any other city in the country. It is equaled only by the flour mills of this rapidly growing western giant. Minneapolis stands at the head of the flour manufacturing of the world. She has no equal in this branch of manufacture either on this continent or in Europe. The wheat raised in such immense quantities in the Northwest is here ground into flour and shipped to every part of the United States; while vast quantities are exported to Europe. The banks of the river are lined with immense flour mills, which furnish employment to thousands of hands.

Minneapolis is more a manufacturing than a commercial city. Saint Paul monopolizes much of the commerce of the Upper Mississippi. Steamboats can only ascend to Fort Snelling, some miles below the Falls, hence Minneapolis depends largely upon the railroads for transportation. But while Saint Paul measures miles of streets lined with stores and warehouses, Minneapolis can show an equal number of mills and factories. It is also a city of residences—a beautiful city. The streets are broad and amply shaded, and the houses are, many of them, very handsomely built and surrounded by ornamental gardens.

(Glazier, *Down the Great River*, 172, 176–78)

In a book on America's economic progress, the author considers the status and prospects of Minneapolis

The city is built on a fine broad plateau, seemingly specially designed by nature for a metropolis. The river makes a fall or descent of 50 feet within a mile, has a perpendicular descent of 18 feet, and has 135,000 horse-power at low-water mark. It is crossed by a fine suspension bridge built in 1876, and three other bridges. There are four fine lakes in the vicinity. Immense manufacturing establishments are conducted by means of water power from the river. The value of the lumber sawed in one year amounted to $3,000,000 and the flour made in one year amounted to nearly $8,000,000. The wholesale grocery business amounts to nearly $6,000,000 a year. An immense amount of grain is milled. Among the other important manufactures are iron, machinery, water-wheels, engines and boilers, agricultural implements, cotton and woolen goods, furniture, barrels, boots and shoes, paper, linseed oil, beer, sashes, doors, and blinds. Pork-packing is conducted on a very extensive scale; and there are numerous saw-mills. . . . The city is ornamented by a series of beautiful parks, boulevards, and parkways, laid out and improved at an enormous expense. . . . Minneapolis is the great railroad centre of the Northwest. All the roads of the Northwest, in fact, touch Minneapolis. It has a line of steamers to St. Cloud. Among the public buildings are a court-house, a city hall erected in 1873, an academy of music, and an opera-house. There are 70 churches. The Athenaeum has a library of 15,000 volumes. Minneapolis is the seat of the University of Minnesota (open to both sexes), organized in 1868, and having a library of 18,000 volumes.

(Beale, *Picturesque Sketches of American Progress*, 110)

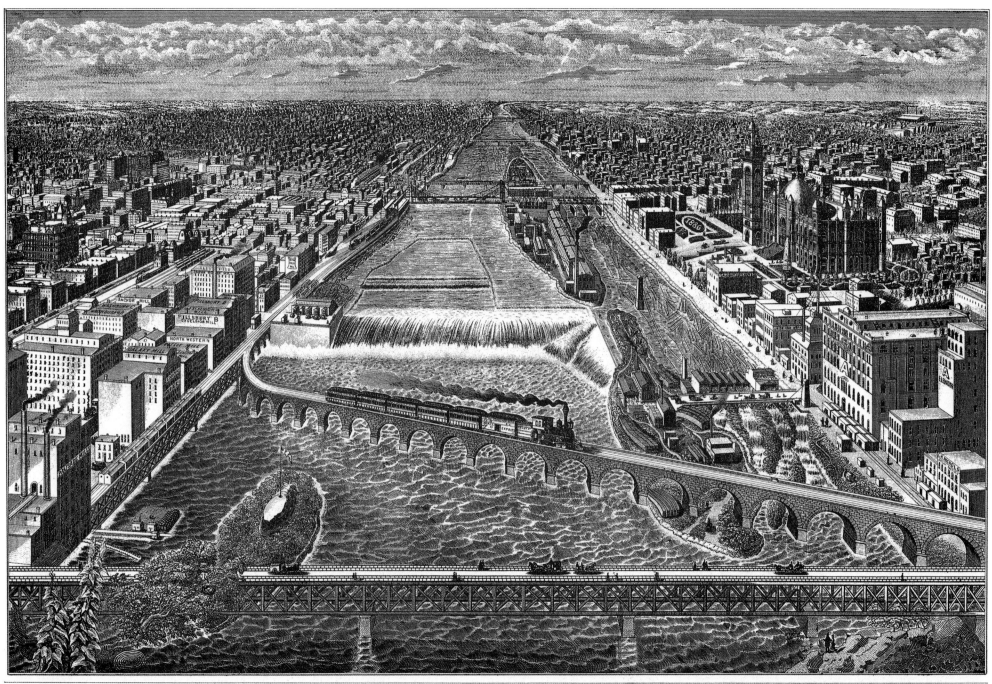

Ent. according to act of Congress in the year 1886 by A. Hageboeck in the office of the Librarian of Congress at Washington, D.C.

ENGRAVED, PRINTED AND PUBLISHED BY A. HAGEBOECK, MINNEAPOLIS, MINN.

VIEW OF MINNEAPOLIS, MINN.

View of Minneapolis, Minn. Unsigned. Engraved, printed, and published by A[ugustus] Hageboeck, Minneapolis, Minn., 1886. Line engraving, 11 1/4 x 16 5/8 in. (28.5 x 42.2 cm).

Geography and Map Division, Library of Congress

Bird's Eye View of Minneapolis. Drawn by F[rank] Pezolt. Printed by F. G. Christoph Lith. Co, Chicago. Copyright by A. M. Smith, [Minneapolis], 1891. Lithograph, 29 x 41 in. (73.7 x 104.2 cm).

Geography and Map Division, Library of Congress

Minneapolis, Minnesota, from the air, July 16, 1989.

Alex MacLean

Folio 65.   Settlers Plat Land for a Town on the Mississippi above St. Paul and Name It St. Cloud

John Wilson surveys his land into streets and lots in the summer of 1854

On the 19th of July, 1853, John L. Wilson . . . proceeded to enclose what he supposed to be three hundred and twenty acres of land, a portion of which is where the business center of St. Cloud now stands. Having thus secured his possession, he went up the river to Little Falls, and was engaged in mill-building until the spring of 1854, when he returned to his claim. . . .

Mr. Wilson surveyed and platted a portion of his claim, and named it St. Cloud. This was the beginning of the present thriving and beautiful city. . . .

Martin Woolley staked out a claim to the south of Mr. Wilson, but made no improvements. He soon afterwards sold it to Anton Edelbrock and J. P. Wilson. . . . A stock company of twelve men was then formed . . . the stock consisting of twelve shares of $1,000 each. This company surveyed and platted the Woolley claim, and gave it the name of St. Cloud City, but it is now more commonly known as Lower Town.

(N. H. Winchell et al., *History of the Upper Mississippi Valley,* 375–76)

A visitor in 1856 describes conditions in the two-year-old town

St. Cloud is favorably located on the west bank of the river, seventy-five miles above St. Paul. It is just enough elevated to have good drainage facilities, should it become densely populous. For many years it was the seat of a trading post among the Winnebagoes. But the date of its start as a town is not more than six months ago; since when it has been advancing with unsurpassed thrift, on a scale of affluence and durability. Its main street is surely a street in other respects than in the name; for it has on either side several neatly built three-story blocks of stores, around which the gathering of teams and of people denotes such an activity of business as to dispel any idea that the place is got up under false pretences [*sic*]. The St. Cloud advertisements in the St. Paul daily papers contain the cards of about forty different firms or individuals, which is a sort of index to the business of the place. A printing press is already in the town, and a paper will in a few days be issued. There are now two hotels. . . . A flourishing saw-mill was destroyed by fire, and in a few weeks another one was built in its place. An Episcopal church is being erected. The steamer "H. M. Rice" runs between here and St. Anthony. It is sometimes said that this is the head of the Upper Mississippi navigation, but such is not the case. The Sauk Rapids which terminate here are an obstruction to continuous navigation between St. Anthony and Crow Wing, but after you get to the latter place (where the river is twenty feet deep) there is good navigation for two hundred miles. There are several roads laid out to intersect at St. Cloud, for the construction of which, I believe, the government has made some appropriation. Town lots are sold on reasonable terms to those who intend to make improvements on them, which is the true policy for any town, but the general market price ranges from $100 to $1000 a lot.

The author reflects on the reasons for the apparent prosperity of St. Cloud and other new settlements in the region

It would not be more surprising to have Eastern people doubt some of the statements concerning the growth of Western towns, than it was for the king of Siam to doubt that there was any part of the world where water changed from liquid to a hard substance. His majesty knew nothing about ice. Now, there are a good many handsome villages in the East which hardly support one store. Not that people in such a village do not consume as much or live in finer style; but the reason is that they are old settlers who produce very much that they live on and who, by great travelling facilities, are able to scatter their trading custom into some commercial metropolis. Suppose, however, one of your large villages to be so newly settled that the people have had no chance to raise anything from their gardens or their fields, and are obliged to buy all they are to eat and all that is to furnish their dwellings, or equip their shops, or stock their farms; then you have a state of things which will support several stores, and a whole catalogue of trades. It is a state of affairs which corresponds with every new settlement in the West; or, indeed, which faintly compares with the demand for everything merchantable, peculiar in such places. Then again, besides the actual residents in a new place, who have money enough in their pockets, but nothing in their cellars, there is generally a large population in the back country of farmers and no stores. Such people come to a place like this to trade, for fifteen or twenty miles back, perhaps; and it being a county seat they have other objects to bring them. At the same time there is an almost constant flow of settlers through the place into the unoccupied country to find preemption claims, who, of course, wish to take supplies with them. The settler takes a day, perhaps, for his visit in town to trade. Time is precious with him, and he cannot come often. So he buys, perhaps, fifty or a hundred dollars worth of goods. These are circumstances which account for activity of business in these river towns, and which, though they are strikingly apparent here, are not peculiar to this town. At first, I confess, it was a mystery to me what could produce such startling and profitable trade in these new towns.

(Andrews, *Minnesota and Dacotah,* 142–45)

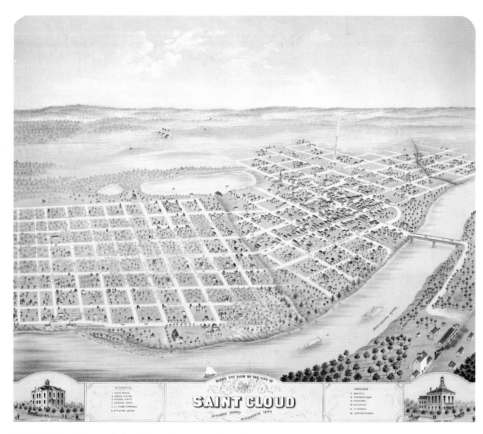

Bird's Eye View of the City of Saint Cloud Stearns County Minnesota 1869. Drawn by A[lbert] Ruger. Printed by Merchant's Lithographing Company, Chicago. Lithograph, 21 x 24 in. (53.4 x 61 cm).

Geography and Map Division, Library of Congress

St. Cloud, Minnesota, from the air, July 16, 1989.

Alex MacLean

Bibliography

Abler, Ronald, John S. Adams, and John R. Borchert. "The Twin Cities of St. Paul and Minneapolis." In John S. Adams, ed., *Contemporary Metropolitan America*, vol. 3, *Nineteenth Century Inland Centers and Ports*, 372–75. Association of American Geographers Comparative Metropolitan Analysis Project. Cambridge: Ballinger Publishing Company, 1976.

Addison, Agnes. *William Strickland: Architect and Engineer, 1788–1854.* Philadelphia: University of Pennsylvania Press, 1950.

Alexander, J. E. *Transatlantic Sketches.* Philadelphia: Key and Biddle, 1833.

Alpers, Svetlana. *The Art of Describing: Dutch Art in the Seventeenth Century.* Chicago: University of Chicago Press, 1983.

Andrews, Christopher Columbus. *Minnesota and Dacotah: In Letters Descriptive of a Tour through the North-West in the Autumn of 1856. With Information Relative to Public Lands, and a Table of Statistics.* Washington: Robert Farnham, 1857.

Anglo-American Art Museum, Louisiana State University. *The Louisiana Landscape, 1800–1969.* Exhibition catalog. [Baton Rouge, 1969.]

Appletons' Cyclopedia of American Biography. 7 vols. New York: D. Appleton and Company, 1887–1900.

Appletons' Illustrated Hand-Book of American Cities; Comprising the Principal Cities in the United States and Canada, with Outlines of Through Routes, and Railway Maps. New York: D. Appleton and Company, 1877.

Asbury, Henry. *Reminiscences of Quincy, Illinois, Containing Historical Events, Anecdotes, Matters Concerning Old Settlers and Old Times, Etc.* Quincy: D. Wilcox & Sons, 1882.

Ashe, Thomas. *Travels in America, Performed in 1806, for the Purpose of Exploring the Rivers Alleghany, Monongahela, Ohio, and Mississippi, and Ascertaining the Produce and Condition of Their Banks and Vicinity.* London: William Sawyer & Co., 1808.

Ashworth, Henry. *A Tour in the United States, Cuba, and Canada.* London: A. W. Bennett and Fred Pitman, [1861?].

Atwater, Caleb. *Remarks Made on a Tour to Prairie du Chien: Thence to Washington City, in 1829.* N.p.: n.p., [1829?].

Ayer, I. Winslow. *Life in the Wilds of America, and Wonders of the West in and beyond the Bounds of Civilization.* Grand Rapids: Central Publishing Company, 1880.

Baily, Francis. *Journal of a Tour in Unsettled Parts of North America in 1796 & 1797.* London, Baily Brothers, 1856. Reprint, edited by Jack D. L. Holmes. Carbondale and Edwardsville: Southern Illinois University, 1969.

[Baird, Robert]. *View of the Valley of the Mississippi, or the Emigrant's and Traveller's Guide to the West. Containing a General Description of That Entire Country; and Also Notices of the Soil, Productions, Rivers, and Other Channels of Intercourse and Trade: and Likewise of the Cities and Towns, Progress of Education, &c. of Each State and Territory.* 2d ed. Philadelphia: H. S. Tanner, 1834.

Banvard, John. "Adventures of the Artist" and "Description of Banvard's Panorama." In John Francis McDermott, ed., *Before Mark Twain: A Sampler of Old, Old Times on the Mississippi*, 112–39. Carbondale and Edwardsville: Southern Illinois University Press, 1968.

Barber, John Warner, and Henry Howe. *Our Whole Country. A Panorama and Encyclopedia of the United States, Historical, Geographical and Pictorial.* 2 vols. Cincinnati: Charles Tuttle, 1863.

Bates, George E., Jr., et al. *Historic Lifestyles in the Upper Mississippi River Valley.* Lanham, Md.: University Press of America, 1983.

Bay, J. Christian. "Introduction." In Henry Lewis, *Das Illustrirte Mississippithal,* iii-xii. Leipzig: H. Schmidt & C. Günther, 1923.

Beale, J. H. *Picturesque Sketches of American Progress. Comprising Official Descriptions of Great American Cities Prepared under the Supervision of the Authorities of the Respective Cities, Showing Their Origin, Development, Present Condition, Commerce and Manufactures. Illustrated Sketches of American Scenery, and Celebrated Resorts. With Historical Sketches of the Wonderful Achievements of Our Country, under the Various Administrations.* New York: The Empire Co-operative Association, 1889.

Beck, Lewis C[aleb]. *A Gazetteer of the States of Illinois and Missouri.* Albany: Charles R. and George Webster, 1823.

Beckman, Thomas. "The Beck & Pauli Lithographing Company." *Imprint* 9 (Spring 1984): 1–6.

———. *Milwaukee Illustrated: Panoramic and Bird's-eye Views of a Midwestern Metropolis, 1844–1908.* Milwaukee: Milwaukee Art Center, 1978.

"The Belize." *Ballou's Pictorial* 11 (August 30, 1856): 133.

Bishop, Harriet E. *Floral Home or, First Years of Minnesota. Early Sketches, Later Settlements, and Further Developments.* New York: Sheldon, Blakeman and Company, 1857.

Bissell, Richard. *How Many Miles to Galena?* Boston: Little, Brown and Company, 1968.

Bonnemains, Jacqueline. "Charles-Alexandre Lesueur en Amérique du Nord (1816–1837)." *Annales du Muséum du Havre* 29 (March 1984).

Boutros, David. "The West Illustrated: Meyer's Views of Missouri River Towns." *Missouri Historical Review* 80 (April 1986): 304–20.

Broderick, James L. *The Character of the Country: The Iowa Diaries of James L. Broderick, 1876–1877.* Edited by Loren N. Horton. Iowa City: Iowa State Historical Department, Division of the State Historical Society, 1976.

Brown, Col. James. "Early Reminiscences of Memphis and West Tennessee." *The Old Folks' Record* 1 (June 1875): 403–7.

Bryant, William Cullen, ed. *Picturesque America, or The Land We Live In.* 2 vols. New York: D. Appleton, 1872–1874.

Buckingham, J[ames] S[ilk]. *The Eastern and Western States of America.* 3 vols. London: Fisher, Son, & Co., 1842.

Bunnell, Lafayette Houghton. *Winona (We-No-Nah) and Its Environs on the Mississippi in Ancient and Modern Days.* Winona, Minn.: Jones & Kroeger, Printers and Publishers, 1897.

Burghardt, Andrew. "The Location of River Towns in the Central Lowland of the United States." *Annals of the Association of American Geographers* 49 (September 1959): 305–23.

"Burlington, Iowa." *Ballou's Pictorial* 8 (April 21, 1855): 252.

Butts, Porter. *Art in Wisconsin: The Art Experience of the Middle West Frontier.* Madison: Madison Art Association, 1936.

Capers, Gerald M., Jr. *The Biography of a River Town, Memphis: Its Heroic Age.* Chapel Hill: University of North Carolina Press, 1939.

Carleton, Mark T. *River Capital: An Illustrated History of Baton Rouge.* Woodland Hills, Calif.: Windsor Publications, 1981.

Cazden, Robert. *A Social History of the German Book Trade in America to the Civil War.* Columbia, S.C.: Camden House, 1984.

"Cities of the Valley of the Mississippi and Ohio." *The Commercial Review of the South and West* 1 (February 1846): 145–53.

"City of Dubuque, Iowa." *Ballou's Pictorial Drawing-Room Companion* 13 (October 31, 1857): 280.

"City of Muscatine, Iowa." *Ballou's Pictorial Drawing-Room Companion* 9 (August 4, 1855): 73.

Claiborne, J[ohn] F[rancis] H[amtramck]. *Life and Correspondence of John A. Quitman, Major-General, U.S.A., and Governor of the State of Mississippi.* 2 vols. New York: Harper & Brothers, 1860.

Cochran, Carl M. "James Queen Philadelphia Lithographer." *Pennsylvania Magazine of History and Biography* 82 (April 1958): 139–75.

Coen, Rena Neumann. *Painting and Sculpture in Minnesota, 1820–1914.* Minneapolis: University of Minnesota Press, 1976.

Coffin, Charles Carleton. *The Seat of Empire.* Boston: Fields, Osgood, & Co., 1870.

Colden, Cadwallader. *Memoir Prepared at the Request of the Committee of the Common Council of the City of New York, and Presented to the Mayor of the City, at the Celebration of the Completion of the New York Canal.* [New York]: Printed by Order of the Corporation of New York, 1825 [1826].

Collot, Georges Henri Victor. *A Journey in North America, Containing a Survey of the Countries Watered by the Mississippi, Ohio, Missouri, and Other Affluing Rivers. . . .* 3 vols. Paris: Arthur Bertrand, 1826. Facsimile edition. Florence: O. Lange, 1924.

Conclins' New River Guide, or A Gazetteer of all the Towns on the Western

Waters: Containing Sketches of the Cities, Towns, and Countries Bordering on the Ohio and Mississippi Rivers, and Their Principal Tributaries; Together with Their Population, Products, Commerce, &c., in 1848; and Many Interesting Events of History Connected with Them. Compiled from the Latest and Best Authority. Cincinnati: J. A. and U. P. James, 1850.

Coulter, Fredrick Lee. *Memphis, 1800–1900.* 3 vols. New York: Nancy Powers & Company, 1982.

Crawford, Charles W. *Yesterday's Memphis.* Miami: E. A. Seemann Publishing, 1976.

"The Creole Sketchbook of A. R. Waud." *American Heritage* 15 (December 1963): 33–48.

Crescent City Silver: An Exhibition of Nineteenth-Century New Orleans Silver. [New Orleans]: Historic New Orleans Collection, 1980.

Crozier, William L. "From Rural to Urban: Nineteenth Century Industrialization and Urbanization in the Upper Mississippi River Valley." In George E. Bates, Jr., et al. *Historic Lifestyles in the Upper Mississippi River Valley,* 513–64. Lanham, Md.: University Press of America, 1983.

Cumming, John. "Albert Ruger and His Views." Unpublished essay. Clarke Historical Library, Central Michigan University, Mount Pleasant, Mich.

Cunningham, John T. "Barber and Howe: History's Camp Followers." *New Jersey History* 102 (Spring/Summer 1984): 65–72.

Currie, James T. *Enclave: Vicksburg and Her Plantations, 1863–1870.* Jackson: University Press of Mississippi, 1980.

Davis, James D. *History of Memphis. The History of the City of Memphis, Being a Compilation of the Most Important Documents and Historical Events Connected with the Purchase of Its Territory, Laying off of the City and Early Settlement. Also, the "Old Times Papers. . . ."* Memphis: Hite, Crumpton & Kelly, 1873.

Davis, Keith F. " 'A Terrible Distinctness': Photography of the Civil War Era." In Martha A. Sandweiss, ed., *Photography in Nineteenth-Century America,* 130–79. Fort Worth: Amon Carter Museum; New York: Harry N. Abrams, 1991.

Davis, Reuben. *Recollections of Mississippi and Mississippians.* Boston: Houghton, Mifflin and Company, 1891.

Deák, Gloria Gilda. *Picturing America, 1497–1899: Prints, Maps, and Drawings Bearing on the New World Discoveries and on the Developments of the Territory That Is Now the United States from the I. N. Phelps Stokes Collection and Other Collections in the Miriam and Ira D. Wallach Division of Art, Prints, and Photographs of the New York Public Library.*

2 vols. Princeton: Princeton University Press, 1988.

De Leon, T. C. "New Orleans." *Appletons' Journal* 8 (October 26, 1872): 449–54.

de Maré, Eric. *The Victorian Woodblock Illustrators.* London: Gordon Fraser, 1980.

Dennett, John Richard. *The South as It Is: 1865–1866.* Edited by Henry M. Christman. New York: The Viking Press, 1965.

Dicey, Edward. *Six Months in the Federal States.* 2 vols. London: Macmillan and Co., 1863.

Dickens, Charles. *American Notes and Pictures from Italy.* London: Chapman & Hall, 1906.

Doffing, Lucille Hammargren. *Hastings on the Mississippi.* Hastings: Hastings Gazette; Kilkenny, Minn.: Hammargren Printing, 1976.

Drumm, Stella M., and Isaac H. Lionberger. "Earliest Picture of St. Louis." *Glimpses of the Past* 8 (1941): 71–98.

Dry, Camille N., and Richard J. Compton. *Pictorial St. Louis: The Great Metropolis of the Mississippi Valley, a Topographic Survey Drawn in Perspective A.D. 1875.* St. Louis: Compton & Co., 1875.

Dunbar, Tony. *Delta Time: A Journey through Mississippi.* New York: Pantheon Books, 1990.

Dupré, E[ugene]. *Atlas of the City and County of St. Louis.* St. Louis: E. Dupré, 1838.

Ekberg, Carl J. *Colonial Ste. Genevieve.* Gerald, Mo.: Patrice Press, ca. 1985.

"Epic of the Towns." *Palimpsest* 12 (March 1931): 114–22.

Espenshade, Edward B., Jr. "Urban Development at the Upper Rapids of the Mississippi." Ph.D dissertation, Department of Geography, University of Chicago, 1943.

Fairbanks, Jonathan. "The Great Platte River Trail in 1853: The Drawings and Sketches of Frederick Piercy." In Ron Tyler, ed., *Prints of the American West,* 67–86. Fort Worth: Amon Carter Museum, 1983.

Falk, Alfred. *Trans-Pacific Sketches: A Tour through the United States and Canada.* Melbourne, Sydney, and Adelaide: George Robertson, 1877.

Farrar, Maurice. *Five Years in Minnesota. Sketches of Life in a Western State.* London: Sampson Low, Marston, Searle, & Rivington, 1880.

Federal Writers' Program, Work Projects Administration. *Arkansas: A Guide to the State.* New York: Hastings House, 1941.

———. *Louisiana: A Guide to the State.* New York: Hastings House, 1941.

———. *Missouri: A Guide to the "Show Me" State,* New York: Duell, Sloan and Pearce, 1941.

———. *Wisconsin: A Guide to the Badger State.* New York: Hastings House, 1941.

Federal Writers' Project, Work Projects Administration. *Illinois: A Descriptive and Historical Guide.* Rev. ed. Chicago: A. C. McClurg & Co., 1947.

———. *Kentucky: A Guide to the Bluegrass State.* New York: Hastings House, 1939.

———. *Tennessee: A Guide to the State.* New York: Hastings House, 1939.

Federal Writers' Project, Works Projects Administration. *Iowa: A Guide to the Hawkeye State.* New York: Hastings House, 1938.

———. *Minnesota: A State Guide.* Rev. ed. New York: Hastings House, 1954.

———. *Mississippi: A Guide to the Magnolia State.* New York: Hastings House, 1938.

———. *New Orleans City Guide.* Boston: Houghton Mifflin Company, 1938.

Ferguson, William. *America by River and Rail; or, Notes by the Way on the New World and Its People.* London: James Nisbet and Co., 1856.

Ferris, Jacob. *The States and Territories of the Great West; Including Ohio, Indiana, Illinois, Missouri, Michigan, Wisconsin, Iowa, Minesota [sic], Kansas, and Nebraska; Their Geography, History, Advantages, Resources, and Prospects; Comprising Their Local History, Institutions, and Laws. Giving a Table of Distances, and the Most Direct Routes and Modes of Conveyance; also Pointing out the Best Districts for Agricultural, Commercial, Lumbering, and Mining Operations. With a Map and Numerous Illustrations.* New York: Miller, Orton, and Mulligan, 1856.

Flagg, Edmund. *The Far West: or, a Tour beyond the Mountains. Embracing Outlines of Western Life and Scenery; Sketches of the Prairies, Rivers, Ancient Mounds, Early Settlements of the French, etc. etc.* 2 vols. New York: Harper & Brothers, 1838.

Flint, Timothy. *Recollections of the Last Ten Years in the Valley of the Mississippi.* Boston: Cummings, Hilliard, and Company, 1826. Reprint, with an Introduction by George R. Brooks and a Foreword by John Francis McDermott. Carbondale and Edwardsville: Southern Illinois University Press, 1968.

Folwell, W. W. "Minneapolis in 1890." *New England Magazine* 3, new ser. (September 1890): 86–109.

Fox, Michael J. "Joseph John Stoner, 1829–1918." *Mapline: A Quarterly Newsletter,* Herman Dunlap Smith Center for the History of Cartography at the Newberry Library, no. 9 (March 1978): unpaged.

Gambee, Budd Leslie, Jr., *Frank Leslie and His Illustrated Newspaper, 1855–1860.* Ann Arbor: University of Michigan, Department of Library Science, 1964.

Garczynski, R. E. "The Upper Mississippi, from St. Louis to St. Anthony's Falls." In William Cullen Bryant, ed., *Picturesque America, or The Land We Live In,* 2:318–52. New York: D. Appleton, 1872–1874.

Gaylor, Charles. *Lewis' Panorama. A Description of Lewis' Mammoth Panorama of the Mississippi River, from the Falls of St. Anthony to the City of St. Louis: Containing an Account of the Distances, and Settlements of the Country; the Names and Population of the Various Cities, Towns and Villages on the River, with Historical Remarks, &c. Compiled from Various Authentic Sources.* Cincinnati: Printed at the Dispatch Office, 1849.

Gilchrist, Agnes Addison. *William Strickland: Architect and Engineer, 1788–1854.* New York: Da Capo Press, 1969.

Glazier, Willard. *Down the Great River; Embracing an Account of the Discovery of the True Source of the Mississippi, together with Views, Descriptive and Pictorial, of the Cities, Towns, Villages and Scenery on the Banks of the River, as Seen during a Canoe Voyage of over Three Thousand Miles from Its Head Waters to the Gulf of Mexico.* Philadelphia: Hubbard Brothers, 1888.

———. *Headwaters of the Mississippi; Comprising Biographical Sketches of Early and Recent Explorers of the Great River and a Full Account of the Discovery and Location of Its True Source in a Lake Beyond Itasca.* Chicago: Rand, McNally & Company, 1894.

———. *Peculiarities of American Cities.* Philadelphia: Hubbard Brothers, 1886 [copyright and preface dated 1883].

Greenough, William W. "Tour to the Western Country." *Proceedings of the Massachusetts Historical Society* 44 (1911): 339–554.

Guernsey, Alfred H., and Henry M. Alden. *Harper's Pictorial History of the Great Rebellion.* 2 vols. New York: Harper & Bros. Publishers, 1868.

Haberly, Loyd. *Pursuit of the Horizon, a Life of George Catlin, Painter & Recorder of the American Indian.* New York: Macmillan, 1948.

Haefner, Marie. "Rivalry among the River Towns." *Palimpsest* 38 (May 1937): 160–74.

Hall, Basil. *Travels in North America, in the Years 1827 and 1828.* 3 vols. Edinburgh: Cadell and Co., 1829.

Hamy, E.-T. *Les Voyages du naturaliste Ch. Alex. Lesueur dans L'Amérique du Nord (1815–1837) d'après les manuscrits et les oeuvres d'art conservés au Muséum d'Histoire Naturelle de Paris et au Muséum d'Histoire Naturelle du Havre.* Paris: Au Siège de la Société des Américanistes, 1904.

Hartshorne, Richard. "The Twin City District. A Unique Form of Urban Landscape." *Geographical Review* 22 (July 1932): 431–32.

Heilbron, Bertha L. "Making a Motion Picture in 1848: Henry Lewis on the Upper Mississippi." *Minnesota History* 17 (June 1936): 131–49.

———. *Making a Motion Picture in 1848: Henry Lewis' Journal of a Canoe Voyage from the Falls of St. Anthony to St. Louis.* St. Paul: Minnesota Historical Society, 1936.

Hesse-Wartegg, Ernst von. *Travels on the Lower Mississippi, 1879–1880.* Edited and translated by Frederic Trautmann. Columbia: University of Missouri Press, 1990.

Hetherington, H. S. "Inaugural Address as Mayor of Dubuque," April 1858. In Franklin T. Oldt and P. J. Quigley, *History of Dubuque County Iowa.* Chicago: Goodspeed Historical Association, n.d.

Historic New Orleans Collection. *Alfred R. Waud, Special Artist on Assignment: Profiles of American Towns and Cities, 1850–1880.* New Orleans: Historic New Orleans Collection, 1979.

———. *Encyclopaedia of New Orleans Artists, 1718–1918.* New Orleans: Historic New Orleans Collection, 1987.

The History of Dubuque County, Iowa, Containing a History of the County, Its Cities, Towns, &c. . . . Chicago: Western Historical Company, 1880.

History of La Crosse County, Wisconsin. Chicago: Western Historical Company, 1881.

History of Lee County, Iowa, Containing a History of the County, Its Cities, Towns, &c. Chicago: Western Historical Company, 1879.

History of Lewis, Clark, Knox and Scotland Counties, Missouri. St. Louis and Chicago: Goodspeed Publishing Co., 1887.

History of Muscatine County, Iowa, Containing a History of the County, Its Cities, Towns, &c. . . . Chicago: Western Historical Company, 1879.

[Hoffman, Charles F.]. *A Winter in the West.* 2 vols. New York: Harper & Brothers, 1835.

[Hogan, John.] *Thoughts about the City of St. Louis, Her Commerce and Manufactures, Railroads, &c.* St. Louis: Republican Steam Press Print, 1854.

Horton, Loren Nelson. "Town Planning, Growth, and Architecture in Selected Mississippi River Towns of Iowa, 1833–1860." Ph.D. dissertation, University of Iowa, 1978.

Hunt, John Warren. *Wisconsin Gazetteer, Containing the Names, Location, and Advantages, of the Counties, Cities, Towns, Villages, Post Offices, and Settlements, Together with a Description of the Lakes, Water Courses, Prairies, and Public Localities, in the State of Wisconsin.* Madison: Beriah Brown, 1853.

Illustrated Historical Atlas of the State of Iowa. Chicago: Andreas Atlas Co., 1875. Reprint, Iowa City: Iowa State Historical Society, 1970.

Illustrated Historical Atlas of the State of Minnesota. Chicago: A. T. Andreas, 1874.

[Ingraham, Joseph Holt.] *The South-West. By a Yankee.* 2 vols. New York: Harper & Brothers, 1835.

Jackson, Mason. *The Pictorial Press: Its Origin and Progress.* London: Hurst and Blackett, 1885.

Jacobs, W. W. "A History of Guttenberg." In *The Guttenberg Press*, February 27, 1974, section two, 2–20.

James, Edwin, comp. *Account of an Expedition from Pittsburgh to the Rocky Mountains Performed in the Years 1819, 1820. By Order of the Hon. J. C. Calhoun, Secretary of War, under the Command of Maj. S. H. Long, of the U.S. Top. Engineers.* Edited by Reuben Gold Thwaites. 4 vols. New York: AMS Press, 1966.

James, Preston. "Vicksburg: A Study in Urban Geography." *Geographical Review* 21 (April 1931): 234–43.

Johnson, Lila M. "Found (and Purchased): Seth Eastman Water Colors." *Minnesota History* 42 (Fall 1971): 258–67.

"Journal of Canoe Voyage from the Falls of St. Anthony to St. Louis." *Minnesota History* 17 (June 1936): 150–58; (September 1936): 288–301; (December 1936): 421–36.

Keeler, Ralph, and Alfred R. Waud. "From Memphis to St. Louis." *Every Saturday* n.s. 3 (September 30, 1871): 329–33.

———. "From Vicksburg to Memphis, with Some Account of an Explosion." *Every Saturday* n.s. 3 (August 19, 1871): 284–85.

———. "New Orleans. I.—The Heart of the City." *Every Saturday* n.s. 3 (July 1, 1871): 6.

———. "New Orleans. III. On the Levee." *Every Saturday* n.s. 3 (July 22, 1871): 92–94.

———. "On the Mississippi. Natchez and Vicksburg." *Every Saturday* n.s. 3 (August 19, 1871): 185, 188–90.

———. "St. Louis. II. Rambling about the City," *Every Saturday* n.s. 3 (October 28, 1871): 412–15.

———. "Up the Mississippi to Baton Rouge." *Every Saturday* n.s. 3 (August 5, 1871): 140–42.

Kessinger, L. *History of Buffalo County, Wisconsin.* Alma: n.p., 1888.

King, Edward. *The Great South: A Record of Journeys in Louisiana, Texas, the Indian Territory, Missouri, Arkansas, Mississippi, Alabama, Georgia, Florida, South Carolina, North Carolina, Kentucky, Tennessee, Virginia,*

West Virginia, and Maryland. 2 vols. 1875. Reprint. New York: Burt Franklin, 1969.

[Kingsford, William]. *Impressions of the West and South, during a Six Weeks' Holiday*. Toronto: A. H. Armour & Co., 1858.

Landsden, John M. *A History of the City of Cairo, Illinois*. Chicago: R. R. Donnelley & Sons Co., 1910.

Lanman, Charles. *A Summer in the Wilderness; Embracing a Canoe Voyage up the Mississippi and around Lake Superior*. New York: D. Appleton & Company, 1847.

Lapham, I. A. *Wisconsin: Its Geography and Topography, History, Geology, and Mineralogy: Together with Brief Sketches of Its Antiquities, Natural History, Soil, Productions, Population, and Government*. 2d ed. Milwaukee: I. A. Hopkins, 1846.

Larpenteur, August L. "Recollections of the City and People of St. Paul, 1843–1898." *Collections of the Minnesota Historical Society* 9 (1901): 363–94.

Latrobe, Benjamin Henry Boneval. *Impressions Respecting New Orleans: Diary and Sketches, 1818–1820*. Edited with an introduction and notes by Samuel Wilson, Jr. New York: Columbia University Press, 1951.

Latrobe, Charles Joseph. *The Rambler in North America: MDCCCXXXII.—MDCCCXXXIII*. 2 vols. 2d ed. London: R. B. Seeley and W. Burnside, 1836.

Lea, Albert M. *Notes on Wisconsin Territory, with a Map*. Philadelphia: Henry S. Tanner, 1836. Reprint. *Annals of Iowa* 11 (July–October 1913): 115–67.

LeCheminant, Wilford Hill. " 'Entitled to Be an Artist': Landscape and Portrait Painter Frederick Piercy." *Utah Historical Quarterly* 48 (Winter 1980): 49–65.

Lewis, G. *Impressions of America and the American Churches: From Journal of the Rev. G. Lewis, One of the Deputation of the Free Church of Scotland to the United States*. Edinburgh: W. P. Kennedy, 1848.

Lewis, Henry. *The Valley of the Mississippi Illustrated*. Düsseldorf: Arnz and Company, 1854–1857. Translated from the German by A. Hermina Poatgieter. Edited with an introduction and notes by Bertha L. Heilbron. St. Paul: Minnesota Historical Society, 1967.

Lewis, Peirce F. *New Orleans—The Making of an Urban Landscape*. Cambridge: Ballinger Publishing Co., 1976.

Lincoln, Nebraska, *Daily Nebraska State Journal*. June 2, 1889.

Linton, William James. *The History of Wood Engraving in America*. Boston: Estes and Lauriat, 1882.

Lithography in Cincinnati: Presented by Young and Klein, Inc. Pts. 1–2. [Cincinnati: Young and Klein, Inc., 1958?–1959].

Louisville *Daily Journal*. August 5, 1855.

Lyell, Charles. *A Second Visit to the United States of America*. 2 vols. New York: Harper & Bros., 1849.

McDermott, John Francis. "J. C. Wild, Western Painter and Lithographer." *Ohio State Archaeological and Historical Quarterly* 60 (April 1951): 111–25.

———. "John Caspar Wild: Some New Facts and a Query." *Pennsylvania Magazine of History and Biography* 83 (October 1959): 452–55.

———. "Leon Pomarede, 'Our Parisian Knight of the Easel.' " *Bulletin of the City Art Museum of St. Louis* 34 (Winter 1949): 8–18.

———. *The Lost Panoramas of the Mississippi*. Chicago: University of Chicago Press, 1958.

———. "Portrait of the Father of Waters: Leon Pomarede's Panorama of the Mississippi." *Bulletin de l'Institut Française de Washington*, n.s. 2 (December 1952): 46–58.

———. *Seth Eastman's Mississippi: A Lost Portfolio Recovered*. Urbana: University of Illinois Press, 1973.

McElroy's Philadelphia Directory. Philadelphia, E. C. & John Biddle, 1846.

Mackay, Alex. *The Western World; or, Travels in the United States in 1846–47: Exhibiting Them in Their Latest Development, Social, Political, and Industrial; Including a Chapter on California*. 2 vols. Philadelphia: Lea & Blanchard, 1849.

Mackay, Charles. *Life and Liberty in America; or, Sketches of a Tour in the United States and Canada in 1857–8*. New York: Harper and Brothers, 1859.

Madden, Betty I. *Art, Crafts, and Architecture in Early Illinois*. Urbana: University of Illinois Press, 1974.

Magill, John T. "Pelican's-eye Views of New Orleans." *Imprint* 15 (Autumn 1990): 20–31.

Mahoney, Timothy R. "Down in Davenport: A Regional Perspective on Antebellum Town Economic Development." *Annals of Iowa* 50, 3d ser. (Summer 1990): 451–69.

———. "Down in Davenport: The Social Response of Antebellum Elites to Regional Urbanization." *Annals of Iowa* 50, 3d ser. (Fall 1990): 611.

———. *River Towns in the Great West: The Structure of Provincial Urbanization in the American Midwest, 1820–1870*. Cambridge: Cambridge University Press, 1990.

———. "Urban History in a Regional Context: River Towns on the Upper Mississippi, 1840–1860." *Journal of American History* 72 (September 1985): 318–39.

Martineau, Harriet. *Retrospect of Western Travel.* 2 vols. New York: Charles Lohman, 1838.

Marzio, Peter. *The Democratic Art: Pictures for a 19th-Century America.* Boston: David R. Godine, in association with the Amon Carter Museum of Western Art, Fort Worth, 1979.

Mayor, A. Hyatt. "Aquatint Views of Our Infant Cities." *Antiques* 88 (September 1965): 314–18.

Mazzuchelli, Samuel. *The Memoirs of Father Samuel Mazzuchelli, O.P.* Chicago: Priory Press, 1967.

Memphis, Tennessee, *Avalanche.* May 10, 1887.

Merryman, Robert M. *A Hero Nonetheless: Albert Miller Lea, 1808–1891.* Lake Mills, Iowa: Graphic Publishing Co., ca. 1983.

Miller, Henry B. "The Journal of Henry B. Miller." Edited by Thomas Maitland Marshall. *Missouri Historical Society Collections* 6 (1931): 213–87.

Millichap, Joseph R. *George Catlin.* Boise: Boise State University, [1977].

Mitchell, W. H. *Dakota County. Its Past and Present, Geographical, Statistical and Historical, Together with a General View of the State.* Minneapolis: Tribune Printing Company, 1868.

———. *Geographical and Statistical Sketch of the Past and Present of Goodhue County, Together with a General View of the State of Minnesota.* Minneapolis: O. S. King's Book and Job Printing House, 1869.

Mohr, Nicolaus. *Excursion through America.* Edited by Ray Allen Billington. Translated by La Verne J. Rippley with the collaboration of Klaus Lanzinger. Chicago: Lakeside Press, R. R. Donnelley & Sons, 1973.

Monkkonen, Eric. *America Becomes Urban: The Development of U.S. Cities and Towns, 1780–1980.* Berkeley: University of California Press, 1988.

Montulé, Edouard de. *Travels in America, 1816–1817.* Translated by Edward D. Seeber. Bloomington: Indiana University Press, 1951.

———. *A Voyage to North America, and the West Indies, in 1817.* London: Sir Richard Phillips and Co., 1921.

Mott, Frank Luther. *A History of American Magazines.* 5 vols. Cambridge: Harvard University Press, 1957–1968.

Murray, Charles Augustus. *Travels in North America during the Years 1834, 1835, & 1836. Including a Summer Residence with the Pawnee Tribe of Indians, in the Remote Prairies of the Missouri, and a Visit to Cuba and the Azore Islands.* 2 vols. New York: Harper & Brothers, 1839.

Nau, John Fredrick. *The German People of New Orleans, 1850–1900.* Leiden: E. J. Brill, 1958.

Newhall, J[ohn] B. *A Glimpse of Iowa in 1846, or the Emigrant's Guide and Territorial Directory.* Burlington: Thurston and Tizzard, 1846. Reprint. Iowa City: State Historical Society of Iowa, 1957.

Nichols, George Ward. "Down the Mississippi." *Harper's New Monthly Magazine* 41 (November 1870): 835–45.

Nichols, Thomas L. *Forty Years of American Life.* 2 vols. London: John Maxwell and Company, 1864.

Norton, Bettina A. *Edwin Whitefield: Nineteenth-Century North American Scenery.* Barre, Mass.: Barre Publishing, 1977.

Oldt, Franklin T., editor-in-chief. *History of Dubuque County Iowa.* Chicago: Goodspeed Historical Association, [1915].

Oliphant, J. Orin, ed. *Through the South and West with Jeremiah Evarts in 1826.* Lewisburg: Bucknell University Press, 1956.

Oliphant, Laurence. *Minnesota and the Far West.* Edinburgh and London: William Blackwood and Sons, 1855.

Olmsted, Frederick Law. *A Journey in the Back Country.* 1860. Reprint. New York: Burt Franklin, 1970.

Overton, John. Letter to James Winchester, Nashville, October 25, 1818. *Tennessee Historical Magazine* 1 (September 1915): 196–97, n. 14.

Parker, N. Howe. *Iowa as It Is in 1855; A Gazetteer for Citizens, and a Hand-book for Immigrants, Embracing a Full Description of the State of Iowa.* Chicago: Keen and Lee, 1855.

Parker, Nathan H. *Missouri as It Is in 1867; an Illustrated Historical Gazetteer of Missouri.* Philadelphia: J. B. Lippincott & Co., 1867.

The Past and Present of Rock Island County, Ill. Chicago: H. F. Kett & Co., 1877.

Peattie, Donald Culross, ed. *Audubon's America: The Narratives and Experiences of John James Audubon.* Boston: Houghton Mifflin, 1940.

Peters, Harry T. *America on Stone: The Other Printmakers to the American People.* Garden City, N.Y.: Doubleday, Doran and Co., 1931.

Petersen, William J. *Mississippi River Panorama: Henry Lewis Great National Work.* Iowa City: Clio Press, 1979.

———. "A Town of Many Names." *Palimpsest* 20 (November 1939): 348–54.

Peyton, John Lewis. *Over the Alleghanies and across the Prairies. Personal Recollections of the Far West One and Twenty Years Ago.* 2d ed. London: Simpkin, Marshall and Co. 1870.

Pierce, Sally, and Catharina Slautterback. *Boston Lithography, 1825–1880: The Boston Athenaeum Collection.* Boston: The Boston Athenaeum, 1991.

Piercy, Frederick. *Route from Liverpool to Great Salt Lake Valley.* Edited by James Linforth. Liverpool: Franklin D. Richards, 1855. Reprint. Edited by Fawn M. Brodie. Cambridge: Harvard University Press, 1962.

Plumbe, John, Jr. *Sketches of Iowa and Wisconsin.* St. Louis: Chambers, Harris and Knapp, 1839. Reprint. Iowa City: State Historical Society of Iowa, 1948.

Powell, Lyman P. *Historic Towns of the Western States.* New York: G. P. Putnam's Sons, 1901.

"Prospectus" of the Cairo Company. Quoted in J[ohn] C[aspar] Wild, *The Valley of the Mississippi Illustrated in a Series of Views.* St. Louis: The Artist [J. C. Wild], 1841.

Quigley, Iola B. "A Metropolis of the Fifties." *Palimpsest* 12 (January 1931): 20–33.

Quincy Argus and Illinois Bounty Land Register. November 8, 1836.

Raban, Jonathan. *Old Glory: An American Voyage.* New York: Simon and Schuster, 1981.

Rathbone, Perry T., ed. *Mississippi Panorama: The Life and Landscape of the Father of Waters and Its Great Tributary, the Missouri; with 188 Illustrations of Paintings, Drawings, Prints, Photographs, Bank Notes, River Boat Models, Steamboat Appurtenances and the Dickeson-Egan Giant Moving Panorama of the Mississippi.* Rev. ed. St. Louis: City Art Museum of St. Louis, 1950.

———. *Westward the Way: The Character and Development of the Louisiana Territory as Seen by Artists and Writers of the Nineteenth Century.* St. Louis: City Art Museum of St. Louis, 1954.

Ray, Frederic E. *Alfred R. Waud: Civil War Artist.* New York: Viking Press, 1974.

Register, James. *Views of Old Natchez [Early 1800s].* Shreveport: Mid-South Press, 1969.

Reid, Robert W., and Charles Rollinson. *William Rollinson, Engraver.* New York: privately printed, 1931.

Reid, Whitelaw. *After the War: A Tour of the Southern States 1865–1866.* Reprinted as edited and with an introduction and notes by C. Vann Woodward. New York: Harper & Row, 1965.

Reps, John W. "Great Expectations and Hard Times: The Planning of Cairo, Illinois." *Journal of the Society of Architectural Historians* 16 (December 1957): 14–21.

———. *The Making of Urban America: A History of City Planning in the United States.* Princeton: Princeton University Press, 1965.

———. *Saint Louis Illustrated: Nineteenth-Century Engravings and Lithographs of a Mississippi River Metropolis.* Columbia: University of Missouri Press, 1989.

———. "Upstate Cities on Paper and Stone: Urban Lithographs of Nineteenth-Century New York." In David Tatham, ed., *Prints and Printmakers of New York State, 1825–1940.* Syracuse: Syracuse University Press, 1986.

———. *Views and Viewmakers of Urban America: Lithographs of Towns and Cities in the United States and Canada, Notes on the Artists and Publishers, and a Union Catalog of Their Work, 1825–1925.* Columbia: University of Missouri Press, 1984.

Ristow, Walter W. *American Maps and Mapmakers: Commercial Cartography in the Nineteenth Century.* Detroit: Wayne State University Press, 1985.

Rodgers, Thomas L. "Recollections of St. Louis—1857–1860." *Glimpses of the Past* 9 (1941): 111–21.

Roper, James. "The Earliest Pictures of Memphis: Charles Lesueur's Drawings, 1828–1830." *West Tennessee Historical Society Papers* 25 (1971): 5–25.

Rose, George. *The Great Country; or, Impressions of America.* London: Tinsley Brothers, 1868.

Rutter, Frank. "Rare American Colour Prints: Early Views of American Cities now in Favour with Collectors: W. J. Bennett—a Notable English Craftsman among Makers of American Prints." *The Antique Collector: A Journal for Lovers of the Old, Rare & Beautiful* 2 (August 22, 1931), 329–31.

"St. Louis: This Year's Convention City." *Review of Reviews* 13 (June 1896): 672–78.

"St. Louis of To-Day." *Harper's Weekly* 32 (June 4, 1888): supplement, 421–24.

Sandweiss, Martha A. "Undecisive Moments: The Narrative Tradition in Western Photography." In Martha A. Sandweiss, ed., *Photography in Nineteenth-Century America,* 98–129. Fort Worth: Amon Carter Museum; New York: Harry N. Abrams, 1991.

Sanford, Albert H. "Four Pictures Portray La Crosse of Early Day." La Crosse *Tribune & Leader-Press,* July 21, 1938.

Sanford, Albert H., and H. J. Hirshheimer, assisted by Robert F. Fries. *A History of La Crosse, Wisconsin, 1841–1900.* La Crosse: La Crosse County Historical Society, 1951.

Scharff, Maurice R. "Collecting Views of Natchez." *Antiques* 65 (March 1954): 217–19.

Seymour, E. S. *Sketches of Minnesota, the New England of the West. With Incidents of Travel in that Territory during the Summer of 1849.* New York: Harper & Brothers, 1850.

"Sketches on the Upper Mississippi." *Harper's New Monthly Magazine* 38 (July 1853): 177–90.

Smith, F. B. *Radical Artisan.* Manchester: Manchester University Press, 1973.

Smith, Joseph. *History of the Church of Jesus Christ of Latter-Day Saints. Period I. History of Joseph Smith, the Prophet. By Himself.* Vol 3. Revised. Introduction and notes by B. H. Roberts. Salt Lake City[?]: published by the church, 1948.

Snyder, Martin. "J. C. Wild and His Philadelphia Views." *Pennsylvania Magazine of History and Biography* 77 (January 1953): 32–75.

"Steamboat Travel on the Upper Mississippi in 1849." *Minnesota History* 7 (March 1926): 54–61.

Steele, [Eliza R.] *A Summer Journey in the West.* New York: John S. Taylor, 1841.

Stoddard, Amos. *Sketches, Historical and Descriptive, of Louisiana.* Philadelphia: Mathew Carey, 1812.

Stuart, James. *Three Years in North America.* 2 vols. Edinburgh: Robert Cadell, 1833.

Taft, Robert. *Artists and Illustrators of the Old West, 1850–1900.* New York: Charles Scribner's Sons, 1953.

Tasistro, Louis Fitzgerald. *Random Shots and Southern Breezes, Containing Critical Remarks on the Southern States and Southern Institutions, with semi-Serious Observations on Men and Manners.* 2 vols. New York: Harper & Brothers, 1842.

Tatham, David. "John Henry Bufford, American Lithographer." Part 1. *Proceedings of the American Antiquarian Society* 86 (April 1976): 47–73.

————. "The Pendleton-Moore Shop—Lithographic Artists in Boston, 1825–1840." *Old Time New England: The Bulletin of The Society for the Preservation of New England Antiquities* 62 (Fall 1971): 29–46.

Tatham, David, ed. *Prints and Printmakers of New York State, 1825–1940.* Syracuse: Syracuse University Press, 1986.

Tillson, John. *History of the City of Quincy, Illinois.* Revised and corrected by Hon. William H. Collins by direction of the Quincy Historical Society. Chicago: Printed for the Society by The S. J. Clarke Publishing Co., n.d.

Tracy, E. C. *Memoir of the Life of Jeremiah Evarts.* Boston: Crocker and Brewster, 1845.

Trewartha, Glenn T. "French Settlement in the Driftless Hill Land." *Annals of the Association of American Geographers* 28 (September 1938): 179–200.

Trollope, Anthony. *North America.* New York: Alfred A. Knopf, 1951.

Trollope, Mrs. [Frances]. *Domestic Manners of the Americans.* London: Whittaker, Treacher, & Co., 1832.

Trowbridge, J. T. *The South: A Tour of Its Battle-Fields and Ruined Cities.* Hartford: L. Stebbins, 1866. Reprint. New York: Arno Press and The New York Times, 1969.

Tuttle, Charles R. *An Illustrated History of the State of Iowa, Being a Complete Civil, Political and Military History of the State, from its First Exploration down to 1875.* Chicago: Richard S. Peale and Company, 1876.

Twain, Mark. *Life on the Mississippi.* Boston: James R. Osgood and Company, 1883.

U.S. Census Office. *Report on the Social Statistics of Cities.* Compiled by George E. Waring, Jr. 2 vols. Washington: Government Print Office, 1887.

"The Upper Mississippi." *Harper's New Monthly Magazine* 16 (March 1858): 433–54.

Usher, Isaac Lane. "Letters of a Railroad Builder." *Palimpsest* 3 (January 1922): 16–28.

Vail, R. W. G. "The American Sketchbooks of a French Naturalist, 1816–1837: A Description of the Charles Alexandre Lesueur Collection, with a Brief Account of the Artist." *Proceedings of the American Antiquarian Society* 48, new series, pt. 1 (1938): 48–155.

Vessey, John Henry. *Mr. Vessey of England: Being the Incidents and Reminiscences of Travels in a Twelve Weeks' Tour through the United States and Canada in the Year 1859.* Edited by Brian Waters. New York: G. P. Putnam's Sons, 1956.

"View of Vicksburg, Miss." In *Ballou's Pictorial Drawing-Room Companion* 9 (25 August 1855): 121.

Wainwright, Nicholas B. *Philadelphia in the Romantic Age of Lithography: An Illustrated History of Early Lithography in Philadelphia with a Descriptive List of Philadelphia Scenes Made by Philadelphia Lithographers before 1866.* Philadelphia: Historical Society of Pennsylvania, 1958.

Warner, Charles Dudley. *Studies in the South and West with Comments on Canada.* New York: Harper & Brothers, 1889.

Warren, James Raymond. "Thaddeus Mortimer Fowler, Bird's-eye-View Artist." Special Libraries Association, Geography and Map Division, *Bulletin*, no. 120 (June 1980): 27–35.

Waud, A[lfred R.] "Sketches of New Orleans." *Harper's Weekly* 11 (March 9, 1867): 158.

W[aud], A[lfred] R. "Pictures of the South: Mobile . . . Baton Rouge." *Harper's Weekly* 10 (September 8, 1866): 566.

———. "Pictures of the South: Vicksburg." *Harper's Weekly* 10 (July 14, 1866): 442.

Weimar, Wilhelm. *Die Daguerrotypie in Hamburg, 1839–1860*. Hamburg: O. Meissner, 1915.

Wells, William. *Western Scenery; or, Land and River, Hill and Dale in the Mississippi Valley*. Cincinnati: O. O. Onken, 1851.

Wild, J[ohn] C[aspar]. *The Valley of the Mississippi Illustrated in a Series of Views*. St. Louis: The Artist [J. C. Wild], 1841.

Wilkie, Franc B. Davenport Past and Present; Including the Early History, and Personal and Anecdotal Reminiscences of Davenport. Davenport: Luse, Lane & Co., 1858.

Williams, Absalom B. "Moline." In George W. Hawes, comp., *Illinois State Gazetteer and Business Directory, for 1858 and 1859*. Chicago: George W. Hawes, 1859.

Williams, Edward F. III. "Memphis' Early Triumph over Its River Rivals." *West Tennessee Historical Society Papers* 22 (1968): 12.

Winchell, N. H., Edward D. Neill, J. Fletcher Williams, and Charles S. Bryant. *History of the Upper Mississippi Valley*. Minneapolis: Minnesota Historical Co., 1881.

Wisconsin Gazetteer. Wilmington, Del.: American Historical Publications, 1991.

Acknowledgments

Many persons and organizations have helped make this book possible. I am especially grateful for financial help from two sources. A travel grant from the American Philosophical Society allowed me to visit a great many towns along the Mississippi, to find images of those places in local libraries, museums, and historical societies, and to photograph them for study and reproduction purposes.

The Graham Foundation for Advanced Study in the Visual Arts provided the funds that allowed me to retain the services of Alex MacLean, who took the splendid air photos of two dozen towns along the river. The Graham Foundation also allowed me to use a portion of the grant to pay the very substantial sums for rental of color transparencies and for permission to reproduce their images that now face all authors of heavily illustrated books. At both organizations the staff must have doubted that they would ever see tangible results from their generosity.

It is a pleasure also to offer my thanks here to Alex MacLean. Not only is he an expert pilot and photographer, but he also shares my interest in and fascination with urban patterns. He fulfilled my every hope in finding ways to match nineteenth-century bird's-eye views with modern photographs. His recent book, *Look at the Land: Aerial Reflections on America*, demonstrates his artistry as a photographer and his skill as a pilot.

One unforgettable portion of my travels was aboard the *Viking Explorer*, owned and piloted by Captain William Bowell, who offered his friendship and shared with me his vast knowledge of Mississippi River lore and history. Seeing many places on the upper river from the water, as did many of the artists whose work this book displays, gave me a heightened appreciation for their skills.

That weeklong voyage resulted from an invitation extended by William Morrish and Catherine Brown, joint directors of a special summer program of the University of Minnesota Design Center for American Urban Landscape. They gathered a talented and energetic group of students to explore the design possibilities of towns and cities along what they referred to as American's Fourth Coast. My gratitude to them, to Captain Bowell, and to Carol Swenson, who managed many of the details of this expedition, is unbounded.

The preparation of this book took me by less exotic means of transportation to many other towns and cities along the Mississippi River as well as to collections of graphic and written materials in other places. Several other sources were queried by mail or telephone. Without exception, my requests for help were met willingly and skillfully, and I am grateful to all those who responded.

What follows is surely only a partial list of those who aided my research, in order as one proceeds upriver from New Orleans. In that city John T. Magill, Associate Curator of the Historic New Orleans Collection, and the late John A. Mahe II, also of that institution, guided me to several items I would otherwise have overlooked. Wilbur Meneray, Assistant University Librarian for Special Collections, and Joan G. Caldwell, Head, Louisiana collection, Howard-Tilton Memorial Library, Tulane University, also responded to several queries.

In Baton Rouge, H. Parrot Bacot, Director and Curator of what has become the Louisiana State University Museum of Art, provided images and information about Adrien Persac. Gordon A. Cotton, Director, Old Court House Museum, Vicksburg, the staff of the Memphis Public Library, and librarians of Memphis State University also assisted my search for accounts about and images of those three important places on the lower Mississippi.

In and near St. Louis several highly competent curators of print and documentary collections extended their help. They include Jan Broderick, curator of the A. G. Edwards and Sons collection; Louisa Bowen, Archivist, Lovejoy Library, Southern Illinois University, Edwardsville; Duane Sneddeker, Curator of Prints and Photographs, Missouri Historical Society; John Neal Hoover, Associate Librarian, Saint Louis Mercantile Library Association; and Holly Hall, Head, Special Collections, Olin Library, Washington University.

Others who assisted in my search for material included Philip Germann, Director, Historical Society of Quincy and Adams County; Ann King, Local History Librarian, St. Charles, Missouri; Barbara Longtin, Director, and William A. McGonagle, former Director, Muscatine Art Center; Michael Gibson, Archivist, Center for Dubuque History at Loras College; Roger Osborne, Curator, Dubuque County Historical Society; Carol Hunt, former Registrar, and Scott Roller, Collections Manager, Putnam Museum, Davenport, Iowa; Elizabeth Haaw of Fort Madison, Iowa; Eric Austin, Manuscripts Archivist, State Historical Society of Iowa; and Mary Bennett, Curator of Prints and Photographs, State Historical Society of Iowa.

I am also grateful to Daryl Watson, Executive Director, Galena/Jo Daviess County History Museum, Galena, Illinois; Andy Kraushaar, Iconographic Collections, State Historical Society of Wisconsin; Carley Robison, Archivist, Henry W. Seymour Library, Knox College, Galesburg, Illinois; Mary Wussow, Reference Librarian, Dakota County Library, Hastings, Minnesota; Anita Taylor Doering, Archivist, La Cross Public Library, Winding Rivers Library System, La Cross, Wisconsin.

At the Minnesota Historical Society in St. Paul I have been helped by Jon Walstrom, Map Curator; Thomas O'Sullivan, Art Curator; Dona Sieden, Library Assistant; and Tracey Baker, Reference Specialist, among others. I also owe thanks to my former Cornell colleague and now Deputy Director of the Society, Dr. Ian Stewart. Others helped my search for materials in the public libraries of St. Paul and Minneapolis and in the Hennepin County Historical Society. Elsewhere, I have benefited from information provided or help extended by Gary Fitzpatrick, Geography and Map Division, Library of Congress, and two former staff members there: Richard Stephenson and Patrick Dempsey; Bernard Reilly and Helena Zinkham, Division of Prints and Photographs, Library of Congress; Roberta Waddell, Curator of Prints, New York Public Library; Wendy Shadwell, Curator of Prints and Photographs, New-York Historical Society; and Larry Viskochil, Curator of Prints and Photographs, Chicago Historical Society.

Also, I would like to thank Melissa Thompson, Registrar, Amon Carter Museum; Alfred Kleine-Kreutzmann, Curator of Rare Books & Special Collections, Public Library of Cincinnati & Hamilton County; Fran Schell, Director, Public Services, Tennessee State Library and Archives, Nashville; and for information about Charles Alexandre Lesueur, C. Douglas Lewis, Curator of Sculpture, National Gallery of Art, Washington, D.C., and Mme J. Bonnemains, Conservateur de la Collection Lesueur, Museum d'Histoire Naturelle, Le Havre, France.

I also acknowledge with thanks permission from copyright holders to publish short extracts from these books: Tony Dunbar, *Delta Time: A Journal through Mississippi,* issued by Pantheon books Division of Random House, Inc.; Jonathan Raban, *Old Glory,* a publication of Aitken & Stone, Ltd.; and Richard Bissell, *How Many Miles to Galena?* published by Little, Brown and Co.

This book reproduces engravings, lithographs, and wood engravings from more than two dozen public collections, with the source of each indicated in its caption. My thanks go to the museums, libraries, and historical societies who are thus identified, as well as to the A. G. Edwards Co. and Eric Newman, both of St. Louis, for allowing me to use some of the images in these private collections.

At Cornell I have enjoyed, as in the past, the skilled help of many librarians. In the Fine Arts Library, Judith Holiday; and in Olin Library, Barbara Berthelsen, former map librarian; Marie Gast, former newspaper librarian; and a team of knowledgeable reference librarians headed by Caroline Spicer: Christopher Brown, Peter Campbell, Faith Fleming, Robert Kibbee, Fred Muratori, Nancy Skipper, Susan Szasz, Anne Carson, and all the others on the reference desk who answered my questions during the past several years.

I am also grateful to Olin Library for the use of a library study, for permission to reproduce several illustrations from its general collection, and to Mark Dimunation, Curator of Rare Books, for allowing the use of two illustrations from that collection. To all others whose names I may have overlooked but who made my task easier I offer both thanks and apologies.

This is my fifth book to be issued by the University of Missouri Press, and it is a pleasure to express my deep appreciation to its staff for their many contributions toward its publication. No author could have enjoyed better treatment. I feel especially grateful to Beverly Jarrett, Director and Editor-in-Chief, for her determination to produce such an elaborate and expensive volume, to Rhonda Miller, for her skills in typographic design, and to Jane Lago, Managing Editor, for her editorial talents in saving me from mistakes. The flaws that remain are mine.

Once again I thank my wife, Constance Peck Reps, for her encouragement throughout the several years of research and writing as well as for her companionship on two research journeys on or along parts of the Mississippi.

Index